Visual Basic® for Applications By EXAMPLE

que

William J. Orvis

Visual Basic for Applications By Example

Copyright ©1994 by Que® Corporation

All rights reserved. Printed in the United States of America. No part of this book may be used or reproduced in any form or by any means, or stored in a database or retrieval system, without the written permission of the publisher except in the case of brief quotations in critical articles and reviews. Making copies of any part of this book for any purpose other than your own personal use is a violation of United States copyright laws. For information, address Que Corporation, 201 W. 103rd Street, Indianapolis, IN, 46290.

Library of Congress Catalog Number: 94-65318

ISBN: 1-56529-553-6

This book is sold *as is*, without warranty of any kind, either express or implied, respecting the contents of this book, including but not limited to implied warranties for the book's quality, performance, merchantability, or fitness for any particular purpose. Neither Que Corporation nor its dealers or distributors shall be liable to the purchaser or any other person or entity with respect to any liability, loss, or damage caused directly or indirectly by this book.

96 95 94   6 5 4 3 2 1

Interpretation of the printing code: The rightmost double-digit number is the year of the book's printing; the rightmost single-digit number, the number of the book's printing. For example, a printing code of 94-1 shows that the first printing of the book occurred in 1994.

Publisher: *David P. Ewing*

Associate Publisher: *Michael Miller*

Managing Editor: *Michael Cunningham*

Product Marketing Manager: *Ray Robinson*

Publishing Director
Joseph B. Wikert

Product Development Specialist
Bryan Gambrel

Production Editors
Lori Cates
Andy Saff

Technical Editor
Russell L. Jacobs

Book Designer
Amy Peppler-Adams

Cover Designer
Dan Armstrong

Production Team
Angela Bannan
Kim Cofer
Brook Farling
Carla Hall
Greg Kemp
Andrea Marcum
Aren Munk
Ryan Rader
Caroline Roop
Kris Simmons
Tina Trettin
Donna Winter
Robert Wolf

Editorial Assistants
Michelle Williams
Jill Stanley

Indexer
Charlotte Clapp

Imprint Manager
Kelli Widdifield

Composed in *Palatino* and *MCPdigital* by Prentice Hall Computer Publishing. Screen reproductions in this book were created by using Collage Plus from Inner Media, Inc., Hollis, New Hampshire.

Dedication

*To Barry, Kit, Amy, Jody, and Laura.
Your help and support over the years is most appreciated.*

About the Author

William J. Orvis is an electronics engineer at the University of California's Lawrence Livermore National Laboratory, where he is involved in the large-scale numerical modeling of solid-state devices, development of micron-sized vacuum microelectronic devices, and computer security research. (He describes himself as a computer virus smasher.) He is a member of CIAC, the Department of Energy's computer incident response team. Orvis received both his B.S. and M.S. degrees in Physics and Astronomy at the University of Denver in Colorado. He is the author of *Excel 4 for Scientists and Engineers* (Sybex, 1993), *Do-It-Yourself Visual Basic for MS-DOS* (Sams Publishing, 1992), *Do-It-Yourself Visual Basic* (for Windows) (Sams Publishing, 1992, 2nd ed. 1993), *ABC's of GW-BASIC* (Sybex, 1990), *Excel Instant Reference* (Sybex, 1989), *1-2-3 for Scientists and Engineers* (Sybex, 1987, 2nd ed. 1991), and *Electrical Overstress Protection for Electronic Devices* (Noyes Data Corporation, 1986). His books have been translated into Japanese, Italian, and Greek. He also has written for *Computers in Physics* and *IEEE Circuits and Devices* magazines.

Acknowledgments

No project of this size is the work of one person. Although I might like to think that this book is "All Mine," a whole organization at Que helped put it together, and I could not have done it without them. You sometimes wonder why you thank the editors for several months of nights without sleep and weekends tied to a computer, but when you see the final product, you realize that it was all worth it. Then, if people actually buy the darn thing, you realize that maybe you have actually done something worthwhile.

At the top of the list is Joe Wikert, who twisted my arm to take this project (he didn't have to twist it very far) and cracked the whip over me to get it done. Next are Bryan Gambrel, Lori Cates, and Andy Saff, who coordinated the project and kept things on track.

I also want to thank Danny and Tien at Today Computers in Pleasanton, California, who keep my system operating and who can be counted on for personal service whenever I call.

Finally, I want to thank B.J., Skye, Sierra, and Shane for not solving all the puzzles in MYST before I get a chance to play it. And, I want to thank Julie for keeping the kids off my back while I worked on the manuscript.

Trademark Acknowledgments

All terms mentioned in this book that are known to be trademarks or service marks have been appropriately capitalized. Que cannot attest to the accuracy of this information. Use of a term in this book should not be regarded as affecting the validity of any trademark or service mark.

Visual Basic is a registered trademark of Microsoft Corporation.

Overview

Introduction

Part I Introducing Visual Basic for Applications
1 Welcome to Visual Basic for Applications
2 Objects, Properties, and Methods
3 Accessing Excel Objects with Visual Basic

Part II The Primary Language Elements
4 Understanding Data Types and Variables
5 Using Assignment Statements and the Built-In Functions

Part III Functions and Procedures
6 Creating and Using Procedures
7 Creating and Using Functions

Part IV Controlling Execution
8 Understanding Decision Making
9 Using Block If Structures
10 Using Select Case
11 Don't Use Unstructured Branching

Part V Loops and Repeated Structures
12 Using Counted Loops
13 Using Logically Terminated Loops
14 Using Object Type Loops

Part VI Performing Input and Output
15 Using Built-In Dialog Boxes
16 Using a Worksheet as a Data Form
17 Creating Custom Dialog Boxes
18 Saving Data in a Sequential Disk File
19 Saving Data in a Random Access File
20 Saving Data in Other Places

Part VII Debugging a Procedure
  21 What To Do When Your Code Crashes
  22 Using Breakpoints and Watch Points
  23 Using Error Trapping To Handle Unforeseen Events

Part VIII Advanced Language Features
  24 Creating Custom Menus and Toolbars
  25 Creating Custom Objects
  26 Interapplication Communications

Appendixes
  A Answers to the Review Questions
  B Table of ANSI Codes
  C Visual Basic Error Codes
  Glossary
  Index

Contents

Introduction

Who Should Use This Book? 1
The Book's Philosophy 2
    Use the Online Help for Complete Command Syntax 2
    Extend the Examples 3
    A Short Word about the Introductory Examples 3
An Overview of This Book 3
    Part I: Introducing Visual Basic for Applications 3
    Part II: The Primary Language Elements 3
    Part III: Functions and Procedures 4
    Part IV: Controlling Execution 4
    Part V: Loops and Repeated Structures 4
    Part VI: Performing Input and Output 4
    Part VII: Debugging a Procedure 4
    Part VIII: Advanced Language Features 4
    The Appendixes and the Glossary 5
Conventions Used in This Book 5
    Code Lines 5
    Reader Level Icons 5
    Note, Tips, and Cautions 6
    Excel Toolbar Buttons 6
    Use of the Term *Visual Basic* 6

Part I Introducing Visual Basic for Applications

1 Welcome to Visual Basic for Applications   9

What Is Visual Basic for Applications? 9
What Visual Basic for Applications Can Do for You 10
Recording a Visual Basic Procedure 10
    Preparing To Record a Procedure 11
    Setting the Type of References Recorded 11
    Starting the Recorder 11
    Creating the Worksheet 12
Running the Procedure 18
Adding an Omission to the Procedure 18
Understanding and Editing the Procedure 22

Contents

Attaching the Procedure to Worksheet Objects 26
    Attaching the Procedure to a Button 27
    Attaching the Procedure to a Button on a Toolbar 28
    Attaching the Procedure to a Menu 28
    Attaching the Procedure to a Graphics Object 29
Summary 29
Review Questions 29
Review Exercises 29

2 Objects, Properties, and Methods   31

What Are Objects? 31
Properties and Methods 33
Inheritance 34
Classes 35
Locating Objects 35
    Online Help 35
    The Object Browser 36
    Macro Recorder 37
Summary 37
Review Questions 37
Review Exercises 38

3 Accessing Excel Objects with Visual Basic   39

Using Object Collections 39
    Getting Information about a Collection 40
    Adding Members to a Collection 42
    Removing Members from a Collection 42
Accessing Cells with Range Objects 43
    The Range Method 43
    The Cells Method 45
    The Offset Method 46
    The Range Method Shortcut 47
Using the Active Properties 47
Using Content Properties 50
Applying Formatting Properties 51
Executing Worksheet Methods 54
Summary 55
Review Questions 55
Review Exercises 55

Part II The Primary Language Elements

4 Understanding Data Types and Variables 59

What Are Data Types? 59
Understanding Built-In Data Types 60
Understanding Variables 63
Declaring Variables...63
    Forcing Yourself To Declare Variables 64
    Declaring Variables with Dim 64
    Understanding the Scope of Variables 64
    Declaring Global Variables 65
Understanding Arrays 66
Using Constants To Enhance a Code's Readability 67
    Creating and Using Constants..67
    Locating Built-In Constants 68
Creating Custom Data Types 68
Summary 69
Review Questions 69
Review Exercises 69

5 Using Assignment Statements and the Built-In Functions 71

What Are Assignment Statements? 71
Using Comment Statements 72
Declaring and Assigning Object Variables 73
Using Visual Basic Operators 74
    Understanding the Precedence of Operators 74
    Experimenting with Operators 75
Using Visual Basic Functions 77
    Mathematical Functions 78
    String Functions 82
    Date and Time Functions 86
Converting Data Types in Visual Basic 88
Summary 89
Review Questions 89
Review Exercises 90

Contents

Part III Functions and Procedures

6 Creating and Using Procedures — 93

What Are Procedures? 93
Types of Procedures 94
    General Procedures 94
    Command Procedures 94
    Event Procedures 95
Calling a Procedure 95
    Calling a Procedure in a Different Module 96
    Calling a Procedure in a Different Workbook 96
    Preventing Access to Modules and Procedures 97
Passing Values to Procedures 98
    Declaring Variables in the Procedure Header 98
    Using a Comma-Delimited List 99
    Using a Named Argument List 100
    Passing Values by Address 100
    Passing Values by Value 100
    Using Optional Arguments 103
    Using an Indeterminate Number of Arguments 104
Making Procedure Variables Persist 105
Summary 106
Review Questions 106
Review Exercises 106

7 Creating and Using Functions — 109

What Are Functions? 109
Creating a Function 110
    Setting a Function's Data Type 110
    Calling a Function 111
Creating Custom Worksheet Functions 112
Using Worksheet Functions in a Procedure 114
Passing an Array to a Custom Worksheet Function 116
Passing an Array to the Worksheet from a Function 120
Using Functions in DLL Libraries 122
Summary 124
Review Questions 124
Review Exercises 125

Part IV Controlling Execution

8 Understanding Decision Making — 129

What Is Decision Making? 129
Using an If Statement 130
Understanding Logical Values 131

	Understanding Logical Tests 134
	Understanding Logical Expressions 135
	Summary 136
	Review Questions 136
	Review Exercises 137

9 Using Block If Structures — 139

Executing Single Blocks with the If-Then Statement 139
Executing Multiple Blocks with If-Then-ElseIf 144
Including an Else Clause 146
Summary 149
Review Questions 150
Review Exercises 150

10 Using Select Case — 151

Defining the Cases 151
Including a Case Else Clause 154
Summary 158
Review Questions 158
Review Exercises 159

11 Don't Use Unstructured Branching — 161

What Is Unstructured Branching? 161
The Problems with Unstructured Branching 162
Use Structured Branching Whenever Possible 167
Summary 167
Review Question 167
Review Exercise 167

Part V Loops and Repeated Structures

12 Using Counted Loops — 171

What Is a Counted Loop? 171
Using For-Next Loops 171
Using the Loop Counter 172
Summary 177
Review Questions 177
Review Exercises 177

13 Using Logically Terminated Loops — 179

What Are Logically Terminated Loops? 179
Using Do-Loop Loops 180
    Using While or Until 181
    Using Exit Do 181

xiii

Contents

        Placing the Condition at the Beginning of the Loop 181
        Placing the Condition at the End of the Loop 182
    Using While-Wend Loops 183
    Summary 184
    Review Questions 184
    Review Exercises 184

14 Using Object Type Loops   185

    What Are Object Type Loops? 185
    Applying the For Each Loop to Collections 186
    Applying the For Each Loop to Arrays 188
    Summary 190
    Review Questions 190
    Review Exercises 190

Part VI Performing Input and Output

15 Using Built-In Dialog Boxes   195

    Using the MsgBox( ) Function 195
        Creating a Simple Message Box 196
        Creating a Dialog Box by Adding Buttons
           to a Message Box 197
        Receiving Values from the MsgBox Function 199
        Adding a Title to the Dialog Box 200
    Using the InputBox Function 201
    Using Other Built-In Dialog Boxes 205
    Calling Application Dialog Boxes 206
    Summary 207
    Review Questions 208
    Review Exercises 208

16 Using Worksheet as a Data Form   209

    Defining Input Ranges 209
    Putting Buttons on a Worksheet 218
    Locking the Worksheet 222
    Summary 223
    Review Questions 223
    Review Exercises 224

17 Creating Custom Dialog Boxes   225

    Opening a New Dialog Sheet 225
    Using Objects on a Form 228
        The Button Object 228
        The Label Object 229

	The Edit Box Object	231
	The Group Box Object	231
	The Check Box Object	231
	The Option Button Object	231
	The List Box Object	232
	The Drop-Down Object	234
	The Combination List-Edit Object	234
	The Combination Drop-Down Edit Object	235
	The Scroll Bar Object	235
	The Spinner Object	235
Attaching Procedures to Custom Dialog Box Objects		236
Displaying a Custom Dialog Box		236
Adding a Custom Dialog Box to the Contacts Database		237
Using Dialog Box Objects on a Worksheet		248
Summary		249
Review Questions		249
Review Exercises		250

18 Saving Data in a Sequential Disk File — 251

Sequential and Random Access Files	251
Reading and Writing Sequential Files	252
Opening a File	252
Closing a File	253
Printing to a File	254
Writing to a File	257
Inputting from a File	258
Saving the Personal Contacts Database in a Sequential File	262
Summary	276
Review Questions	277
Review Exercises	278

19 Saving Data in a Random Access File — 279

Reading and Writing Random Access Files	279
Opening a File	280
Closing a Random Access File	281
Using the Type Statement To Define a Record	281
Putting Data into a Record	282
Getting Data from a Record	282

Contents

Reorganizing Data in Random Access Files 283
Saving the Personal Contacts Database
  in a Random Access File 284
Summary 304
Review Questions 304
Review Exercises 304

20 Saving Data in Other Places — 307

Saving Data in a Worksheet 307
  Opening or Creating a Worksheet or Workbook 307
  Writing Data to Worksheet Ranges 309
Storing the Personal Contacts Database on a Worksheet 310
Saving Data in an External Database 322
Summary 325
Review Questions 325
Review Exercises 325

Part VII Debugging a Procedure

21 What To Do When Your Code Crashes — 329

What Is Debugging? 330
When Your Code Crashes 331
Examining and Changing Variables in the Immediate Pane ..332
Examining a Variable with Instant Watch 333
Examining Variables in the Watch Pane 334
Listing Procedures in the Calls Dialog Box 335
Summary 337
Review Questions 337
Review Exercise 338

22 Using Breakpoints and Watch Points — 339

Understanding Break Mode 339
Breaking a Program with Ctrl-Break or a Stop Statement 340
Setting and Removing Breakpoints 342
Running a Program after a Breakpoint 344
Setting Watch Points 345
Using Debug.Print To Track Changes in Values 347
Using Beep To Track the Progress of a Program 348
Summary 349
Review Questions 349
Review Exercises 349

23 Using Error Trapping To Handle Unforeseen Events — 351

What Is an Error Trap? 351
Why Trap Errors? 352
Enabling the Trap 353
Which Trap Responds? 354
Creating the Error Handler 355
Returning from the Error Handler 358
Handling Unexpected Errors 359
Creating User-Defined Errors 359
Passing Error Values in Variables 360
Using Excel's Error Values 360
Passing User-Defined Errors in Variables 361
Trapping User Interrupts 361
Delayed Error Processing 362
Using an Error Handler To Count Array Dimensions 363
Adding an Error Handler to the Personal Contacts
    Database 363
Summary 378
Review Questions 378
Review Exercises 379

Part VII Advanced Language Features

24 Creating Custom Menus and Toolbars — 383

The Layout of a Menu Bar 383
Creating Menus with the Menu Editor 386
    Adding a Menu Item to an Existing Menu 387
    Adding a Menu to an Existing Menu Bar 389
    Adding a New Menu Bar 390
    Displaying a Custom Menu Bar 391
    Removing a Custom Menu Bar 391
Creating Menus with Code 393
    Accessing Menu Bars, Menus, and Menu Items 393
    Adding a Menu Item to an Existing Menu 393
    Adding a Menu to an Existing Menu Bar 395
    Adding a New Menu Bar 395
Changing the Properties of Menus and Menu Items 396
Adding a Shortcut Key to a Menu Command 397
Modifying Shortcut Menus 399
Accessing Toolbars 401

Contents

Adding Buttons to a Toolbar 402
Creating Custom Toolbars 403
Creating Buttons with the Button Image Editor 404
Attaching a Toolbar to a Workbook 405
Using Code To Control Toolbars and Toolbar Buttons 406
Summary 408
Review Questions 409
Review Exercises 409

25 Creating Custom Objects   411

Defining the Custom Object 411
Creating the Custom Properties 412
    The Property Let Procedures 412
    The Property Get Procedures 414
    The Property Set Procedure 415
Creating the Custom Methods 416
Using a Custom Object 416
Summary 429
Review Questions 429
Review Exercises 429

26 Interapplication Communications   431

What Is Interapplication Communication? 431
What Is DDE? 433
Using Dynamic Data Exchange 433
    Opening a DDE Communication Channel 434
    Closing a DDE Channel 435
    Getting Information from a Server 435
    Sending Information to a Server 437
    Sending Commands to a Server 439
Using Object Linking and Embedding 440
    Using OLE Automation 440
    Creating and Opening Objects 442
    Embedding an Object with Code 443
Passing Keystrokes to Windows Applications 446
Summary 449
Review Questions 449
Review Exercises 450

A Answers to the Review Questions   451

Chapter 1 Answers 451
Chapter 2 Answers 452
Chapter 3 Answers 452
Chapter 4 Answers 453
Chapter 5 Answers 453
Chapter 6 Answers 453
Chapter 7 Answers 454
Chapter 8 Answers 455
Chapter 9 Answers 455
Chapter 10 Answers 456
Chapter 11 Answer 456
Chapter 12 Answers 457
Chapter 13 Answers 457
Chapter 14 Answers 457
Chapter 15 Answers 458
Chapter 16 Answers 458
Chapter 17 Answers 458
Chapter 18 Answers 459
Chapter 19 Answers 460
Chapter 20 Answers 460
Chapter 21 Answers 461
Chapter 22 Answers 461
Chapter 23 Answers 462
Chapter 24 Answers 463
Chapter 25 Answers 464
Chapter 26 Answers 464

B Table of ANSI Codes   467

C Visual Basic Error Codes   475

Glossary   485

Index   493

Introduction

Visual Basic for Applications By Example is one of several books in Que's *By Example* series. The basic philosophy of these books is that programming is best taught with many examples. Complicated descriptions of command syntax and structure are likely to bore a beginning programmer, and does little for the more advanced programmer. Therefore, this book emphasizes short, straightforward, common examples in which you actually execute the commands and functions to see how they perform.

Who Should Use This Book?

This book teaches how to program with Visual Basic for Applications at three different levels: beginning, intermediate, and advanced. The first few chapters of the book describe in detail the operation of each example. However, later chapters describe only generally the details that should be obvious to the beginning programmer, and the detailed discussion is limited to only the new features being examined in the current chapter.

This book is primarily for the user of Excel who would like to use Visual Basic for Applications to expand the capabilities of Excel and to link Excel with other applications such as Word and Project. The reader of this book should be familiar with the Excel application and with using worksheets to list and calculate values. If you do not know how to start Excel, insert values in cells, insert formulas in cells, and format a worksheet, you would do well to learn that first. However, a knowledge of the Excel 4 macro language is not a prerequesite for using this book.

Introduction

If you are an advanced programmer, or even an advanced BASIC programmer, you should get a lot out of this book, because Visual Basic for Applications is decidedly different from most implementations of the BASIC programming language. While having all the features of traditional BASIC languages, Visual Basic for Applications also has extensions that enable it to control Excel and the other members of the Microsoft Office suite of programs using the objects of each of these programs. This is quite different from traditional methods of remote control, in which one program usually controls another by mimicking a person typing at the keyboard. Visual Basic for Applications has direct access to the commands themselves. Advanced programmers will want to learn about these features so that they can effectively use Visual Basic for Applications to expand the capabilities of other programs.

The Book's Philosophy

The goal of this book is to teach you to use modern programming practice to produce modular, easy-to-understand code. Repeatedly, the point is made that some coding practice makes the code more obvious and more readable. If it is obvious what a piece of code is doing, you won't have to spend much time figuring it out the next time you have to work with it.

There are important reasons for wanting to write code that is easy to understand, the first of which is so that you can understand what you have done. This benefits you as you create your code, by helping you ensure that it is doing what you want it to do. It also benefits you later when you need to make changes or correct a bug. If you keep in mind that debugging code often takes more time than you spend designing and programming it, the extra time that you spend inserting comments and making your code easy to understand won't seem like such a burden.

In addition to benefiting you, writing easy-to-understand code benefits anyone else who must change or correct your code.

Use the Online Help for Complete Command Syntax

This book does not describe every possible command and syntax variation in the Visual Basic for Applications language. What is included are the modern programming constructs and the more common options and syntax. Using the commands described in this book, you should have no problem creating nearly any type of application. To see all the commands and the complete syntax for the commands given here, look up the commands in the online help. (However, don't try to learn every command and statement in the Visual Basic for Applications online help. Many statements are included only for compatibility with older versions of BASIC.)

Extend the Examples

The examples given in this book are not ends in themselves, but working blocks of code that demonstrate specific tasks. You are encouraged to expand and modify these examples to suit your own needs whenever possible. Try variations of the examples, and try different options. It is unlikely that you will destroy anything permanently by experimenting with the language. (You periodically back up your files anyway, don't you?) You are also encouraged to create your own examples to experiment with different commands and capabilities. The more coding you do on your own, the faster you will learn the language.

A Short Word about the Introductory Examples

Some of the examples in the early parts of the book contain statements and commands that have not been described yet. These were used to make the examples more useful than they would have been if the commands were not used. When any advanced commands are used, their use is noted and their function is briefly described. If you want more information, check the chapter that describes the command in question, or use the online help.

An Overview of This Book

Visual Basic for Applications By Example is divided into eight parts. Part I is a brief introduction to Visual Basic for Applications and to object-oriented programming. Later sections examine different types of language elements so that after you learn the language you can easily use this book as a reference.

Part I: Introducing Visual Basic for Applications

Part I is an introduction to Visual Basic for Applications. An introductory example gives you a feel for the language and how it interacts with Excel. This part of the book also describes of how Visual Basic differs from more traditional BASIC languages and introduces Visual Basic's version of object-oriented programming.

Part II: The Primary Language Elements

Part II describes the primary language elements of the Visual Basic for Applications language. These elements include the variable and data types. Also in this part of the book you learn how data is stored in memory, and are introduced to the functions that are built into Visual Basic for Applications.

Part III: Functions and Procedures

Part III explains how to use Visual Basic for Applications to create your own procedures and functions, including simple procedures, command procedures, event procedures, functions, and custom worksheet functions.

Part IV: Controlling Execution

Part IV describes control structures and how you use them to change a program from a simple sequential calculator to a logic-driven program. Included in this part are descriptions of logical values and formulas, If statements, block If structures, and Select Case structures. All these structures use logical conditions to select the code to be executed.

Part V: Loops and Repeated Structures

Part V discusses repeated structures, which are blocks of code that execute repeatedly according to some condition or counter. Although you can use block If statements to create repeated structures, such structures are used so often that all programming languages provide built-in methods for producing them. This part of the book includes discussion of For-Next counted loops, Do-Loop logically terminated loops, and For Each object type loop structures.

Part VI: Performing Input and Output

Part VI explains how you send data into and out of your Visual Basic for Applications program. Worksheet access is emphasized throughout this book, so this part of the book focuses on creating user input forms and storing data in disk files.

Part VII: Debugging a Procedure

Part VII discusses the art of debugging procedures and using Visual Basic for Applications' debugging tools. The amount of time that you spend debugging procedures often exceeds the time that you spend planning and writing the procedures. Visual Basic for Applications has an impressive array of debugging tools to assist you in determining the cause of a particular bug.

Part VIII: Advanced Language Features

The advanced language features are those features that go beyond a traditional programming language. These features include creating custom menus and toolbars, creating custom objects, and remote control of other applications using Dynamic Data Exchange and Object Linking and Embedding.

The Appendixes and the Glossary

The appendixes contain information that supports the rest of the book. Included in the appendixes are an ASCII/ANSI character code table and a list of the Visual Basic for Applications error codes. Also included are the answers to the review questions for each chapter. Following the appendixes is a comprehensive glossary.

Conventions Used in This Book

Several typographic conventions, icons, notes, tips, and cautions are used throughout this book to enhance its readability and expand the information content.

Code Lines

The following typographic conventions are used in this book:

- Code lines and syntax lines are presented in `monospace` type.
- Placeholders for variables or literal values on syntax lines and some examples are in *`italic monospace`*.
- Text that you are expected to type is in **boldface type**.
- File names are all uppercase letters. For example: MYFILE.TXT.
- New terms defined in the text and in the glossary are in *italic*.

Reader Level Icons

Three icons appear in the margins to mark the difficulty of the examples, the review questions, and the review exercises. In the body of each chapter, each example is marked near its beginning. At the end of the chapter, the review questions and exercises are sorted according to difficulty, with one of the following icons marking the first question at each difficulty level:

Level 1 examples and questions are for the beginning programmer. These examples tend to be restricted to showing the basic concept described in the chapter. Most anyone who has read the chapter should be able to understand these examples and answer the questions.

Level 2 examples and questions are for the intermediate programmer. The examples are a little more complex and include more than the basic concepts.

Level 3 examples and questions are for the more advanced programmer. The examples tend to be much more complex, and include programming constructs and tricks that are straightforward but not necessarily described in the chapter. Some of the level 3 review problems will be an interesting challenge for the advanced programmer, although none should take more than an evening to work out.

Note, Tips, and Cautions

Occasionally you will see boxed text that expands on a topic not directly related to the current chapter, or expounding special tips and cautions for using some command or method just described in the chapter. These boxes are marked in the margin with three different icons that indicate the type of information contained in the box:

Notes expand on different topics related to the current item being discussed that may not fit into the general flow of the chapter's discussion.

Tips indicate shortcuts and easier ways to perform some actions that may not be obvious from the text.

Cautions warn you about possible problems you might encounter when using the code or methods described in the current section of the book. Pay attention to these cautions, because they can save you a lot of headaches.

Excel Toolbar Buttons

When the use of a toolbar button is mentioned in the text as a shortcut to a command, the image of that button appears in the margin for identification. In most cases when you are using Visual Basic for Applications, the use of the toolbar buttons significantly speeds program development, by making commonly used commands conveniently available.

Use of the Term *Visual Basic*

This book uses the terms *Visual Basic* and *Visual Basic for Applications* synonymously, even though *Visual Basic* should apply to the Visual Basic for Windows package. Because I dislike using acronyms and get tired of typing *Visual Basic for Applications*, I have settled on using the shortened though slightly inaccurate term. In any discussion in which the distinction between the Visual Basic for Windows package and Visual Basic for Applications is important, the full names are used. Otherwise, whenever you see the term *Visual Basic* used in this book, it refers to Visual Basic for Applications.

Part I

Introducing Visual Basic for Applications

CHAPTER 1

Welcome to Visual Basic for Applications

For many years, Bill Gates of Microsoft has expressed a vision of using the BASIC computer language as a common macro language for all applications. That vision has finally manifested itself in Visual Basic for Applications. First available in Excel and Project, Visual Basic for Applications will eventually span all of Microsoft's major applications, including Word, Mail, and PowerPoint. The first part of this book introduces you to the Visual Basic language and its intimate connection with Excel. In later parts, you learn the intricacies of the language and of programming with Visual Basic. In this chapter, you will learn the following:

- ♦ What Visual Basic is
- ♦ How to record a Visual Basic procedure
- ♦ How to edit a procedure
- ♦ How to attach a procedure to a button

What Is Visual Basic for Applications?

Visual Basic for Applications is the newest embodiment of Microsoft's Visual Basic 3.0 for Windows. Microsoft removed the Forms Designer from Visual Basic, attached Visual Basic to Excel, and then added dialog sheets to replace the Forms Designer. In addition, Microsoft made all the commands and objects (cells, worksheets, and so forth) of Excel accessible to Visual Basic. Because of this, Visual Basic can control all of Excel's functions. Thus, Visual Basic is now a super macro language for Excel that follows the well-known commands and syntax of the BASIC programming language.

In addition to Excel, Visual Basic is also the macro language for Project and will soon be the macro language for Word, Mail, and PowerPoint. If you are suffering from language and operating system overload, this should come as a great relief. Over the last few years, it seems like almost every major application has been released with its own macro language, and that each macro language was different from all the others and also different from all the established programming languages. By making one language the universal macro language, Microsoft has significantly reduced the headaches involved in developing custom commands and procedures.

If you are familiar with older versions of BASIC, such as BASICA and GW-BASIC, you might assume that Visual Basic is a primitive programming language, lacking the constructs and structures expected in a modern language. However, Visual Basic is nothing of the sort. Although it does abide by the syntax and rules of BASIC programming and runs most GW-BASIC or BASICA programs, Visual Basic is a fully implemented, modern programming language, with all the structured statements and data types that you would expect in such a language. In addition, Visual Basic uses objects, which makes it significantly more understandable and thus much easier to use to develop applications. Although not quite up to C++'s level of object-oriented programming (OOP), Visual Basic controls Excel by manipulating Excel's objects. However, you cannot use the Visual Basic programming language to create new classes of objects, though you can come close.

What Visual Basic for Applications Can Do for You

In addition to making it easier to program macro procedures, Visual Basic, combined with OLE 2.0, enables you to create "mega-applications" that combine and coordinate the strengths of multiple major applications. For example, you can create a document preparation program that uses Excel to access a database and generate charts and tables, Word to combine those charts and tables with text to produce a report, and Mail to distribute that report, all with the push of a single button. Visual Basic is the glue that binds all this together and orchestrates the procedure. Because the applications are object-oriented, any Visual Basic application can access all the data and commands in the compliant applications by accessing the compliant application's objects.

Recording a Visual Basic Procedure

To understand how a Visual Basic procedure works, let Excel create the first one for you. Using Excel's Macro Recorder, you can record all the steps necessary to create a worksheet. Later, you can replay the procedure to re-create the worksheet.

The first example is an amortization table. When you are paying off a loan, the amount of interest and principal paid each month changes from month to month, depending on the amount that you paid and the balance due in the account. As is usually the case, you pay the same amount each month and the interest rate is a constant, so you can create an amortization table that calculates the amount of principal and the interest paid, and the reduction in the principal balance each month.

Preparing To Record a Procedure

The first step in recording a procedure is to determine where in the creation of a worksheet you want the recording to begin, and to prepare the worksheet up to that point. After you turn on the recorder, everything you do becomes part of the recording. For a complete worksheet, you probably should start with a blank sheet. If you are creating a procedure to perform some special formatting of some cells, you should fill the cells with data before starting the recording.

Setting the Type of References Recorded

The next step is to set the type of references stored in the procedure. Excel has two types of references: relative and absolute. *Relative references* specify a worksheet cell's location as an offset from the currently active cell. The advantage of relative references is that you can use them to format different regions of a worksheet, relative to the currently selected cell. *Absolute references* always refer to an explicit cell. When you run a procedure that uses absolute references, it always accesses the same cell, no matter which cell is selected.

The default is to use absolute references, so if you want to use relative references in your procedure, you must choose the **T**ools **R**ecord Macro **U**se Relative References command before recording the procedure. To change back to absolute references, choose the **T**ools **R**ecord Macro **U**se Absolute References command.

Starting the Recorder

There are two ways to start the recorder, depending on where you want it to store the recording. If you want to store the recording in a new module sheet, choose the **T**ools **R**ecord Macro **R**ecord New Macro command. If you want to start recording on an existing module, place the cursor where you want the recording to begin and execute the **T**ools **R**ecord Macro **M**ark Position for Recording command, then start the recording with the **T**ools **R**ecord Macro R**e**cord At Mark command.

Chapter 1 ◆ Welcome to Visual Basic for Applications

Creating the Worksheet

To prepare to record the creation of an amortization table, perform the following steps:

1. Start Microsoft Excel, if it is not already running. If it was already running, create a new workbook with the File New command.

2. Choose the Tools Record Macro Record New Macro command. The Record New Macro dialog box then appears.

3. In the Macro Name box, type **AmortTable**. In the Description box, type **Creates a 180 month amortization table**, and click the Options button. The dialog box then expands as shown in figure 1.1.

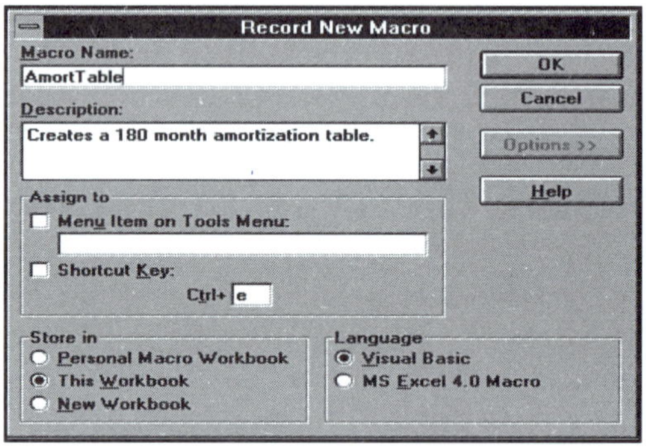

Figure 1.1

The Record New Macro dialog box is where you set the options for recording the macro.

In the Record New Macro dialog box, you can set many of the options to include in the procedure that you are going to record. You can also set or reset most of these options after you record the procedure, by choosing the Tools Macro and the Tools Assign Macro commands.

The Macro Name field contains the name that you want to give this procedure. You should keep the name short but descriptive. The name must be a single word, or multiple words connected with underscores (_). In the Description box you can describe what the macro does. Any text you place here also appears as a comment in the header of the procedure. The Assign To box enables you to attach this new procedure to an item on the Tools menu or to a shortcut key. You will do this later with the Tools Assign Macro command.

The Store In box gives you three options as to where you want to store the new procedure. The most common option is This Workbook, which places the procedure in a new module attached to the current workbook. The Personal Macro Workbook option places the procedure in a special, hidden workbook that is opened every time you start Excel. Thus, any procedures that you place there are available globally to any open workbook. To see the personal workbook, choose the Window Unhide command. The third option is New Workbook, which places the procedure in a new module on a new workbook.

Visual Basic for Applications By EXAMPLE

The last box on the dialog box is the Language box, in which you can choose Visual Basic or the MS Excel 4.0 Macro language as the language to use when creating the procedure. You will almost always use the Visual Basic option. You would choose the MS Excel 4.0 Macro language option only when creating a macro to be used by someone who has not yet upgraded to Excel 5.

To record the creation of the amortization table, perform these steps:

1. Choose OK to close the dialog box. The Stop button then appears on a floating toolbar. Later you click this button to stop recording the procedure.

2. Select cell A1 and type **Amortization Table**.

3. Select cell D1 and type **Interest Rate**.

4. Select cell D2 and type **Principal**.

5. Select cell D3 and type **Payment**.

6. Select cell E1, type **0.0675**, and then press Enter. This is the interest rate per year as a fraction.

7. Choose the Format Cells command, select the Number tab, the Percentage Category, and the `0.00%` code. Choose OK. This formats the cell as a percentage so it appears as a percent instead of a fraction.

8. Select cell E2 and type **10000**. This is the initial principal.

9. Choose the Format Cells command, and then select the Number tab, the Currency Category, and the code `$#,##0.00_);($#,##0.00)`. Then choose OK. This formats the principal as currency.

10. Select cell E3 and type **=PMT(E1/12,180,E2,0)**. This function calculates the correct payment for paying off the loan in 180 months. The interest rate in E1 is divided by 12 to get the interest rate per month. Excel knows that this is a currency value and automatically formats the cell as currency. The value is negative, because a payment is an expense for you.

11. Select cell B5 and type **Month**.

12. Select cell C5 and type **Interest**.

13. Select cell D5 and type **Principal Paid**.

14. Select cell E5 and type **Principal Balance**.

15. Select the bar between the D and E column headers, then drag it right to widen column D until the whole label in cell D5 is showing in the cell.

16. Select the bar between the E and F column headers and drag it right to widen column E until the whole label in cell E5 is showing in the cell.

17. Select cell B6 and type **1**. You need two starting numbers so that Excel knows how to fill the selection when you use the fill handle in step 19.

18. Select cell B7 and type **2**.

19. Select cells B6:B7, and then select the fill handle at the bottom-right corner of the selection and drag it down to cell B185. This creates in column B a series of integers from 1 through 180.

20. Select cell C6 and type **=ROUND(E1*E2/12,2)**. Calculate the interest paid in a month by multiplying the interest divided by 12 times the principal. Round the number to the nearest whole cent.

21. Select cell D6 and type **=-E3-C6**. The principal paid in a month is simply the payment minus the interest. Excel's PMT function calculates a payment as a negative number (because it is money paid out), so you must use a minus sign here.

22. Select cell E6 and type **=E2-D6**. The principal balance is simply the previous balance minus the principal paid this month.

23. Select cell C7 and type **=ROUND(E1*E6/12,2)**.

24. Select cell D6, click the fill handle, and drag down to D7.

25. Select cell E7 and type **=E6-D7**.

26. Select cells C7:E7, click the fill handle, and drag it down to cell E185.

27. Scroll the worksheet back to the top. In the following steps, you'll make the worksheet look a bit more presentable by boxing in the tables and turning off gridlines and column headings.

28. Select cells D1:E3, choose the **F**ormat **C**ells command, select the Border tab, click the **L**eft, **R**ight, **T**op, and **B**ottom check boxes, and choose OK.

29. Select cells B5:E5, choose the **F**ormat **C**ells command, select the Border tab, click the **O**utline check box, and choose OK.

30. Select cells **B6:E185**, choose the **F**ormat **C**ells command, select the Border tab, click the **O**utline check box, and choose OK.

31. Select cell A1.

32. Choose the **T**ools **O**ptions command and select the View tab. Then, in the Window Options box, uncheck the **G**ridlines and Row & Column **H**eadings check boxes and choose OK.

The worksheet should now look like figure 1.2.

Figure 1.2

The completed worksheet for the amortization table.

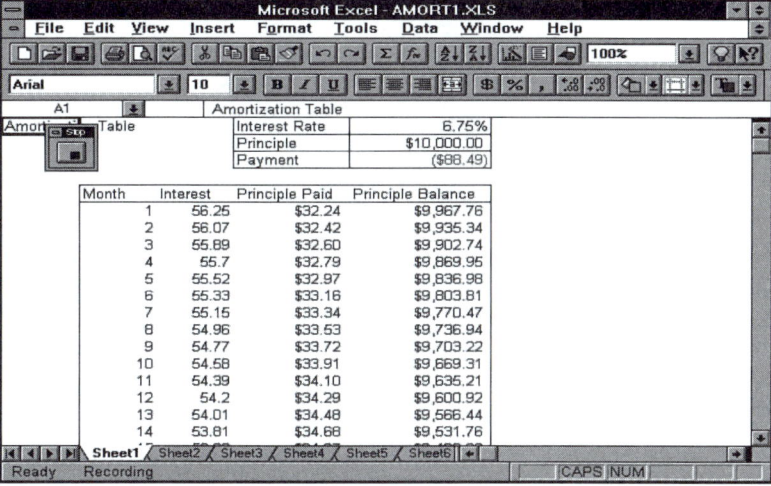

Note the Stop button on the floating toolbar on the upper-left corner of the worksheet. You press this button to stop the recorder. Save the workbook as AMORT1.XLS. Using the tabs along the bottom of the workbook, find and select the Module1 tab, and you see your new procedure as shown in figure 1.3 and in the following listing:

Figure 1.3

The recorded procedure in Module1 that re-creates the amortization table.

```
' AmortTable Macro
' Creates a 180 month amortization table.
'
Sub AmortTable()
    Range("A1").Select
    ActiveCell.FormulaR1C1 = "Amortization Table"
    Range("D1").Select
    ActiveCell.FormulaR1C1 = "Interest Rate"
    Range("D2").Select
    ActiveCell.FormulaR1C1 = "Principle"
    Range("D3").Select
    ActiveCell.FormulaR1C1 = "Payment"
    Range("E1").Select
    ActiveCell.FormulaR1C1 = "0.0675"
    Range("E1").Select
    Selection.NumberFormat = "0.00%"
    Range("E2").Select
    ActiveCell.FormulaR1C1 = "10000"
```

Chapter 1 ◆ Welcome to Visual Basic for Applications

```
'
' AmortTable Macro
' Creates a 180-month amortization table.
'
'
Sub AmortTable()
    Range("A1").Select
    ActiveCell.FormulaR1C1 = "Amortization Table"
    Range("D1").Select
    ActiveCell.FormulaR1C1 = "Interest Rate"
    Range("D2").Select
    ActiveCell.FormulaR1C1 = "Principal"
    Range("D3").Select
    ActiveCell.FormulaR1C1 = "Payment"
    Range("E1").Select
    ActiveCell.FormulaR1C1 = "0.0675"
    Range("E1").Select
    Selection.NumberFormat = "0.00%"
    Range("E2").Select
    ActiveCell.FormulaR1C1 = "10000"
    Range("E2").Select
    Selection.NumberFormat = "$#,##0.00_);($#,##0.00)"
    Range("E3").Select
    ActiveCell.FormulaR1C1 = "=PMT(R[-2]C/12,180,R[-1]C,0)"
    Range("B5").Select
    ActiveCell.FormulaR1C1 = "Month"
    Range("C5").Select
    ActiveCell.FormulaR1C1 = "Interest"
    Range("D5").Select
    ActiveCell.FormulaR1C1 = "Principal Paid"
    Range("E5").Select
    ActiveCell.FormulaR1C1 = "Principal Balance"
    Range("E6").Select
    Columns("D:D").ColumnWidth = 13
    Columns("E:E").ColumnWidth = 16
    Range("B6").Select
    ActiveCell.FormulaR1C1 = "1"
    Range("B7").Select
    ActiveCell.FormulaR1C1 = "2"
    Range("B6:B7").Select
    Selection.AutoFill Destination:=Range("B6:B185"), _
        Type:=xlFillDefault
```

```
Range("B6:B185").Select
ActiveWindow.ScrollRow = 1
Range("C6").Select
ActiveCell.FormulaR1C1 = "=ROUND(R[-5]C[2]*R[-4]C[2]/12,2)"
Range("D6").Select
ActiveCell.FormulaR1C1 = "=-R3C5-RC[-1]"
Range("E6").Select
ActiveCell.FormulaR1C1 = "=R[-4]C-RC[-1]"
Range("C7").Select
ActiveCell.FormulaR1C1 = "=ROUND(R1C5*R[-1]C[2]/12,2)"
Range("D6").Select
Selection.AutoFill Destination:=Range("D6:D7"), _
    Type:=xlFillDefault
Range("D6:D7").Select
Range("E7").Select
ActiveCell.FormulaR1C1 = "=R[-1]C-RC[-1]"
Range("C7:E7").Select
Selection.AutoFill Destination:=Range("C7:E185"), Type _
    :=xlFillDefault
Range("C7:E185").Select
ActiveWindow.ScrollRow = 1
Range("D1:E3").Select
With Selection.Borders(xlLeft)
    .Weight = xlThin
    .ColorIndex = xlAutomatic
End With
With Selection.Borders(xlRight)
    .Weight = xlThin
    .ColorIndex = xlAutomatic
End With
With Selection.Borders(xlTop)
    .Weight = xlThin
    .ColorIndex = xlAutomatic
End With
With Selection.Borders(xlBottom)
    .Weight = xlThin
    .ColorIndex = xlAutomatic
End With
Selection.BorderAround LineStyle:=xlNone
Range("B5:E5").Select
Selection.Borders(xlLeft).LineStyle = xlNone
Selection.Borders(xlRight).LineStyle = xlNone
```

```
        Selection.Borders(xlTop).LineStyle = xlNone
        Selection.Borders(xlBottom).LineStyle = xlNone
        Selection.BorderAround Weight:=xlThin, _
            ColorIndex:=xlAutomatic
    Range("B6:E185").Select
        Selection.Borders(xlLeft).LineStyle = xlNone
        Selection.Borders(xlRight).LineStyle = xlNone
        Selection.Borders(xlTop).LineStyle = xlNone
        Selection.Borders(xlBottom).LineStyle = xlNone
        Selection.BorderAround Weight:=xlThin, _
            ColorIndex:=xlAutomatic
    Range("A1").Select
    With ActiveWindow
        .DisplayGridlines = False
        .DisplayHeadings = False
    End With
End Sub
```

> **Note:** Note that five of this listing's lines end with an underscore. This is Excel's line continuation character. When a line ends with the continuation character, the line that follows it is processed as though it appears on the right side of the line that precedes it.

Running the Procedure

Now that you have created this procedure, you probably want to run to it to see whether it really re-creates the amortization table. To do this, switch to an empty worksheet, such as Sheet2 in your workbook, and choose the **T**ools **M**acro command. In the Macro dialog box, select the AmortTable macro and choose **R**un. The worksheet is re-created automatically.

Adding an Omission to the Procedure

If you look closely at the worksheet you just created, you will note a small problem. When you placed the formula in column C to calculate the interest paid each month, you didn't format the column as currency. Do you have to record the macro all over again to insert the missing part? No, let Excel do it for you by changing the recording point and recording the missing piece. You need only to format cells C6 and C7 as Currency just before C7 is copied into the rest of the table (between steps 25 and 26).

Visual Basic for Applications *By* EXAMPLE

To add the missing part to the procedure, follow these steps:

1. Select the Module1 tab, and locate the statement that selects cells C7:E7, as shown in the second statement of the following:

```
ActiveCell.FormulaR1C1 = "=R[-1]C-RC[-1]" _
    Range("C7:E7").Select
Selection.AutoFill Destination:=Range("C7:E185"), _
    Type:=xlFillDefault
```

2. Place the cursor at the beginning of the statement `Range("C7:E7").Select`.

3. Choose the **T**ools **R**ecord Macro **M**ark Position for Recording command. This tells Excel where you want to start recording.

4. Select the Sheet1 tab.

5. Choose the **T**ools **R**ecord Macro R**e**cord At Mark command. The recorder is now running.

6. Select cells C6:C7, choose the **F**ormat **C**ells command, select the Number tab, choose the Currency **C**ategory command, and then select the code `$#,##0.00_);($#,##0.00)`. Then choose OK.

7. Click the Stop button to stop the recorder. Then save the workbook.

The worksheet does not look exactly right yet, because only cells C6 and C7 have the correct formatting. In the code procedure in the Module1 sheet, notice that the code for formatting those two cells was inserted where you placed the cursor in step 2. The following is the corrected procedure, with the added lines indicated with boldface type:

```
'
' AmortTable Macro
' Creates a 180-month amortization table.
'
'
Sub AmortTable()
    Range("A1").Select
    ActiveCell.FormulaR1C1 = "Amortization Table"
    Range("D1").Select
    ActiveCell.FormulaR1C1 = "Interest Rate"
    Range("D2").Select
    ActiveCell.FormulaR1C1 = "Principal"
    Range("D3").Select
    ActiveCell.FormulaR1C1 = "Payment"
    Range("E1").Select
```

Chapter 1 ♦ Welcome to Visual Basic for Applications

```
ActiveCell.FormulaR1C1 = "0.0675"
Range("E1").Select
Selection.NumberFormat = "0.00%"
Range("E2").Select
ActiveCell.FormulaR1C1 = "10000"
Range("E2").Select
Selection.NumberFormat = "$#,##0.00_);($#,##0.00)"
Range("E3").Select
ActiveCell.FormulaR1C1 = "=PMT(R[-2]C/12,180,R[-1]C,0)"
Range("B5").Select
ActiveCell.FormulaR1C1 = "Month"
Range("C5").Select
ActiveCell.FormulaR1C1 = "Interest"
Range("D5").Select
ActiveCell.FormulaR1C1 = "Principal Paid"
Range("E5").Select
ActiveCell.FormulaR1C1 = "Principal Balance"
Range("E6").Select
Columns("D:D").ColumnWidth = 13
Columns("E:E").ColumnWidth = 16
Range("B6").Select
ActiveCell.FormulaR1C1 = "1"
Range("B7").Select
ActiveCell.FormulaR1C1 = "2"
Range("B6:B7").Select
Selection.AutoFill Destination:=Range("B6:B185"), _
    Type:=xlFillDefault
Range("B6:B185").Select
ActiveWindow.ScrollRow = 1
Range("C6").Select
ActiveCell.FormulaR1C1 = "=ROUND(R[-5]C[2]*R[-4]C[2]/12,2)"
Range("D6").Select
ActiveCell.FormulaR1C1 = "=-R3C5-RC[-1]"
Range("E6").Select
ActiveCell.FormulaR1C1 = "=R[-4]C-RC[-1]"
Range("C7").Select
ActiveCell.FormulaR1C1 = "=ROUND(R1C5*R[-1]C[2]/12,2)"
Range("D6").Select
Selection.AutoFill Destination:=Range("D6:D7"), _
    Type:=xlFillDefault
Range("D6:D7").Select
Range("E7").Select
ActiveCell.FormulaR1C1 = "=R[-1]C-RC[-1]"
**Range("C6:C7").Select**
```

```
        Selection.NumberFormat = "$#,##0.00_);($#,##0.00)"
        Range("C7:E7").Select
        Selection.AutoFill Destination:=Range("C7:E185"), _
            Type:=xlFillDefault
        Range("C7:E185").Select
        ActiveWindow.ScrollRow = 1
        Range("D1:E3").Select
        With Selection.Borders(xlLeft)
            .Weight = xlThin
            .ColorIndex = xlAutomatic
        End With
        With Selection.Borders(xlRight)
            .Weight = xlThin
            .ColorIndex = xlAutomatic
        End With
        With Selection.Borders(xlTop)
            .Weight = xlThin
            .ColorIndex = xlAutomatic
        End With
        With Selection.Borders(xlBottom)
            .Weight = xlThin
            .ColorIndex = xlAutomatic
        End With
        Selection.BorderAround LineStyle:=xlNone
        Range("B5:E5").Select
        Selection.Borders(xlLeft).LineStyle = xlNone
        Selection.Borders(xlRight).LineStyle = xlNone
        Selection.Borders(xlTop).LineStyle = xlNone
        Selection.Borders(xlBottom).LineStyle = xlNone
        Selection.BorderAround Weight:=xlThin,ColorIndex:=xlAutomatic
        Range("B6:E185").Select
        Selection.Borders(xlLeft).LineStyle = xlNone
        Selection.Borders(xlRight).LineStyle = xlNone
        Selection.Borders(xlTop).LineStyle = xlNone
        Selection.Borders(xlBottom).LineStyle = xlNone
        Selection.BorderAround Weight:=xlThin,ColorIndex:=xlAutomatic
        Range("A1").Select
        With ActiveWindow
            .DisplayGridlines = False
            .DisplayHeadings = False
        End With
End Sub
```

Chapter 1 ◆ Welcome to Visual Basic for Applications

To run this corrected procedure, switch to a blank worksheet such as Sheet3, choose the **Tools Macro** command, select the AmortTable procedure, and then choose **Run**. This creates a worksheet that contains all the correct formatting and looks like figure 1.4. Note the formatting in column C (the Interest column).

Figure 1.4

The amortization table produced by the corrected procedure.

Month	Interest	Principle Paid	Principle Balance
		Amortization Table	
	Interest Rate		6.75%
	Principle		$10,000.00
	Payment		($88.49)
1	$56.25	$32.24	$9,967.76
2	$56.07	$32.42	$9,935.34
3	$55.89	$32.60	$9,902.74
4	$55.70	$32.79	$9,869.95
5	$55.52	$32.97	$9,836.98
6	$55.33	$33.16	$9,803.81
7	$55.15	$33.34	$9,770.47
8	$54.96	$33.53	$9,736.94
9	$54.77	$33.72	$9,703.22
10	$54.58	$33.91	$9,669.31
11	$54.39	$34.10	$9,635.21
12	$54.20	$34.29	$9,600.92
13	$54.01	$34.48	$9,566.44
14	$53.81	$34.68	$9,531.76

Understanding and Editing the Procedure

In this next section, you review the procedure piece by piece to see how it works, and how you might edit it. Editing a recorded procedure normally involves removing unnecessary statements that the recorder includes. For example, when you close a dialog box, the procedure might include all the dialog box's settings even though you changed only one. Also, when you type in a cell and then press Enter, the insertion point moves down one cell, so that you have to reselect the cell in order to format it. The procedure inserts text directly into the selected cell, and does not require that you press Enter. If you press Enter, the statement that selects the next statement down is included in the procedure and is not needed.

> **Tip:** If you click the check box instead of pressing Enter, the insertion point does not move down and the extra statements are not inserted into your procedure.

The first five lines of the procedure are comment lines. On a line of code, anything that follows a single quotation mark is a comment and is ignored by Visual Basic. Comments can appear almost anywhere in a procedure, including on the right side of an executable statement. Note that the name and description set in the Record New Macro dialog box are included here.

Following the five comment lines is the procedure header, which is the statement that actually names the procedure and controls its recording:

```
'
' AmortTable Macro
' Creates a 180-month amortization table.
'
'
Sub AmortTable()
```

The next two statements select cell A1 and place in it the text "Amortization Table":

```
Range("A1").Select
ActiveCell.FormulaR1C1 = "Amortization Table"
```

The `Range().Select` statement uses the Range object to address cell A1 on the current worksheet, and the Select method selects that cell. The next few chapters discuss objects and methods in greater detail. The second line uses the ActiveCell property to reference cell A1, the current active cell, and uses the FormulaR1C1 property to insert the text into the cell. Properties are also discussed in the next few chapters.

The next six statements do the same for cells D1, D2, and D3:

```
Range("D1").Select
ActiveCell.FormulaR1C1 = "Interest Rate"
Range("D2").Select
ActiveCell.FormulaR1C1 = "Principal"
Range("D3").Select
ActiveCell.FormulaR1C1 = "Payment"
```

The next two statements insert the number 0.0675 in cell E1 in the same manner as before, but the two statements following them reselect cell E1 and then format it so that it displays its value as a percentage:

```
Range("E1").Select
ActiveCell.FormulaR1C1 = "0.0675"
Range("E1").Select
Selection.NumberFormat = "0.00%"
```

The Selection property addresses the current selection and the NumberFormat property sets the format for the selection. This is where you pressed Enter after typing **0.0675** into the cell, causing the active cell to move down one row. Cell E1 then had to be reselected to have its formatting changed. Because the Visual Basic statements do not change the active cell, you can remove the statement highlighted in boldface type without changing what the procedure does.

Chapter 1 ♦ Welcome to Visual Basic for Applications

The following four statements place the number 10,000 in cell E2 and format it as currency:

```
Range("E2").Select
ActiveCell.FormulaR1C1 = "10000"
Range("E2").Select
Selection.NumberFormat = "$#,##0.00_);($#,##0.00)"
```

Again, you could remove the boldface line.

The next two lines select cell E3, and insert a formula (in the same way as you insert labels and numbers) to calculate the loan payment:

```
Range("E3").Select
ActiveCell.FormulaR1C1 = "=PMT(R[-2]C/12,180,R[-1]C,0)"
```

The next few lines insert labels in cells B5, C5, D5, and E5:

```
Range("B5").Select
ActiveCell.FormulaR1C1 = "Month"
Range("C5").Select
ActiveCell.FormulaR1C1 = "Interest"
Range("D5").Select
ActiveCell.FormulaR1C1 = "Principal Paid"
Range("E5").Select
ActiveCell.FormulaR1C1 = "Principal Balance"
Range("E6").Select
```

You caused the selection of E6 in the last line by pressing Enter. You can delete this line.

These two statements change the column width of columns D and E:

```
Columns("D:D").ColumnWidth = 13
Columns("E:E").ColumnWidth = 16
```

The Columns collection selects the column, and the ColumnWidth property changes the column width.

The next four statements place a 1 in B6 and a 2 in B7. The fifth statement selects the range of cells B6:B7, and the sixth executes the Edit Fill Down command, creating the list of months by automatically filling the cells with the integers from 1 to 180:

```
Range("B6").Select
ActiveCell.FormulaR1C1 = "1"
Range("B7").Select
ActiveCell.FormulaR1C1 = "2"
Range("B6:B7").Select
Selection.AutoFill
Destination:=Range("B6:B185"),Type:=xlFillDefault
Range("B6:B185").Select
```

The following lines do the same for cells C6, D6, E6, C7, D7, and E7, and then copy those formulas into the body of the table. You can remove the lines highlighted in boldface type without changing what the procedure does.

```
ActiveWindow.ScrollRow = 1
Range("C6").Select
ActiveCell.FormulaR1C1 = "=ROUND(R[-5]C[2]*R[-4]C[2]/12,2)"
Range("D6").Select
ActiveCell.FormulaR1C1 = "=-R3C5-RC[-1]"
Range("E6").Select
ActiveCell.FormulaR1C1 = "=R[-4]C-RC[-1]"
Range("C7").Select
ActiveCell.FormulaR1C1 = "=ROUND(R1C5*R[-1]C[2]/12,2)"
Range("D6").Select
Selection.AutoFill Destination:=Range("D6:D7"),Type:=xlFillDefault
Range("D6:D7").Select
Range("E7").Select
ActiveCell.FormulaR1C1 = "=R[-1]C-RC[-1]"
Range("C6:C7").Select
Selection.NumberFormat = "$#,##0.00_);($#,##0.00)"
Range("C7:E7").Select
Selection.AutoFill Destination:=Range("C7:E185"),Type:=xlFillDefault
Range("C7:E185").Select
```

Note that the formulas in lines 3 and 5 are in the R1C1 format instead of the A1 format. Excel automatically makes this change, even if you are using A1 formatting on the workbook.

The next line scrolls back to the top of the window. Following that are several lines containing With statements.

```
ActiveWindow.ScrollRow = 1
Range("D1:E3").Select
With Selection.Borders(xlLeft)
    .Weight = xlThin
    .ColorIndex = xlAutomatic
End With
With Selection.Borders(xlRight)
    .Weight = xlThin
    .ColorIndex = xlAutomatic
End With
With Selection.Borders(xlTop)
    .Weight = xlThin
```

```
        .ColorIndex = xlAutomatic
End With
With Selection.Borders(xlBottom)
    .Weight = xlThin
    .ColorIndex = xlAutomatic
End With
```

The With statements decrease the amount of typing you have to do when you apply several formats to the same cell. Everything between the With and End With statements behave as though the text to the right of With is attached to the left of the decimal in the other statements. Again, you can remove all the statements in boldface type without changing the operation of the procedure.

The rest of the procedure places borders around the cells, turns off the gridlines and headings, and makes A1 the active cell. Again, the boldfaced lines can be removed.

```
Selection.BorderAround LineStyle:=xlNone
Range("B5:E5").Select
Selection.Borders(xlLeft).LineStyle = xlNone
Selection.Borders(xlRight).LineStyle = xlNone
Selection.Borders(xlTop).LineStyle = xlNone
Selection.Borders(xlBottom).LineStyle = xlNone
Selection.BorderAround Weight:=xlThin,ColorIndex:=xlAutomatic
Range("B6:E185").Select
Selection.Borders(xlLeft).LineStyle = xlNone
Selection.Borders(xlRight).LineStyle = xlNone
Selection.Borders(xlTop).LineStyle = xlNone
Selection.Borders(xlBottom).LineStyle = xlNone
Selection.BorderAround Weight:=xlThin,ColorIndex:=xlAutomatic
Range("A1").Select
With ActiveWindow
    .DisplayGridlines = False
    .DisplayHeadings = False
End With
End Sub
```

Attaching the Procedure to Worksheet Objects

The Tools Macro command is sufficient for executing procedures that you seldom use, but would become quite inconvenient if you need to execute them often. To alleviate this problem, you can attach a procedure to a menu or any other worksheet object.

Visual Basic for Applications **By**
EXAMPLE

Attaching the Procedure to a Button

Actually, you can attach a procedure to almost any worksheet object. To attach the procedure to a button, follow these steps:

1. Select the Sheet4 tab.

2. Choose the **View Toolbars** command, check the Drawing Toolbar check box, and choose OK.

3. Select the Create Button button and draw a button on the upper-right side of the worksheet, by clicking the button and then dragging it to the desired location. When the Assign Macro dialog box appears, select AmortTable and choose OK.

4. If the new button isn't already selected, select it by clicking the Select button on the toolbar to turn on the selection tool, and then select the new button. If you don't turn on the selection tool first, clicking the new button executes the attached procedure instead of selecting the button.

5. Change the button caption to **Amort Table**, then deselect it.

6. Save the workbook.

Now when you press the button, the procedure executes and creates the amortization table as shown in figure 1.5. Try it.

Figure 1.5
By pressing the button on the worksheet, you produce the amortization table.

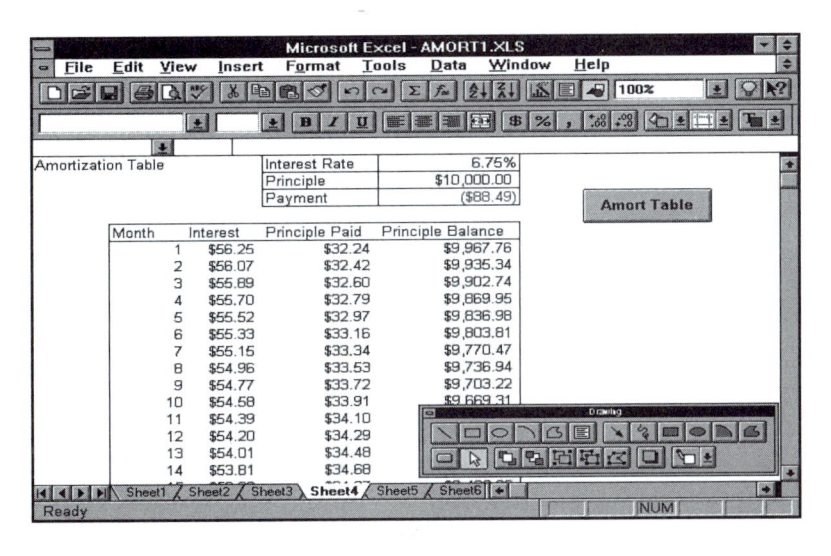

After you place all the drawing objects on the worksheet, you can hide the Drawing toolbar.

27

Chapter 1 ◆ Welcome to Visual Basic for Applications

Attaching the Procedure to a Button on a Toolbar

You attach a procedure to a toolbar by placing a new tool button on the toolbar and then attaching the procedure to it. To attach a procedure to a toolbar, follow these steps:

1. Select the Sheet5 tab.

2. Choose the **V**iew **T**oolbars command and then click the Customize button. When the Customize dialog box opens, first select the Custom category, and then select a custom button and drag it to an empty space on the Drawing toolbar. The Assign Macro dialog box automatically appears when you place a new button on a toolbar. Select AmortTable and then choose OK. When the Customize dialog box reappears, select Close.

3. Save the worksheet.

The Drawing toolbar now has a new button on it. When you press that button, the amortization table is again created on the active worksheet as shown in figure 1.6. The new button is the smiley face on the lower-right corner of the toolbar.

Figure 1.6
By pressing the button on the Drawing toolbar, you produce the amortization table.

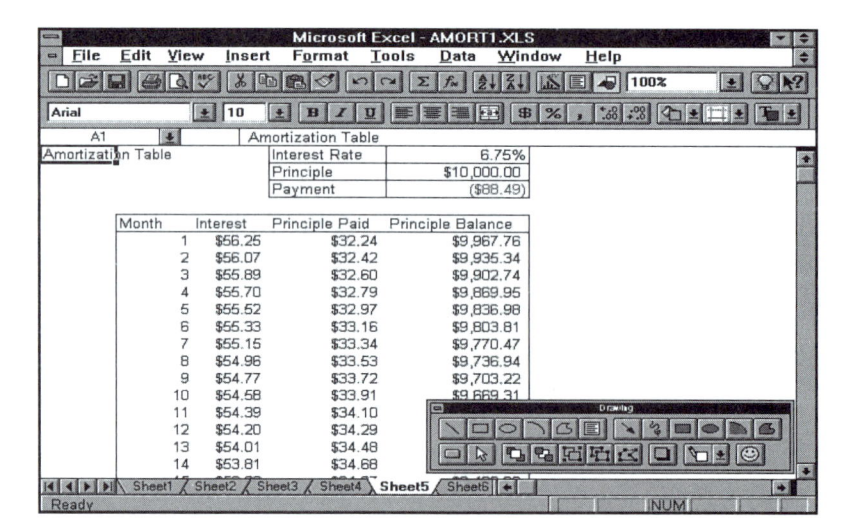

Attaching the Procedure to a Menu

When you first created the amortization table procedure, you had the option of placing it on a menu. To do that now, use the **T**ools **M**acro command, select the macro, and then click the Options button. A dialog box similar to that in figure 1.1 appears. In the Assign To box, check the Men**u** Item on Tools Menu check box, type **Amort** in the text box just below the check box, and then choose OK. When the Macro dialog box appears, choose Close. Menu Item Amort now appears at the bottom of the **T**ools menu. Selecting it re-creates the amortization table as before.

Attaching the Procedure to a Graphics Object

In the same manner that you attached the procedure to a button, you can attach a procedure to any graphics object on the worksheet. This includes all the lines, circles, and boxes that you can create with the Drawing toolbar, and also includes graphs. Simply select the object and choose the Tools Assign Macro command, select the procedure, and then choose OK.

After you assign a graphics object to a procedure, you can no longer simply click the object and drag it around the screen. Now whenever you click the drawing object, you execute the procedure attached to it. To select the drawing object so that you can move or change it, or unassign the macro, turn on the selection tool by choosing the Select button on the Drawing toolbar. You can now select the graphics object without executing its attached procedure. Additionally, you can press Ctrl while clicking the object to select it without executing its attached procedure.

Summary

This chapter has introduced the Visual Basic for Applications language and the extensions that allow it to connect to and control Excel. You used the Macro Recorder to record a custom procedure, edited that procedure, and then attached it to several different buttons. In the next chapter you learn about Microsoft's implementation of objects in Visual Basic, and the actual language statements in the procedure that you recorded.

Review Questions

Answers to review questions are in Appendix A.

1. What is Visual Basic's continuation character for continuing a statement on more than one line?

2. What are the three places where a new macro can be stored?

3. Explain the difference between absolute and relative references.

Review Exercises

1. With the Macro Recorder turned on, re-create one of your favorite Excel worksheets. Then examine the procedure listing and compare it to the steps that you took when creating your favorite worksheet.

2. Turn on the Macro Recorder, type some numbers on the worksheet, and then use them to create a graph. Examine the code recorded by the Macro Recorder while you created a graph and edited it.

CHAPTER 2

Objects, Properties, and Methods

The last chapter gave you a glimpse of the Visual Basic language and how you can apply it to Excel objects to control a worksheet. But what are objects? Is this some new programming jargon term to impress your friends with, or is it something real? In this chapter, you learn about Visual Basic's implementation of object-oriented programming (OOP—another one of those jargon terms) and its application to Excel. In this chapter you learn the following:

- What a programming object is
- How Visual Basic uses objects
- How to use an object's properties
- How to use an object's methods
- How to locate usable objects

What Are Objects?

What is an object in a computer code? You know what physical objects are. Your mouse, keyboard, and computer are physical objects, as is your coffee cup. So how does the code inside your computer become an object?

Chapter 2 ◆ Objects, Properties, and Methods

Object-oriented programming (OOP) is the latest style for designing computer programs. This style is used because modern program design endeavors to achieve several specific goals for computer programs. That is, computer programs should be

- Verifiable
- Revisable
- Reusable
- Transportable

Programs must be verifiable so that you can ensure that they are doing what they are supposed to be doing. Programs must be revisable so that you or someone else can later understand a program well enough to make corrections or changes. Programs should be reusable so that you only have to write a procedure once, and then can reuse it later when you need the same functionality again. Finally, programs should be transportable so that they can be moved to a different platform with a minimum of recording.

Most modern programming practice seeks to achieve these goals by *modularizing* computer programs. Modular computer programs are divided into discrete chunks called *modules*. Each module has a specific, well-defined function to perform, and has access to only the data that it needs to perform that function. Modular code, designed with well-defined interfaces to the other modules in a program, is much easier to debug, maintain, and understand. Another aspect of modularity is isolation, which ensures that any changes that you make to a module's code affects only the operation of that module, and no other. Again, this enhances your ability to debug, maintain, and understand the code.

Object-oriented programming is modularizing to the extreme. In object-oriented programming, a code object is a *container*. A container includes data and the code that knows how to manipulate that data. Although a code object is simply a block of code and data, it is visualized as a real, physical thing such as a button. A code object has a specific function to perform and contains all the code and data necessary to perform that function, but its inner workings are often hidden from view.

In more traditional programming, computer programs are designed as in an assembly line, in which a block of data is passed from module to module, with each module modifying or using that data in some way. Modules did not contain data, only code to modify whatever data you passed to them. If you accidentally pass a procedure the wrong data or the wrong amount of data, the procedure processes it anyway, returning garbage or even crashing your system.

In object-oriented programming, the data and the code that manipulates that data are combined together into a structure called an object. Instead of passing the data from module to module to perform different calculations with it, you send messages to the object containing the data, asking the object to perform the calculation. You are less likely to pass bad data to an object, because the data that the object manipulates is contained within the object. Furthermore, you don't call or execute an object; instead, you pass it a message, politely asking it to perform one of its tasks. (Of course, if it lacks the capability to perform the manipulation, the object may politely tell you that it can't fulfill your request.)

Common examples of Visual Basic and Excel objects include worksheets, ranges (cell ranges), buttons, text boxes, workbooks, chart sheets, and module sheets.

Properties and Methods

A code object contains properties and methods. The *properties* are the object's visible data, and the *methods* are the tasks that the object knows how to perform. *Visible data* is that data that can be accessed from outside of the object. Properties can be the data that an object manipulates, or they can control how an object looks or behaves. For example, the Value property of a text box contains the text that is typed in the box, the Color property of a font controls how it looks, and the Enabled property of a menu item controls whether you can select it.

You don't call an object in the same way that you call a subroutine. Instead, you send it a message to change one of its properties or to execute one of its methods. You access the properties and methods contained in an object by appending a dot and the property's or method's name to the object. For example, if Power is a Button object, the following is the construct to access the Value property of Power:

```
Power.Value
```

If you follow this construct with an equals sign (=) and a number, the object changes the value of the property within the object. To retrieve the value of the property, you place the construct on the left side of a formula.

When a method executes, it applies only to the properties contained within the object; it cannot directly change the value of another object's properties. However, the method can ask some other object to change the value of the other object's properties.

Consider as an example of an object the push button that turns on the power to your monitor (maybe you have a switch instead, but if so bear with me and imagine that your monitor has a button). If you push the button, the internal mechanical linkages connect the output to the input, and the switch is on. Pushing it a second time causes the mechanical linkages to disengage, and the power is turned off. Therefore, the switch is like an object, in that it is a totally self-contained device with well-defined interfaces. One interface, the button, enables you to turn it on or off. The second interface, the terminals, communicates the state of the switch to other objects within the monitor. It does not matter how the internal linkages make or break the connection between the terminals. Likewise, although there are many different kinds of switches, from purely mechanical to solid state, the kind that your monitor uses is unimportant. You need not access the internal workings of the switch (and the plastic case prevents you from doing so anyway). What is important is that the input is either connected or not connected to the output, depending on the state of the switch.

A code version of this switch operates in much the same manner. When you press it with the mouse pointer, its state changes from on to off, or from off to on.

Instead of having a mechanical connection, the code switch has a property named Value that can equal on or off, but both interfaces serve the same purpose in their respective environments.

When you press the button by clicking it with the mouse pointer, you change the value of the Value property from on to off or from off to on. The button also responds by changing its image to mimic a real button being pressed.

Pressing the button itself does not turn something on, as pressing the button on your monitor does not turn the monitor on all by itself. The button on your monitor depends on the line cord object to bring power to the switch. The mechanical switch simply connects the input to the output. The code button does the same thing: It does not turn your virtual monitor on or off, it only changes its Value property on and off. Some other object, such as a virtual screen object, must examine the switch object and determine whether to turn it on or not.

Inheritance

Just as a switch object is part of a monitor object, code objects can be made part of other larger code objects. When objects are combined, a special property known as *inheritance* comes into play. When an object is made part of another object, that other object inherits all the properties and methods of the former. This principle is the same for the mechanical switch; when it becomes part of your monitor, that monitor inherits the on/off property of the switch and the method for changing that property when the button is pressed.

To access an object's properties or methods when the object is contained within one or more larger objects, you specify each of the container objects starting with the outermost container, followed by a dot and the next inner container object, followed by another dot and the next inner container object, and so forth until you reach the object whose properties and methods you are trying to access. Thus you have a list of objects from left to right that progresses from the outermost object to the one you are interested in. Follow this construct with a final dot and the property or method that you want to access. For example, the MyMonitor monitor object contains the Power button object, so MyMonitor inherits the Value property of Power. To access this Value property, you would use the following construct:

```
MyMonitor.Power.Value
```

If MyMonitor is contained in the MyHouse object, you access Value using the following construct:

```
MyHouse.MyMonitor.Power.Value
```

And so you would continue for each enclosing object. The MyHouse object now has inherited the capabilities of a button.

Classes

Each object is a specific, unique thing. A *class*, however, describes all objects of a specific type. Thus, classes are at the highest level of object definitions. You use a class to create an object. For example, you use the class Button to create specific Button objects. Each Button object that you create is distinct and unique from all the other Button objects that you create. The button Power1 is an object of the class Button, as is the button Power2. Although both Power1 and Power2 are of the class Button, they are separate, distinct objects.

Locating Objects

Locating objects for Visual Basic to use can often be difficult. This is because a Visual Basic program can apply to multiple applications, and each application has its own libraries of objects.

Online Help

One of the best ways to locate objects is with the online help facility. The Help window not only lists the objects but also tells you what they are for and how to use them. Help runs as a separate application under Windows, so you can have Help files open for several applications at the same time. In addition, when a Help topic is displayed, you can press the On Top button to keep displaying the Help window on top of your worksheet so that you can continue reading it as you work on your worksheet.

To access Excel's online help, choose the **Help** **C**ontents command. In the Help window that appears, Visual Basic has its own separate section, "Programming with Visual Basic." To get the contents of the Visual Basic section shown in figure 2.1, click the "Programming with Visual Basic" section. Within the Visual Basic section, the "Programming Language Summary" and its subsections list the Excel objects that are available to Visual Basic.

> **Note:** To use the search capability of online help to locate Visual Basic topics, you must be in the Visual Basic section of the online help facility. If you are in the Excel section, you locate Excel topics only.

Chapter 2 ◆ Objects, Properties, and Methods

Figure 2.1
The Visual Basic section of Excel's online help.

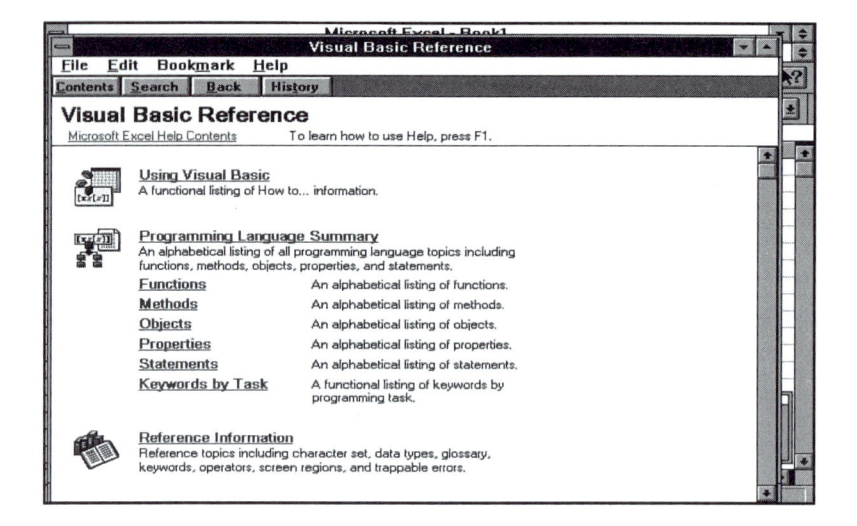

The Object Browser

The second way to locate objects is to use the Object Browser. The Object Browser enables you to see all the available objects in Excel, Visual Basic, any attached sheets, and any other open applications that register their objects with the operating system.

To start the Object Browser in Excel, make a module sheet active and choose the **V**iew **O**bject Browser command, or click the Object Browser button on the Visual Basic toolbar. The Object Browser dialog box like that shown in figure 2.2 appears.

Figure 2.2
Visual Basic's Object Browser.

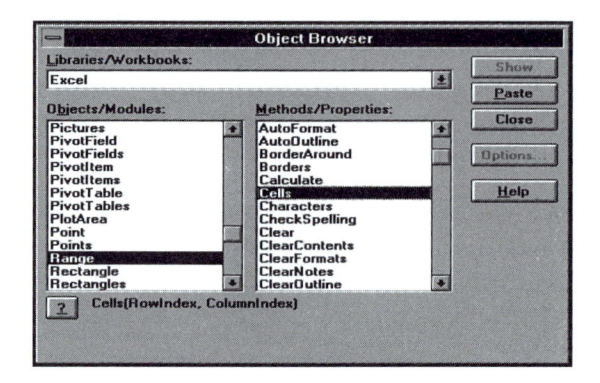

At the top of the Object Browser is a drop-down list of all the open libraries. Excel and Visual Basic for Applications (VBA) are considered libraries of objects. In figure 2.2, the Excel application is selected. On the left side of the Object Browser is a list of the names of all the objects in the selected library. On the right side is a list of the properties and methods in the selected object. In figure 2.2, the Range object is selected, which is used to select cell ranges on a worksheet. If you select a method, such as the Cells method as shown in figure 2.2, its syntax is displayed at the bottom of the Object Browser. If you click the ? button, the online help facility displays more information about the selected method.

When you find the object that you want, choose **P**aste. Then the syntax line shown at the bottom of the box is inserted into your program at the current cursor location.

Macro Recorder

The simplest way to learn how to use worksheet objects is to use the Macro Recorder as you did in Chapter 1. This is especially useful when you want to insert values or apply formatting to cells. Place the insertion point in your module where you want to insert the code, and choose the **T**ools **R**ecord Macro **M**ark Position for Recording command. Switch to the worksheet in which you want to insert data, and choose the **T**ools **R**ecord Macro R**e**cord at Mark command. When you finish recording your macro, click the Stop button on the floating toolbar.

The steps that you recorded are now inserted into your procedure as Visual Basic code, which includes all the objects, methods, and procedures that you need to perform those steps. Edit the code to remove any unneeded steps or to change what the procedure does.

Summary

In this chapter, you learned about Visual Basic's implementation of object-oriented programming, and how objects are used to access an Excel worksheet. You also learned about an object's properties and methods, and how to apply them. In the next few chapters, you examine these parts of Visual Basic in much more detail.

Review Questions

Answers to review questions are in Appendix A.

1. Objects are considered containers. What two things do they contain?
2. Describe a programming object.
3. Describe a method and explain how you access it in code.
4. Describe a property and explain how you access it in code.

Chapter 2 ◆ Objects, Properties, and Methods

Review Exercises

1. Use the Object Browser to locate the syntax of the Cells method for Excel's Range object, as shown in figure 2.2.

2. Use the Object Browser to locate the syntax of the Cos function in the VBA library's Math module.

3. Use the online help facility to locate the same function as in exercise 2.

4. Use the Macro Recorder to format some cells, then compare the recording to the steps that you took to make the recording. Try this several times with different types of formatting and changes to a cell's contents and appearance.

CHAPTER 3

Accessing Excel Objects with Visual Basic

Microsoft Excel is a library of objects within the Excel application container. As you might expect, Excel objects include worksheets, workbooks, charts, and cell ranges. The libraries of Excel worksheet functions are also objects, as are menus and toolbars. Visual Basic for Applications is the method for modifying the operation of Excel. In this chapter, you look more closely at the Visual Basic/Excel interface, to see exactly how to access and control the different objects in Excel. In this chapter, you will learn the following:

- ♦ How to use collections to access objects
- ♦ How to use Range objects to access worksheet cells
- ♦ How to use the special active properties to make procedures more general
- ♦ How to change the contents and format cells
- ♦ How to access worksheet methods

Using Object Collections

You use collections to access most worksheet objects in Visual Basic. A *collection* is a container for all the objects of a specific class. For example, the Workbooks collection contains all the currently open workbooks, and the Worksheets collection contains all the worksheets in an open workbook. Because Visual Basic cannot access workbooks or worksheets by name, you must use the collections to connect a name of an object to the actual object. The following are several frequently used collections:

Sheets	All the sheets of any type in a workbook
Workbooks	All the currently open workbooks
Worksheets	All the worksheets in a workbook
Charts	All the chart sheets in a workbook

You access a member of a collection in two ways: with an integer or with the member's name. For example, if you have a workbook named Sales, the following code accesses a worksheet in that workbook:

```
Workbooks("Sales").Worksheets(2)
Workbooks("Sales").Worksheets("West")
```

If West were the second worksheet in the Worksheets collection, both of these references would point to the same sheet. When you use the explicit name of an object when accessing a collection, you ensure that you receive a specific object every time that you access that collection. However, you must know the name of the object before you access the collection.

Using the integer method, you can cycle through all the elements of a collection simply by changing the value of the integer. You don't have to know the name of an object to access it.

Finally, if you don't specify the member of a collection, the reference specifies all the members of the collection. By specifying all the members of a collection in this way, you can change some global properties of the members, or add or remove members.

A useful Visual Basic statement for accessing the elements of a collection is the For Each statement, which is described in Chapter 14, "Using Object Type Loops." The For Each statement applies a block of statements to each member of a collection.

> **Caution:** If you add or remove a member of a collection, the numbering of the other elements of the collection may change. If you access this changed collection with the same integer as you used a previous time, you may get a different member.

Getting Information about a Collection

Several properties enable you to access information about a collection. Most collections have a Count property that contains the number of members in the collection. To get the name of a member, extract a single object from the collection

Visual Basic for Applications By EXAMPLE

and examine the Name property of the object. Another useful property is Parent, which contains the name of the object that contains the collection.

To see how these properties work, follow these steps:

1. Create a new workbook with the **File New** command.

2. Create a module with the **Insert Macro Module** command.

3. Type the following procedure into the module:

   ```
   Sub GetInfo()
   'Get information about collections.
   Worksheets("Sheet1").Range("B2").Value = Worksheets.Count
   Worksheets("Sheet1").Range("B3").Value = Worksheets.Parent.Name
   Worksheets("Sheet1").Range("B4").Value = Worksheets(3).Name
   End Sub
   ```

4. Run the procedure by choosing the **Tools Macro** command, selecting GetInfo, and choosing Run, or by clicking somewhere in the procedure and clicking the Run icon on the Visual Basic toolbar.

This procedure gets the value of the Count property of the Worksheets collection and places it in cell B2 on the Sheet1 worksheet. It then gets the name of the Parent object and places it in cell B3, then gets the name of the third worksheet in the collection and places it in cell B4. If you switch to Sheet1, it should look like figure 3.1, with the values displayed in cells B2, B3, and B4. The first is the number of worksheets in this workbook, the second is the name of the workbook, and the third is the name of the third worksheet.

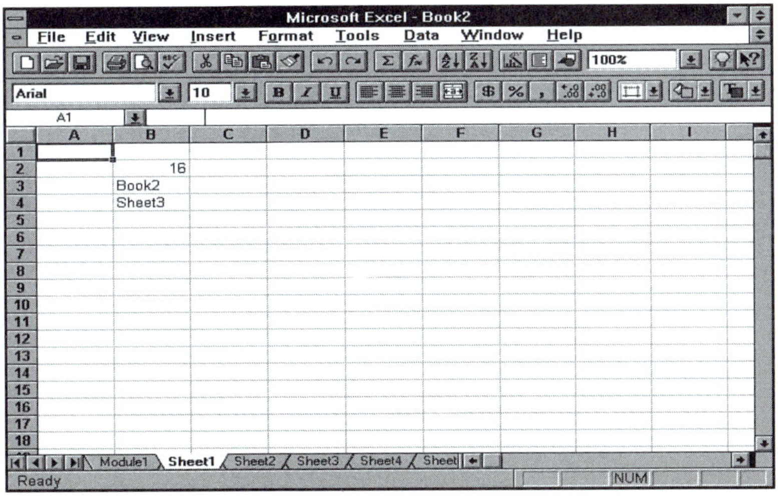

Figure 3.1
The changes in Sheet1 caused by the GetInfo procedure.

Chapter 3 ◆ Accessing Excel Objects with Visual Basic

Adding Members to a Collection

To add members to a collection, use the Add method. The format of the Add method depends on the type of collection with which you are working. For example, when using the Add method with the Workbooks collection, you can add an argument that determines which kind of worksheets are in the new workbook. In most cases, if you use the Add method, you get whichever worksheet or workbook is the current default.

When working with the Workbooks collection, you can also use the Open method to open an existing workbook. If you open or add another workbook by some other means, such as using the **File O**pen command, it is automatically added to the collection.

Removing Members from a Collection

To remove members from the Workbooks collection, use the Delete method or the Close method. If you apply the Delete method to a collection without selecting a specific member, all the members in the collection are deleted. The Close method operates the same as closing a workbook with the **File C**lose command. If you close workbooks by any means, they are automatically removed from the Worksheets collection.

To see how adding and deleting members of a collection works, add the following steps to the previous example:

1. Select the Module1 sheet and change the procedure to the following (changes to the previous procedure are indicated by boldface type):

```
Sub GetInfo()
'Get information about collections
Worksheets("Sheet1").Range("B2").Value = Worksheets.Count
Worksheets("Sheet1").Range("B3").Value = Worksheets.Parent.Name
Worksheets("Sheet1").Range("B4").Value = Worksheets(3).Name
'Add and delete members from a collection
Worksheets.Add   'Add a new worksheet
Worksheets("Sheet1").Range("B6").Value = Worksheets.Count
Worksheets("Sheet1").Range("B7").Value = Worksheets(3).Name
Worksheets(3).Delete   'Delete sheet number 3
Worksheets("Sheet1").Range("B8").Value = Worksheets(3).Name
Worksheets("Sheet1").Range("B9").Value = Worksheets.Count
End Sub
```

2. Run the procedure as before, using either the **T**ools **M**acro command or the Run icon on the Visual Basic toolbar.

Switch back to Sheet1, which should now look like figure 3.2. Note that the Add method added another worksheet to the beginning of the list of sheets. The Count property then returned 16 sheets, and sheet number 3 changes from Sheet3 to Sheet2. This change is caused by the new sheet being inserted at the beginning of the list. Next, the Delete method is used to delete sheet number 3, which reduces the count by 1 and changes sheet number 3 to Sheet3 again.

Figure 3.2
Adding and deleting worksheets changes the Count and Name properties.

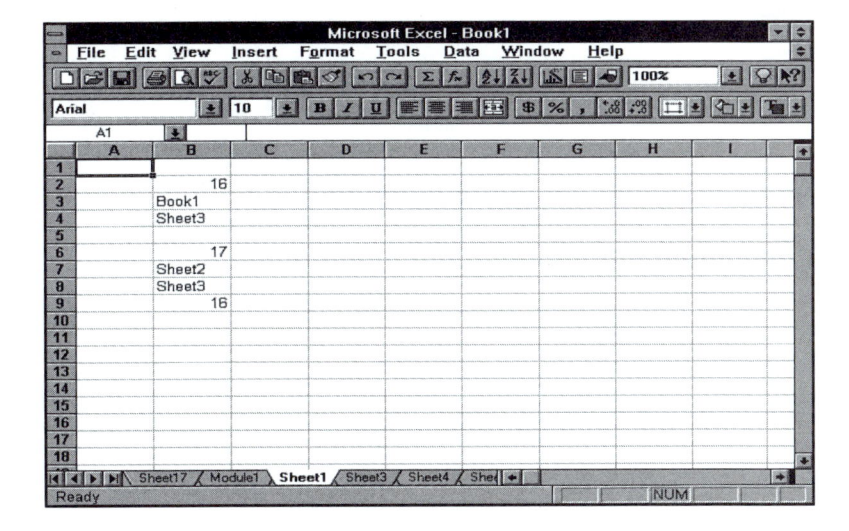

Note in the tabs at the bottom of the screen that the new sheet, Sheet17, was added at the beginning and that Sheet2 was deleted.

Accessing Cells with Range Objects

You might expect that individual cells on a worksheet are objects. However, this isn't the case. Individual cells on a worksheet are accessed as Range objects. A *Range object* is any cell or rectangular group of cells on a worksheet. The Union method is used to combine unconnected groups of cells into a single Range object. Three methods are available for producing Range objects: Range, Cells, and Offset. A shortcut method that uses square brackets is also available.

The Range Method

The Range method, which is the most versatile method, takes one or two cell references as arguments and returns a Range object. The cell references must be strings in the A1 style (which is the familiar column-letter-row-number notation), a named range on the worksheet, or another Range object. To display the values returned by the Count and Name properties, you must place the values into cells. In the previous example, you accomplish this by using the Range method and references to single cells.

A single cell reference as an argument returns a Range object for that single cell. Two single cell references return a Range object for the rectangular region between those two cells. A reference to a rectangular cell range in normal Excel format is also allowed (A7:D9, for example), as are the names of named ranges on a worksheet.

> **Tip:** Named ranges are useful when selecting Range objects, because the code in the procedure still applies to the correct range even if you move the affected range to a different location on a worksheet. If the code uses explicit cell references to define a range, however, you must edit the procedure before moving it.

To see more examples of the Range method, open a new workbook, create a new module sheet, and type the following procedure:

```
Sub theRanges()
'Accessing cells with the Range method
Worksheets("Sheet1").Range("B1").Value = 1    'A single cell
Worksheets("Sheet1").Range("A3", "C4").Value = 2 'A range of cells
Worksheets("Sheet1").Range("B7:C9").Value _
    = 3    'Another range of cells
'An unconnected range
Union(Worksheets("Sheet1").Range("D1:F2"), _
    Worksheets("Sheet1").Range("E7:G9")).Value = 4
'Another unconnected range
Worksheets("Sheet1").Range("D11:F12,D15:E17").Value = 5
End Sub
```

Run this procedure and then switch to Sheet1 to see the results. Sheet1 should now look like figure 3.3. The first example of the Range method accesses the single cell B1, in which it places the value 1; the second and third examples access rectangular ranges of cells, in which they place the numbers 2 and 3. The fourth example uses the Union method to combine two Range objects into a single Range object that references two unconnected ranges and places the number 4 in them. The fifth example also references two unconnected ranges created with a single Range method and places the number 5 in them.

> **Note:** If you apply the Range method to a Range object, the reference is relative to the upper-left corner of the Range object, even though the cell reference is an explicit cell name. For example, `Range("B5").Range("B2")` references cell C6 because the range B2 (one row down and one column right from cell A1) is determined relative to cell B5.

Figure 3.3
The procedure theRanges places numbers in cell ranges.

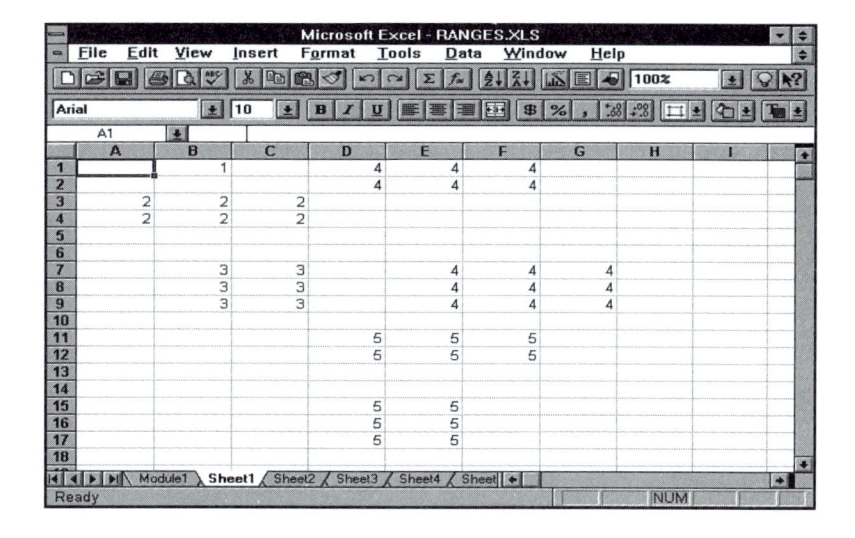

The Cells Method

The Cells method takes two integers as arguments and returns a Range object containing a single cell. The two integer arguments determine the row and column number of the selected cell. You can also use a quoted string that contains the column letter for the second argument, but doing so is not very useful. The Cells method is most useful for selecting groups of cells, one cell at a time, simply by changing the value of the integers. You can also use the Cells method as an argument to the Range method. This enables you to use integers to select cell ranges larger than one cell.

> **Note:** The Cells method is like the Range method, in that if you apply it to an existing range, the returned range is relative to the upper-left corner of the existing range. Thus `Range("B7:D12").Cells(3,2)` references cell C9. However, for such cases, the Offset method does the same thing, but is more obvious in what it is doing—that is, the cell selected with the Offset method is an offset from the existing Range object.

To see more examples of the Cells method, open a new workbook, create a new module sheet, and type the following procedure:

```
Sub theCells()
'Accessing cells with the Cells method
Worksheets("Sheet1").Cells(1, 2).Value = 1    'A single cell
Worksheets("Sheet1").Range(Worksheets("Sheet1").Cells(3, 1), _
    Worksheets("Sheet1").Cells(4, 3)).Value = 2 'A range of cells
```

Chapter 3 ♦ Accessing Excel Objects with Visual Basic

```
Worksheets("Sheet1").Cells(1, "D").Value = 3    'Another single cell
For I = 1 To 10
Worksheets("Sheet1").Cells(I + 5, 2).Value = I
Next I
End Sub
```

Run the procedure and switch to Sheet1 to see the results as shown in figure 3.4. The first Cells example in the preceding procedure places the number 1 in cell B1 (row 1, column 2). The second Cells example uses the Cells method twice as arguments to the Range method to produce a reference to the cell range A3:C4. The numbers used in these references can be replaced with variables or formulas, as the last example demonstrates. The last example uses a For-Next loop, which Chapter 12, "Using Counted Loops," explains in more detail. The loop executes the statements between the For and Next statements ten times, with the value of I increasing by 1 for each iteration of the loop. The Cells method uses the value of I to calculate the row number, which moves the selected row down one with each iteration of the loop. The value of I is then placed in the selected cell.

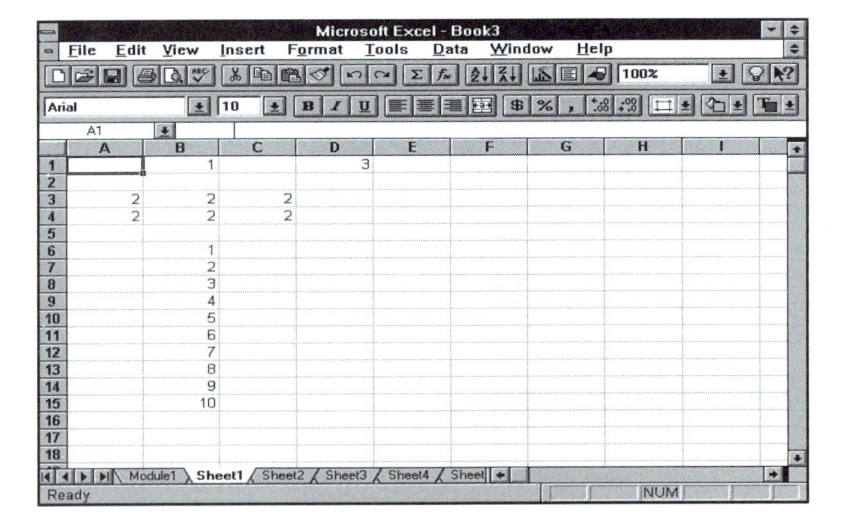

Figure 3.4
Results of the procedure theCells placing numbers in cell ranges.

The Offset Method

The Offset method works much like the Cells method, except that the Range object returned is always relative to the upper-left corner of the current Range object. The Offset method is most often used to create a Range object relative to the current active cell on a worksheet. The Offset method takes two arguments—a row index and a column index—but the indexes are the offsets from the current Range object.

If you compare the Cells and the Offset methods, you see that their row and column indexes differ by 1 when they reference the same cell. For example, the two following statements both reference cell E3:

```
Worksheets("Sheet1").Range("A1").Cells(3,5)

Worksheets("Sheet1").Range("A1").Offset(2,4)
```

When creating Range objects that are relative to some other Range object, use the Offset method rather than a Range or Cells method to make your code more intuitive.

The Range Method Shortcut

Placing a cell reference between two square brackets is a shortcut for using the Range method with the same cell reference as an argument. Thus, the following two statements both reference the same cell:

```
Worksheets("Sheet1").Range("E7")

Worksheets("Sheet1").[E7]
```

Although this shortcut requires less typing, its syntax is less readable than that of the full Range method. For this reason, you should avoid using the shortcut.

Using the Active Properties

Visual Basic has several special properties of the Application object that significantly simplify Visual Basic programs. These active properties always evaluate to the currently active object of a specific class. The *active object* is the topmost sheet for workbooks and worksheets, the active cell for Range objects, or the selected object for graphics objects.

The active properties are often used with the Select and Activate methods. The Select method selects a range of cells or a sheet. The Activate method makes a single cell within the current selection the active cell. When applied to a sheet, Activate works the same as Select.

The ActiveWorkbook property evaluates to the workbook that is currently being displayed. The ActiveSheet property evaluates to the topmost sheet in the active workbook. The topmost sheet can be a worksheet, chart sheet, macro sheet, or module sheet, depending on which object is currently visible or on top.

The ActiveCell property always evaluates to a single-celled Range object that contains the active cell on the topmost worksheet. In any group of selected cells on a worksheet, only one is the active cell. The active cell is distinguishable by its white background, because the rest of the selection has a black background. When a group of cells is first selected on a worksheet, the active cell is at the top-left corner of the

Chapter 3 ◆ Accessing Excel Objects with Visual Basic

selection. Every time you press Enter while typing values into a selection, the active cell moves down to the next cell of the selection. When the active cell reaches the bottom of the selection, it moves right one column and up to the top of the selection. When the active cell reaches the lower-right corner of the selection, it moves back up to the upper-left corner.

The Selection property is closely related to the ActiveCell property, but evaluates to the whole selection rather than the single active cell. If only one cell is selected, the Selection and the ActiveCell are the same. The active cell is always within the current selection and is usually the cell in the upper-left corner of the selection.

To see more examples of these properties, open a new workbook, create a new module sheet, and type the following procedure:

```
Sub ACProp()
    'Use the Active properties to format a cell.
    ActiveWorkbook.Worksheets("Sheet1").Select
    ActiveSheet.Range("B3").Select
    ActiveCell.Value = 23
    ActiveCell.NumberFormat = "0.00"
    ActiveCell.HorizontalAlignment = xlCenter
    ActiveCell.BorderAround Weight:=xlThick, ColorIndex:=4
    ActiveCell.Interior.ColorIndex = 6

    'Now use the same properties to format a selection.
    ActiveSheet.Range("C5:F7").Select
    Selection.Value = 23
    Selection.NumberFormat = "0.00"
    Selection.HorizontalAlignment = xlCenter
    Selection.BorderAround Weight:=xlThick, ColorIndex:=4
    Selection.Interior.ColorIndex = 6
    ActiveSheet.Range("A1").Select
End Sub
```

Run this procedure, and it will switch to the Sheet1 worksheet, insert 23 in cell B3, outline it in green, and color the background yellow. Next it selects the range C5:F7 and does the same to each cell in the range. The worksheet should now look like figure 3.5.

The first block of statements selects Sheet1 and then selects cell B3 on Sheet1 using the ActiveSheet property. The next few lines insert the number 23, give it a numeric format, center the number, draw a green border around it, and make the interior of the cell yellow. Each of these lines uses the ActiveCell property to select cell B3.

The next block of statements does the same thing to the range of cells C5:F7. This time the Range object is a range of cells rather than a single cell, and the Select method selects the whole range. In addition, the Selection property is used to apply the changes to the whole selection rather than just to the active cell.

Figure 3.5

The results of the ACProp procedure placing numbers in cell ranges and formatting those ranges.

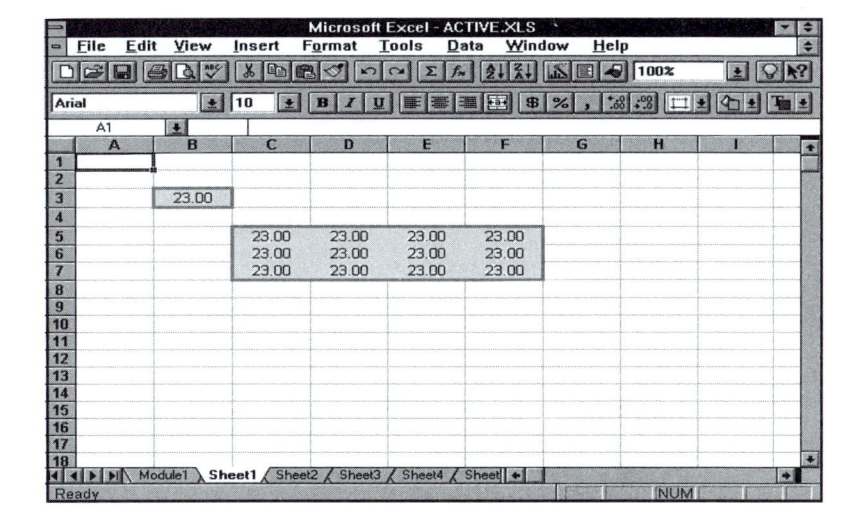

Notice that this procedure repeats some of the objects several times. You can simplify such a procedure by using the With statement. To do so, you follow the With keyword with a list of objects, which you separate with periods. All statements between the With and the End With statements are assumed to have this list of objects attached at any period dangling on the left side of a word. For example, you could rewrite the preceding procedure as follows, and it would still operate the same:

```
Sub ACProp()
    'Use the Active properties to format a cell
    ActiveWorkbook.Worksheets("Sheet1").Select
    ActiveSheet.Range("B3").Select
    With ActiveCell
        .Value = 23
        .NumberFormat = "0.00"
        .HorizontalAlignment = xlCenter
        .BorderAround Weight:=xlThick, ColorIndex:=4
        .Interior.ColorIndex = 6
    End With

    'Now use the same properties to format a selection
    ActiveSheet.Range("C5:F7").Select
    With Selection
        .Value = 23
        .NumberFormat = "0.00"
        .HorizontalAlignment = xlCenter
        .BorderAround Weight:=xlThick, ColorIndex:=4
```

```
        With .Interior
            .ColorIndex = 6
        End With
    End With
    ActiveSheet.Range("A1").Select
End Sub
```

In the second block of code that applies to the selection, note that a second With statement is nested within the first. When you nest multiple With statements, as in this example, each With value builds on the last.

> **Note:** In many cases the objects returned by the ActiveWorkbook, ActiveSheet, or ActiveCell properties are equal to the default objects, and thus are not required in the code. However, if you include the Active properties, your code is much more readable and, if a situation occurs in which these objects are not equal to the default objects, you are assured of getting the correct object.

Using Content Properties

In most of the examples shown so far, whenever you want to place a value in a worksheet cell, you use the Value property of the Range object. Range objects provide two ways by which you can change the contents of a cell: the Value property and the Formula property.

The Value property contains the cell's current value, which is the current numeric or textural contents. When you view a cell on the screen, what you see as the contents of the cell is the value as modified by the current cell format. If you reference a cell in another cell within the same formula, the cell's value is that which it receives from the other cell. When you set the value of a cell, you equate the Value property to a numeric or string value.

The Formula property contains what you actually type into a cell to produce the value. If you type a number into a cell, the value and the formula are the same. If you type a formula into a cell, the Formula property contains the formula, and the Value property contains the result of the formula.

The Formula property offers two variations that determine how you write cell references in the formula. If you use the Formula property, Excel assumes that the string that you insert into the cell is a formula with cell references in the A1 style, which is the familiar column-letter-row-number notation. If you use the FormulaR1C1 property, Excel assumes that you wrote the formula using the R1C1 format for addressing other cells. The R1C1 method of cell addressing is a row-column notation; using this method, for example, R2C3 references the cell on the second row and the third column.

Visual Basic for Applications **By**
EXAMPLE

Applying Formatting Properties

In addition to setting the contents of a cell, you can set the font, style, formatting, color, patterns, and border of the cell. By setting the font and style of a cell, you specify the font of the text and whether it is bold or italic. Formatting consists of a template that describes how a number is displayed in a cell. Choose the Format Cells command and select the Number tab for a list of available numeric formats. Color, patterns, and borders are also listed under the Format Cells command.

The best way to write Visual Basic code to format cells is to use the Macro Recorder. Because so many options and variations are possible with the different formatting commands, it can be difficult to get the correct formatting simply by typing the formats. By using the Macro Recorder, you can adjust the style and format of a cell until it is displayed the way you want it and then use the recorded macro in your code.

For example, start the Macro Recorder and type some text in one cell and a number in another, and then play with the formatting, color, size, borders, and other settings. Then see what results in the recorded macro. I produced the following macro while creating the worksheet shown in figure 3.6. The comments were inserted after the procedure was recorded. The comments marked Default were not changed in the dialog boxes, but are included in the recording because they are set in the same box as other options.

Code	Comment
`' StylePlay Macro`	Start the recorder.
`' Playing with styles`	Name the procedure **StylePlay**.
`Sub StylePlay()`	
`    Range("C4").Select`	Select cell C4.
`    ActiveCell.FormulaR1C1 = "Sierra"`	Type **Sierra**.
`    Range("C6").Select`	Select cell C6.
`    ActiveCell.FormulaR1C1 = "1234"`	Type **1234**.
`    Range("C4").Select`	Select cell C4.
`    With Selection.Font`	Choose the **Format Cells** command and select the Font tab.
`        .Name = "Times New Roman"`	Select the Times New Roman font.
`        .FontStyle = "Bold Italic"`	Set the style to bold italics.
`        .Size = 36`	Set the size to 36 points.
`        .Strikethrough = False`	Default.
`        .Superscript = False`	Default.

51

Chapter 3 ♦ Accessing Excel Objects with Visual Basic

`.Subscript = False`	Default.
`.OutlineFont = False`	Default.
`.Shadow = False`	Default.
`.Underline = xlNone`	Default.
`.ColorIndex = 7`	Set the color to pink.
`End With`	Choose OK.
`Columns("C:C").ColumnWidth = 20`	Widen column C.
`Range("C4").Select`	Select cell C4.
	Choose the **Format Cells** command and select the Border tab.
`Selection.Borders(xlLeft)._`	
`    LineStyle = xlNone`	Default.
`Selection.Borders(xlRight)._`	
`    LineStyle = xlNone`	Default.
`Selection.Borders(xlTop)._`	
`    LineStyle = xlNone`	Default.
`Selection.Borders(xlBottom)._`	
`    LineStyle = xlNon`	Default.
`Selection.BorderAround _`	Select Outline.
`    Weight:=xlMedium, _`	Select the medium line.
`    ColorIndex:=xlAutomatic`	
`With Selection.Interior`	Select the Patterns tab.
`    .ColorIndex = 8`	Select light blue color.
`    .Pattern = xlSolid`	Default.
`    .PatternColorIndex = xlAutomatic`	
`End With`	Choose OK.
`Rows("6:6").RowHeight = 50.`	Make row 6 50-points tall.
`Range("C6").Select`	Select cell C6.
`Selection.NumberFormat = _`	Choose **Format Cells**, and select the Number tab.
`   "$#,##0.00_);($#,##0.00)"`	Select the Currency format with two trailing zeros.
`With Selection`	Select the Alignment tab.
`    .HorizontalAlignment = xlCenter`	Select Horizontal centered.
`    .VerticalAlignment = xlCenter`	Select Vertical centered.
`    .WrapText = False`	Default.
`    .Orientation = xlHorizontal`	Default.
`    .AddIndent = False`	Default.
`End With`	Select the Font tab.
`With Selection.Font`	

Visual Basic for Applications *By* EXAMPLE

```
        .Name = "Arial"                    Default.
        .FontStyle = "Bold"                Select bold.
        .Size = 24                         Select 24 point.
        .Strikethrough = False             Default.
        .Superscript = False               Default.
        .Subscript = False                 Default.
        .OutlineFont = False               Default.
        .Shadow = False                    Default.
        .Underline = xlNone                Default.
        .ColorIndex = xlAutomatic          Default.
    End With
    With Selection.Interior                Select the Patterns tab.
        .ColorIndex = 4                    Select green.
        .Pattern = 17                      Select a light gray dot
                                               pattern.
        .PatternColorIndex = xlAutomatic   Default.
    End With                               Choose OK.
    Columns("C:C").ColumnWidth = 29.86     Widen column C.
End Sub
```

Figure 3.6
Results of the StylePlay procedure.

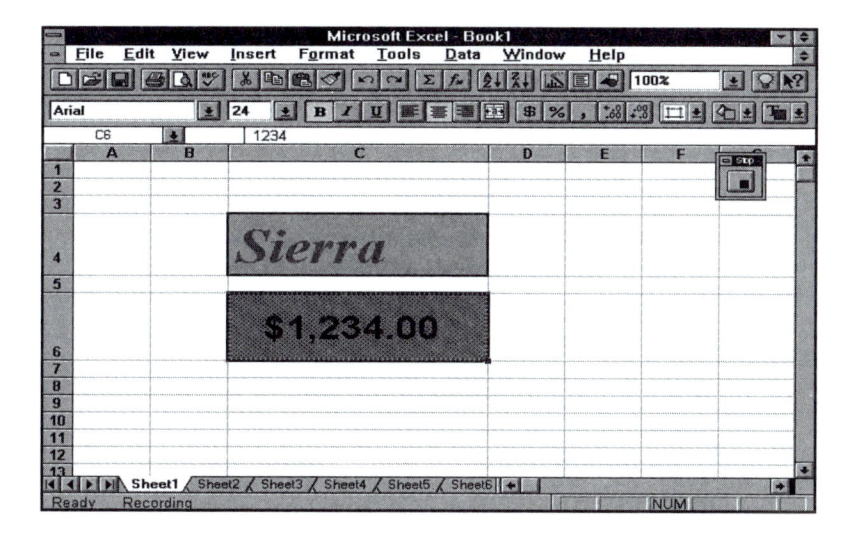

The text "Sierra" is hot pink on a blue background with a black border. The text "$1,234.00" is black on a green background.

As you review this procedure, notice that you can see the different formatting elements applied to the different parts of the cell. Font formatting is applied to the Font object, Borders are applied directly to the Range object, and the cell colors are applied to the Interior object.

This procedure sets several of the properties with values such as xlAutomatic, xlNone, or xlCenter. These are all Excel constants. You use them in place of the numeric values, because when you read the procedure the constants are more meaningful than a list of numbers. To see a list of constants, use the Object Browser to select the Excel library and then the Constants object.

Executing Worksheet Methods

Executing methods on the worksheet is similar to applying formatting. In fact, you apply several of the formats using methods rather than properties.

The last example uses the BorderAround method to change the properties of the borders surrounding a selection, as follows:

```
Selection.BorderAround Weight:=xlMedium,ColorIndex:=xlAutomatic
```

Note the difference between executing the BorderAround method and assigning a value to the LineStyle property of a border, as follows:

```
Selection.Borders(xlRight).LineStyle = xlNone
```

When you change the value of a property, you equate it to a new value (in this example, the xlNone constant). When you execute a method, you give it values by passing it arguments. You follow the method with the names of the arguments, and then equate the arguments to their values by using a colon equals sign (:=) rather than an equals sign. In this example, the Weight argument is set equal to the xlMedium constant, and the ColorIndex argument is set equal to the xlAutomatic constant.

Some useful Range object methods include Cut, Copy, and Paste. These three methods do not take any arguments, they simply transfer the contents of the Range object either to or from the clipboard. Also useful are the Clear and ClearContents methods, which either clear everything from a cell or remove only the formula and value.

The PrintOut method is useful for sending a Range object to the printer. You can select the range, define it as the print area, and then print the object, or you can pass a range to the PrintOut method, which handles all this for you. If you have to print many small sections on a worksheet, create a button on the worksheet and attach the following short routine to it; then all you have to do is select a range and press the button to print it:

```
'
'PrintIt
'
Sub PrintIt()
    Selection.PrintOut
End Sub
```

Summary

In this chapter you learned how to access and change the contents and formatting of cells on the worksheet. In addition, you learned about Excel's objects and methods, and examined how to access and use them. This completes Part I of this book. In Part II you begin to learn about the Visual Basic for Applications language and how you use it to calculate things.

Review Questions

Answers to the review questions are in Appendix A.

1. What is a collection?
2. What two ways do you access the contents of a collection?
3. How can you find out how many members are in a collection?
4. What are the three main methods for selecting Range objects on the worksheet?
5. If the current active cell is B7 and you want to access cell F12, what would you use for arguments to

    ```
    ActiveCell.Cells(?,?)
    ```

    and to

    ```
    ActiveCell.Offset(?,?)
    ```

Review Exercises

1. Run the Macro Recorder and try all the different formatting commands to see what is inserted in the recorded procedure. If you encounter any commands or statements that you don't understand, look them up in the online help.
2. Create a procedure that changes the current selection to red and puts a green border around it.
3. Create a procedure that adds a new default workbook with 16 worksheets to the Workbooks collection and then deletes worksheets 4 through 16 from that workbook's Worksheets collection.

Part II

The Primary Language Elements

CHAPTER 4

Understanding Data Types and Variables

Variables and data types control where and how data is stored in your computer's memory. In a strictly typed language, you must declare the type of every variable before you use it. Although Visual Basic is not a strictly typed language, you can manage the use of your memory much more efficiently by forcing all your variables to be of an explicit type. In this chapter, you will learn the following:

- ♦ All about data types
- ♦ How to create new data types
- ♦ How to store data in variables
- ♦ How to create and use arrays
- ♦ The scope of variables

What Are Data Types?

A *data type* specifies how a data value is stored in the memory of your computer. Specifying a data type also sets some limitations on the stored value, such as how big it can be, how many digits it can have, and whether it can have a fractional part.

If you want to fit a number into a fixed number of bytes of memory, there are several ways that you can do it. For example, you can pick a data type that uses all the bytes as a single integer, which results in numbers with the highest resolution (that is, the largest number of digits). However, integers cannot have fractional parts, and cannot represent very large numbers. To have fractions and larger

Chapter 4 ♦ Understanding Data Types and Variables

numbers, you must use some of the bytes to store the location of the decimal point, and the remainder to store the numeric part of the number. You thus exchange some resolution for the capability to store larger numbers and to have fractions. You could simply use more bytes to store the same resolution number with an exponent, but that requires the use of more memory.

When you specify the data type of a number, you specify a trade-off among resolution, size, and memory usage.

Understanding Built-In Data Types

Visual Basic has 11 built-in data types, each of which is listed in table 4.1.

Table 4.1. Visual Basic's built-in data types.

Data Type	Size (bytes)	Resolution (digits)	Range
Boolean	2	1	True or False
Integer	2	5	–32,768 to 32,767
Long	4	10	–2,147,483,648 to 2,147,483,647
Single	4	7	-3.402823×10^{38} to $-1.401298 \times 10^{-45}$ and 1.401298×10^{-45} to 3.402823×10^{38}
Double	8	15	$-1.79769313486232 \times 10^{308}$ to $-4.94065645841247 \times 10^{-324}$ and $4.94065645841247 \times 10^{-324}$ to $1.79769313486232 \times 10^{308}$
Currency	8	19	–922,337,203,685,477.5808 to 922,337,203,685,477.5807
Date	8		1/1/100 to 12/31/9999
String	1 + 1 per character		0 to 65,535 characters
Object	4		Any defined object

Data Type	Size (bytes)	Resolution (digits)	Range
Array	Number of elements times the number of bytes in the data type of the array		
Variant	Depends on the data stored		Any built-in data type

The Boolean data type uses two bytes (16 bits) of memory for storage. The Boolean data type has only two possible values, True or False, which could be represented with a single bit, but the Boolean type is actually stored as an Integer, with a value of 0 for False, and –1 for True. Although this wastes some memory, Microsoft probably did this to make the Boolean type compatible with the other data types when it is used in a formula.

The Integer data type uses two bytes of memory to store a biased integer value. A *simple integer* has only positive values, but a *biased integer* is one that has positive or negative values. The Integer data type uses one bit to signify positive or negative values, and the remaining 15 for the number.

The Long data type is a double-sized integer that uses four bytes, or 32 bits, of memory. This data type is also a biased integer, so it uses 31 bits for the number and 1 for the sign. The Long data type has twice the resolution of the Integer type, but also uses twice as much memory.

The Single data type represents a real, floating-point number. To store a floating-point number, you divide it into two pieces: the mantissa and the exponent. The *mantissa* is the numeric part of the number, and the *exponent* indicates where the decimal point is. Be careful of the Single data type, especially if you are calculating currency, because it has only seven digits of resolution. If you use two of those digits for cents, that leaves only five digits for dollars, or a maximum value of $34,028.23. Trying to store any numbers larger than that results in an overflow error.

The Double data type is a double-sized Single, with twice the resolution and eight times the numeric range. It also uses twice as much memory.

The Currency data type is a special eight-byte integer in which the decimal is between the fourth and fifth digits from the right. This data type is especially set up to minimize roundoff errors so that it gives the correct number of dollars and cents after a calculation. When you use the floating-point data types, a roundoff error might result in a value that equals 4.999999999 rather than 5.0. Although in most cases such a difference is negligible, it is not negligible for such purposes as accounting. The Currency data type prevents these problems.

The Date data type stores dates and times in eight bytes of memory. Dates are stored as an integer number of days from 1/1/1900, and times are stored as fractional parts of a day. Thus, a value of 34398.75 stored as a Date refers to March 5, 1994 at 6:00 PM. When using this data type, keep in mind that although Visual Basic's range extends from 1/1/100 to 12/31/9999, Excel's range is 1/1/1900 to 12/31/2078. Also, to maintain compatibility with Lotus 1-2-3, Excel has an error built in to the date system: it includes 2/29/1900, a date that does not exist. Because of this error, dates between 1/1/1900 and 2/29/1900 are off by one day. However, unless you are an astronomer, you probably won't notice that this discrepancy exists.

The String data type is used to store strings of text. It uses one byte of memory for each character, plus one to mark the end of the string. Characters are stored in memory as ANSI codes (see Appendix B). The first 128 codes are the standard keyboard characters, punctuation, numbers, and control characters. The second 128 codes are the graphics characters. Note that the ANSI graphics characters used in Windows applications and the graphics characters used in DOS applications differ.

The Object data type uses four bytes of memory and stores a reference to any Visual Basic object.

An Array data type is not really a different data type, but a specification for an indexed list of values of one of the other data types. Arrays are discussed in much more detail later in this chapter.

The Variant data type is the default data type for Visual Basic. Essentially, you can store almost anything as a Variant. If you don't specify the data type for storing a value, the Variant data type is used. The Variant data type checks what is being stored and then adjusts itself so that the data fits. Because of this checking, the Variant data type tends to waste time and memory. For a simple procedure, this waste is negligible, but for a large procedure that performs many numerical calculations, you should consider specifying the data type.

> **Note:** In table 4.1, you might notice that the ranges of the data types seem to have strange values. The Integer data type, for example, has an upper limit of 32,767. Why that particular number and not some nice round number like 30,000? The answer is that such numbers *are* nice round numbers—in binary, that is. Numbers are stored in memory in binary, not decimal. Therefore, the Integer type uses one bit for the sign and 15 bits for the number, so that the largest decimal number that you can represent with a 15 bit binary number is 32,767, as follows:
>
> $$2^{15} - 1 = 32{,}767$$

Understanding Variables

Variables are named storage locations in a computer's memory. After calculating a value, you must store it in memory so that you can recall it later. You can use absolute memory locations in your code to indicate where to store a value, but while a memory reference like 0380:0004 is not very intuitive, the variable WestCoastSales is. By using variables, you let Visual Basic create a linear mapping between a location in memory and a descriptive name. Then you can use that descriptive name in your code and let Visual Basic take care of storing things in the correct location in memory.

Variable names consist of alphabetic characters, numbers, and some punctuation. Variables must start with an alphabetic character, and cannot contain embedded spaces, periods, or type declaration characters (#, $, %, &, and !). You can use capitalization in your variables, but Visual Basic does not distinguish between variables with or without capitalization. To create descriptive variable names, it is common practice to join together multiple words with the underscore character (_) or with capital letters. For example, each of the following are valid variable names:

    theDate   aDate   Sales_WesternRegion

    MyName   GrossSales   CapitalLoss

    TheAmountNeededToPayOffTheLoan

The last variable name is a little long. Although you can join together a whole sentence to create a very descriptive variable name, consider how much time it will take you to type such a variable name accurately when you create code. Indeed, such long and intricate names can make coding unnecessarily difficult and time-consuming. Instead, you should try to use something more succinct, like PayOff. Try to keep variable names short but descriptive.

Declaring Variables

Variable types are the same as the data types described earlier in this chapter. By declaring a variable to be of a specific type, you tell Visual Basic what data type to use when storing some value in memory. If you don't declare the type of a variable, the default is the Variant data type.

The Variant data type stores most any value, and is useful for short, simple programs. For longer programs, however, you should declare every variable before you use it. There are two benefits to declaring each variable:

- Flags any misspelled variable names. A misspelled variable name in your program becomes a new variable that most likely will cause your program to perform incorrectly. However, if you must declare all variables before using them, an undeclared variable results in a runtime error, which immediately flags the variable as a problem.

♦ Conserves memory and time. Before a variable of the Variant data type actually stores data, Visual Basic must check which kind of data is being stored in the variable and then reserve a piece of memory large enough to hold the data. If you declare a variable beforehand, Visual Basic already knows the data type for the data being stored in the variable and automatically reserves memory for it.

Forcing Yourself To Declare Variables

To force every variable to be declared before it is used, you must place an Option Explicit statement at the top of each module. For each existing module, you must manually type the statement **Option Explicit** at the beginning. Then, to have Visual Basic automatically place an Option Explicit statement at the beginning of each new module, select the **T**ools **O**ptions command, select the Module General tab, and then select the **R**equire Variable Declaration check box.

Declaring Variables with Dim

To declare variables, insert a Dim statement at the top of the procedure that uses the variable. Use the following syntax to declare variables with the Dim statement:

```
Dim variable As type, variable As type,...
```

where variable is a *variable* name and *type* is the data type.

The following are all examples of declaration statements:

```
Dim theName As String
Dim Cost As Currency, I As Integer
Dim ProductNumber As Long
Dim Height As Single, Width As Single
Dim aPicture
```

The last statement declares aPicture as a Variant type variable. Any variable declarations that do not include an explicit type declaration declare Variant type variables.

Understanding the Scope of Variables

The *scope* of a variable consists of those modules and procedures in which the variable is available. For a variable to be available in a procedure, you must be able to use or change its value in that procedure, and any changes made to the value of the variable anywhere in the variable's scope are instantly seen everywhere else in the variable's scope. Figure 4.1 is a diagram showing how to determine the scope of a variable. The lowest level of declaration is in a procedure. Variables declared with the Dim statement in a procedure are available only in that procedure. The variables var1 (in Procedure1), var2, var4, and var5 are all defined at the procedure level and thus are available only in their respective procedures. A variable of the same name declared in a different procedure is a distinct, independent entity. For example, var2 is defined in two different procedures, so changing the value of var2 in Procedure3 does not affect the value of var2 in Procedure2.

Figure 4.1

The scope of variables follows the object-oriented model of containers; variables declared in an outer container are available to the procedures within that container.

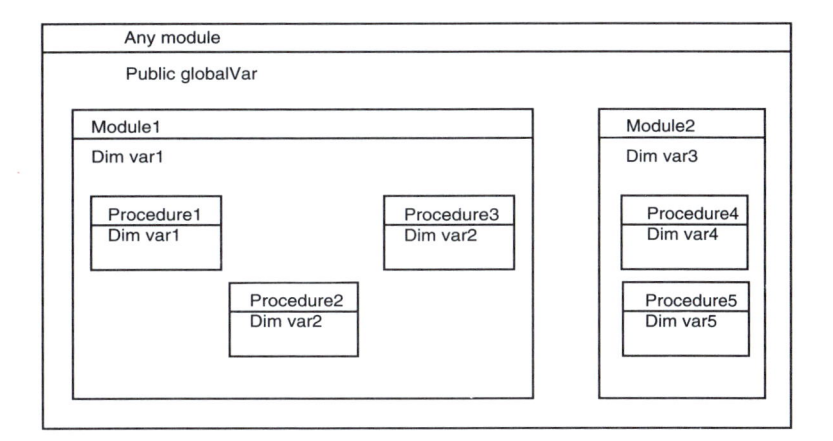

```
Any module
  Public globalVar
  ┌─Module1──────────────────────────────┐   ┌─Module2──────────┐
  │ Dim var1                             │   │ Dim var3         │
  │                                      │   │                  │
  │  ┌Procedure1┐      ┌Procedure3┐      │   │ ┌Procedure4┐     │
  │  │Dim var1  │      │Dim var2  │      │   │ │Dim var4  │     │
  │  └──────────┘      └──────────┘      │   │ └──────────┘     │
  │                                      │   │                  │
  │        ┌Procedure2┐                  │   │ ┌Procedure5┐     │
  │        │Dim var2  │                  │   │ │Dim var5  │     │
  │        └──────────┘                  │   │ └──────────┘     │
  └──────────────────────────────────────┘   └──────────────────┘
```

A declaration at the module level, such as var1 and var3, creates a variable that is available in every procedure in the module. Thus, var3 is available in Procedure4 and Procedure5. The variable var1 is available in Procedure2 and Procedure3, but in Procedure1, another variable var1 is declared that overrides the declaration at the module level. The variable var1 defined in Procedure1 differs from the variable var1 that is available in Procedure2 and Procedure3.

Declaring Global Variables

To make a variable available to all procedures in all modules, declare it at the module level using the keyword Public rather than Dim. A variable declared with Public is available to every procedure in an application. In figure 4.1, the variable globalVar is declared as Public in Module1, and therefore is available in all five procedures.

Understanding Arrays

When you declare a variable, you create a single, named memory location. When you declare an array, you create a list of adjacent memory locations, all with the same name. To access an individual element of an array, you follow the array name with an index number in parentheses. You declare an array with Dim or Public just like any other variable, but follow the array name with a number in parentheses to define the number of elements that the array can have. For example, each of the following statements declare arrays:

```
Dim Sales(5) As Currency
Dim AcctNo(700 To 799) As Integer
Dim theCoords(4,1 to 3) as Single
Dim Birthdays(3 to 23,5 to 7) As Date
```

The first statement creates an array named Sales with a data type of Currency. The default array index starts at 0, so there are six elements in the array:

```
Sales(0), Sales(1), Sales(2), Sales(3), Sales(4), Sales(5)
```

You select an array element by specifying its array index. The second example creates an array of Integers named AcctNo. This statement specifies both the lower and upper limit of the index, so the array contains 100 elements:

```
AcctNo(700), AcctNo(701), AcctNo(702), ... AcctNo(799)
```

The third example creates a two-dimensional array of floating-point numbers named theCoords. Because the declaration specifies two index ranges, the array is two-dimensional. The first index ranges from 0 to 4 and the second ranges from 1 to 3. Specifying an element of a two-dimensional array requires two indexes, as shown in the following examples:

```
theCoords(1,1), theCoords(1,2), theCoords(1,3)
theCoords(2,1), theCoords(2,2), theCoords(2,3)
theCoords(3,1), theCoords(3,2), theCoords(3,3)
theCoords(4,1), theCoords(4,2), theCoords(4,3)
```

Higher-order arrays are possible, but it is difficult to imagine what an array with more than three dimensions would represent.

The last example creates a two-dimensional array of Date type variables, with upper and lower limits specified for both indexes. The first index ranges from 3 to 23, and the second ranges from 5 to 7.

Using Constants To Enhance a Code's Readability

A *constant* is a value that does not change while a program is running. Although you can simply insert the value of a constant where it is required, the resultant code is not terribly intuitive. For example, you can specify the colors red, green, blue, and yellow with the constants 3, 4, 5, and 6. The following procedure changes the background color of cell B5 of the active worksheet:

```
Sub colors1()
    Range("B5").Interior.ColorIndex = 5
End Sub
```

Compare this procedure to the following one, which does the same thing:

```
Sub colors2()
    Const Blue = 5
    Range("B5").Interior.ColorIndex = Blue
End Sub
```

In the second procedure, you can more easily figure out what the code does.

The second most important use for constants is for setting values that might change from one compilation of a program to another, or for a value that you are unsure about. When you use such values in many places in your code and the value changes, you have to change each occurrence. However, if you use a constant, you need only change the constant's definition to change its value globally throughout the code.

Creating and Using Constants

To create a constant, use the keyword Const followed by a constant name, an equals sign, and the value of the constant. The following statements each define constants:

```
Const Red = 3, Green = 4, Blue = 5, Yellow = 6
Const ArrayLimit = 100
Const maxAccounts = 1000
```

You must define constants before they are used. The scope of constants is the same as that of variables. Constants defined in a procedure are available only within that procedure. Constants defined in a module are available in every procedure in the module. Constants declared Public are available to every procedure in every module of a program. You define public constants at the module level by placing the keyword Public before the keyword Const, as in the following example:

```
Public Const ArrayLimit = 100
```

This statement defines a global constant named ArrayLimit with a value of 100. ArrayLimit is thus available throughout the program.

Chapter 4 ◆ Understanding Data Types and Variables

Locating Built-In Constants

Visual Basic and Excel both have a long list of built-in constants that you can use without declaring them. These constants are for setting the values of different properties in Excel or Visual Basic, and for setting values for use with dialog boxes. The online help describes the available constants along with the properties and functions with which they are used.

You also can use the Object Browser to display a list of all the constants. With the Excel library selected, select the Constants object, and the Object Browser displays a list of all the Excel constants. The Excel constants all start with the characters *xl*. With the VBA library selected, select the Constants object to see a list of all the Visual Basic constants. The Visual Basic constants all start with *vb*.

Creating Custom Data Types

The built-in data types cover most situations that you will encounter. However, in some situations it is convenient to combine several existing data types into a single, compound data structure.

For example, if you are creating a client database program, you will likely collect a name, address, and phone number. You could store all this information in five arrays, but it would be much more convenient to combine it all together into a single structure and then create a single array of those structures.

To create the data structure, you use the Type statement. The Type statement has the keyword Type followed by a name for the new type. The next few lines describe the names and types for the elements of the data structure, and are followed by an End Type statement. For example, the following code creates a data structure for the client database:

```
Type ClientType
    Name As String
    Address As String
    CityState As String
    Zipcode As Long
    Phone As String
End Type
```

This statement only defines the structure of the new type. You must now declare a variable of this type before you can use it, as follows:

```
Dim MyClients(1000) As ClientType
```

This statement declares an array of 1,000 ClientType data structures.

To access the elements of a structure, you type the structure name followed by a period, followed by the element name. Thus, to store values in this structure, you could use something like the following:

```
MyClients(10).Name = "John Doe"
MyClients(10).Address = "1234 Somewhere St."
MyClients(10).CityState = "Nowhere, CA"
MyClients(10).Zipcode = 94567
MyClients(10).Phone = 510 123-4567
```

These statements access element 10 of the array MyClients, and set the values of the five elements of the data structure.

Summary

In this chapter you learned about data types, variables, and data structures. These structures determine how data is stored in memory, and form the most basic building blocks of a computer program. In the next chapter, you learn how to combine these variables to perform useful calculations.

Review Questions

Answers to the review questions are in Appendix A.

1. Define a data type, and a variable type.
2. How many bytes of memory does a Currency data type use?
3. What does "scope of a variable" mean?
4. How do you force yourself to declare all variables in a module?

Review Exercises

1. Create the two procedures colors1 and colors2, which were discussed in the section "Using Constants To Enhance a Code's Readability." Select a worksheet, and execute both procedures to ensure that they give the same results.

2. Write a Type statement to create a data structure for a telephone list. Include an element for the last name, first name, telephone number, birthday, and the date of the last contact.

3. Diagram the elements of the three-dimensional array created with the following statement:

   ```
   Dim MyArray(3,3,5).
   ```

CHAPTER 5

Using Assignment Statements and the Built-In Functions

Now that you know all about variables, it's time to start using them to do useful work. In this chapter, you learn how to combine the concepts of objects and variables to move data around and calculate useful numbers.

In this chapter, you will learn the following:

- What assignment statements are
- How to use comment statements
- How to use operators and functions
- How to convert between different data types
- How to create and use object variables

What Are Assignment Statements?

Assignment statements are the basis for all calculations in Visual Basic, because any calculated value must be assigned to a variable for storage. An assignment statement has a variable on the left, an equals sign, and a formula on the right. The formula can be a single value, or a formula consisting of other variables, constants, operators, and functions. The variable on the left can be a simple variable, an array, or an object's property. You have already seen assignment statements in the examples discussed so far in this book—after all, without them, you can't create a program that does anything.

The following are all examples of assignment statements:

```
theFilename = "c:\vba\examples\examp1.xls"
Sales = Units * Price
Profit = Sales - Cost
Coords(3,2) = 19.37
Selection.Value = 25
Range("B5").Formula = "=B4*B3-1"
ActiveCell.FormulaR1C1 = "Amortization Table"
ActiveCell.FormulaR1C1 = "10000"
ActiveCell.FormulaR1C1 = "Principal Balance"
ActiveCell.FormulaR1C1 = "=ROUND(R[-5]C[2]*R[-4]C[2]/12,2)"
ActiveWindow.ScrollRow = 1
With Selection.Borders(xlBottom).Weight = xlThin
ActiveWindow.DisplayGridlines = False
```

The first three statements assign a value to another variable, the fourth assigns a value to an array variable, and all the rest assign values to properties. You can assign any values except objects in this way; objects require a special assignment statement.

Using Comment Statements

In any program you are going to use for more than a day or two, comments are almost as important as assignment statements. A comment is just what its name implies: a comment on the design, operation, or programming of a program. A comment must begin with a single quotation mark ('), and anything that you type to the right of that mark is totally ignored by Visual Basic when it executes your program. Thus, you can add any descriptions or text that explains what you are doing.

Comments do not have to start at the beginning of a line, but can be placed anywhere to the right of a valid statement. It must be to the right of a valid statement, because if it were to the left of a valid statement, that statement would become part of the comment and would be ignored. Actually, this feature is useful for removing a statement from a program without actually having to delete the statement. Simply place a single quotation mark at the beginning of a statement that you don't want executed and it becomes a comment. Later you can restore the statement to the program simply by deleting the single quotation mark.

When you used the Macro Recorder in Chapter 1, Excel automatically inserted a block of comments before the start of the recorded procedure. These comments explain what the procedure does. The comments in the following statements are shown in boldface type, although on your screen they appear in green:

```
'
' AmortTable Macro
' Creates a 180 month amortization table.
'
'
Sub AmortTable()    'Start of the amortization table procedure
    Range("A1").Select    'Select cell A1 on the current worksheet
'Insert a title in that cell
    ActiveCell.FormulaR1C1 = "Amortization Table"    'This is the title
    Range("D1").Select    'A column label goes in cell D1
    ActiveCell.FormulaR1C1 = "Interest Rate"    'The column label
```

Although comments do not affect a program's operation, they substantially affect how well you or someone else is able to understand what the program is doing and why it is doing it. When writing a program, you may not want to take the time to type comments, but do it anyway. The amount of time you spend now writing a few lines of comments is small compared to the amount of time you or someone else may spend later figuring out what you did.

Unless you are sure you are going to delete a program after using it once or twice, be sure to include as many comments as necessary to ensure that anyone can read it and understand exactly what it is doing. Keep in mind, though, that programs that you expect to have a short life span often have a habit of sticking around for years, especially if they do something useful. Invariably, someone will have to make a change or fix a bug, and to do that he or she must be able to read and understand your code. Even if you are the one who needs to do so, most likely you will forget how and why you wrote portions of the code—unless your comments are there to remind you.

Declaring and Assigning Object Variables

You declare object variables in the same way as any of the other variables: You use the keyword Dim, followed by the variable name, and then As Object. To assign a value to an object variable, use the keyword Set, followed by the variable name, an equals sign, and a formula that evaluates to an object.

1 For example, the following procedure creates an object variable, assigns to it a Range object referencing cell B5, and then uses that object variable to assign a value to the cell:

```
Sub ObjVar()
    Dim theRange As Object
    Set theRange = ActiveSheet.Range("B5")
    theRange.Value = 10
End Sub
```

Chapter 5 ♦ Using Assignment Statements and the Built-In Functions

Using Visual Basic Operators

The basic mathematical operations are performed with operators. Addition, subtraction, multiplication, and division are the most common operators. These operators all combine two values, so they are known as binary operators. Most operators are binary operators, though negation is unary, having only one value.

Table 5.1 lists all the mathematical and string operators available in Visual Basic.

Table 5.1. Visual Basic's mathematical and string operators.

Operator	Description
^	Exponentiation
-	Negation
*	Multiplication ⎤
/	Division ⎦ Equal precedence
\	Integer division
Mod	Modulus
+	Addition ⎤
-	Subtraction ⎦ Equal precedence
&	Concatenation (string)

Understanding the Precedence of Operators

Table 5.1 lists the operators in the order of their precedence. *Precedence* determines which operation is performed first in a formula. Note that multiplication and division have equal precedence, as do addition and subtraction.

In any complicated formula, don't depend on the precedence of the operators to calculate your formula in the correct order. Always use parentheses to force the calculation to be performed in the correct order. For example, the following formula calculates the monthly payment required to pay off a loan of `principal` dollars in n months at a monthly interest of `rate`:

```
Payment = principal*rate/(1-(1/(1+rate)^n))
```

The parentheses force 1+rate to be calculated first, and then raised to the power n. Next, the result is divided into 1, and then that result is subtracted from 1. This result is then divided into the product of principal and rate. Without parentheses, the formula is incorrectly calculated in three terms:

```
Payment = principal*rate/1 - 1/1 + rate^n
```

Exponentiation has the highest precedence, so it is applied first to the value rate rather than 1+rate. Next are multiplication and division, so principal is multiplied times rate and then divided by 1 (a wasted calculation), and then 1 is divided by 1 (another wasted calculation). Finally come addition and subtraction, which combine the three terms together. Again, the result is incorrect without parentheses.

Experimenting with Operators

Addition, subtraction, multiplication, division, negation, and exponentiation are well-known operators. Integer division, modulus, and string concatenation operators, however, are not as well known.

To experiment with these operators, use the Immediate pane of the Debug window. To open the Debug window, switch to a module or insert a new one, and choose the **V**iew **D**ebug Window command. Select the Immediate tab to view the Immediate pane. Any Visual Basic command that you can type in a single line can be executed in the Immediate pane. To print the result of a calculation, type **?** or **print**, followed by whatever you want to calculate and print. For example, if you type **? 5\4**, Visual Basic performs the integer division and returns a 1, as shown at the top of the Immediate pane in figure 5.1. If you place several calculations on a line separated by commas, the results are printed every 14 characters. Try some more examples of integer division as shown in the figure, to get a feel for how it works.

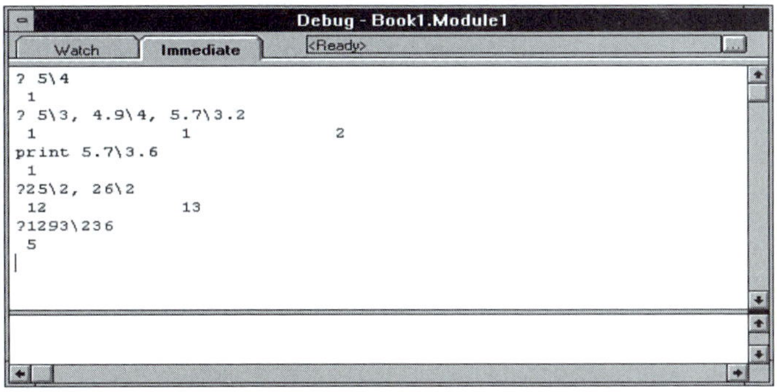

Figure 5.1
Using the Immediate pane of the Debug window to examine the operation of the integer division operator.

Chapter 5 ♦ Using Assignment Statements and the Built-In Functions

> **Tip:** The Immediate pane of the Debug window is useful for testing the operation of almost any Visual Basic operator or function. If you are unsure of what a function does, the Immediate pane is a simple place to try it out. Anything that you can type on a single line can be executed in the Immediate pane. Some multiline expressions also can be calculated if you separate the lines with colons, as in
>
>   For I = 1 to 10: print I: Next I
>
> which starts a three-line For-Next loop that prints the numbers from 1 to 10 on the window.

In integer division, the two numbers are converted to integers by rounding, the division operation is performed, and the result is converted to an integer by truncation. Figure 5.1 shows several examples of the operation of the integer division operator.

The modulus operator complements the integer division operator and returns the remainder. For example, 5 Mod 3 returns 2, because 5 divided by 3 is 1 with a remainder of 2. The modulus is most often used to calculate such things as the day of the week some number of days in the future, or the hour of the day some number of hours in the future. For example, 100 Mod 7 gives the day of the week 100 days from now, assuming that today is day number 1.

Examine some more modulus calculations in the Immediate pane, as shown in figure 5.2.

Figure 5.2

Using the Immediate pane of the Debug window to examine the modulus operator.

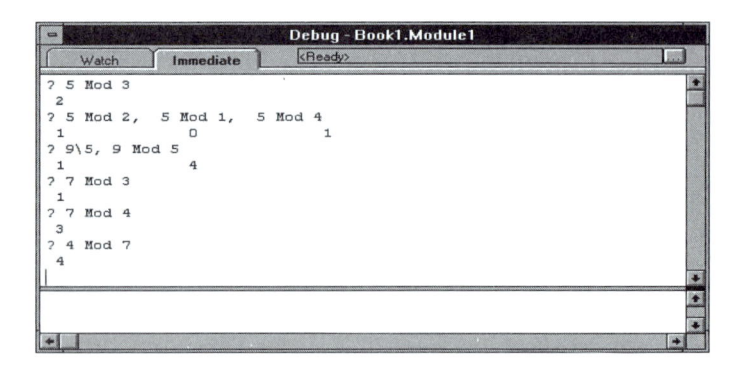

```
Debug - Book1.Module1
 Watch    Immediate    <Ready>
? 5 Mod 3
 2
? 5 Mod 2,  5 Mod 1,  5 Mod 4
 1          0          1
? 9\5, 9 Mod 5
 1          4
? 7 Mod 3
 1
? 7 Mod 4
 3
? 4 Mod 7
 4
```

The last of these operators is the string concatenation operator. The concatenation operator simply combines two strings into one. Use it to build complex strings consisting of pieces of text combined with the output of string functions. Figure 5.3 shows the result of using the concatenation operator with some functions that return strings.

Figure 5.3

Using the Immediate pane of the Debug window to examine the concatenation operator.

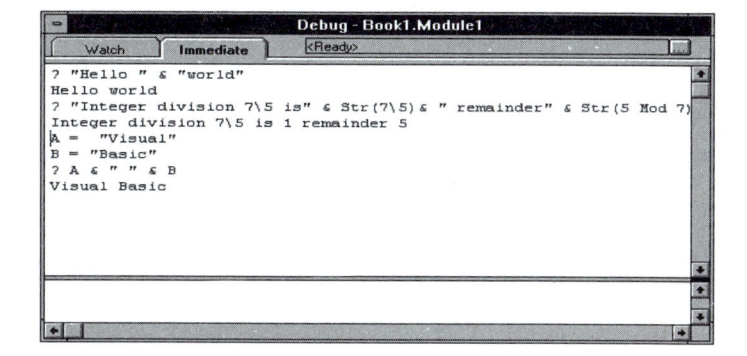

```
Debug - Book1.Module1
Watch   Immediate   <Ready>
? "Hello " & "world"
Hello world
? "Integer division 7\5 is" & Str(7\5) & " remainder" & Str(5 Mod 7)
Integer division 7\5 is 1 remainder 5
A = "Visual"
B = "Basic"
? A & " " & B
Visual Basic
```

In the second example in figure 5.3, the Str() function is used to convert a number into a string. In the third example, the variables A and B are assigned string values, which are then combined in a formula. Functions, including string functions, are described later in this chapter.

> **Note:** If the Option Explicit statement is placed at the top of the module that is behind the Debug window, you must declare variables before you can use them. Because you cannot use the Dim statement in the Immediate pane, you cannot create new variables there. However, you can use variables that are declared in the module behind the Debug window. If Option Explicit is not in the module behind the Debug window, any variables you type in the Immediate pane are automatically created.

Two other types of operators are available in Visual Basic: the comparison operators and the logical operators. Both of these are discussed in Chapter 8, "Understanding Decision Making."

Using Visual Basic Functions

Although the operators provide the basic mathematical operations, the more complicated calculations are provided by the built-in functions. The functions of Visual Basic operate in much the same manner as those of Excel, except that they always return single values. Excel's functions can apply to whole arrays of numbers and return arrays as a result. Visual Basic's functions usually apply to single values and return single values. To apply a Visual Basic function to an array of values, you must apply it individually to each member of the array.

Chapter 5 ◆ Using Assignment Statements and the Built-In Functions

Mathematical Functions

Table 5.2 lists the mathematic functions available in Visual Basic.

Table 5.2. Visual Basic's math functions.

Function	Description
Atn	Returns the arctangent of a number
Sin	Returns the sine of an angle in radians
Cos	Returns the cosine of an angle in radians
Tan	Returns the tangent of an angle in radians
Exp	Returns the exponential of a number e^x
Log	Returns the natural logarithm of a number (base e = 2.71828...)
Sqr	Returns the square root of a number
Randomize	Initializes the seed of the random number generator
Rnd	Returns a random number
Abs	Returns the absolute value of a number
Sgn	Returns the sign of a number
Fix	Converts a number to an integer by truncation
Int	Converts a number to the largest integer less than the number

The mathematical functions listed in table 5.2 usually take a single number as an argument, transform it in some way, and return a single number. The trigonometric functions, Sin(), Cos(), and Tan(), take an angle in radians and convert it into the appropriate trigonometric value. If you want to use degrees rather than radians, multiply the angle in degrees by Π/180 before using it in the function. The Atn() function takes a number as an argument and returns the angle in radians that is the arctangent of that number. To get the angle in degrees, multiply by 180/Π.

For example, using the Immediate pane of the Debug window, calculate the sine of 27 degrees and the arctangent of 5, as follows:

```
? Sin(27*3.1415/180)
0.453978116452753
? Atn(5)
1.37340076694502
```

Next are the two logarithmic functions, Log() and Exp(). Both are natural logarithms with a base of **e** = 2.71828. Following these is Sqr(), which calculates the square root of a number.

Next are the Randomize and Rnd() functions. In a program that uses the Rnd function to calculate random numbers, you also should run Randomize once. The Randomize function initializes the random number generator so that it does not give the same results each time. The random numbers are actually calculated with a formula, so if you use the same seed each time, you get the same set of numbers. The Randomize function uses the system clock to calculate a random seed so that you always get a different set of random numbers. The Rnd() function returns random numbers. If its argument is negative, it uses the argument as the seed. If its argument is 0, it returns the previous random number again; if the argument is positive or missing, it returns the next random number in the sequence.

Examine the Rnd() function in the Immediate pane (the numbers you get should be different from those shown in the following example listing):

```
Randomize
? Rnd, Rnd, Rnd
    0.4425265      0.6843034       0.5414312
? Rnd, Rnd, Rnd
    0.6601722      0.9210758       0.2244858
? Rnd, Rnd, Rnd
    0.243394       0.8367548       0.7939159
? Rnd, Rnd, Rnd
    0.6482016      9.553748E-02                  0.1604512
? Rnd(-1), Rnd(-1), Rnd(-1)
    0.224007       0.224007        0.224007
? Rnd
    3.584582E-02
? Rnd(0), Rnd(0), Rnd(0)
    3.584582E-02                   3.584582E-02                  3.584582E-02
? Rnd(1), Rnd(1), Rnd(1)
    8.635235E-02                   0.1642639       0.1797358
```

The Abs() function returns the absolute value, and the Sgn() function returns the sign of a number. The last two functions, Fix() and Int(), convert floating-point numbers to integers. The Fix() function uses truncation to convert the floating-point number to the nearest integer, and the Int() function rounds down to the nearest integer less than the number. Be careful of these two functions when the argument is negative, because they may not do what you expect.

Examine these functions in the Immediate pane. The following examples of output from the Immediate pane include the CInt() type conversion function (discussed later in this chapter), which uses rounding to the closest integer to make the conversion.

Chapter 5 ◆ Using Assignment Statements and the Built-In Functions

```
? Abs(-4), Abs(4), Sgn(-4), Sgn(4)
4            4          -1           1
? Fix(3.7),Fix(3.3),Fix(-3.7), Fix(-3.3)
3            3          -3          -3
? Int(3.7),Int(3.3),Int(-3.7), Int(-3.3)
3            3          -4          -4
? CInt(3.7),CInt(3.3),CInt(-3.7), CInt(-3.3)
4            3          -4          -3
```

Notice that the list of functions in table 5.2 is somewhat limited. Only four built-in trigonometric functions are listed, but there are about 24 trigonometric functions, including the hyperbolic functions, that you commonly use. Table 5.3 lists some standard formulas that use built-in functions to calculate the missing ones. These formulas should work for both positive and negative values of x. The few that contain the ± symbol are double valued. Use the plus sign (+) to calculate the first value and the minus sign (–) to calculate the second.

Table 5.3. Formulas for common math functions not included with Visual Basic.

Function	Formula
Secant	Sec(x) = 1/Cos(x)
Cosecant	Csc(x) = 1/Sin(x)
Cotangent	Cot(x) = 1/Tan(x)
Arcsine	Asin(x) = Atn(x/Sqr(1 - x^2))
Arccosine*	Acos(x) = 1.5708 - Atn(x/Sqr(1 - x^2))
Arcsecant*	Asec(x) = Atn(Sqr(x^2 - 1)) + (Sgn(x) - 1)*1.5708
Arccosecant*	Acsc(x) = Atn(1/Sqr(x^2 - 1)) + (Sgn(x) - 1)*1.5708
Arccotangent	Acot(x) = 1.5708 - Atn(x)
Hyperbolic Sine	Sinh(x) = (Exp(x) - Exp(-x))/2
Hyperbolic Cosine	Cosh(x) = (Exp(x) + Exp(-x))/2

Function	Formula
Hyperbolic Tangent	Tanh(x) = (Exp(x) - Exp(-x))/ (Exp(x) + Exp(-x))
Hyperbolic Secant	Sech(x) = 2/(Exp(x) + Exp(-x))
Hyperbolic Cosecant	Csch(x) = 2/(Exp(x) - Exp(-x))
Hyperbolic Cotangent	Coth(x) = (Exp(x) + Exp(-x))/(Exp(x) - Exp(-x))
Inverse Hyperbolic Sine	ASinh(x) = Log(x + Sqr(x^2 + 1))
Inverse Hyperbolic Cosine	ACosh(x) = Log(x ± Sqr(x^2 - 1))
Inverse Hyperbolic Tangent	ATanh(x) = Log((1 + x)/(1 - x))/2
Inverse Hyperbolic Secant	ASech(x) = Log((1 ± Sqr(1 - x^2))/x)
Inverse Hyperbolic Cosecant	ACsch(x) = Log(1 ± Sqr(1 + x^2))/x)
Inverse Hyperbolic Cotangent	ACoth(x) = Log((x + 1)/(x - 1))/2
Logarithm to base n	LogN(x) = Log(x)/Log(n)

The number 1.5708 is Π/2.

To see how these formulas work, try using a few in the Immediate pane. In the following example, you first assign a value to the variable *x* and then calculate a formula that uses it:

```
x = 5
? Atn(Sqr(x^2 - 1)) + (Sgn(x) - 1)*1.5708  'Arcsecant
 1.36943840600457
x = -5
? Atn(Sqr(x^2 - 1)) + (Sgn(x) - 1)*1.5708  'Arcsecant
-1.77216159399543
x = 7
? (Exp(x) - Exp(-x))/(Exp(x) + Exp(-x))   'Hyperbolic Tangent
 0.999998336943945
```

Chapter 5 ♦ Using Assignment Statements and the Built-In Functions

String Functions

Visual Basic has an extensive set of string functions for searching and manipulating strings. Table 5.4 lists the string functions available in Visual Basic.

Table 5.4. String functions.

Function	Description
StrComp	Compares two strings
LCase	Converts a string to lowercase
UCase	Converts a string to uppercase
Space	Creates a string of multiple spaces
String	Creates a string of multiple characters
Len	Finds the length of a string
Instr	Locates a substring
LSet	Left-justifies a string in a fixed-length string
RSet	Right-justifies a string in a fixed-length string
Left	Extracts the left side of a string
Right	Extracts the right side of a string
Mid	Extracts or replaces a substring
LTrim	Removes blank spaces from the left side of a string
RTrim	Removes blank spaces from the right side of a string
Trim	Removes blank spaces from both sides of a string
Asc	Gets the ASCII code for a character
Chr	Gets the character for an ASCII code
Str	Converts a number to a string
Format	Converts a number to a string using a format
Val	Converts a string to number
Hex	Converts a number to hex string
Oct	Converts a number to octal string

Visual Basic for Applications   *By* EXAMPLE

The StrComp() function compares two strings, and LCase() and UCase() convert a string to all lowercase or all uppercase. The Space() function creates a string consisting of spaces, and the String() function creates a string that consists of a single character repeated many times. Len() gets the length of a string and Instr() locates a substring. LSet() and RSet() are normally used with fixed-length strings to left- or right-justify a substring within a fixed-length string.

To examine these string functions in the Immediate pane, first define two strings to which you can apply the functions:

```
A = "The small brown puppy ran away."
B = "JanFebMarAprMayJunJulAugSepOctNovDec"
? LCase(B)
janfebmaraprmayjunjulaugsepoctnovdec
? UCase(B)
JANFEBMARAPRMAYJUNJULAUGSEPOCTNOVDEC
? Len(B)
 36
? Instr(B,"Jul")
 19
```

To examine LSet() and RSet(), you first need a fixed-length string. Normal strings are variable-length; that is, they are as long as is necessary to hold whatever text is placed in them. To declare a fixed-length string, insert the length into the Dim statement that declares the string. The Dim statement cannot be executed in the Debug window, so you must use it in a procedure first to declare your variables.

The following is a short "dummy" procedure to run and declare the string. Close the Debug window and type the following procedure in a module. The Stop statement causes the program to stop executing, but does not end the program, so the variables are still available for you to examine and use. Click anywhere in the procedure and choose the **R**un **S**tart command. The procedure should run until it reaches the Stop statement and then open the Debug window.

```
Dim D As String * 10
Sub StrTst()
D = "123456789012345"
Stop
End Sub
```

In the Debug window, examine the value of D. Note that it contains only 10 characters and not the 15 that you assigned to it. Using LSet() and RSet() inserts the indicated substrings at either end of the fixed-length string:

83

Chapter 5 ♦ Using Assignment Statements and the Built-In Functions

```
?D
1234567890
LSet D = "abc"
? D
abc
RSet D = "def"
? D
      def
```

The Left(), Right(), and Mid() functions each extract parts of a string. LTrim(), RTrim(), and Trim() remove blank characters from the left side, right side, or both sides of a string. The Asc() and Chr() functions work as a pair to convert between printed characters and the ASCII and ANSI codes. Finally, the Str(), Val(), Hex(), and Oct() functions convert between numbers and text representations of numbers.

Try these functions in the Immediate pane as well, using the same string constants as before:

```
A = "The small brown puppy ran away."
B = "JanFebMarAprMayJunJulAugSepOctNovDec"
```

The Left() and Right() functions take two arguments: a string and a number. The number indicates the number of characters to extract and return from the respective sides of the string. The Mid() function takes three arguments: the string, a starting character, and the number of characters to extract. For example, the function Mid(B,10,3) extracts three characters from string B beginning at the tenth character from the left. Using the string B as just defined, that function returns the text "Apr". You can also use the Mid() function on the left side of a formula, in which case it becomes the Mid statement. The Mid statement replaces the indicated substring instead of extracting it. Thus the statement Mid(B,10,3) = "Vacation" replaces "Apr" with "Vac".

```
? Left(A,5)
The s
? Right(A,5)
away.
? Mid(B,10,3)
Apr
? B
JanFebMarAprMayJunJulAugSepOctNovDec
Mid(B,10,3) = "Vacation"
? B
JanFebMarVacMayJunJulAugSepOctNovDec
```

Note that only the indicated number of characters is replaced from the string on the right. To insert a longer or shorter string for a substring, use the following construct:

```
? Left(B,9)&"Vacation"&Right(B,Len(B)-12)
JanFebMarVacationMayJunJulAugSepOctNovDec
```

To examine the trim functions, LTrim, RTrim, and Trim, first create a string that includes many extra spaces on the left and right. Actually, the trim functions are most often used with numbers that are converted to strings, because the conversion functions often place spaces before and after the converted number. So that you can see where the spaces begin and end, place a vertical bar on either end of the trimmed strings. The trim functions remove all white space, including tabs, from the respective sides of the strings.

```
C = "       hello world      "
? "|"&LTrim(C)&"|"
|hello world      |
? "|"&RTrim(C)&"|"
|       hello world|
? "|"&Trim(C)&"|"
|hello world|
```

The conversion routines convert numbers into text and text representations of numbers into numbers. The Str() function does not appear to do much, because it converts the number 27, for example, into the decimal string 27. The Oct() and Hex() functions convert the number into octal (base 8) and hexadecimal (base 16) format numbers. The Val() function does the opposite conversion, converting a number in a string. Val() ignores any white space on the left and converts the text into a number until it reaches a character that cannot be part of a number. The function ignores any other text or numbers in the string. Note that Val() also ignores any white space within a number. You define octal and hexidecimal strings by placing &o or &h before the number. The Val() function correctly converts these types of numbers as well.

```
? Str(27),Oct(27),Hex(27)
 27            33           1B
? Val(" 234abc567")
 234
? Val("   12 3abc  ")
 123
? Val("   1.2e10abc")
 12000000000
?Val("abc")
 0
?Val(" &o33")
 27
?Val("   &h1B")
 27
```

Date and Time Functions

The date and time functions listed in table 5.5 handle conversions between a textual version of a date or time and a serial date number (or serial time number if the number includes only the time). A serial date number stores dates and times in a single floating-point number. Dates are stored as the number of days since the start of 1/1/1900, and times are stored as fractional parts of a day. Thus, 0.5 is noon, and 0.75 is 6:00 in the evening. If you subtract two serial date numbers, you get the number of days between the two dates.

Table 5.5. Date and time functions.

Function	Description
Date	Gets or sets the current date
Time	Gets or sets the current time
Now	Gets the current date and time
DateSerial	Gets a serial date from three integers: month, day, and year
DateValue	Gets a serial date from a string representation of a date
TimeSerial	Gets a serial date from three integers: hour, minute, and second
TimeValue	Gets a serial date from a string representation of a time
Timer	Gets the elapsed time
Day	Converts a serial date to a date
Month	Converts a serial date to a month in a year
Weekday	Converts a serial date to a day in the week
Year	Converts a serial date to a year
Hour	Converts a serial date to an hour of the day
Minute	Converts a serial date to a minute of the hour
Second	Converts a serial date to a second of a minute

The first two functions, Date() and Time(), get or set the current system date. If the function is on the right side of an assignment statement, it gets the date or time; if it is on the left, it sets the date or time. The Now() function returns both the current date and time as a serial date number.

In the Immediate pane, use the Format() function to display the serial date number as a date and time, or the CDbl() function to convert it into a double precision, floating-point number:

```
? Format(Date,"mm/dd/yy hh:mm")
11/19/93 00:00
? Format(Time," hh:mm")
 00:25
? Format(Now,"mm/dd/yy hh:mm")
11/19/93 00:25
? CDbl(Now)
 34292.0210416667
```

The DateSerial() function takes three integer arguments—the year, month, and day (note the order)—and converts them into a serial date number. The DateValue() function converts a date as a string into a serial date number. TimeSerial() and TimeValue() perform the same action, but for times.

```
? Format(DateSerial(94,12,27),"mm/dd/yy hh:mm")
12/27/94 00:00
? Format(DateValue("12/27/94"),"mm/dd/yy hh:mm")
12/27/94 00:00
? Format(TimeSerial(12,18,27),"hh:mm:ss")
12:18:27
? Format(TimeValue("13:44"),"hh:mm")
13:44
```

The Timer function returns the number of milliseconds since midnight the previous day. By calling Timer before and after a procedure, you can determine how fast your procedure is running.

```
? Timer
 2761.98
```

The Day(), Month(), Weekday(), Year(), Hour(), Minute(), and Second() functions all take a serial date number as an argument. They then return the day of the month, the month of the year, and so on, as an integer.

```
? Day(Now)
 19
? Month(Now)
 11
? Year(Now)
 1993
? Weekday(Now)
 6
```

```
? Hour(Now)
 0
? Minute(Now)
 54
? Second(Now)
 8
```

Converting Data Types in Visual Basic

Conversion of data types from one type to another is usually done automatically by Visual Basic. When calculating a formula, Visual Basic converts all the numbers in a formula to the most accurate type, calculates the formula, and then converts the result to the type of the variable on the left. The type conversion functions in table 5.6 have two basic uses: to document the type conversion and to perform an unconventional conversion.

Table 5.6. Numeric conversion functions.

Function	Description
CBool	Converts the data type to Boolean
CCur	Converts the data type to Currency
CDate	Converts the data type to Date
CDbl	Converts the data type to Double
CInt	Converts the data type to Integer
CLng	Converts the data type to Long
CSng	Converts the data type to Single
CStr	Converts the data type to String
CVar	Converts the data type to Variant
CVErr	Converts the data type to an error number

If the type conversion isn't obvious but is important to a calculation, you can use the type conversion functions to perform the conversion instead of letting Visual Basic do it for you. Although you are not required to perform conversions in this way, by doing so you make it obvious what is being converted to what.

When you want to make an unconventional calculation, you must use these functions to make the conversions. Unconventional calculations are necessary to accomplish such tasks as viewing a date as a serial date number rather than a date, or converting a floating-point number to an integer to truncate its value. In the section "Date and Times Functions" earlier in this chapter, the CDbl() function was used to convert a date to a serial date number so that you could see how the date and time are stored in a single number. If you try to display the date value without either converting it to a text representation of a date or converting it to a number, you get an error.

In addition to these functions, you also use the Int() and Fix() mathematical functions and the Str(), Val(), and Format() string functions to convert between different data types.

Summary

In this chapter you have examined assignment statements, comment statements, and the built-in functions of Visual Basic. Most work in a computer program is done through assignment statements. They calculate new values from existing values and functions and assign storage in memory. You use comment statements to reveal what your assignment statements are supposed to do. The built-in functions provide the basic numerical and string functions necessary to do most common calculations. In the next two chapters, "Creating and Using Procedures" and "Creating and Using Functions," you learn to create your own procedures and functions.

Review Questions

Answers to review questions are in Appendix A.

1. What does an assignment statement do?
2. How does Visual Basic convert data types when calculating a formula?
3. How do you create and assign a value to an object variable?
4. What do operators do?
5. What is the precedence of the operators, and how do you change the order of the calculation of a formula?
6. What function would you use to round −3.4 to −2?

Chapter 5 ♦ Using Assignment Statements and the Built-In Functions

Review Exercises

1. Convert 1.34 radians to degrees.

2. Calculate the value of 355/113 in the Immediate pane. This is a popular approximation to Π, and is easy to remember because it uses each of the first three odd integers twice.

3. Calculate the inverse hyperbolic cotangent of 25 in the Immediate pane of the Debug window.

4. Define three variables in the Immediate pane. Variable A is the string "My name is", B is your first name in quotation marks, and C is your last name in quotation marks. Write a formula to combine these three strings into a sentence.

5. Write a formula that uses the Now function to get the date and time, extracts the fractional part of the decimal fraction, and multiplies by the number of minutes in a day. The result should be the number of minutes from midnight until the current time.

6. Write a formula to determine the day of the week 327 days from now.

Part III

Functions and Procedures

CHAPTER 6

Creating and Using Procedures

You've been using things named procedures throughout this book. For example, in Chapter 1, you let Excel create a procedure for you. Now it's time to look at procedures in detail, to see how they work and how you create them.

In this chapter, you will learn the following:

- What a procedure is
- The different types of procedures
- How to call a procedure and pass data to it
- What an event procedure is

What Are Procedures?

A *procedure* is the smallest usable computer program that you can write in Visual Basic. A procedure is a grouping of one or more Visual Basic statements to accomplish a particular task. A complete application can consist of one or many procedures, depending on its complexity. Normally, you should try to keep the tasks that a procedure must perform simple and straightforward. If the tasks become complicated, break your program into more procedures, with each procedure taking care of a smaller part of the task.

Chapter 6 ◆ Creating and Using Procedures

Every procedure begins with a procedure declaration statement and ends with an End Sub statement, as follows:

```
Sub procedure_name (arguments)
    .
    procedure body
    .
End Sub
```

The procedure declaration statement names the procedure, marks its beginning, and lists any arguments that may be passed between the procedure and a calling program. The End Sub statement marks the end of the procedure. Everything between these two statements is the procedure body, which performs the task of the procedure.

The argument list is a connection between a calling procedure and the procedure being called. Although any globally defined values are available to both procedures, any specific values that must be passed are sent in the argument list.

Types of Procedures

There are essentially four kinds of procedures:

- ◆ General procedures
- ◆ Command procedures
- ◆ Event procedures
- ◆ Functions

Functions, which are analogous to Visual Basic's built-in functions, are discussed in detail in Chapter 7. The distinctions among the other three types of procedures mainly concern the tasks that they perform.

General Procedures

General procedures, which are also known simply as *procedures*, are the standard Visual Basic procedures that do not normally change things outside of themselves. These procedures calculate values, display documents, send messages to other applications, and manipulate disk files.

Command Procedures

Command procedures augment the capabilities of applications outside of Visual Basic. In particular, command procedures expand the capabilities of Excel by affecting workbooks or their contents. In effect, the functionality of the command procedures is analogous to that of the Excel menu commands. The procedures created by the Macro Recorder are examples of command procedures because they are all recordings of actions applied to a worksheet.

Command procedures usually are not sent any arguments; if they need data from the user, they display a dialog box to get it directly.

Event Procedures

Event procedures are tied to specific events, and are executed when the event occurs. Events include pressing a button, executing a menu command, opening or closing a worksheet, opening or closing Excel, and changing the contents of a dialog box. Note that an event procedure can also be a command procedure or a general procedure.

To make a procedure an event procedure, you simply attach the procedure to an event. For example, in the first chapter, you attached a procedure to a button. That procedure then became an event procedure tied to the button click event.

To have an event procedure activate whenever the user opens or closes a workbook, name it Auto_Open or Auto_Close. To have an event procedure run whenever the user activates a worksheet, equate the procedure name to the OnSheetActivate property of that particular sheet object. For example, the statement

```
Worksheets("Sheet1").OnSheetActivate = "InitIt"
```

runs the InitIt procedure whenever the user activates Sheet1. If you use the Application object, then the procedure executes whenever the user activates a sheet.

You can use the OnSheetDeactivate property similarly, to execute a procedure whenever the user deactivates a sheet. (You deactivate a sheet by closing it or by making another sheet the active sheet.)

Calling a Procedure

So far in this book, you have executed a procedure by selecting it in the Macro dialog box or by attaching it to a button. However, procedures can be executed by other procedures; this is known as *calling* a procedure.

To call a procedure, simply place its name where you want to call it within another procedure. If the called procedure needs arguments, place them after the procedure name. For example, in the following procedure outline, the Proc1 procedure calls the Proc2 procedure:

```
Sub Proc1 ()
    'Some statements.
    Proc2
    'Some other statements.
End Sub

Sub Proc2 ()
    'Proc2 body.
End Sub
```

Chapter 6 ◆ Creating and Using Procedures

Calling a Procedure in a Different Module

When you call a procedure, Visual Basic first looks in the module containing the calling procedure and then looks in all the other modules attached to the current workbook. So, to call any other procedure in the current workbook, you usually don't have to do anything special. However, if the current workbook contains more than one procedure with the same name, you must attach the module name to the procedure name to indicate which module to search for the procedure.

To attach a module name to a procedure name, you surround the module name with square brackets followed by a period and then the procedure name. For example, if Proc1 is in Module1, Proc2 is in Module5, and another Proc2 is in Module2, calling the Proc2 procedure in Module5 from within Proc1 would require code similar to the following:

```
Sub Proc1 ()
    'Some statements.
    [Module5].Proc2
    'Some other statements.
End Sub
```

If the workbook includes only one Proc2, you don't need the reference to the module. However, if you have many modules and procedures in a workbook, you should include the module name to enhance your code's readability, so that you can more easily find the called procedure.

Calling a Procedure in a Different Workbook

If the procedure that you want to call is in another workbook, you need only attach that workbook to the current workbook to make all its modules and procedures available.

To attach another workbook to your current workbook, perform the following steps:

1. Make sure that the other workbook has been saved. You cannot attach an unsaved workbook.

2. With a module in your current workbook active, choose the **T**ools References command.

3. In the References dialog box, select the check box next to the name of the other workbook, as shown in figure 6.1, and then choose OK. If the workbook is not listed, use the Browse button to locate it.

Figure 6.1

Attaching a workbook in the References dialog box.

After you attach a workbook, Visual Basic searches the modules in the workbook if it does not locate a called procedure in your current workbook.

As with using a procedure in another module, if more than one workbook has procedures of the same name, you must attach the workbook name to the procedure name, or to the procedure and module names, to specify both the workbook and module to search for the procedure. For example, if Proc1 must call Proc2, and Proc2 is in the Module5 module in the MYSTUFF.XLS workbook, you must add the module and workbook name to the Proc2 call, as follows:

```
Sub Proc1 ()
    'Some statements.
    [MYSTUFF.XLS].[Module5].Proc2
    'Some other statements.
End Sub
```

Again, if only one Proc2 is in all the attached workbooks, you do not have to insert the workbook name. However, doing so considerably improves the readability of your programs, and also ensures that if two procedures have the same name, you can easily determine which procedure you want.

Preventing Access to Modules and Procedures

Now that you have seen how to access procedures in other modules and workbooks, how can you prevent a procedure from being accessed from outside of its module? This question becomes critical in several scenarios. Often you will create subprocedures for the other procedures in a module, and those procedures should not be accessed from outside their module. Or, you may have a set of similar but different procedures with the same names in two or more modules.

For example, in a stock analysis program, you might create a module for each stock that you want to analyze, and design a trend analysis procedure explicitly for each individual stock. Rather than worrying about a bunch of procedures with the name Trend, you can make each such procedure *private* to the module in which it resides.

To make a procedure private to a module, place the keyword Private at the beginning of the procedure declaration statement. For example, to make the Proc1 procedure accessible exclusively to other procedures in the same module, use the following procedure header:

```
Private Sub Proc1 ()
    .
    .
    .
End Sub
```

To protect a whole module from being accessed by a procedure in another workbook, place the following statement at the top of the module:

```
Option Private Module
```

Passing Values to Procedures

The arguments of the procedure header enable you to define the names and types of values that can be passed to a procedure. Except for global variables, and variables defined at the module level, all variables in a procedure are private to that procedure. That is, the variables defined in a procedure cannot be read or changed outside of that procedure unless the arguments in the procedure header pass them in or out.

Declaring Variables in the Procedure Header

In addition to declaring the variables in a procedure that are passed between a procedure and an external calling procedure, you also declare the type of those variables. You use the same type of constructs as you use to define the types of variables in a Dim statement.

For example, consider the following simple procedure. which does nothing more than take the first two arguments, multiply them, and return the product in a third argument:

```
Sub MultiplyEm(Value1 As Single, Value2 As Single, Product As Single)
    Product = Value1 * Value2
End Sub
```

Note that all three arguments are defined as Single type. As in the Dim statement, if you don't specify the type of an argument, it defaults to the Variant type.

To call this procedure from a second procedure, you would use code similar to the following:

```
Sub TestProc()
    Dim Result As Single
    MultiplyEm 5, 7, Result
    Debug.Print Result
End Sub
```

This procedure defines a variable as Single type, passes the numbers 5 and 7 to the MultiplyEm procedure, and receives the result back in the variable named Result. The Print method of the Debug object prints the result on the Immediate pane of the Debug window. To run this procedure, open the Debug window and enter the following into the Immediate pane:

Run("TestProc")

Figure 6.2 shows the printed value of Result, immediately below the Run command.

Figure 6.2
Running a procedure from the Immediate pane of the Debug window.

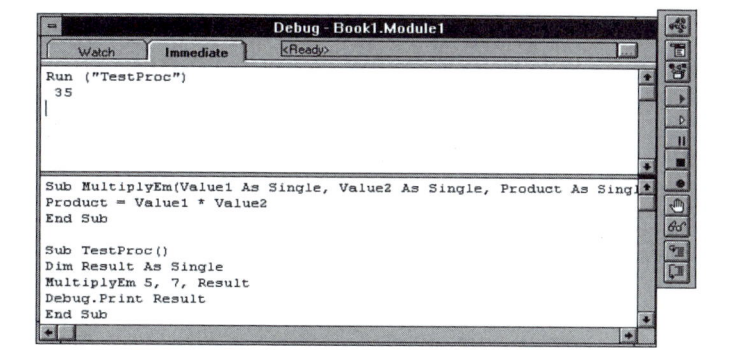

```
Debug - Book1.Module1
Watch    Immediate    <Ready>
Run ("TestProc")
 35

Sub MultiplyEm(Value1 As Single, Value2 As Single, Product As Singl
Product = Value1 * Value2
End Sub

Sub TestProc()
Dim Result As Single
MultiplyEm 5, 7, Result
Debug.Print Result
End Sub
```

Using a Comma-Delimited List

When you call a procedure and place the arguments in a comma-separated list, there is a one-to-one mapping of the values to the variables in the procedure header. For example, in the MultiplyEm procedure, the variable Value1 is given the value 5, Value2 is given the value 7, and the result contained in Product is passed to the variable Result.

You don't have to use literal values for the arguments to the procedure, but you can use variables as shown in the following example:

```
Sub TestProc()
    Dim Result As Single, ValA As Single, ValB As Single
    ValA = 5
    ValB = 7
    MultiplyEm ValA, ValB, Result
    Debug.Print Result
End Sub
```

Executing this procedure yields the same result as the previous version of TestPtoc, which uses literal values in the procedure call.

Using a Named Argument List

In addition to placing the arguments in a comma-delimited list, you can use a named list. In a named list, you use the variable name from the procedure header, followed by colon equals (:=), which you then follow with the value or variable that you want to pass. If you use a named list, the arguments do not have to be in order as they must in a comma-delimited list.

For example, the following version of TestProc yields exactly the same results as the previous two:

```
Sub TestProc()
    Dim Result As Single, ValA As Single, ValB As Single
    ValA = 5
    ValB = 7
    MultiplyEm Product:=Result, Value1:=ValA, Value2:=ValB
    Debug.Print Result
End Sub
```

Named arguments are most useful for clarifying what you are passing to a procedure. This is especially useful for procedures with many arguments, where it is not always obvious which values are being passed to which variables.

Passing Values by Address

When you call a procedure and pass a variable to it as an argument, you are not really passing the value to the procedure; instead, you are actually passing the address to the place in memory at which the value is stored. When a procedure needs you to pass a value to it in an argument, it uses the address that you pass to it in the procedure header to access the original value in memory. When a procedure needs to return a value, it does essentially the same thing: it uses the address passed to it to find the location in memory at which the value is to be stored.

Passing a value by address doesn't require any additional coding, because it is the default method of passing arguments.

Passing Values by Value

When you pass an argument to a procedure by address, the procedure can change the argument's value. Sometimes you want to ensure that a called procedure does not change the value of an argument that you pass to it. To handle these cases, pass the argument by value instead of by address.

You can pass an argument by value in two ways: by modifying the procedure header or by making the argument a formula. Either of these methods protects the value of an argument from change.

Modifying the Procedure Header

To modify the procedure header to pass an argument by value, you precede the argument name with the keyword ByVal.

For example, to ensure that its two input arguments are not changed, you would modify the MultiplyEm procedure as follows:

```
Sub MultiplyEm(ByVal Value1 As Single, ByVal Value2 As Single, _
        Product As Single)
    Product = Value1 * Value2
    Value1 = 99
End Sub
```

Notice that a statement has also been inserted to try and change the value of Value1. Make sure that you don't place the ByVal keyword before the argument that returns the result, or nothing will be returned.

To print the value of ValA, the variable that is passed to the Value1 argument, modify TestProc as follows:

```
Sub TestProc()
    Dim Result As Single, ValA As Single, ValB As Single
    ValA = 5
    ValB = 7
    MultiplyEm Product:=Result, Value1:=ValA, Value2:=ValB
    Debug.Print Result
    Debug.Print ValA
End Sub
```

If you run this procedure from the Debug window before inserting the ByVal keywords, you get the following result:

```
Run ("TestProc")
    35
    99
```

After you insert the keywords to pass the arguments by value, the result changes as follows:

```
Run ("TestProc")
    35
    5
```

Making the Argument a Formula

The second way to pass an argument by value is to make it a formula. Instead of being a single value, an argument can be a formula that evaluates to a value of the correct type. When you use a formula as an argument to a procedure, the formula is evaluated, the result is placed in a temporary memory storage location, and the address to that temporary location is passed to the procedure being called. If the called procedure changes the value of the argument, it changes only the value in the temporary storage location, not the original value.

Chapter 6 ◆ Creating and Using Procedures

To make a single value into a formula, simply surround it with parentheses. Use the previous example to experiment with this. Try removing the ByVal keyword from the procedure header and then calling the procedure without the keyword, and then try calling it with the parentheses around the ValA argument. Without the parentheses, the procedures and result are as follows:

```
Sub TestProc()
    Dim Result As Single, ValA As Single, ValB As Single
    ValA = 5
    ValB = 7
    MultiplyEm Product:=Result, Value1:=ValA, Value2:=ValB
    Debug.Print Result
    Debug.Print ValA
End Sub

Sub MultiplyEm(Value1 As Single, Value2 As Single, Product As Single)
    Product = Value1 * Value2
    Value1 = 99
End Sub

Run ("TestProc")
 35
 99
```

When you insert the parentheses, the procedure and result changes as follows:

```
Sub TestProc()
    Dim Result As Single, ValA As Single, ValB As Single
    ValA = 5
    ValB = 7
    MultiplyEm Product:=Result, Value1:=(ValA), Value2:=ValB
    Debug.Print Result
    Debug.Print ValA
End Sub

Sub MultiplyEm(Value1 As Single, Value2 As Single, Product As Single)
    Product = Value1 * Value2
    Value1 = 99
End Sub

Run ("TestProc")
 35
 5
```

> **Note:** All data structures, including arrays, must be passed by address, and only single values can be passed by value. To pass a data structure by value, you would have to duplicate the whole structure before passing it to the procedure.

Using Optional Arguments

In some cases you might want to allow a user to not specify an argument and use a default value instead. To do this, preface the argument name in the procedure header with the keyword Optional. Then the procedure must check for a missing argument and insert the default value if necessary.

The following procedure makes the second input argument optional, and inserts a default value if the user chooses to omit it:

```
Sub MultiplyEm(Product As Single, Value1 As Single, Optional Value2)
    If IsMissing(Value2) Then Value2 = 10
    Product = Value1 * Value2
End Sub
```

Note that you change the argument order to make the optional argument the last one, and that you remove the argument's type, making it the Variant type. You make these changes because when you use the Optional keyword, all arguments to its right must also be optional and of the Variant data type.

The second line of the procedure uses an If statement to test for a missing value. (Chapter 8, "Understanding Decision Making," discusses If statements in detail.) If no argument was passed, the IsMissing() function returns True; otherwise it returns False. If the argument is missing, the If statement inserts 10, the default value, into Value2.

Try calling the procedure as follows, with the one argument missing:

```
Sub TestProc()
    Dim Result As Single, ValA As Single, ValB As Single
    ValA = 5
    ValB = 7
    MultiplyEm Product:=Result, Value1:=ValA
    Debug.Print Result
    Debug.Print ValA
End Sub
```

The result in the Debug window is as follows:

```
Run ("TestProc")
 50
  5
```

Using an Indeterminate Number of Arguments

Many of Excel's built-in worksheet functions can take one or more arguments, with the actual number of arguments indeterminate until runtime. You can create a procedure with a similar capability by placing the keyword ParamArray before the last argument in the procedure header, and making the last argument an array of Variant type variables. Within the procedure, you must determine how many elements of the array contain data and then work with those elements. Use the UBound() function to find the highest defined array element, and the For Each loop (described in Chapter 14, "Using Object Type Loops") to operate on every element in the array.

The following MultiplyEm2 procedure takes an indeterminate number of arguments and returns the product of all those arguments:

```
Sub TestProc()
    Dim Result As Single, ValA As Single, ValB As Single
    Dim ValC As Single, ValD As Single, ValE As Single
    ValA = 5
    ValB = 7
    ValC = 3
    ValD = 12
    ValE = 4
    MultiplyEm2 Result, ValA, ValB, ValC, ValD, ValE
    Debug.Print Result
End Sub

Sub MultiplyEm2(Product As Single, ParamArray Values())
    Product = 1
    For Each Value In Values
        Product = Product * Value
    Next Value
End Sub

Run("TestProc")
 5040
```

The TestProc procedure calls MultiplyEm with five variable arguments, plus one for the returned value. The MultiplyEm procedure then initializes the variable Product to 1, and then the For Each statement steps through all the values in the array Values and multiplies the value of Product by each value it finds. The returned value is the product of the five input values.

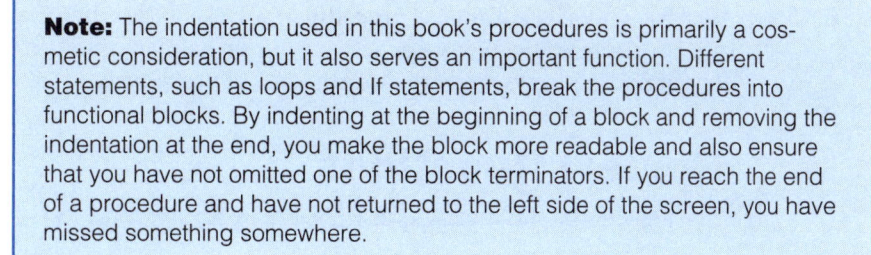

> **Note:** The indentation used in this book's procedures is primarily a cosmetic consideration, but it also serves an important function. Different statements, such as loops and If statements, break the procedures into functional blocks. By indenting at the beginning of a block and removing the indentation at the end, you make the block more readable and also ensure that you have not omitted one of the block terminators. If you reach the end of a procedure and have not returned to the left side of the screen, you have missed something somewhere.

Making Procedure Variables Persist

When a procedure completes and returns to the calling procedure, all variables declared within that procedure disappear, never to be seen again. If the procedure is called a second time, a new set of variables is declared, used, and then discarded when the procedure ends. Of course, this does not apply to variables that you declare outside of the procedures; those survive until the procedure that originally declared them ends. Variables declared at the module level persist until the program ends.

Sometimes, though, you want the variables in a procedure to persist until the next time that the procedure is called—for example, to gather statistics about procedure calls, or to use values from a previous calculation as the starting point for the next. You could declare all the variables in the procedure at the module level, or you can declare them as static in the procedure. You use the Static statement to declare variables in a procedure in the same manner as you use the Dim statement. However, unlike Dim-declared variables, Static-declared variables do not go away when the procedure ends.

For example, instead of using the following in a procedure

```
Dim Result As Single
```

you would use the subsequent Static statement, which enables Result to persist after the procedure in which it is declared returns to its calling procedure:

```
Static Result As Single
```

Chapter 6 ◆ Creating and Using Procedures

Summary

In this chapter, you learned all about three of the four types of procedures: general procedures, command procedures, and event procedures. General procedures are normal procedures that calculate or display things, and command procedures manipulate other applications such as Excel or Word. Event procedures, which can also be general or command procedures, are executed when a specific event occurs, such as a worksheet being opened or a button being pressed. In Chapter 7 you learn about functions, which is the fourth kind of procedure.

Review Questions

The answers to the review questions are in Appendix A.

1. What is a procedure?
2. Define the three types of procedures described in this chapter. How do they differ?
3. What statements must come at the beginning and end of a procedure?
4. What kind of procedures does the Macro Recorder create?
5. What does it mean to call a procedure? How do you call a procedure?
6. How do you make variables retain their value from one calling of a procedure to the next?
7. How do you hide procedures from other modules?
8. What does passing an argument by address mean?
9. What does passing an argument by value mean?
10. How do you pass an argument by address? How do you pass it by value?
11. How do you call a procedure in another workbook?

Review Exercises

1. Write a procedure named AddIt that adds the value of two arguments and returns the result in a third.
2. Write a procedure named SumIt that adds a variable list of floating-point numbers and returns the sum.

3. In a second module, create a second SumIt procedure that sums a list of integers. Then, from another workbook, write a procedure that uses the two SumIt procedures, first to sum a list of real numbers (2.7, 5.9, 23.85, 19.6, 8.4) and print the result on the Immediate pane of the Debug window, and then to sum a list of integers (3, 45, 27, 15, 5, 14, 1) and print that total as well. Be sure to select the right version of the SumIt procedure.

4. Create a startup procedure that runs when you start Excel and prints "Good Morning" in the center of the active worksheet.

CHAPTER 7

Creating and Using Functions

Chapter 6 introduced three types of procedures that Visual Basic offers: general procedures, command procedures, and event procedures. This chapter covers the fourth type of Visual Basic procedure, functions. Visual Basic offers many functions, and you can access many more in external libraries. In addition, Visual Basic enables you to create your own custom functions. In this chapter, you will learn how to do the following:

- Create and use functions
- Set the data type of a function
- Create custom worksheet functions
- Use worksheet functions
- Use functions in external libraries

What Are Functions?

Functions are procedures that return values in the procedure name. Other than that, functions behave much the same as subprocedures. The main advantage that functions offer over subprocedures is that you can use functions in a formula directly, just like a variable. To use a value returned by a subprocedure in a formula, you must assign the returned value to a variable and then use the variable in the formula.

Because functions can be used in a formula, the syntax that you use to create and use them is slightly different from that of the subprocedures described in Chapter 6; however, the same basic properties and constraints still apply.

Creating a Function

The way that you create functions is similar to that of subprocedures, with some important differences. The function header and footer are similar to the subprocedure header and footer, but you use the word Function rather than Sub:

```
Function function_name (arguments) As type
.
.   function body
.
function_name = something
End Function
```

The function header declares the function name and any arguments. Additionally, because a formula uses a function like a variable, the function has a data type just like a variable. You specify the data type in the header. Following the header is the function body, which performs the function's task. A special requirement of functions is that an assignment statement that assigns a value to the function's name appear somewhere before the end of the function procedure. The function ends with an End Function statement.

Setting a Function's Data Type

The function header contains a space for arguments and a declaration for the function's data type. You declare the argument list for a function exactly as you do for a procedure. Each variable in the argument list has an As *type* clause that defines the type of the function's arguments. Arguments either send data to a function, receive data from a function, or both. As with Dim and Sub statements, if you don't declare an argument, the data type is Variant by default.

The data type of the value that the function returns is set with the As *type* clause on the right side of the function header. The data types are identical to those used in an argument list or Dim statement.

For example, you can easily rewrite the MultiplyEm procedure examples in Chapter 6 as functions, with the data types specified in the headers:

```
'
'   A function to multiply two values.
'
Function MultiplyEm(Value1 As Single, Value2 As Single) As Single
```

```
        MultiplyEm = Value1 * Value2
End Function
'
'   A function to multiply a list of values.
'
Function MultiplyEm2(ParamArray Values()) As Single
    Dim Product As Single
    Product = 1
    For Each Value In Values
        Product = Product * Value
    Next Value
    MultiplyEm2 = Product
End Function
```

Calling a Function

Calling a function differs from calling a procedure, because you call a function as part of a formula rather than as a stand-alone statement. Because a function is part of a formula, you must enclose its argument list in parentheses to bind the arguments to the function. Without the parentheses, distinguishing the formula from the function is difficult or even impossible.

Aside from this use of parentheses, you call a function the same way that you call a procedure: the methods of using arguments, passing by value or by address, using default values for missing arguments, and using lists of arguments are all the same. For example, to call the previous functions, you would use the following procedure:

```
Sub TestProc()
    Dim Result As Single, ValA As Single, ValB As Single
    Dim ValC As Single, ValD As Single, ValE As Single
    ValA = 5
    ValB = 7
    ValC = 3
    ValD = 12
    ValE = 4
    Debug.Print MultiplyEm(3, 5), MultiplyEm(ValA, ValB)
    Debug.Print MultiplyEm2(ValA, ValB, ValC, ValD, ValE)
    Result = MultiplyEm(ValC, ValD) / 2 + _
        MultiplyEm2(ValA, ValB, ValC)
    Debug.Print Result
End Sub
```

The first two functions are called as arguments of the the Debug object's Print method. Each of the two calls to the function calculates a single value and returns it to the Print method. The next statement makes a single call to the MultiplyEm2

Chapter 7 ◆ Creating and Using Functions

procedure as an argument of the Print method. The next statement is an assignment statement with a formula that uses both of the functions and returns a value in the variable Result. The variable Result is then printed in the next statement.

Running this procedure in the Immediate pane of the Debug window yields the following result with three output lines, one for each of the Print methods:

```
Run("TestProc")
    15              35
    5040
    123
```

Creating Custom Worksheet Functions

You can use Visual Basic functions in worksheets as well as in Visual Basic programs. However, when you use functions in a worksheet, they must return values only. Also, they cannot execute commands like a command procedure and must not directly modify cell contents.

To use a custom Visual Basic function in a worksheet, type its name into a worksheet formula, as you would for any built-in worksheet function. You can also select the function and its argument list from the Function Wizard in the User Defined category (as described later in this chapter).

For example, the two MultiplyEm functions used in the last example are available for use in a worksheet. If you switch to a blank sheet, type **=MultiplyEm(5,7)** in a cell, and then press Enter, the result (35) appears in the cell. Figure 7.1 shows several more examples of using the two MultiplyEm functions. Note that the functions work with cell references as arguments as well as literal values, but do not work with a range reference. The next section describes how you pass range references.

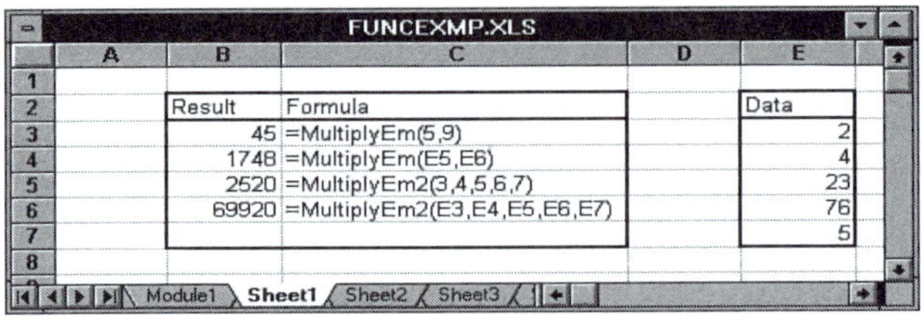

Figure 7.1
Using custom functions in a worksheet.

	A	B	C	D	E
1			FUNCEXMP.XLS		
2		Result	Formula		Data
3		45	=MultiplyEm(5,9)		2
4		1748	=MultiplyEm(E5,E6)		4
5		2520	=MultiplyEm2(3,4,5,6,7)		23
6		69920	=MultiplyEm2(E3,E4,E5,E6,E7)		76
7					5
8					

Note: In each of the worksheets created in this chapter, column B contains the result, and column C displays the function or formula that generates that result.

For another example, consider the following equation, which calculates the required payment on a loan with an initial balance of presval, a rate of rate, for nper periods. This equation should give results that are the same as the Pmt() worksheet function, except that it gives a positive value for the payment and assumes that the loan is completely paid off in nper periods.

$$LPmt = \frac{presval * rate}{1 - \left[\frac{1}{1 + rate}\right]^{nper}}$$

The built-in function Pmt() takes as input the rate per period and the number of periods, although for most loans it is more common to state the interest per year and the number of years even though the payments are made every month. The following function uses this formula, the rate (as a fraction) per year, and the number of years, and returns the monthly payment:

```
'
'   Calculate the payment on a loan from the yearly rate
'   the number of years and the principal.
'
Function LPmt(presval As Currency, theRate As Single, _
    theYears As Integer) As Currency
    Dim nper As Integer, rate As Single
    nper = theYears * 12    'Convert years to months
    rate = theRate / 12     'Convert yearly rate to monthly rate
    LPmt = presval * rate / (1 - (1 / (1 + rate)) ^ nper)
End Function
```

You first must define the variables nper and rate, because Excel already has functions with these names and you need the declarations to override the Excel function names. If you don't declare the variables, Visual Basic tries to insert the functions, gets confused, and returns an error message. After defining the variables, the function converts the yearly rates to monthly rates and then calculates the payment.

If you type this function into a module, and then switch to a worksheet and open the Function Wizard, the new function appears in the User Defined category, as shown in figure 7.2. Figure 7.3 shows the application of this function with three different interest rates.

Chapter 7 ♦ Creating and Using Functions

Figure 7.2
The LPmt() custom function displayed in the Function Wizard window along with its arguments.

Figure 7.3
Using the LPmt() custom function to calculate a loan payment for three different interest rates.

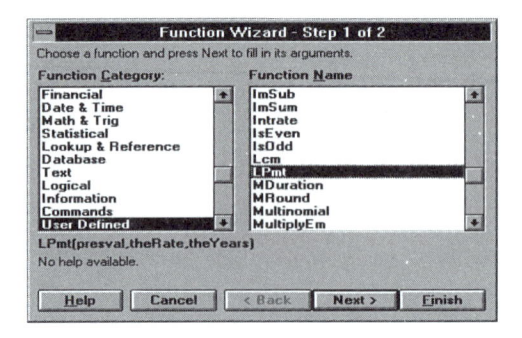

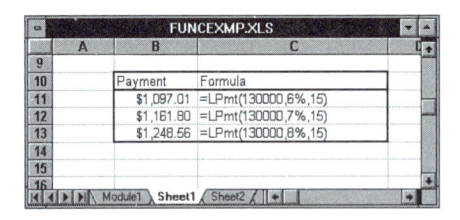

> **Note:** When you type **6%** into a worksheet function, Excel actually inserts the number `0.06`, the fractional interest rate, rather than the percentage rate.

Using Worksheet Functions in a Procedure

As you can use Visual Basic functions in a worksheet, you can also use worksheet functions in a procedure. All of Excel's worksheet functions are available and attached to the Application object. Use the Object Browser to select the Excel library and the Application object. This not only results in the display of a complete list of all special functions and calculations, but also makes each listed function and calculation available for use in Visual Basic. Be careful, though; some of the worksheet functions have the same name as a Visual Basic function, but have different arguments or yield different results. For example, the Visual Basic zLog() function returns the natural logarithm (base **e** = 2.71828...), but the Excel Log() function returns the common logarithm (base 10).

To access the Excel worksheet functions, preface the function name with the Application object followed by a period. If you leave out the Application object, you get the Visual Basic function. For example, to use the Excel Log() function in a formula, you would use a statement such as the following:

```
theLog = Application.Log(someValue)
```

This statement calculates the common logarithm of someValue and stores it in the variable theLog.

A good use for this capability, beyond making the many Excel functions available for use in your Visual Basic programs, is to create glue functions that modify the Excel functions for use in a worksheet. A *glue function* is a function procedure that rearranges or modifies the arguments of a function to make it easier to use.

Excel's annuity functions all take as input the interest rate per period and the number of periods, although most annuities, even though they have a monthly payment schedule, are stated in yearly interest and years to payoff. The next example is a useful set of glue functions that convert the four Excel annuity functions to yearly inputs. Make sure that you use a slightly different name for the functions so that they are not confused with the built-in functions.

```
'
'Glue function for calculating the interest rate.
'
Function theRate(nyrs As Integer, pmt As Currency, _
    pv As Currency) As Single
    Dim nper As Integer, fv As Currency, guess As Single
    fv = 0      'Assume the loan is paid off.
    guess = 0.1 'An initial guess
    nper = nyrs * 12 'Convert the years to months.
    'Calculate the interest rate per period and convert to
    'yearly interest.
    theRate = 12 * Application.rate(nper, -pmt, pv, fv, 0, guess)
End Function
'
'Glue function for calculating the payment.
'
Function thePmt(theRate As Single, nyrs As Integer, _
    pv As Currency) As Currency
    Dim nper As Integer, fv As Currency, rate As Single
    fv = 0      'Assume the loan is paid off.
    nper = nyrs * 12 'Convert the years to months.
    rate = theRate / 12 'Convert rate per year to rate per month.
    'Calculate the payment and convert to a positive number.
    thePmt = -Application.pmt(rate, nper, pv, fv)
End Function
'
'Glue function for calculating the present value.
```

Chapter 7 ♦ Creating and Using Functions

```
Function thePv(theRate As Single, nyrs As Integer, _
    thePmt As Currency) As Currency
    Dim nper As Integer, fv As Currency, rate As Single
    fv = 0     'Assume the loan is paid off.
    nper = nyrs * 12 'Convert the years to months.
    rate = theRate / 12 'Convert rate per year to rate per month.
    'Calculate the present value.
    thePv = Application.pv(rate, nper, -thePmt, fv)
End Function
'
'Glue function for calculating the number of years.
'
Function theNyrs(theRate As Single, thePmt As Currency, _
    pv As Currency) As Integer
    Dim nper As Integer, fv As Currency, rate As Single
    fv = 0     'Assume the loan is paid off.
    nper = nyrs * 12 'Convert the years to months.
    rate = theRate / 12 'Convert rate per year to rate per month.
    'Calculate the months and convert to years.
    theNyrs = Application.nper(rate, -thePmt, pv, fv) / 12
End Function
```

In each function, it is assumed that the future value is 0, and the results are all converted to positive values. Figure 7.4 shows the application of these functions with some common values.

Figure 7.4
Using the annuity glue functions.

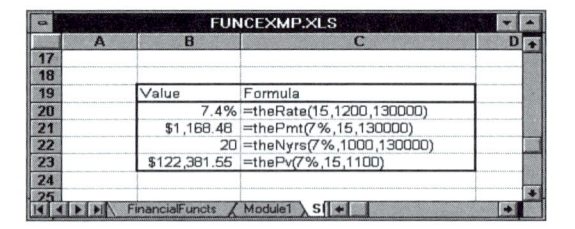

	Value	Formula
20	7.4%	=theRate(15,1200,130000)
21	$1,168.48	=thePmt(7%,15,130000)
22	20	=theNyrs(7%,1000,130000)
23	$122,381.55	=thePv(7%,15,1100)

Passing an Array to a Custom Worksheet Function

Although most functions deal with single values, you often need to pass an Excel array or a range reference to a function. The function used in figure 7.1 can take only single values as arguments, and not range references. However, as you can see in the figure, the procedure handles range references that consist of a single cell. This is because Excel automatically replaces single range references with their values before passing them to a function. A larger reference requires some extra handling to pass the values to the function correctly.

An Excel array is enclosed in curly brackets and separates columns with commas, and rows with semicolons. For example, the following is a two-dimensional, three-by-three array:

$$\{1,2,3;4,5,6;7,8,9\} = \begin{vmatrix} 1 & 2 & 3 \\ 4 & 5 & 6 \\ 7 & 8 & 9 \end{vmatrix}$$

When you pass an Excel array to a Visual Basic function, it is automatically converted into a Visual Basic array. However, if you pass an Excel range reference such as C2:E4, it is passed as a Range object. If your function is always going to receive arrays as arguments, you can define the function argument as a Visual Basic array. However, you are more likely to want to pass range references to a worksheet function.

To pass an Excel range reference to a Visual Basic function, the argument of the function must be of the Variant type. The value passed to the function is then a Variant containing a Range object. If you pass an Excel array to a function with a Variant type argument, the argument becomes a Variant that contains an array. Note that this differs from an array of Variants. If the value passed is a Variant containing an array, then you can access the array exactly as you would any other array (with parentheses and an index) because Excel arrays are translated directly into Visual Basic arrays when you pass them as an argument.

If the value passed is a Variant that contains a Range object, you can extract the values from each element in the range, using the Cells method and the Value property. However, a simpler way to access these values is to use the For Each loop, which executes once for each element of the argument. If the argument is a range, then each element is a Range object for a single cell, which is automatically converted to the value in the cell. A second benefit of this loop is that if the argument is an array, the loop executes once for each element of the array and returns the value of that element, so that this construct works with both the Excel arrays and Range objects.

For example, the following version of the MultiplyEm() function takes either Excel arrays or range references and correctly multiplies the values:

```
'
'   A function to multiply an array of values
'
Function MultiplyEm3(theArray) As Single
    Dim Product As Single, Value
    Product = 1
```

Chapter 7 ♦ Creating and Using Functions

```
    For Each Value In theArray
        Product = Product * Value
    Next Value
    MultiplyEm3 = Product
End Function
```

Figure 7.5 shows the results of using this function with different arguments.

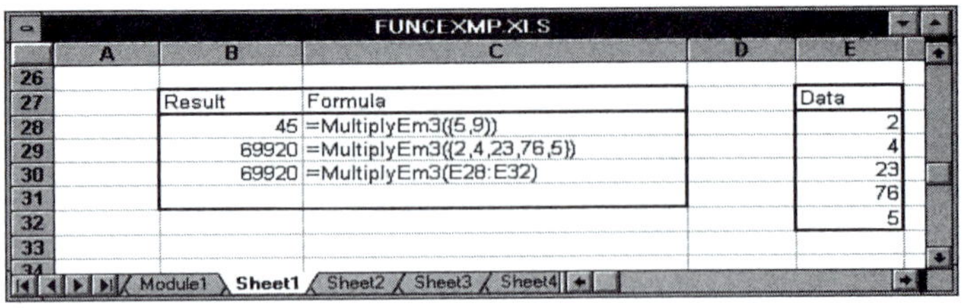

Figure 7.5
Using the MultiplyEm4 function to pass Excel arrays and range references.

	A	B	C	D	E
26					
27		Result	Formula		Data
28		45	=MultiplyEm3({5,9})		2
29		69920	=MultiplyEm3({2,4,23,76,5})		4
30		69920	=MultiplyEm3(E28:E32)		23
31					76
32					5
33					

This procedure cannot handle a compound range reference such as B2:C3,D2:E3. To handle such a reference, you use the same method that you used in Chapter 6 to send multiple arguments to a procedure: Use the ParamArray keyword and make the Variant argument an array. To extract the values, you need two For Each loops: one to extract the element from the array of Variant variables, and the second to extract the element from the array or object contained in each Variant variable.

For example, the following variation of the MultiplyEm() function takes any number of arrays or range references and correctly multiplies all the elements:

```
'
'   A function to multiply an array of arrays of values
'
Function MultiplyEm4(ParamArray theArray()) As Single
    Dim Product As Single, Part, Value
    Product = 1
    For Each Part In theArray
        For Each Value In Part
            Product = Product * Value
        Next Value
    Next Part
    MultiplyEm4 = Product
End Function
```

Visual Basic for Applications By EXAMPLE

The function header declares the argument as a parameter array of Variant type variables. The Dim statement declares the local variables, and then the variable Product is initialized to a value of 1. The first For Each loop extracts the elements of theArray, which is itself an array or a Range object, and stores them in the variable Part. The second For Each loop extracts from Part each of the elements, which are individual values, and then multiplies them. The two Next statements end the two For Each loops, and finally, the value stored in Product is returned.

Figure 7.6 shows the result of using this function with several different arguments.

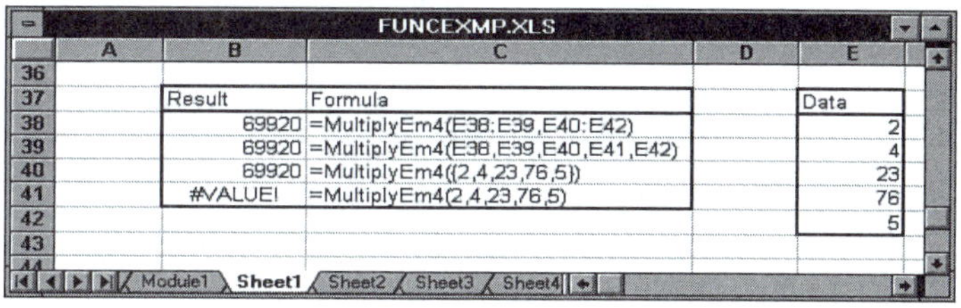

Figure 7.6
Using the MultiplyEm4 function to pass multiple Excel arrays and range references.

	A	B	C	D	E
36					
37		Result	Formula		Data
38		69920	=MultiplyEm4(E38:E39,E40:E42)		2
39		69920	=MultiplyEm4(E38,E39,E40,E41,E42)		4
40		69920	=MultiplyEm4({2,4,23,76,5})		23
41		#VALUE!	=MultiplyEm4(2,4,23,76,5)		76
42					5
43					

Note that the last example in figure 7.6 returns an error value. That example sends a simple list of numbers to the function. When the function receives the list, the first For Each loop extracts an element of the list, and then the second For Each loop attempts to extract an element from a simple value, resulting in an error.

To create a function that handles single values, lists of values, cell ranges, lists of cell ranges, and Excel arrays, you must test the value passed to the function to see which type of value is returned, and then select the appropriate method for extracting the values. To see which type of value is returned, use the TypeName() function, which returns a string that contains the name of the type of the variable used as an argument. If the variable is an array, the function returns the type name followed by a pair of empty parentheses. For example, if the argument is an array of Single type variables, TypeName() returns Single().

After you have determined the type of the variable, use a block If statement to select the correct method for calculating the product. Chapter 9, "Using Block If Structures," discusses this type of statement in detail. A block If statement tests whether a value is True. If so, the block of code between the If and Else statements is executed. If the value is False, the block of code between the Else and End If statements is executed.

For example, the following function accepts any type of list or array, and then calculates the product:

```
'
' A function to multiply any list of values
'
Function MultiplyEm5(ParamArray theArray()) As Single
    Dim Product As Single, Part, Value
```

Chapter 7 ♦ Creating and Using Functions

```
      Product = 1
      For Each Part In theArray
        If TypeName(Part) = "Range" Or _
            Right(TypeName(Part), 2) = "()" Then
          For Each Value In Part
            Product = Product * Value
          Next Value
        Else
          Product = Product * Part
        End If
      Next Part
      MultiplyEm5 = Product
    End Function
```

This function is almost identical to the MultiplyEm4() function, except for the addition of the block If statement. The If statement uses the TypeName() function to test for a Range object or an array. The statement tests for the Range object directly, but because it cannot use a direct test for an array, it extracts the two rightmost characters and checks whether they are a pair of parentheses. If they are, you infer that they are part of an array. If the block If statement detects a range or array, the block of code containing the second For Each statement is executed to extract the parts of the range or array. If the statement does not detect a range or array, it infers that it has a single value, so the statement between the Else and End If statements is executed to multiply the value by Product.

Figure 7.7 shows an example that uses this function with several different arguments.

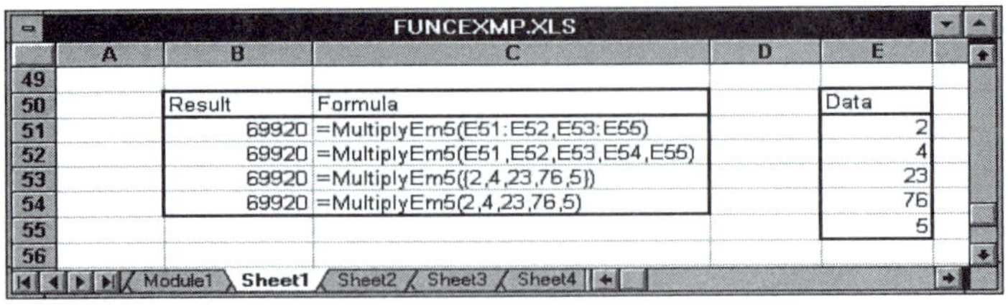

Figure 7.7
Using the MultiplyEm5 function to pass multiple Excel arrays, range references, and individual values to a function.

	A	B	C	D	E
49					
50		Result	Formula		Data
51		69920	=MultiplyEm5(E51:E52,E53:E55)		2
52		69920	=MultiplyEm5(E51,E52,E53,E54,E55)		4
53		69920	=MultiplyEm5({2,4,23,76,5})		23
54		69920	=MultiplyEm5(2,4,23,76,5)		76
55					5
56					

Passing an Array to the Worksheet from a Function

The opposite problem is to pass a Visual Basic array back to the worksheet. To do this, the function must be of the Variant type, and you must store the array as a Variant type. When you use the function, insert it into a range of cells on the worksheet.

Visual Basic for Applications By EXAMPLE

> **Note:** To insert an array function into a range of worksheet cells, select a range on the worksheet, type the function into the first cell, and hold down Ctrl-Shift when pressing Enter or clicking the check box.

For example, the following function returns the abbreviations for all the months of the year as a 12-element horizontal array:

```
'
' A function to return the months of the year
'
Function theMonths()
' The function has no arguments, and is a Variant type.
    theMonths = Array("Jan.", "Feb.", "Mar.", "Apr.", "May", _
        "Jun.", "Jul.", "Aug.", "Sep.", "Oct.", "Nov.", "Dec.")
End Function
```

Figure 7.8 shows the results of using the function on a worksheet in different ways. In all three cases, you select 12 cells, type the formula above the cells, and hold down Ctrl-Shift while pressing Enter.

Figure 7.8
Using the theMonthsfunction to pass a Visual Basic array to a worksheet.

The example on the top-left inserts the horizontal array in a vertical array of cells, which results in only the first element of the array being inserted in each cell. The example on the top-right uses the TRANSPOSE() worksheet function to transpose the horizontal array into a vertical array so it can be correctly inserted into the cells. The example at the bottom inserts the array into a horizontal array of cells, so you do not have to transpose it to insert it correctly.

Chapter 7 ◆ Creating and Using Functions

Using Functions in DLL Libraries

The use of Dynamic Link Libraries (DLLs) is a cornerstone of the Windows operating system. A *Dynamic Link Library* is a special kind of library that is stored in .DLL files and linked to an executing program at runtime rather than when the program is compiled. Programs that need library functions load them into memory only when they need them. The main reason for using DLLs is to share code among multiple applications. In this way, you need to store only one copy of the library on disk, which significantly reduces the amount of disk memory that you use. DLLs also make it easier to maintain your code, because you need only maintain a single copy of the library. Without DLLs, or a similar code-sharing capability, every program would have to store within its executable file all the functions that it uses, and every time that you change a function, you would also have to recompile each application that uses the function.

Nearly every function that you might want to use is already available within Visual Basic or Excel, so you may never need to use DLLs. You are most likely to use DLLs to call a special function or procedure created with a fully compiled language such as C or FORTRAN. This is possible to do because most modern compilers can produce DLLs. You might also want to call a system function that is unavailable in Visual Basic, such as one that accesses the keyboard buffers or that directly communicates with a device driver.

> **Caution:** Be careful when using external libraries, because a system crash can result if you call one incorrectly. While experimenting with DLLs, be sure to save your programs often.

The most difficult part of using Dynamic Link Libraries is to obtain the declaration information. If you want to access Windows system functions, you need a copy of the Windows Software Development Kit (SDK), which contains descriptions of the library functions and the function declarations.

To use a function or procedure in a DLL, you simply place the function's declaration statement at the top of a module. The declaration statement contains the function name, the library name, and the argument types. The declaration statement tells Visual Basic where to find the function and what kinds of arguments the function expects to see. After you declare a function, you can use it on the worksheet or in any Visual Basic program.

The following are examples of function or procedure declarations:

```
Declare Sub MessageBeep Lib "USER" (ByVal N As Integer)

Declare Function GetCurrentTime Lib "USER" () As Long

Declare Sub GetKeyboardState Lib "USER" (lpKeyState As Any)
```

The first example declares the MessageBeep( ) function in the library file USER.DLL. The function has a single integer argument that it passes to the library as a value. The second statement declares the function GetCurrentTime( ), which is also in USER.DLL. This function has no arguments and returns a Long integer. The last statement declares a procedure named GetKeyboardState in the USER.DLL file. The procedure requires one argument that can be of any type.

> **Note:** The file USER.DLL is part of the Windows 3.1 runtime package and is located in your WINDOWS/SYSTEM directory.

> **Note:** The data type Any is a special type that normally is for use only with external procedures. It disables type checking so that you can use different variable types to create the type that the external function or procedure needs. You must be careful, though, to ensure that you are passing the correct values to the procedure.

After you declare a library function or procedure, you can use them like any other functions and procedures. For example, the GetCurrentTime( ) function returns the number of milliseconds since you started Windows. You could use this function in a program that logs how much time you spend running programs in Windows. To call that function and display its result in the Immediate pane of the Debug window, you could create a procedure such as the following:

```
Declare Function GetCurrentTime Lib "USER" () As Long

Sub TimeUsed()
Debug.Print GetCurrentTime()
End Sub
```

Running this procedure in the Immediate pane results in the following output:

```
Run("TimeUsed")
6211633
```

This output indicates that Windows has been running for 6,211 seconds, or about 103 minutes.

Like any other function, GetCurrentTime can be used in a worksheet formula, as shown in figure 7.9. In that formula, the function is called twice: once to get the number of milliseconds that Windows has been operating, and a second time as part of a formula that calculates the number of minutes that Windows has been operating.

Chapter 7 ◆ Creating and Using Functions

Figure 7.9
Using the GetCurrentTime function from the USERS.DLL to get the number of microseconds since Windows was started and then display the result as minutes.

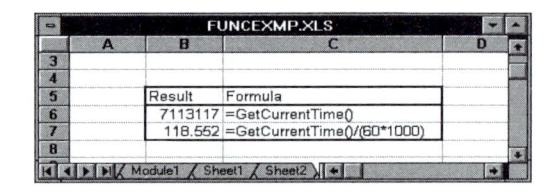

Summary

In this chapter, you have examined functions, one of the four types of procedure available in Visual Basic. A function is a special type of procedure that returns a value in the function's name. In Visual Basic, you can create your own functions for use in your Visual Basic programs or create worksheet functions that you can use in a worksheet. In addition, a Visual Basic program can use all the functions available to Excel. If you need to, you can access the many functions available in different Dynamic Link Libraries and use them in your programs.

This chapter completes Part III of this book. In the first three parts, you learned the basic structure of Visual Basic programs and the linkage between Visual Basic and a worksheet. Now that you understand procedures, statements, and variables, the next part will teach you about the control structures that make decisions within a procedure and control the flow of execution.

Review Questions

The answers to the review questions are in Appendix A.

1. What is a function and how does it differ from the other procedures?
2. How do you set the data type of a function?
3. What special statement must you place before the end of a function procedure?
4. How do you execute a procedure in the Debug window?
5. What restrictions are there on functions to be used on a worksheet?

Review Exercises

1. Create a custom worksheet function that mimics the Sum( ) function. Compare your function with the Sum( ) function to ensure that they yield the same results with different types of arguments.

2. Write a procedure that declares the MessageBeep procedure in the USERS.DLL library and executes it both in a worksheet and in a procedure. Use 0 for the Integer argument.

3. Write a glue function that calculates the future value of an investment given the present value, the interest rate per year, and the number of years. Assume that interest is calculated and credited quarterly, and use the built-in worksheet function as a basis for your procedure.

4. Write a function that returns the days of the week to a worksheet as an array function.

5. Write a function to invert a 2-by-2 matrix. The procedure must get the 2-by-2 matrix from the worksheet, invert it, and return the inverted matrix to the worksheet. The inverse of a matrix (A^{-1}) is the matrix that, when multiplied times the original matrix (**A**), returns the identity matrix (**I**). Compare the results to those returned by the MINVERSE( ) worksheet function.

$$A = \begin{vmatrix} a & b \\ c & d \end{vmatrix}, \quad A^{-1} = \begin{vmatrix} \frac{d}{da-bc} & \frac{-b}{da-bc} \\ \frac{-c}{da-bc} & \frac{a}{da-bc} \end{vmatrix}, \quad A^{-1}A = I = \begin{vmatrix} 1 & 0 \\ 0 & 1 \end{vmatrix} \checkmark$$

6. Write a procedure to invert a 3-by-3 matrix. Use the worksheet function MINVERSE( ) as a basis for your procedure.

Part IV

Controlling Execution

CHAPTER 8

Understanding Decision Making

Decision making in computer programs is what separates the computer from a simple calculator. Although a calculator performs only the calculations that you give it, a computer can compare two values and change its thread of execution according to the results of that comparison. In this chapter, you will learn the following:

- How a computer makes decisions
- How to make decisions in Visual Basic
- How to change the thread of execution based on a decision
- How to create logical expressions to make decisions

What Is Decision Making?

Decision making in computers consists of comparing two values and then changing the thread of execution based on the result of that comparison. The comparison of two values has three possible results: greater than, equal to, or less than. By combining multiple comparisons, you can create complex logical expressions. You can then use a complex expression to examine multiple pieces of data, make a decision, and then change the thread of execution based on that decision.

Chapter 8 ◆ Understanding Decision Making

If a program didn't include any decision making, the thread would start at the first statement, execute each statement in turn, reach the last statement in the program, and end. However, if a program includes decision making, the thread jumps from place to place in the code, skipping some statements and executing others multiple times. With decision making, the calculations that a program makes are no longer fixed at design time, but can change at runtime because of changes in its numerical environment. With decision making, a program is no longer a slightly more powerful calculator but a machine capable of complex logic.

> **Note:** The *thread of execution* is the sequence of steps a program executes as it goes from start to finish. The "thread" metaphor refers to the practice of drawing a line (or thread) from statement to statement in a code's printout, to indicate which statements are executed in which order.

Using an If Statement

The simplest decision-making statement is the If statement. The syntax of the If statement is as follows:

```
If logical Then statement
```

Here, `logical` is a logical expression of some sort, usually a comparison between two values or a formula with a logical result (True or False), or a value that is zero (False) or nonzero (True). Finally, `statement` is any Visual Basic statement or a compound statement.

> **Note:** You form a compound statement by placing several statements together on one line separated with colons. For example, the following two statements
>
>   aVal = 25
>   MyName = "Bill"
>
> could be put together on a single line as the following compound statement:
>
>   aVal = 25: MyName = "Bill"
>
> You should avoid forming compound statements if possible, because they tend to make a program confusing and difficult to read.

The If statement operates by testing the value of `logical`. If that value is True, `statement` is executed; if it is False, `statement` is not executed and execution continues with the next statement in the program. When an If statement is encountered, the thread of execution can take a slight detour, either executing the attached statement or not. Note that the statement can be a procedure name, in which an entirely different block of code could be executed before execution continues in the statement that follows the If statement.

A common use of the If statement is range checking, especially if a range has an upper or lower limit. For example, if you want to ensure that an index value is less than a particular maximum value, you can test it with an If statement, and if the index is above that value, you can then make it equal to the maximum value. One way to do this is as follows:

```
If Index > MaxVal Then Index = MaxVal
```

Here, the logical expression is a comparison of the value of Index and that of MaxVal. If Index is greater than (>) MaxVal, the logical value is True, and the statement Index = MaxVal is executed. If Index is less than or equal to MaxVal, the rest of this statement is skipped.

Understanding Logical Values

Logical values are Logical type variables or expressions that result in a value of True or False. Most expressions that expect a logical value accept a value of 0 for False and any nonzero value for True.

The simplest logical values are the two predefined logical constants True and False. The next most common logical expressions are simple comparisons that use the logical comparison operators, which are listed in table 8.1. After simple comparisons, the next most common logical expressions are those discussed in the section "Understanding Logical Expressions," later in this chapter.

Table 8.1. The logical comparison operators in Visual Basic.

Operator	Description
=	Equal
<>	Not equal
<	Less than
>	Greater than
<=	Less than or equal to
>=	Greater than or equal to
Is	Identical to (objects only)
Like	Equal to using wild cards

The first six operators (=, <>, <, >, <=, and >=), when applied to numeric data, return True if the condition is met or False if it is not. Be careful, though, when comparing two variables with different numeric types; in such an instance, you must convert one of the variables to the type of the other variable. Normally, the conversion is to the more accurate type, but in the case of Currency, the numbers being compared are truncated to four places after the decimal. To ensure that two variables are compared the way that you expect, convert them both to the same type by using the conversion functions (which are listed in table 5.6). If either of the values being compared equals Null, the expression returns Null. The value Null indicates that a variable holds no valid value.

When you compare strings, however, the comparison is less clear-cut. Two methods of comparing strings are available: binary and text. The default mode is a binary comparison of the characters' ANSI codes (see Appendix B), in which b is greater than a and A is less than a. If you place the statement "Option Compare Text" at the top of a module, then the comparison changes to text. A text comparison is not case-sensitive, so a equals A and b equals B, but b is still greater than a.

The Like operator is a special operator that enables you to use wild-card characters when comparing strings. The comparison is done much like wild-card file selection in DOS. Table 8.2 lists the wild-card characters and what they match.

Table 8.2. The wild-card characters for use with the Like operator.

Wild Card	Matches
*	Zero or more characters
?	Any single character
#	Any single digit (0–9)
[*charlist*]	Any single character in *charlist*
[!*charlist*]	Any single character not in *charlist*

The first two wild cards (* and ?) you might recognize from DOS. Both have the same effect in Visual Basic. To use the wild-card characters as part of the comparison string, you enclose them in square brackets ([]). This works for all but the right square bracket (]), which would terminate the list instead of being part of the string. To match the right square bracket, use it outside of a *charlist* group.

In addition to the comparison operators, another function is available for comparing strings. The StrComp() function takes three arguments: two strings and a numeric code. The following is the function's syntax:

```
Result = StrComp(string1, string2, compare)
```

The function returns +1 (*string1* > *string2*), 0 (*string1* = *string2*) or -1 (*string1* < *string2*), depending on the result of the comparison. The numeric code *compare* determines whether the comparison is binary (0) or text (1).

> **Note:** When comparing strings to numbers, Visual Basic tries to do the comparison in a reasonable way, such as converting the string to a number and then making the comparison. However, relying on Visual Basic to handle the conversion is poor programming practice, because then in the resultant code it's not always obvious how the comparison was made. To compare strings and numbers correctly, convert one value to the other type before making the comparison, to ensure that you know what is being compared.

The following are examples of logical values that you can create by making comparisons. The comparisons were done in the Immediate pane of the Debug window.

```
? 1 = 1, 1 > 2, 1 < 2, 2 <= 2
True           False          True           True
? "Skye" < "Sierra", "Shane" > "B.J."
False          True
? "Bill" > "Bil"
True
? "Bill" > "bill"
False
? StrComp("Bill","bill",1)    'text comparison
 0
A = 25.7
B = 35.9
? A >= B, A <= B, A = B, A < B, A > B
False          True           False          True           False
? "Sierra" Like "S*"
True
? "Shane" Like "??a?*"
True
? "Sierra" Like "S?[aeiou]?*", "Shane" Like "S?[aeiou]?*"
True      True
? "Sierra" Like "S?[!a]*", "Shane" Like "S?[!a]*"
True      False
? "Box[*]" Like "Bo?[[]??", "Box[*]" Like "????[*]]"
True      True
```

Chapter 8 ♦ Understanding Decision Making

To compare two objects, use the Is operator. The Is operator returns True only if the two compared variables refer to the same object—not similar objects, but the same identical object. To test for different types of objects, use the TypeName( ) function, which is used in the example in Chapter 7. To test for different types of values, use the VarType( ) function or the logical tests described in the next section. For a complete description of TypeName( ) and VarType( ), see the online help.

Understanding Logical Tests

A special set of functions is available in Visual Basic for testing values. You use these functions to ensure that values are of the right type before you use them in calculations or for testing for error values or missing data.

Table 8.3 lists the logical tests available in Visual Basic.

Table 8.3. The logical tests available in Visual Basic.

Function	Description
IsArray( )	Returns True if the argument is an array
IsDate( )	Returns True if the argument is a date
IsEmpty( )	Returns True if the argument is an empty string
IsError( )	Returns True if the argument is an error value
IsMissing( )	Returns True if an optional argument was not passed to a procedure
IsNull( )	Returns True if the argument is Null
IsNumeric( )	Returns True if the argument is a number
IsObject( )	Returns True if the argument is an object

These functions return True if the argument is of the specified type; otherwise they return False. One exception is the IsMissing( ) function, which you use in a procedure with optional arguments to test whether the argument was passed to the procedure.

Understanding Logical Expressions

Logical expressions are simply extensions of the simple comparison expressions discussed in the last few sections. To create a logical expression, combine one or more logical comparisons and the Boolean operators (logical operations) listed in table 8.4.

Table 8.4. The Boolean operators available in Visual Basic.

Function	Description
Not	Inverse or negation
And	And
Or	Or
XOr	Exclusive Or
Imp	Implies
Eqv	Equivalence

The Boolean operators combine logical values according to explicit truth tables. A *truth table* shows the logical output of a function for all possible input. Table 8.5 is a truth table for all the Boolean operators.

Table 8.5. Truth table for the Boolean operators (T = True and F = False).

A	B	Not A	A And B	A Or B	A Xor B	A Imp B	A Eqv B
T	T	F	T	T	F	T	T
T	F	F	F	T	T	F	F
F	T	T	F	T	T	T	F
F	F	T	F	F	F	T	T

The Not, And, Or, Xor, and Eqv operators are relatively straightforward and easy to understand. The Not operator reverses the logical value, And returns True if both A and B are True, Or returns True if either A or B (or both) is True, Xor returns True only if A or B (but not both) is True, and Eqv returns True if A and B are the same. A statistician would have to explain why the Imp operator is called "implies," but you need only understand that you can use Imp to form a complete set of operators that yields all possible combinations of two logical values.

Chapter 8 ◆ Understanding Decision Making

The following are all logical expressions evaluated in the Immediate pane:

```
? (1 = 1) and (2 > 1)
True
NumOpen = 2
Filename = "MYFILE.XLS"
? (Filename = "MYFILE.XLS") And (NumOpen < 3)
True
numPeople = " 127 "
? 127 = numPeople   'Not good, comparison is not obvious.
True
? 127 = Val(numPeople)   'Do it this way, comparison is obvious.
True
theLogicalValue = (Val(numPeople) < 130) or (Val(numPeople) > 100)
? theLogicalValue
True
```

When you use the Boolean operators, be sure to use parentheses for any but the simplest operation. Because the Boolean operators all have the same precedence, omitting the parentheses can yield very different results. For example, try the following code in the Immediate pane:

```
A = True
B = False
? A or B and B and A
True
? (A or B) and B and A
False
```

Summary

In this chapter, you have learned about logical values and formulas, and about the simplest form of branching in a Visual Basic program. You learned how to use the comparison operators and how to use the Boolean operators to combine these comparisons into complex logical expressions. In the next few chapters, you will use these logical expressions to do more complex branching in a program.

Review Questions

The answers to the review questions are in Appendix A.

1. What differentiates a simple calculator from a computer?
2. What is the thread of execution?

3. What is a compound Visual Basic statement?

4. How does a binary comparison differ from a text comparison? Which is the default?

5. What is the value of the following comparison operations?

```
5 >= 5
9 < 7
27.8 = 27.85
13.5 <> 11.3
"X" = "x"      (binary comparison)
"Y" < "y"      (text comparison)
";" > "a"      (binary comparison)
"Pat" <= "Wilbur"   (binary comparison)
```

Review Exercises

1. Write a pair of If statements that restrict a value to the range 25 to 75. If a value is outside of that range, change it to the value of the nearest limit. That is, change values less than 25 to 25, don't change values between 25 and 75, and change values greater than 75 to 75.

2. Write a single If statement that limits a value to the range –50 to 50 and sets any values that are out of that range to 0.

3. Write an If statement that checks the value of a string variable named FileName, and if the value is blank, calls a function named GetFileName( ) to get a file name and store it in FileName.

4. Write a single logical formula that uses the Like operator to match the names Jenny, Michelle, Skye, Ashley, and Kelley but not Kristina, Crystal, Melissa, Elisabeth, Danielle, or Casie.

5. Create a truth table that shows that the following two logical expressions are identical:

```
Not (A And B)
    (Not A) Or (Not B)
```

and the converse expressions:

```
Not (A Or B)
    (Not A) And (Not B)
```

CHAPTER 9

Using Block If Structures

Block If structures are the most powerful of the logical branching structures. With them, you can create all the other logical structures in Visual Basic, including branches and loops.

In this chapter, you will learn how to do the following:

- Create single-block structures
- Create multiblock structures
- Use an Else clause

Executing Single Blocks with the If-Then Statement

The last chapter introduced the If-Then statement, which enables you to execute a single statement if a logical value is True. You can expand that single statement into a structure that executes a block of code if a logical value is True. A *block of code* or *code block* is generally a contiguous group of statements designed to be executed together as a block.

The structure of a single-block If structure is as follows:

```
If logical Then
    block of statements
End If
```

Chapter 9 ◆ Using Block If Structures

The first part of the block If structure is the same as an If-Then statement. The difference is that nothing follows the word Then on the first line. When *logical* is True, and nothing follows Then, the block of statements is executed down to the End If statement. If *logical* is False, the block is not executed and execution continues with the statement after the End If statement.

1

For example, in a procedure with optional arguments, you must test the optional arguments to see whether a value was passed to the procedure. If no value was passed to the procedure in an optional argument, you must supply a default value for that argument. The following function procedure calculates an employee's pay from his hours and pay rate. If you omit the pay rate, the function uses a default rate of $5.25 per hour. Note the Option Explicit statement at the beginning of the function. This statement forces you to declare all variables before you use them.

```
Option Explicit
'
' Procedure to calculate pay.
'
Function thePay(hours As Single, Optional PayRate) As Currency
  Const DefaultRate = 5.25
  If IsMissing(PayRate) Then
    PayRate = DefaultRate
  End If
  thePay = hours * PayRate
End Function
```

Note this function's use of the constant DefaultRate. You could just as easily have inserted the value for the default rate into the assignment statement for PayRate. However, by using the named constant, your actions are much more obvious, making the code more readable and understandable. Another benefit of using constants is that if you use one in multiple places in a procedure, you need only change its declaration to change the value used in each place.

Another option is to place all the constant declarations for pay rates and bonuses at the top of the module that uses them, which makes them even easier to find and change. To try this technique, create the following short procedure to insert some values and then print the results on the Immediate pane of the Debug window:

```
'
' Procedure to test the functions.
'
Sub TestProc1()
  Dim theHours As Single, theRate As Currency
  Dim Pay1 As Currency, Pay2 As Currency
  theHours = 40
  theRate = 8.75
```

```
    Pay1 = thePay(theHours)    'One argument.
    Pay2 = thePay(theHours, theRate)    'Two arguments.
    Debug.Print Format(Pay1, "$#,##0.00"), Format(Pay2,
"$#,##0.00")
End Sub
```

This procedure calls the function twice: once without a pay rate and once with it. In this procedure, the Format() function is used to format the results before printing them. The Format() function uses a formatting string similar to that which is used to format numbers in worksheet cells. In this procedure, the formatting string inserts a dollar sign at the beginning of the number, requires commas every three decimal places, and requires a number or 0 in the one character position to the left of the decimal and in the two positions to its right. See the online help for more information on the formatting codes that you can use in a formatting string. Running this program from the Immediate pane results in the following output:

```
Run("TestProc1")
$210.00        $350.00
```

Tip: When you try to use the Run statement to run a new procedure from the Immediate pane of the Debug window, if any errors are in any of the procedures, Visual Basic indicates that it cannot find the procedure. To remedy this, switch back to the module that contains the procedure, place the cursor somewhere in the procedure that you want to run, and click the Run Macro button. When Visual Basic finds the error, it displays an error dialog box. To display the offending statement, click the Go To button. After you fix the statement, click the Run Macro button to run it again. When the procedure finally runs without error, you can use the Run statement to run it from the Immediate pane.

The following variation of this procedure also checks for the inclusion of a sales figure and calculates a bonus if the sales are greater than a specified threshold:

```
'
' Procedure to calculate pay
' and test for a bonus.
'
Function thePay2(hours As Single, Optional PayRate, _
    Optional Sales) As Currency
  Dim Bonus As Currency
  Const DefaultRate = 5.25
  Const BonusThreshold = 5000
```

Chapter 9 ◆ Using Block If Structures

```
   Const BonusValue = 500
   If IsMissing(PayRate) Then 'Set default rate if none given.
      PayRate = DefaultRate
   End If
   Bonus = 0
   If Not IsMissing(Sales) Then
      If Sales > BonusThreshold Then    'Give bonus if sales > $5000
         Bonus = BonusValue
      End If
   End If
   thePay2 = hours * PayRate + Bonus 'Figure the pay
End Function
```

To handle the bonus calculation, this function adds two nested block If structures. When you nest block If structures, the inner block If is not executed unless the outer one has a True argument. You might think that you can create a logical expression by combining both of the logical comparisons in the two nested block If structures and then calculate the bonus with a single-block If structure, as follows:

```
If (Not IsMissing(Sales)) And (Sales > BonusThreshold) Then
   Bonus = BonusValue
End If
```

However, this solution doesn't work if the value for Sales is missing. When Sales is missing, this statement tries to compare a missing value with a number and then returns an error. By using two nested block If structures, you ensure that you never attempt to make the comparison when Sales is missing.

Now create a procedure that tests this function in the Immediate pane, and then run the procedure. The easiest way to do this is to copy and then modify the previous procedure as follows:

```
'
'  Procedure to test the functions.
'
Sub TestProc2()
   Dim theHours As Single, theRate As Currency, theSales As Currency
   Dim Pay1 As Currency, Pay2 As Currency, Pay3 As Currency
   theHours = 40
   theRate = 8.75
   theSales = 8500
   Pay1 = thePay2(theHours)
   Pay2 = thePay2(theHours, theRate)
   Pay3 = thePay2(theHours, theRate, theSales)
```

```
Debug.Print Format(Pay1, "$#,##0.00"),Format(Pay2,"$#,##0.00"), _
    Format(Pay3, "$#,##0.00")
End Sub


Run("TestProc2")
$210.00        $350.00        $850.00
```

You can also use a single-block If structure during the debugging process. For example, to determine whether a program is working correctly, you may have to insert code at different locations to perform a test or display a value. When you finish using this debugging code, you must either remove it from the program or disable it. A simple way to disable the code is to place it inside of a single-block If structure with a global value as the logical argument. Setting the global variable to True enables the debugging code, and setting it to False disables it.

For example, as you develop the function thePay2( ), you might want to print a message in the Immediate window whenever a bonus is calculated. If you use a single-block If statement to print the message, and use DoDebugging as the logical condition, when you finish developing your procedures you can simply change the value of DoDebugging to False to stop printing the message. The following thePay3( ) function and TestProc3 procedure demonstrate this capability:

```
Option Explicit
Const DoDebugging = True    'Turn on/off debugging code.
'
'  Procedure to test the functions.
'
Sub TestProc3()
  Dim theHours As Single, theRate As Currency, theSales As Currency
  Dim Pay1 As Currency, Pay2 As Currency, Pay3 As Currency
  theHours = 40
  theRate = 8.75
  theSales = 8500
  Pay1 = thePay3(theHours)
  Pay2 = thePay3(theHours, theRate)
  Pay3 = thePay3(theHours, theRate, theSales)
  Debug.Print Format(Pay1, "$#,##0.00"), _
      Format(Pay2, "$#,##0.00"), Format(Pay3, "$#,##0.00")
End Sub
'
'  Procedure to calculate pay
'  and test for a bonus.
'
```

Chapter 9 ◆ Using Block If Structures

```
Function thePay3(hours As Single, Optional PayRate, _
    Optional Sales) As Currency
  Dim Bonus As Currency
  Const DefaultRate = 5.25
  Const BonusThreshold = 5000
  Const BonusValue = 500
  If IsMissing(PayRate) Then 'Set default rate if none given.
    PayRate = DefaultRate
  End If
  Bonus = 0
  If (Not IsMissing(Sales)) Then
    If Sales > BonusThreshold Then   'Give bonus if sales > $5000
      Bonus = BonusValue
      If DoDebugging Then   'This is debugging code
        Debug.Print "***Bonus Calculated***"
      End If
    End If
  End If
  thePay3 = hours * PayRate + Bonus 'Figure the pay
End Function
```

Note that the declaration of the DoDebugging constant is placed at the top of the module. This makes the constant available to all procedures in the module, and also makes it easy to find.

The result of running this procedure in the Immediate pane is as follows:

```
Run("TestProc3")
***Bonus Calculated***
$210.00        $350.00        $850.00
```

Note that even though the function thePay3() is called three times in the test procedure, the bonus is calculated only the one time that the sales value is included and is greater than $5,000.00. Try different values for the value theSales in the test procedure to see when the bonus is calculated.

Executing Multiple Blocks with If-Then-ElseIf

You can extend the single-block If structure to multiple blocks by adding ElseIf clauses. The syntax of a multiblock If structure is as follows:

```
If logical1 Then
    block of statements1
ElseIf logical2
    block of statements2
ElseIf logical3
    block of statements3
.
.  (more blocks)
.
End If
```

When a multiblock If structure is encountered, Visual Basic calculates *logical1* and if it is True, executes *block of statements1*. If *logical1* is False, Visual Basic skips over *block of statements1*, calculates *logical2*, and if it is True, calculates *block of statements2*. If *logical2* is False, Visual Basic skips over *block of statements2* and calculates *logical3*. This decision making continues for all the ElseIf clauses down to the End If statement. When a True logical value is found, and the block of statements that follows it is calculated, Visual Basic skips to the statement that follows the End If statement. Visual Basic ignores any other blocks in a multiblock If structure after it finds a block with a True logical value.

You can use multiblock If structures whenever you must consider several different possibilities in a particular order. For example, to ensure that Sales is available before you attempt to compare it with the threshold for receiving a bonus, the function thePay2( ) uses two nested If structures. You can rewrite that nested block as a multiblock If structure, as follows:

```
'
' Procedure to calculate pay
' and test for a bonus.
'
Function thePay4(hours As Single, Optional PayRate, _
    Optional Sales) As Currency
  Dim Bonus As Currency
  Const DefaultRate = 5.25
  Const BonusThreshold = 5000
  Const BonusValue = 500
  If IsMissing(PayRate) Then 'Set default rate if none given.
    PayRate = DefaultRate
  End If
  Bonus = 0
  If IsMissing(Sales) Then
    'Do nothing if Sales is missing.
  ElseIf Sales > BonusThreshold Then    'Give bonus if sales >$5000
```

Chapter 9 ♦ Using Block If Structures

```
        Bonus = BonusValue
    End If
    thePay4 = hours * PayRate + Bonus 'Figure the pay
End Function
```

The first line of this multiblock If structure tests whether Sales was passed to the procedure. If not, the first block of the If structure is executed. In this case, the block consists of only a comment statement. If Sales is available, the logical expression in the first line of the If structure is False, and Visual Basic moves on to the ElseIf statement and tests its logical expression. In this case, if Sales is greater than BonusThreshold, the block following the ElseIf statement is executed and the employee receives a bonus. This procedure runs identically to the procedure thePay2( ).

Including an Else Clause

There is one more clause that you can add to an If statement: an Else clause. The Else clause must head the last block of a logical If structure, and executes when ever none of the other blocks is executed. The full syntax of a block If structure, including the Else clause, is as follows:

```
If logical1 Then
    block of statements1
ElseIf logical2
    block of statements2
ElseIf logical3
    block of statements3
.
.   (more blocks)
.
Else
    else block of statements
End If
```

In this syntax, one or more If and ElseIf statements are calculated, and if none of the logical values are True, Visual Basic executes the *else block of statements*. Use the Else clause when you want the program to do something whenever no matches are found, to select a second block of code when *logical1* is False, or to handle unexpected situations, default cases, error messages, and so forth.

You can use an Else clause to write the function thePay4(), which brings all the statements related to calculating the bonus inside the block If structure:

Visual Basic for Applications By EXAMPLE

```
'
' Procedure to calculate pay
' and test for a bonus.
'
Function thePay5(hours As Single, Optional PayRate, _
     Optional Sales) As Currency
  Dim Bonus As Currency
  Const DefaultRate = 5.25
  Const BonusThreshold = 5000
  Const BonusValue = 500
  If IsMissing(PayRate) Then  'Set default rate if none given.
    PayRate = DefaultRate
  End If
  If IsMissing(Sales) Then
    Bonus = 0      'No bonus if Sales is missing.
  ElseIf Sales > BonusThreshold Then    'Give bonus if sales >$5000
    Bonus = BonusValue
  Else
    Bonus = 0      'No bonus if Sales is less than BonusThreshold.
  End If
  thePay5 = hours * PayRate + Bonus 'Figure the pay
End Function
```

Note that all the statements that change the value of Bonus are within a single-block If structure. In the previous versions of the function thePay, you assume that the employee does not deserve a bonus, set Bonus to 0, and then change it if the employee does deserve a bonus. You never check for a situation in which the employee does not deserve a bonus. In the preceding procedure, you now test for each situation and set the value of Bonus accordingly, making the function much more straightforward and easier to understand.

You can revise this procedure to include overtime in the calculation. This revision requires a block If structure that calculates the different cases. In this function, the employee is paid straight time for up to 40 hours a week, time and a half for the hours over 40 and up to 50, and then double time for hours over 50:

```
'
' Procedure to calculate pay and overtime
' and then test for a bonus.
'
Function thePay6(hours As Single, Optional PayRate, _
      Optional Sales) As Currency
```

147

Chapter 9 ◆ Using Block If Structures

```
    Dim Bonus As Currency, Wages As Currency
    Const DefaultRate = 5.25
    Const BonusThreshold = 5000
    Const BonusValue = 500
    If IsMissing(PayRate) Then 'Set default rate if none given.
       PayRate = DefaultRate
    End If
    If IsMissing(Sales) Then
       Bonus = 0      'No bonus if Sales is missing.
    ElseIf Sales > BonusThreshold Then   'Give bonus if sales > $5000
       Bonus = BonusValue
    Else
       Bonus = 0      'No bonus if Sales is less than BonusThreshold.
    End If
    If hours <= 40 Then
       Wages = hours * PayRate
    ElseIf (hours > 40) And (hours <= 50) Then
       Wages = 40 * PayRate + (hours - 40) * 1.5 * PayRate
    Else
       Wages = 40 * PayRate + 10 * 1.5 * PayRate _
            + (hours - 50) * 2 * PayRate
    EndIf
    thePay6 = Wages + Bonus 'Figure the pay
End Function
```

> **Note:** The formula for calculating the wages in this example is written exactly as it was described, with straight time up to 40 hours, time and a half from 40 to 50 hours, and double time for hours over 50. The formula for 40 to 50 hours is as follows:
>
>   Wages = 40 * PayRate + (hours - 40) * 1.5 * PayRate
>
> With a little algebra, this formula can be rewritten in the following simpler form:
>
>   Wages = (hours * 1.5 - 20) * PayRate
>
> Both statements accomplish the same task, but you would have difficulty determining that by reading the second version. Unless you must optimize this section of code for speed, you should use the first version of the statement; although slightly longer, this form of the statement is much more obvious.

To try using the overtime calculation, you can copy the preceding test procedure and then modify it to create the following procedure:

```
Option Explicit
'
'  Procedure to test the overtime calculation.
'
Sub TestProc4()
  Dim theHours1 As Single, theHours2 As Single, theHours3 As Single
  Dim theRate As Currency
  Dim Pay1 As Currency, Pay2 As Currency, Pay3 As Currency
  theHours1 = 40
  theHours2 = 45
  theHours3 = 60
  theRate = 8.75
  Pay1 = thePay6(theHours1, theRate)
  Pay2 = thePay6(theHours2, theRate)
  Pay3 = thePay6(theHours3, theRate)
  Debug.Print Format(Pay1, "$#,##0.00"), _
      Format(Pay2, "$#,##0.00"), Format(Pay3, "$#,##0.00")
End Sub
```

Running this procedure in the Immediate pane results in the following:

```
Run ("TestProc4")
$350.00         $415.63         $656.25
```

Try other combinations of hours and wages to see whether the procedure works as expected.

Summary

In this chapter, you learned about the different variations of the block If structure. This structure enables you to create almost any required control structure.

In the next few chapters, you will learn about some other control structures that make setting up some of the more standard control situations much easier. This is particularly true of the loops that are discussed in Part V, "Loops and Repeated Structures." Although you can implement such loops with the block If structure, you can implement them much more easily with the supplied loop structures.

Chapter 9 ♦ Using Block If Structures

Review Questions

The answers to the review questions are in Appendix A.

1. How do you test for missing optional arguments in a procedure or function call?
2. Why should you use in procedures constants like DefaultRate rather than literal values?
3. How many ElseIf clauses can you use in a block If structure?
4. How many Else clauses can you use in a block If structure?

Review Exercises

1. Rewrite the following nested block If structure as a single-block If structure:

   ```
   If theValue = 7 Then
     If yourValue > 5 Then
       DoSomethingInteresting
     End If
   End If
   ```

2. Create a thePay procedure that has two levels of bonuses: $500 for sales between $5,000 and $10,000, and $1,000 for sales over $10,000.

3. Create a thePay procedure that uses the default pay rate when the value of PayRate is equal to 0 as well as when it is missing.

CHAPTER 10

Using Select Case

The Select Case structure is a special case of the block If control structure. You use it in situations in which a single value is the object of all the logical comparisons that determine whether to execute a block. Although you can implement the same functionality with a block If structure, using Select Case usually makes it easier.

In this chapter, you will learn how to do the following:

- ♦ Use Select Case
- ♦ Set up the cases
- ♦ Use a Case Else clause

Defining the Cases

The Select Case structure is a special control structure that you use to handle situations in which the value being compared is the same for multiple blocks. You use the structure most often when the value you are comparing is an integer that represents some sort of a selector or index. The value of this selector or index selects the block of code to be processed.

The syntax of the Select Case structure is as follows:

```
Select Case value
  Case compare1
    block of code 1
..Case compare2
    block of code 2
 .
 . more cases
 .
End Select
```

In this syntax, *value* is a variable or expression that evaluates to some numeric or string value, and the *compare* expressions are lists of one or more values to compare to *value*. When the Select Case statement is executed, *value* is calculated and compared to the *compare1* list. If there is a match, *block of code 1* is executed; if there isn't a match, Visual Basic goes to the next Case statement and compares *value* to the values in *compare2*, and then executes *block of code 2* if there is a match, and so on. If nothing matches *value*, execution resumes after the End Select statement. As with the block If statement, Visual Basic executes only the block of code following the first Case statement that matches *value*, even if some of the later Case statements match it as well.

The format of the *compare* values is very flexible, allowing for many different possibilities. If *compare* is a list of values separated with commas, then for that Case statement to have a match, one of the listed values must match *value*. An element of the list could be *value1* To *value2*, which specifies that *value* must be between *value1* and *value2* inclusive. An element can also be Is *oper value3*, in which *oper* can be any one of the comparison operators from table 8.1 except for Is and Like.

For example, the following are all valid Case statements:

```
Case 25
Case 1, 3, 5, 7
Case "Jessica"
Case 1, 2, 7 To 9, 11
Case 3, 5, Is >= 7
Case Is < 0, 1, 2, 3, 5 To 7, Is > 10
```

The first Case statement is selected only if *value* is equal to 25. The second is selected if *value* equals 1, 3, 5, or 7. The third is selected if *value* equals the text "Jessica." The fourth is selected if *value* equals 1, 2, 11, or any number between 7 and 9. The fifth is selected if *value* is 3 or 5, or any number greater than or equal to 7. The last Case statement is selected if *value* is less than 0, equal to 1, 2, or 3, in the range 5 to 7, or greater than 10.

Although you can use the Select Case statement to select any type or range of values, the most common use is for selecting a calculation from a list of enumerated values. A list of *enumerated values* is a list of options, with each option given an integer value to identify it. You then identify the values with constants, which you can use in your calculations.

For example, in Chapter 7, "Creating and Using Functions," you created a glue function for calculating the payment on a loan. This function was set up for monthly payments, but other possibilities are bimonthly, quarterly, semiannually, and yearly. To make the function more versatile, add a list of enumerated values that selects the length of the period, and then make the list an argument of the function. Then use Select Case to adjust the calculation for the selected period.

First you must declare the definitions of the enumerated values:

```
Option Explicit
Const yearly = 0
Const monthly = 1
Const bimonthly = 2
Const quarterly = 3
Const semiannually = 4
```

Next you create the new function, as follows. Note that the procedure uses constants rather than explicit values.

```
'
'Glue function for calculating the payment.
'
Function thePmt2(theRate As Single, nyrs As Integer, _
    pv As Currency, PeriodType As Integer) As Currency
    ' PeriodType is a code for the length of a period
    '  PeriodType = 0  yearly payments
    '             = 1  monthly
    '             = 2  bimonthly
    '             = 3  quarterly
    '             = 4  semiannually
    Dim nper As Integer, fv As Currency, rate As Single
    fv = 0     'Assume the loan is paid off.
    Select Case PeriodType
      Case yearly
        nper = nyrs
        rate = theRate
      Case monthly
        nper = nyrs * 12
        rate = theRate / 12
      Case bimonthly
        nper = nyrs * 6
        rate = theRate / 6
      Case quarterly
        nper = nyrs * 4
        rate = theRate / 4
      Case semiannually
        nper = nyrs * 2
        rate = theRate / 2
    End Select
    'Calculate the payment and convert to a positive number.
    thePmt2 = -Application.pmt(rate, nper, pv, fv)
End Function
```

Chapter 10 ♦ Using Select Case

The Select Case structure selects the correct calculation for the indicated period and adjusts the values of the arguments accordingly.

Now create a procedure to test the output of the new function:

```
'
'  Procedure to test the thePmt calculation.
'
Sub TestProc5()
  Dim rate As Single, theYears As Integer, presval As Currency
  Dim Pay1 As Currency, Pay2 As Currency, Pay3 As Currency
  Dim Pay4 As Currency, Pay5 As Currency
  rate = 0.07    '7% per year
  theYears = 15    '15 year loan
  presval = 130000   'Loan amount is $130,000
  Pay1 = thePmt2(rate, theYears, presval, yearly)
  Pay2 = thePmt2(rate, theYears, presval, monthly)
  Pay3 = thePmt2(rate, theYears, presval, bimonthly)
  Pay4 = thePmt2(rate, theYears, presval, quarterly)
  Pay5 = thePmt2(rate, theYears, presval, semiannually)
  Debug.Print "Yearly = " & Format(Pay1, "$#,##0.00")
  Debug.Print "Monthly = " & Format(Pay2, "$#,##0.00")
  Debug.Print "Bimonthly = " & Format(Pay3, "$#,##0.00")
  Debug.Print "Quarterly = " & Format(Pay4, "$#,##0.00")
  Debug.Print "Semiannually = " & Format(Pay5, "$#,##0.00")
End Sub
```

This procedure calculates the payment for the same loan, but for five different payment periods. Running this function in the Immediate pane results in the following output:

```
Run ("TestProc5")
Yearly = $14,273.30
Monthly = $1,168.48
Bimonthly = $2,340.79
Quarterly = $3,516.94
Semiannually =$7,068.27
```

Including a Case Else Clause

As with the block If structure, you can insert a special Case statement that catches any values that do not match any of the other Case statements. To do this, insert a Case Else clause as the last block before the End Select statement. Any values that do not match the other Case statements match the Case Else statement.

For example, the function thePmt2() displays a list of enumerated values from which you can select the payment period, but if you insert a number that isn't part of the list, you exit the function and it returns an error value. To capture these error values, the function uses a Case Else statement; to insert an error value into the value to be returned, thePmt2() uses the CVErr() function. The following revision of the function thePmt2(), thePmt3(), uses a constant that returns the Excel error value #VALUE!, so you can use thePmt3() both with other Visual Basic procedures and as an Excel worksheet function. This revision also introduces another change to the function: it now returns the Variant type, which enables the function to return error values as well as numeric values. The revised function is as follows:

```
'
'Glue function for calculating the payment.
'
Function thePmt3(theRate As Single, nyrs As Integer, _
    pv As Currency, PeriodType As Integer) As Variant
    ' PeriodType is a code for the length of a period
    '   PeriodType = 0  yearly payments
    '              = 1  monthly
    '              = 2  bimonthly
    '              = 3  quarterly
    '              = 4  semiannually
    ' Any other value gives an error.
    Dim nper As Integer, fv As Currency, rate As Single
    fv = 0     'Assume the loan is paid off.
    Select Case PeriodType
      Case yearly
        nper = nyrs
        rate = theRate
      Case monthly
        nper = nyrs * 12
        rate = theRate / 12
      Case bimonthly
        nper = nyrs * 6
        rate = theRate / 6
      Case quarterly
        nper = nyrs * 4
        rate = theRate / 4
      Case semiannually
        nper = nyrs * 2
        rate = theRate / 2
      Case Else   'Error
```

Chapter 10 ◆ Using Select Case

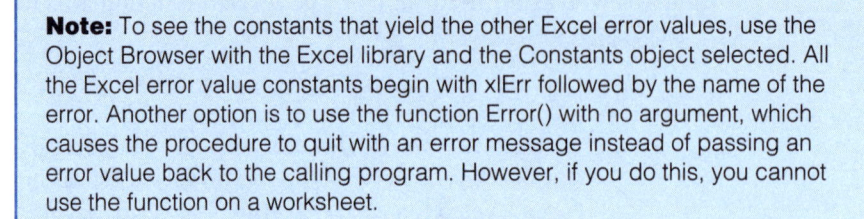

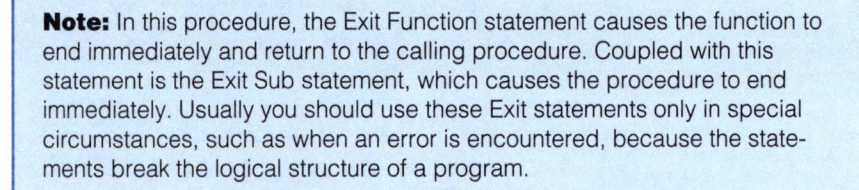

```
            thePmt3 = CVErr(xlErrValue)    'Set the return value
                                           'to an error.
        Exit Function    'Exit the function
    End Select
    'Calculate the payment and convert to a positive number.
    thePmt3 = -Application.pmt(rate, nper, pv, fv)
End Function
```

> **Note:** To see the constants that yield the other Excel error values, use the Object Browser with the Excel library and the Constants object selected. All the Excel error value constants begin with xlErr followed by the name of the error. Another option is to use the function Error() with no argument, which causes the procedure to quit with an error message instead of passing an error value back to the calling program. However, if you do this, you cannot use the function on a worksheet.

> **Note:** In this procedure, the Exit Function statement causes the function to end immediately and return to the calling procedure. Coupled with this statement is the Exit Sub statement, which causes the procedure to end immediately. Usually you should use these Exit statements only in special circumstances, such as when an error is encountered, because the statements break the logical structure of a program.

You must also change the test procedure to allow the return of an error value. You must check whether the value that the function returns is an error before you try to use it in a function. If you don't check the value, it causes an additional error when the function tries to process the error value.

The following procedure tests two values with the function: one good value and one out-of-range value. A separate procedure, PrintIt( ), does the actual testing and printing of the results on the Immediate pane. The IsError( ) function does the testing, returning True if the argument is an error value.

```
Option Explicit
Const yearly = 0
Const monthly = 1
Const bimonthly = 2
Const quarterly = 3
Const semiannually = 4
'
'   Procedure to test the thePmt calculation.
'
```

```
Sub TestProc6()
  Dim rate As Single, theYears As Integer, presval As Currency
  Dim Pay1, Pay2    'These must be of the Variant type to
                    'be able to receive an error value.
  rate = 0.07    '7% per year
  theYears = 15    '15 year loan
  presval = 130000    'Loan amount is $130,000
  Pay1 = thePmt3(rate, theYears, presval, yearly)
  Pay2 = thePmt3(rate, theYears, presval, 5)    'Insert an error value
  PrintIt Pay1
  PrintIt Pay2
End Sub

Sub PrintIt(aValue)
  'See if aValue is an error before trying to print it.
  If IsError(aValue) Then
    Debug.Print "Error Value = "; aValue
  Else
    Debug.Print Format(aValue, "$#,##0.00")
  End If
End Sub
```

Running the procedure in the Immediate pane yields the following results:

```
Run ("TestProc6")
$14,273.30
Error Value = Error 2015
```

You can also use the procedure in a worksheet, which yields the expected results shown in figure 10.1.

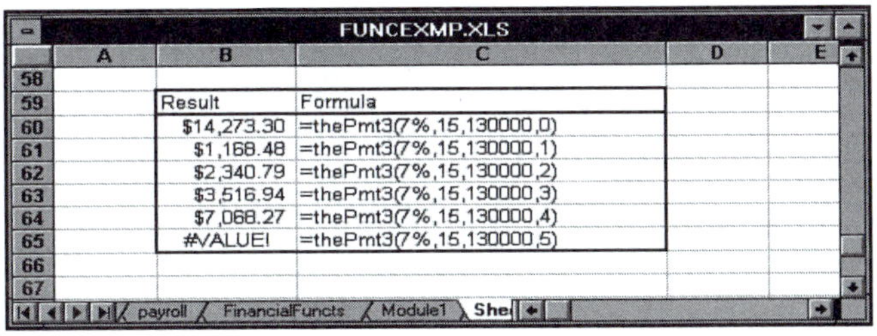

Figure 10.1

The function thePmt3() used in a worksheet, with a good value for the period length selector and an out-of-range value.

	B	C
59	Result	Formula
60	$14,273.30	=thePmt3(7%,15,130000,0)
61	$1,168.48	=thePmt3(7%,15,130000,1)
62	$2,340.79	=thePmt3(7%,15,130000,2)
63	$3,516.94	=thePmt3(7%,15,130000,3)
64	$7,068.27	=thePmt3(7%,15,130000,4)
65	#VALUE!	=thePmt3(7%,15,130000,5)

Chapter 10 ◆ Using Select Case

Summary

In this chapter you learned about the Select Case control structure. The Select Case structure is a special structure for selecting a code block based on comparisons to a single value. In the last three chapters, you have learned about structured control structures. In the next chapter, you will learn about unstructured control structures, and why you should not use them.

Review Questions

The answers to the review questions are in Appendix A.

1. Is the following a valid Case statement?

   ```
   Case Is Like "??[aeiou]*"
   ```

2. Given the following two Case statements, which block(s) are executed if Value = 13? If Value = 17?

   ```
   Select Case Value
       Case 11, 14, 15 To 19
           Block 1
       Case 11 To 15, 17
           Block 2
   End Select
   ```

3. What are enumerated values? What are they good for?

4. What can you use the Case Else statement for?

5. What is the name of the Excel constant that gives a #NUM! error with the CVErr( ) function?

Review Exercises

1. Rewrite the other financial glue functions from Chapter 7, "Creating and Using Functions," to take a different payment period into account.

2. Rewrite the function thePay6( ) from the last chapter to calculate overtime, using a Select Case structure rather than the block If structure.

3. Write a block If structure that accomplishes the same task as the Select Case structure in the function thePmt3( ).

CHAPTER 11

Don't Use Unstructured Branching

Unstructured branches have been part of BASIC since its inception. In fact, structured control structures are only a recent addition. Programming languages originally included unstructured branches because they mimicked the computer's underlying electronic capabilities. However, unstructured branching can make a program difficult if not impossible to figure out, while structured control structures create code that is much easier to understand and validate—hence the title of this chapter.

In this chapter, you will learn the following:

- ♦ What unstructured branching is
- ♦ Why you should try to avoid it

What Is Unstructured Branching?

An *unstructured branch* is a structure that can branch anywhere in a procedure. The simplest of the unstructured branches is the GoTo statement. The GoTo statement has the following syntax:

```
GoTo label
```

where `label` is the name of a label or marker at some line in the procedure. You create a label by starting a line with the label name followed by a colon. However, you don't include the colon in the label name that appears in the GoTo statement.

Another unstructured branch is the *logical branch*, which has the following syntax:

```
If logical Then GoTo label
```

This branch is similar to the simple GoTo statement, but the branch is taken only if `logical` is True.

The *GoSub-Return* statements are the original procedure-calling convention in BASIC. The GoSub statement has the following syntax:

```
GoSub label
```

where `label` is the same as for the GoTo statement. The difference between the GoTo and the GoSub statements is that when a Return statement is encountered in the GoSub statement, the execution point returns to the statement following the last GoSub statement encountered.

Two variations of GoTo and GoSub are the *calculated branches*:

```
On value GoTo label1, label2, label3,...

On value GoSub label1, label2, label3,...
```

In these statements, `value` is an integer. If `value` equals 1, the branch is to `label1`; if `value` equals 2, the branch is to `label2`; and so on.

The Problems with Unstructured Branching

As you have seen, a structured branch divides a code into adjacent blocks and selects a block according to some logical criteria. With a structured branch, you know where to look for the code that is to be executed when a certain logical value is True. With an unstructured branch, you have no idea where to look for the code that is executed when the branch is taken. If you are editing someone else's code and you encounter a GoTo statement, where do you look to find the other end of the branch? If you are lucky, the target of the branch is nearby, but it does not have to be.

Although you can create structured code with the unstructured branch, doing so requires much self discipline. For example, you could use unstructured branches when writing the function thePay6() in Chapter 10. To do so, you would have to revise the code as follows:

```
'
'Glue function using unstructured branches.
'
Function thePmt4(theRate As Single, nyrs As Integer, _
    pv As Currency, PeriodType As Integer) As Variant
```

```
    ' PeriodType is a code for the length of a period
    '  PeriodType = 0   yearly payments
    '             = 1   monthly
    '             = 2   bimonthly
    '             = 3   quarterly
    '             = 4   semiannually
    ' Any other value gives an error.
    Dim nper As Integer, fv As Currency, rate As Single
    fv = 0     'Assume the loan is paid off.
    If PeriodType <> yearly Then GoTo lmonth
        nper = nyrs
        rate = theRate
    GoTo getval
lmonth:
    If PeriodType <> monthly Then GoTo lbimonth
        nper = nyrs * 12
        rate = theRate / 12
    GoTo getval
lbimonth:
    If PeriodType <> bimonthly Then GoTo lquarter
        nper = nyrs * 6
        rate = theRate / 6
    GoTo getval
lquarter:
    If PeriodType <> quarterly Then GoTo lsemiannual
        nper = nyrs * 4
        rate = theRate / 4
    GoTo getval
lsemiannual:
    If PeriodType <> semiannually Then GoTo lelse
        nper = nyrs * 2
        rate = theRate / 2
    GoTo getval
lelse:
        thePmt4 = CVErr(xlErrValue)    'Set the return value
                                       'to an error.
        GoTo done     'Exit the function
getval:
    'Calculate the payment and convert to a positive number.
    thePmt4 = -Application.pmt(rate, nper, pv, fv)
done:
End Function
```

Chapter 11 ♦ Don't Use Unstructured Branching

In this case the enumerated values are consecutive, so you could alternatively write the function as follows:

```
'
'Glue function using unstructured branches.
'
Function thePmt5(theRate As Single, nyrs As Integer, _
    pv As Currency, PeriodType As Integer) As Variant
    ' PeriodType is a code for the length of a period
    '   PeriodType = 0  yearly payments
    '              = 1  monthly
    '              = 2  bimonthly
    '              = 3  quarterly
    '              = 4  semiannually
    ' Any other value gives an error.
    Dim nper As Integer, fv As Currency, rate As Single
    fv = 0    'Assume the loan is paid off.
    On PeriodType + 1 GoTo lyear, lmonth, lbimonth, _
        lquarter, lsemiannual
    'Go here if out of range.
    thePmt5 = CVErr(xlErrValue) 'Set the return value to an error.
    GoTo done    'Exit the function
lyear:
        nper = nyrs
        rate = theRate
    GoTo getval
lmonth:
        nper = nyrs * 12
        rate = theRate / 12
    GoTo getval
lbimonth:
        nper = nyrs * 6
        rate = theRate / 6
    GoTo getval
lquarter:
        nper = nyrs * 4
        rate = theRate / 4
    GoTo getval
lsemiannual:
        nper = nyrs * 2
        rate = theRate / 2
```

```
getval:
    'Calculate the payment and convert to a positive number.
    thePmt5 = -Application.pmt(rate, nper, pv, fv)
done:
End Function
```

Although this revised function does not look too terrible, remember that creating such a function or procedure requires strong discipline and great care. Often a procedure is written over the course of many years, with new options being added at various times during the process. Programmers often are tempted to take the quickest, easiest route when revising a procedure, and thus they might add a new option to the end of the existing procedure and then place unstructured branches wherever necessary to tie them together. When this happens, a procedure like the following may result:

```
'
'Glue function using spaghetti code.
'
Function thePmt6(theRate As Single, nyrs As Integer, _
    pv As Currency, PeriodType As Integer) As Variant
    ' PeriodType is a code for the length of a period
    '    PeriodType = 0  yearly payments
    '               = 1  monthly
    '               = 2  bimonthly
    '               = 3  quarterly
    '               = 4  semiannually
    ' Any other value gives an error.
    Dim nper As Integer, fv As Currency, rate As Single
    fv = 0    'Assume the loan is paid off.
    If PeriodType = monthly Then GoTo lmonth
    If PeriodType <> yearly Then GoTo lelse
        nper = nyrs
        rate = theRate
    GoTo getval
lmonth:
        nper = nyrs * 12
        rate = theRate / 12
    GoTo getval
```

Chapter 11 ♦ Don't Use Unstructured Branching

```
lelse:
    If PeriodType = bimonthly Then GoTo lbimonth
    If PeriodType = quarterly Then GoTo lquarter
    If PeriodType = semiannually Then GoTo lsemiannual
        thePmt6 = CVErr(xlErrValue) 'Set the return value to an error.
        GoTo done      'Exit the function
getval:
    'Calculate the payment and convert to a positive number.
    thePmt6 = -Application.pmt(rate, nper, pv, fv)
    GoTo done
lbimonth:
        nper = nyrs * 6
        rate = theRate / 6
lgogetval:
    GoTo getval
lquarter:
        nper = nyrs * 4
        rate = theRate / 4
lqtr:
    GoTo lgogetval
lsemiannual:
        nper = nyrs * 2
        rate = theRate / 2
    GoTo lqtr
done:
End Function
```

All three of these functions yield the same results. However, it is very difficult to figure out what the last one does or even to follow the steps in a single calculation, because the execution point jumps unpredictably all over the procedure. Such coding is known disdainfully as *spaghetti code*, because if you drew the thread of execution on a printout of such a procedure, the result would look as tangled as a plate of spaghetti. Imagine how difficult it would be to follow this procedure if it consisted of several thousand lines of code.

You might wonder why unstructured branches are even available in Visual Basic. The answer is simply to maintain compatibility with older versions of BASIC. A program written in GW-BASIC or BASICA probably will run in a Visual Basic module with only minor modifications. Also, Visual Basic's error-trapping procedures often require the use of unstructured branches.

Use Structured Branching Whenever Possible

In very few situations do you need to use unstructured branches. You can do any normal calculation with a structured branch just as easily as with an unstructured branch, but the code of the structured branch is much more understandable.

The only procedures that may require unstructured branches are error-handling procedures. Such procedures may have to jump over large blocks of code to bypass a normal calculation and handle the error. However, where possible, you should use structured branching for error handling.

Summary

This chapter demonstrated the effects of unstructured programming, and explained why you should avoid using unstructured programming.

This admonishment completes Part IV of this book. Now that you know all about logical structures, you will learn about repeating structures in Part V.

Review Question

The answers to the review questions are in Appendix A.

1. If you have a choice between an unstructured branch and a structured branch, and it looks as though the unstructured branch will be easier to code, which should you choose?

Review Exercise

1. Run the examples in this chapter to check whether they all yield the same results.

Part V

Loops and Repeated Structures

CHAPTER 12

Using Counted Loops

In this part of the book you learn about repeating structures, and how to use them to reduce significantly the amount of code that you must write to accomplish a task. Repeating structures are collectively known as *loops*, and come in three different types: counted, logically terminated, and object type. This chapter covers counted loops, and the next two chapters cover logically terminated and object type loops.

In this chapter, you will learn about the following:

- ♦ What counted loops are
- ♦ How to use the For-Next loop
- ♦ How to use the loop counter

What Is a Counted Loop?

A counted loop repeats a single block of code a specified number of times. You use counted loops when you know beforehand how many times you need to execute a block of code. For example, if you want to change the formatting of 10 consecutive cells on a worksheet, you would use a counted loop to apply the code block that changes the formatting to each cell in turn.

Using For-Next Loops

The For-Next loop structure implements counted loops in Visual Basic. The structure's syntax is as follows:

Chapter 12 ♦ Using Counted Loops

```
For loopvariable = start To end Step stepsize
  .
  . block of code
  .
  Exit For
  .
  . block of code
  .
Next loopvariable
```

In this syntax, *loopvariable* is a variable name that counts the number of times that the loop is executed. The *start* and *end* variables are the starting and ending values for *loopvariable*, and *stepsize* is the amount to increase *loopvariable* each time the loop executes.

When a For-Next loop is encountered in a program, *loopvariable* is given the value *start*, and the block of code down to the Next statement is executed. The value of *loopvariable* is then increased by *stepsize* and compared to the value of *end*. If the value of *loopvariable* is greater than the value of *end*, the loop terminates and execution continues with the statement following the Next statement. Otherwise, the block of code in the loop is repeatedly calculated until the value of *loopvariable* is greater than *end* and the loop terminates.

When the Exit For statement is encountered, the loop is immediately terminated and execution continues with the statement that follows the Next statement. Usually you use the Exit For statement to terminate a loop that you are using to search for something, when whatever you are searching for is found.

If you omit Step *stepsize*, *loopvariable* is incremented by one each time that the loop is executed. If *end* is less than *start* and *stepsize* is negative, the loop counts down rather than up.

Using the Loop Counter

The loop counter is a normal variable that is available within the loop to select different values or cells to apply to the code in the code block. The loop counter is often an integer that is used as an index for an array variable, or for the Cells method to select a worksheet cell.

When a loop terminates, the value of the loop counter is greater than the value of *end* (or less than *end* if the loop is counting down). This fact is often useful when determining whether a loop completed normally, or was terminated prematurely with an Exit For statement.

> **Caution:** Because the loop variable is a normal variable, you can change it within the block of code that it is repeating. However, you should avoid changing the loop variable because such changes can easily yield unintended results. For example, the following construct runs forever:
>
> ```
> For I = 1 To 10
>     I = I - 1
>     Beep
> Next I
> ```

For example, the following procedure fills the current selection with random numbers, using two nested For-Next loops to span the cells in the current selection. You might use a procedure like this to prepare some cells for use in a probability calculation, or you could use a different function or formula to fill a block of cells with any number of different calculated values, depending on what you need.

```
Option Explicit
'
'   Stick random data in the current selection.
'
Sub StickRandom()
    Dim numRows As Integer, numCols As Integer
    Dim theRow As Integer, theCol As Integer
    'Get the size of the current selection.
    numRows = Selection.Rows.Count
    numCols = Selection.Columns.Count
    Randomize  'Initialize the random number generator.
    For theRow = 1 To numRows
        For theCol = 1 To numCols
            Selection.Cells(theRow, theCol).Value = Rnd
        Next theCol
    Next theRow
End Sub
```

The procedure first gets the number of rows and columns in the current selection by applying the Rows and Columns methods to the Selection Range object. The Rows method returns a collection of all the rows in the current selection, and Columns returns a collection that contains all the columns. The Count property returns the number of objects in each collection. The number of rows and columns sets the upper-limits for the loop variables in two nested loops. The outer loop steps over the rows, and the inner one steps over the columns in the current selection. The loop variables theRow and theCol start with a value of 1 and increment by 1 for each

Chapter 12 ◆ Using Counted Loops

step. First the outer loop selects a row, then the inner loop steps along the row, one column at a time. The Cells method and the Value property are used with the Rnd() function to insert a random number in each cell in the current selection.

To run this procedure, you first select an empty worksheet and then a range of cells. You then choose the **Tools M**acro command, which displays the Macro dialog box. Select the StickRandom procedure and then click Run. As the procedure executes, the random values are inserted in the cells, one by one, as shown in figure 12.1.

Figure 12.1

A worksheet after running the StickRandom procedure, which inserts random numbers in each cell of the current selection.

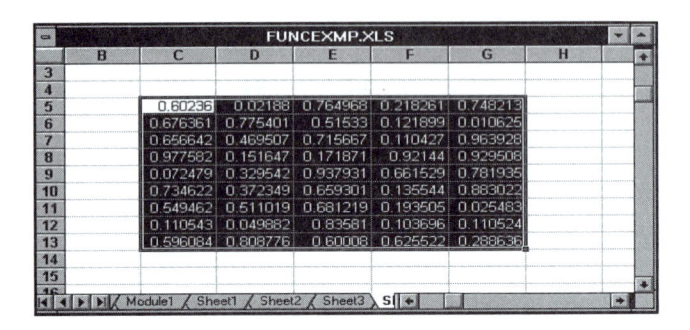

Now that you have a block of cells that contain values, you can create a similar procedure to loop over the contents of the cells, copy the values into an array, average the contents of the array, and display the average in a message box. The following procedure does just that:

```
Option Explicit
'
'   A procedure to average all the values
'   in the current selection and display that
'   average in a dialog box.
'
Sub BlockAverage()
   Dim numRows As Integer, numCols As Integer
   Dim theRow As Integer, theCol As Integer
   Dim I As Integer, J As Integer
   Dim theAverage As Single, theSum As Single
   Dim myArray() As Single
   'Get the size of the current selection.
   numRows = Selection.Rows.Count
   numCols = Selection.Columns.Count
   ReDim myArray(numRows, numCols)
   'Copy the cell contents into an array.
   For theRow = 1 To numRows
```

```
      For theCol = 1 To numCols
        myArray(theRow, theCol) = Selection.Cells(theRow, theCol).Value
      Next theCol
    Next theRow
    'Average the contents of the array.
    theSum = 0
    For I = 1 To numRows
      For J = 1 To numCols
        theSum = theSum + myArray(I, J)
      Next J
    Next I
    theAverage = theSum / (numRows * numCols)
    MsgBox "The Average is: " & Str(theAverage)
End Sub
```

> **Note:** The myArray( ) array variable is dimensioned without any array indices to specify the size. This is a *dynamic array*, which the ReDim statement redimensions at runtime to whatever size is necessary. Dynamic arrays are most useful when you don't know how large an array you need, and you don't want to waste much memory dimensioning an array that is larger than you expect is necessary. Even if you fix the size of such an array to a large value, you invariably will need a larger one. By using dynamic arrays, you can avoid much of the frustration that results from fixing the size of arrays. The only disadvantage is that you must dimension an array twice before you can use it.

This procedure first gets the size of the selection in the same manner as before, and then redimensions the dynamic array myArray( ) so that it is large enough to hold all the values. It next uses two nested loops to copy the values from the cells into the array. When this is complete, a second pair of nested loops steps over each element of the array and sums its value. Finally, the procedure calculates the average value and uses the MsgBox( ) function to display that value in a dialog box.

To run the procedure, select some cells, choose the **T**ools **M**acro command, select the Block Average procedure in the Macro dialog box, and click Run. When the averaging is complete, the result is displayed in a dialog box. The MsgBox( ) function displays the text from its argument in a dialog box with a single OK button, as shown in figure 12.2. To end the procedure, you click OK.

Chapter 12 ◆ Using Counted Loops

Figure 12.2
Averaging the contents of the current selection.

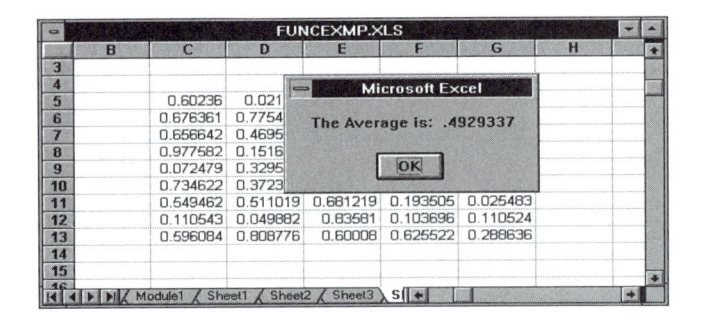

For another example, assume that you need to know how much interest you will pay on the 150th monthly payment of a $130,000 loan for 15 years at 7 percent interest. From figure 7.3, you know that the monthly payment is $1,168.48. To determine the interest paid on the 150th payment, you must calculate the interest in each payment, subtract the interest from the payment to determine the principal paid, and then subtract that from the principal to give the principal amount for the next payment. You then do this calculation 150 times to get the interest on the 150th payment. The following procedure does this:

```
Option Explicit
'
'   Calculate interest on nth payment
'
Function GetInt(ByVal PresVal As Currency, rate As Double, _
    PmtNum As Integer, Pmt As Currency) As Currency
  Dim Interest As Currency, Principle As Currency
  Dim I As Integer
  For I = 1 To PmtNum
    Interest = PresVal * rate      'The interest in this payment.
    Principal = Pmt - Interest     'The principal in this payment.
    PresVal = PresVal - Principal  'The new present value.
  Next I
  GetInt = Interest
End Function
```

The function gets the values from the calling procedure and starts a loop that ranges from 1 to the payment number that you are interested in. You use a counted loop because you want it to execute an explicit number of times. The next two statements calculate the interest and principal in the current payment, and the third calculates the new present value by subtracting the principal payment from the current present value. Because the function reduces the value of PresVal each time it must be passed by value (ByVal) instead of by address, you don't change the value of that argument in the calling procedure.

When the loop completes, the variable Interest contains the interest paid on payment number PmtNum, which is the result that you need. To use the procedure, use GetInt( ) in a worksheet cell, as shown in figure 12.3, and format the cell as currency.

Figure 12.3
Using the GetInt( ) function to calculate the interest on the 150th payment of a $130,000, 15-year loan at 7 percent interest, with a monthly payment of $1,168.48.

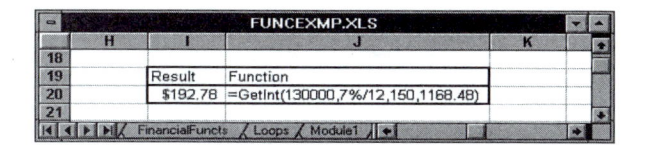

	H	I	J	K
18				
19		Result	Function	
20		$192.78	=GetInt(130000,7%/12,150,1168.48)	
21				

FinancialFuncts / Loops / Module1

Summary

In this chapter, you learned about the For-Next structure, which is a counted repeating structure or loop. You use this structure whenever you want to execute a block of code an explicit number of times. In the next chapter, you learn about logically terminated loops, which execute until something changes.

Review Questions

The answers to the review questions are in Appendix A.

1. What is a counted loop?

2. What does the Exit For statement do?

3. What size step is used if you omit Step *stepsize*?

4. Normally you should avoid changing a loop variable within a loop. But can you think of a situation in which changing a loop variable makes good, logical sense?

Review Exercises

1. Write a function to calculate and return the factorial of its argument. The factorial of *n* (*n!*) is the integer product of all the numbers up to *n*.

```
n! = 1*2*3*...n
```

2. Write a function that calculates the total interest paid on a loan between two payments, such as the total interest paid from payment 120 through 140.

Chapter 12 ◆ Using Counted Loops

3. Consider the MultiplyEm4( ) procedure from Chapter 7, "Creating and Using Functions":

```
'
'  A function to multiply an array of arrays of values
'
Function MultiplyEm4(ParamArray theArray()) As Single
    Dim Product As Single, Part, Value
    Product = 1
    For Each Part In theArray
        For Each Value In Part
            Product = Product * Value
        Next Value
    Next Part
    MultiplyEm4 = Product
End Function
```

Rewrite this procedure using For-Next loops rather than For-Each loops.

CHAPTER 13

Using Logically Terminated Loops

In Chapter 12 you learned about counted loops, which are one of the three types of loops. Logically terminated loops are the second type of repeating structure in Visual Basic. There are two types of logically terminated loops: Do-Loop and While-Wend loops, both of which are discussed in this chapter. The Do-Loop loop is the most versatile of the logical loops, and can handle all logically terminated loop structures. The While-Wend loop is less versatile, and is usually included for compatibility with older versions of BASIC.

In this chapter, you will learn about the following:

- ♦ Logically terminated loops
- ♦ The Do-Loop repeating structure
- ♦ The While-Wend repeating structure

What Are Logically Terminated Loops?

Logically terminated loops are repeating structures that terminate when some condition is met. While counted loops execute a block of code a specific number of times, a logically terminated loop can execute an infinite number of times, or not at all, depending on the state of the logical condition that terminates the loop. You can use the logically terminated loop structure to implement a counted loop by incrementing a variable each time the loop is executed and testing its value for the termination condition—however, it is somewhat cumbersome to do so.

Chapter 13 ♦ Using Logically Terminated Loops

Use logically terminated loops when you don't know how many times you need to execute a loop—for example, when you are reading data from a disk file of unknown length, or communicating with a peripheral device or with another application. In both cases, the termination condition is the lack of any data to process.

You also use a logically terminated loop when creating an event loop. An *event loop* is a logically terminated loop with the literal value True as the condition. Because the condition is a literal, the loop never terminates. The event loop contains calls to procedures that check for the occurrence of an event, such as typing in a cell or executing a command. If one of these events occurs, a procedure is called to handle the event; otherwise the loop continues executing repeatedly, continually checking for the next event to occur. Many applications, such as word processors and spreadsheets, operate in this way, continuously executing an event loop and waiting for you to do something.

Using Do-Loop Loops

The most versatile of the logically terminated loops is the Do-Loop loop. There are actually four configurations for this loop: True condition at the beginning, True condition at the end, False condition at the beginning, and False condition at the end. The syntax for these four configurations are as follows:

```
'
'True condition at beginning.
'
Do While condition
...block of code
.Exit Do
...block of code
Loop

'True condition at end.
'
Do
...block of code
.Exit Do
...block of code
Loop While condition
'
'False condition at beginning.
'
Do Until condition
```

```
...block of code
.Exit Do
...block of code
Loop
'
'False condition at end.
'
Do
...block of code
.Exit Do
...block of code
Loop Until condition
```

Using While or Until

The While and Until keywords determine the logic of the condition, with While indicating that the loop executes while *condition* is True, and the Until keyword indicating that the loop executes until *condition* becomes True. The following relationship exists between While and Until:

```
While condition = Until Not condition
```

Using Exit Do

The Exit Do statement terminates the loop early, and is usually the object of a logical structure (If statement) that tests an alternate condition for terminating the loop, such as an error.

Placing the Condition at the Beginning of the Loop

Placing the condition at the beginning or the end of the loop determines when the condition is checked. If the condition is tested at the beginning of the loop, then the loop will not execute if the condition is initially met. Use this kind of loop when the loop must not be executed unless the condition is met.

For example, when reading a disk file, you use the EOF( ) function to test the next item in the file, to see whether it is the end-of-file marker. If you attempt to read the end-of-file marker, your code stops with an error, so you need to check for the marker before reading any data from the file. To do this, you might use something like the following:

```
Open "Myfile.TXT" For Input As #1     'Open the file
Do Until EOF(1)          'See if you are at the end of the file.
  Input #1,A$            'If not, read some data.
```

Chapter 13 ◆ Using Logically Terminated Loops

```
    .
    .   'Code to do something with A$.
    .
   Loop
   Close #1                'Close the file when done.
```

In this code fragment, the EOF( ) function checks for the end-of-file marker. If you are not at the end of the file, EOF( ) returns False and the loop executes, reading a string from the file and processing it. If EOF( ) detects the end-of-file marker, the function returns True and the loop terminates.

Placing the Condition at the End of the Loop

Placing the condition at the end of the loop ensures that the loop executes at least once. Use this type of loop when your loop must execute once to set the condition so that you can test it. This type of loop is most commonly used when searching for something such as an array of values for a particular value.

For example, the following procedure locates the first positive value in an array:

```
'
'  Find the first positive value in an array.
'
Function FirstPos(theArray) As Single
   Dim J As Integer, Value As Single
   J = LBound(theArray) - 1     'Initialize J.
   Do                           'Begin the loop.
      J = J + 1                 'Increment J.
      Value = theArray(J)       'Get the value.
   Loop Until Value > 0         'Test the value.
   FirstPos = Value
End Function
```

In this procedure, theArray is a Variant, so it can return an array from the worksheet. The LBound( ) function returns the lower bound for the array. J is initialized to one less than that, so that the first time it is incremented, it is equal to the lower bound of the array. The loop starts with the Do statement, J is incremented, and the value of the array at that index is extracted. At the bottom of the loop, the value is tested to see whether it is the one that you want. If it is, the loop terminates with Value equal to the value located in the array, and J equal to the location in the array in which the value resides.

This procedure assumes that you know that there is a value in the array to find. If there may not be such a value, you need to test the value of J as well and break out of the loop if J passes the upper bound of the array. Otherwise you get runtime error 9, "Subscript out of range." To test the value of J, modify the procedure as follows:

Visual Basic for Applications By EXAMPLE

```
'
' Find the first positive value in an array.
'
Function FirstPos2(theArray)
  Dim J As Integer, Value
  J = LBound(theArray) - 1    'Initialize J.
  Do                          'Begin the loop.
    J = J + 1                 'Increment J.
    If J > UBound(theArray) Then  'See whether you have passed
                                  'the upper limit.
      Value = CVErr(xlErrValue)   'Set Value to #VALUE! to indicate
                                  'that no value was found.
      Exit Do                 'Terminate the loop.
    End If
    Value = theArray(J)       'Get the value.
  Loop Until Value > 0        'Test the value.
  FirstPos2 = Value
End Function
```

In this variation of the procedure, each time J is incremented, its value is compared to the upper limit of the array index that the UBound( ) function returns. If J passes the upper limit, Value is set to the #VALUE! error value to indicate that no value was found in the array. The loop is then terminated with the Exit Do statement. Note that the returned value is now a Variant, so that it can contain the error code.

Figure 13.1 shows both the FirstPos( ) and FirstPos2( ) functions used on a worksheet. Note the second use of FirstPos2( ); because the function is given an array argument that does not contain a positive value, it returns an error condition.

Figure 13.1
The FirstPos( ) and FirstPos2( ) functions used on a worksheet.

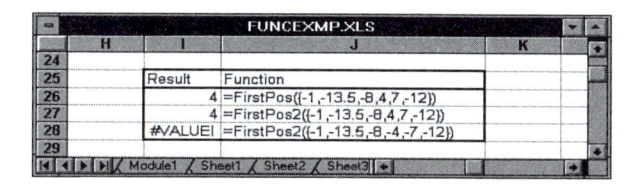

	H	I	J	K
24				
25		Result	Function	
26		4	=FirstPos({-1,-13.5,-8,4,7,-12})	
27		4	=FirstPos2({-1,-13.5,-8,4,7,-12})	
28		#VALUE!	=FirstPos2({-1,-13.5,-8,-4,-7,-12})	
29				

Using While-Wend Loops

The While-Wend loop is a relic of older versions of BASIC. The loop's functionality is fully equivalent to the Do While-Loop structure. The syntax of While-Wend is as follows:

183

```
While condition
  .
  .
  .
Wend
```

Note that the While-Wend structure does not have an Exit statement to terminate the loop early, nor does it allow the termination condition to be at the end of the loop. Otherwise, it works the same as the Do-Loop structure.

Summary

In this chapter you learned about logically terminated loops. Unlike the counted loops, which terminate after a specified number of iterations (see Chapter 12), logically terminated loops continue until a logical condition is met. The next chapter describes the third of the three types of repeating structure, the object type loop.

Review Questions

The answers to the review questions are in Appendix A.

1. What is a logically terminated loop?

2. What is the significance of the While and Until keywords in the Do-Loop structure?

3. Does it matter which end of the loop gets the condition? Why or why not?

Review Exercises

1. Rewrite the FirstPos2( ) function so that it starts at the upper limit of the array index and works down to the lower limit searching for the first positive value.

2. Write a function that receives a string argument and returns the location in the string that contains the last (rightmost) occurrence of the letter A. This function should be similar to the InStr( ) function, but check from the right rather than from the left end of the string.

3. Rewrite the BlockAverage( ) procedure from Chapter 12 using Do-Loop rather than For-Next loops.

CHAPTER 14

Using Object Type Loops

Object type loops are the third of the three types of repeating structures availab[le] in Visual Basic. You use the For Each structure to create object type loops and the[n] apply them to arrays and collections of objects. Actually, you have already se[en] these loops in several of the examples in this book.

In this chapter, you learn the following:

- ♦ How object type loops work
- ♦ How to apply the For Each loop to objects
- ♦ How to apply the For Each loop to arrays

What Are Object Type Loops?

Object type loops are actually much like counted loops (see Chapter 12), in that the[y] are executed a specific number of times. The difference is that when you app[ly] object type loops to a collection of objects, they execute once for each object in t[he] collection. To use object type loops, you don't have to know how many objects a[re] in the collection; that is determined automatically by the loop. The loop counte[r,] instead of containing a value each time the loop is iterated, contains an object fro[m] the collection.

Additionally, you can apply object type loops to arrays. The loops execute on[ce] for each element of the array, and the loop variable contains the element.

Applying the For Each Loop to Collections

You implement object type loops with the For Each structure. To apply the For Each loop to a collection, use the following syntax:

```
For Each element In collection
.
.  Block of code
.
Exit For
.
.  Block of code
.
Next element
```

In this syntax, `element` is a Variant type variable, because it must be capable of containing an object. The variable `collection` is some collection of objects. When the loop executes, an object is selected from the collection and placed in the `element` variable. You can then use the `element` variable in the block of code to do something to the object. Like the For-Next loop, the Exit For statement ends a loop early.

> **Caution:** Be careful if you do something in the body of a For Each loop that changes the number of elements in the collection. The ordering of elements in the collection is somewhat arbitrary and a new element may or may not be included in the loop.

As you have already seen, the For Each structure is useful in several situations, especially when an array or a range of cells is passed to a custom function. Without the For Each structure, you must determine whether an array or a collection of cells (a cell reference) has been passed; any cell reference must then be converted to an array before you process it.

For example, the following function, MultiplyEm6(), uses the For-Next loop to implement the MultiplyEm5() function from Chapter 7. Later you'll see the same function implemented using the For Each statement.

```
'
'  A function to multiply any list of values
'
Function MultiplyEm6(ParamArray theArray()) As Single
```

```
Dim Product As Single
Dim I As Integer, IMax As Integer, IMin As Integer
Dim J As Integer, JMax As Integer, JMin As Integer
Dim K As Integer, KMax As Integer, KMin As Integer
Product = 1
IMax = UBound(theArray)    'Get the upper limit.
IMin = LBound(theArray)    'Get the lower limit.
For I = IMin To IMax    'Loop over the parameter array.
  If TypeName(theArray(I)) = "Range" Then  'Is it a Range?
    JMax = theArray(I).Columns.Count  'Get the number of columns.
    KMax = theArray(I).Rows.Count    'Get the number of rows.
    For J = 1 To JMax     'Loop over the columns.
      For K = 1 To KMax   'Loop over the rows.
        Product = Product * theArray(I).Cells(K, J) 'Calculate
                                                    'the product.
      Next K
    Next J
                                              'Is it an array?
  ElseIf Right(TypeName(theArray(I)), 2) = "()" Then
    JMax = UBound(theArray(I), 1)  'Get the upper limit.
    JMin = LBound(theArray(I), 1)  'Get the lower limit.
    For J = JMin To JMax  'Loop over the array elements.
      Product = Product * theArray(I)(J)  'Calculate the product.
    Next J
  Else    'It's a single value
    Product = Product * theArray(I)  'Calculate the product.
  End If
Next I
MultiplyEm6 = Product
End Function
```

The MultiplyEm6( ) function must first determine the number of elements in the parameter array, and start a loop over those elements. Next, a block If statement tests for a cell range, an array, or a single value, and calculates the product separately for each type.

Chapter 14 ◆ Using Object Type Loops

> **Note:** The MultiplyEm6( ) procedure is actually less capable than the MultiplyEm5( ) procedure. The MultiplyEm6( ) procedure cannot handle vertical arrays like {2;4;23;76;5}, nor can it handle two-dimensional arrays such as {2,4,23,76,5;1,2,3,4,5}, because Visual Basic provides no easy way to determine how many dimensions an array has. To determine the number of dimensions, you must enable an error trap, try some number of dimensions, and see whether you get an error. If you get an error, you have used too many dimensions. An error trap of this type is explored in Chapter 23, "Using Error Trapping To Handle Unforeseen Events."

The following procedure is the same as MultiplyEm6( ) except that this version uses For Each rather than the For-Next loop. Note that the following version is significantly shorter and easier to understand.

```
'
'   A function to multiply any list of values
'
Function MultiplyEm5(ParamArray theArray()) As Single
    Dim Product As Single, Part, Value
    Product = 1
    For Each Part In theArray
      If TypeName(Part) = "Range" Or Right(TypeName(Part), 2) _
          = "()" Then
        For Each Value In Part
          Product = Product * Value
        Next Value
      Else
        Product = Product * Part
      End If
    Next Part
    MultiplyEm5 = Product
End Function
```

Applying the For Each Loop to Arrays

The syntax for applying the For Each loop to an array is nearly identical to that used for collections of objects, except that the *element* variable need not be a Variant, but can be of the same type as the elements of the array. Each time the loop executes, the *element* variable contains a different element than the array.

The For Each statement is often useful when you must do something with all the elements of an array, but don't need to know the shape of the array or which element is being accessed. You can either add all the values in an array or find the smallest value. As long as you don't need the specific elements index, you can use the For Each statement, which usually results in much simpler code.

For example, the following function sums the elements of an array. Note that if you had used the range reference as well as the explicit array, the function would work just as well.

```
'
'   Sum an array
'
Function SumArray(theArray)
    Dim Element, theSum
    theSum = 0
    For Each Element In theArray
        theSum = theSum + Element
    Next Element
    SumArray = theSum
End Function
```

Figure 14.1 shows the result of applying this function to an array of values. To insert this array, you type into the function the range reference of the input array, select the reference you just typed, and press Ctrl-= to replace the reference with the explicit values.

Figure 14.1
Summing an array with the SumArray( ) function.

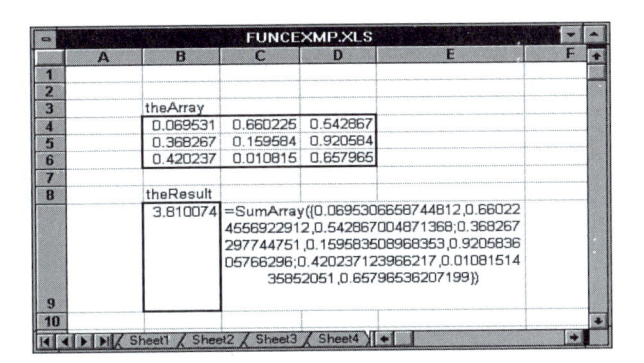

	A	B	C	D	E	F
1						
2						
3		theArray				
4		0.069531	0.660225	0.542867		
5		0.368267	0.159584	0.920584		
6		0.420237	0.010815	0.657965		
7						
8		theResult				
		3.810074	=SumArray({0.0695306658744812,0.66022 4556922912,0.542867004871368;0.368267 297744751,0.159583508968353,0.9205836 05766296;0.420237123966217,0.01081514 35852051,0.65796536207199})			

Note: One thing that you *cannot* do with arrays and the For Each loop that you can do with objects is to change the contents of the object itself. With objects, you can access the Value property and change the original object. With arrays, the loop variable contains the value of the array element, but changing it does not change the corresponding element of the array.

Summary

In this chapter, you learned about the object type loop implemented with the For Each statement. The For Each loop iterates once for each object in a collection or for each element in an array. During each iteration, the loop variable contains the object or the value of the array element.

This chapter completes Part V, which has covered repeating structures. In Part VI you learn about input and output, using dialog boxes and the file system.

Review Questions

The answers to the review questions are in Appendix A.

1. What is an object type loop?
2. When applied to a collection of objects, what does the loop variable in a For Each loop contain during each loop?
3. If the For Each loop is applied to a single object, how many times is the loop calculated?
4. Can you change the value of an array element using a For Each loop?

Review Exercises

1. Rewrite the following FirstPos2() function from Chapter 13 using the For Each loop:

```
'   Find the first positive value in an array.
'
Function FirstPos2(theArray)
  Dim J As Integer, Value
  J = LBound(theArray) - 1    'Initialize J.
  Do                          'Begin the loop.
    J = J + 1                 'Increment J.
    If J > UBound(theArray) Then  'See if you have passed
                                  'the upper limit.
      Value = CVErr(xlErrValue)   'Set Value to #VALUE! to
                                  'indicate that no value
                                  'was found.
      Exit Do                 'Terminate the loop.
    End If
```

```
        Value = theArray(J)        'Get the value.
    Loop Until Value > 0           'Test the value.
    FirstPos2 = Value
End Function
```

2. Write a function that returns the number of positive elements in an array or cell reference.

3. Write a function that returns the standard deviation of all the values in an array or range reference. Use the following formula:

$$\sigma = \sqrt{\frac{\sum_{i=1}^{n} x_i^2}{n-1}}$$

where σ is the standard deviation, n is the number of elements in the array or range reference, and x is the value of an element.

Part VI

Performing Input and Output

CHAPTER 15

Using Built-In Dialog Boxes

Getting data into or out of a program is often difficult to do well. Depending on the application, the code to create the user interface can make up the majority of an application's code. In a well-crafted application, the amount of code used for the user interface is about 90 percent, with only 10 percent used for number crunching. Examining Excel or any other commercial application, you can easily see how that could be so. In this part of the book you learn about the different methods of performing input and output, from dialog boxes to disk files.

Visual Basic is capable of using dialog boxes to get data from users and pass information back to them. In addition to providing several built-in dialog boxes, Visual Basic can use all the dialog boxes available in Excel or Project. Elaborate custom dialog boxes are also available, and are discussed in Chapter 17, "Creating Custom Dialog Boxes."

In this chapter, you will learn how to use the following:

- ♦ The built-in message dialog box
- ♦ The built-in input dialog box
- ♦ Excel's dialog boxes

Using the MsgBox() Function

The MsgBox() function creates a dialog box that is similar to a simple message box. A message box simply displays a message to the user, but a dialog box can also receive input from the user. The dialog box displays a string of text and then waits for the user to click a button. In its simplest form, the dialog box has a single OK button, which the user must click to acknowledge and clear the dialog box. You can expand the capabilities of this dialog box by adding more buttons and having it return a value that indicates which button the user pressed.

Creating a Simple Message Box

You can create a simple message box by using the MsgBox keyword followed by the text that you want to display. When creating a simple message box, you use the function in the statement form; that is, because you ignore any returned values, you do not enclose the arguments in parentheses.

If you need to display numbers, use the Str() or Format() functions to convert them to text first. You have already seen this form of the MsgBox() function in Chapter 12's BlockAverage procedure, which uses the function to display the results calculated by the procedure:

```
Option Explicit
'
'   A procedure to average all the values
'   in the current selection and display that
'   average in a dialog box.
'
Sub BlockAverage()
  Dim numRows As Integer, numCols As Integer
  Dim theRow As Integer, theCol As Integer
  Dim I As Integer, J As Integer
  Dim theAverage As Single, theSum As Single
  Dim myArray() As Single
  'Get the size of the current selection.
  numRows = Selection.Rows.Count
  numCols = Selection.Columns.Count
  ReDim myArray(numRows, numCols)
  'Copy the cell contents into an array.
  For theRow = 1 To numRows
    For theCol = 1 To numCols
      myArray(theRow, theCol) = _
          Selection.Cells(theRow, theCol).Value
    Next theCol
  Next theRow
  'Average the contents of the array.
  theSum = 0
  For I = 1 To numRows
    For J = 1 To numCols
```

```
      theSum = theSum + myArray(I, J)
    Next J
  Next I
  theAverage = theSum / (numRows * numCols)
  MsgBox "The Average is: " & Str(theAverage)
End Sub
```

At the end of the procedure, the Str() function is combined with the text "The Average is: " to convert the numeric average into a string. The string is then passed to the MsgBox function, which displays it as was shown in figure 12.2.

Creating a Dialog Box by Adding Buttons to a Message Box

To expand the capabilities of a simple message box and thus create a dialog box, you can add more buttons to it. You add the buttons by using an optional argument of the MsgBox() function. These extra buttons enable users to choose a course of action or to answer a simple question.

A code for the buttons is added as a second argument, following the text to be displayed in the dialog box, or as the named argument buttons. Table 15.1 lists the codes and constant names available in Visual Basic. Additional codes exist to set the default button, to select an icon, and to make the dialog box modal.

Table 15.1. The codes for setting the buttons and icons on the MsgBox() function.

Code	Constant	Buttons Displayed
Button Codes		
0	vbOKOnly	OK
1	vbOKCancel	OK and Cancel
2	vbAbortRetryIgnore	Abort, Retry, and Ignore
3	vbYesNoCancel	Yes, No, and Cancel
4	vbYesNo	Yes and No
5	vbRetryCancel	Retry and Cancel

continues

Table 15.1. Continued

Code	Constant	Default Button
Default Codes		
0	vbDefaultButton1	First
256	vbDefaultButton2	Second
512	vbDefaultButton3	Third
Icon Codes		
16	vbCritical	Critical Message
32	vbQuestion	Warning Query
48	vbExclamation	Warning Message
64	vbInformation	Information Message
Modal Dialog Codes		
0	vbApplicationModal	Application modal
4096	vbSystemModal	System modal

To use the codes listed in table 15.1, first select the button or buttons that you want to display. Second, if you have more than one button, decide which is to be the default button. The *default button* is the one that is clicked automatically when the user presses Enter while the dialog box is displayed. The codes listed in the Default Codes section of table 15.1 select either the first, second, or third button as the default. The buttons are placed on the dialog box in the same order as they are listed in the Button Codes section of table 15.1.

Third, if you want to add an icon to the dialog box, select the appropriate code from the Icon Codes section of table 15.1.

Fourth, you must decide whether the dialog box is to be modal. If a dialog box is not modal, the user can click another window to hide the dialog box, and then can continue to use the application without clearing the dialog box. If the dialog box is *modal*, however, the user must clear it before continuing with an application. Two types of modal dialog boxes are possible: application modal and system modal. The user must clear an application modal dialog box before continuing to use the application that displayed it, although the user can switch to a different application without clearing the dialog box. A system modal dialog box requires that you clear it before you do anything else.

Finally, you add together the codes for all the buttons and options and then use that sum as the argument to the dialog box.

For example, if you want the dialog box to include Yes and No buttons, to have the No (second) button as the default, to include a warning icon, and make the application modal, you would add the following built-in constants to create the code:

```
theCode = vbYesNo + vbDefaultButton2 + vbExclamation + _
    vbApplicationModal
```

which equals

```
4 + 256 + 48 + 0 = 308
```

However, to ensure that your code indicates more obviously what it does, you should use the constants rather than the numbers.

For example, you could use either of the following MsgBox() statements:

```
MsgBox prompt:="Do you really want to do this?", buttons:=theCode
```

```
MsgBox "Do you really want to do this?", theCode
```

Both of these statements result in the dialog box shown in figure 15.1. To create this figure, try entering either of the preceding statements in the Immediate pane of the Debug window.

Figure 15.1
A dialog box created with button code 308.

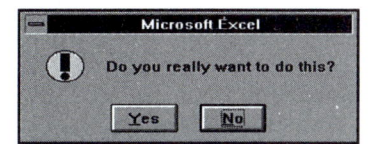

Receiving Values from the MsgBox Function

The dialog box displayed in figure 15.1 is not very useful unless you can determine which button the user pressed to clear the dialog box. To see which button the user pressed, use the function form of MsgBox() and examine the value that the function returns. Table 15.2 lists the possible return values and Visual Basic constants.

Table 15.2. The values returned by the MsgBox() function.

Code	Constant	Button
1	vbOK	OK
2	vbCancel	Cancel

(continues)

Chapter 15 ◆ Using Built-In Dialog Boxes

Table 15.2. Continued

Code	Constant	Button
3	vbAbort	Abort
4	vbRetry	Retry
5	vbIgnore	Ignore
6	vbYes	Yes
7	vbNo	No

For example, to use the dialog box from the last section in a procedure, you might create one like the following:

```
Sub MakeDialog1()
  Dim theCode As Integer, theReply As Integer
  theCode = vbYesNo + vbDefaultButton2 + vbExclamation + _
      vbApplicationModal
  theReply = MsgBox(prompt:="Do you really want to do this?", _
      buttons:=theCode)
  Select Case theReply
    Case vbYes
'      He really wants to do this, so go ahead.
'      Code block for Yes answer.
      Debug.Print "Yes"
    Case vbNo
'      Code block for No answer.
      Debug.Print "No"
  End Select
End Sub
```

This procedure calculates the code for the buttons and icons wanted on the dialog box, displays the dialog box, and stores the returned value in the variable theReply. The Select Case structure is used to select different blocks of code depending on the returned value. Run this procedure in the Immediate pane of the Debug window and it prints Yes or No, depending on which button you press to clear the dialog box.

Adding a Title to the Dialog Box

The default title of a dialog box that you create with the MsgBox() function is "Microsoft Excel." The title is the text displayed in the title bar at the top of the dialog box. To change the title, add to the MsgBox() function another string argument that contains the title you want. If you use the argument list form, the title is the third argument; otherwise use `title:="title text"`.

For example, you can add a title to the dialog box that you created in the last section:

```
Sub MakeDialog1()
  Dim theCode As Integer, theReply As Integer
  theCode = vbYesNo + vbDefaultButton2 + vbExclamation + _
      vbApplicationModal
  theReply = MsgBox(prompt:="Do you really want to do this?", _
    Buttons:=theCode, Title:="You're About To Do Something Dumb")
  Select Case theReply
    Case vbYes
'     He really wants to do this, so go ahead.
'     Code block for Yes answer.
      Debug.Print "Yes"
    Case vbNo
'     Code block for No answer.
      Debug.Print "No"
  End Select
End Sub
```

Figure 15.2 shows the dialog box that this code creates.

Figure 15.2

A dialog box created with the *MsgBox()* function, with a custom title.

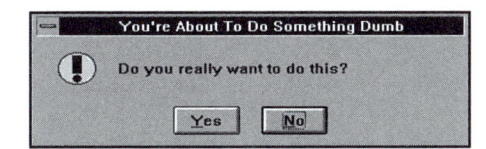

Using the InputBox Function

The InputBox() function creates another type of built-in dialog box. A basic input box includes a text edit window, an OK button, and a Cancel button. When you use the function, any text that you type into the dialog box's text window is returned by the function when you click OK. If you click Cancel, the empty string ("") is returned.

As with the MsgBox() function, the first argument of the InputBox() function is a text string that is used as a prompt in dialog box. The InputBox() function provides no buttons argument, so the second argument is the title. The third argument, default, contains any default text that you want to display in the text edit box when the dialog box opens. All the arguments must be text strings, and the value that the

Chapter 15 ♦ Using Built-In Dialog Boxes

function returns is a text string. If you expect the function to return a number, your procedure must use the Val() function to convert the string version of the number returned by InputBox() function into a binary number that your code can use.

For example, the following procedure displays two dialog boxes—the first to get the user's name, and the second to request his or her age—and then calculates and displays the user's age in days:

```
'
'  Calculate age in days from age in years.
'
Sub AgeCalculator()
  Dim theReply As String, thePrompt As String
  Dim theTitle As String, theDefault As String
  Dim theAge As Single, OkFlag As Boolean
  Dim theName As String
  thePrompt = "Please input your first name."
  theTitle = "Personal Info Dialog"
  theDefault = "Name"
'  Loop until the user inserts a single name.
  Do
  theReply = InputBox(thePrompt, theTitle, theDefault)
  If theReply = "" Then Exit Sub   'The user clicked Cancel.
  theReply = Trim(theReply)    'Get rid of blanks.
  'See if the string is blank, or if there are blanks in the string.
  If (theReply = "") Or (InStr(theReply, " ") <> 0) Then
      MsgBox "I don't understand that, please try again.", , theTitle
    OkFlag = False
     ElseIf theReply = theDefault Then  'The user just pressed Enter.
    MsgBox "Please type something, try again.", , theTitle
    OkFlag = False
  Else
    'Input seems okay.
    theName = theReply
    OkFlag = True
  End If
```

202

```vb
  Loop Until OkFlag
' Now get the user's age.
    thePrompt = "Good Morning " & theReply & ". Please enter your age."
' Loop until the user types a reasonable number.
  Do
  theReply = InputBox(thePrompt, theTitle)
  If theReply = "" Then Exit Sub   'The user clicked Cancel.
  theAge = Val(theReply)    'Convert to a number.
  If Not IsNumeric(theReply) Then   'Did the user type a number?
    MsgBox "This doesn't appear to be a number, _
        please try again.", , theTitle
    OkFlag = False
  'See whether the number is reasonable.
  ElseIf (theAge < 1) Or (theAge > 120) Then
    MsgBox "I don't believe you are " & Str(theAge) & _
        " years old, please try again.", , theTitle
    OkFlag = False
  Else
    'This appears to be an age.
    OkFlag = True
  End If
  Loop Until OkFlag
' Calculate the approximate age in days.
  MsgBox "You are approximately " & _
      Format(theAge * 365, "#,###") & " days old."
End Sub
```

This procedure has two parts. The first part gets the user's first name, and the second gets the user's age and returns the approximate age in days.

The procedure first displays the dialog box shown in figure 15.3, which requests the user's name. When the InputBox() function returns a value, the procedure first checks the returned value for the empty string (""), which indicates that the user pressed Cancel. If so, the procedure terminates with the Exit Sub statement.

Figure 15.3

A dialog box created with the InputBox() function, requesting the user's first name.

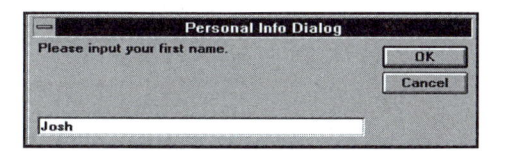

Users occasionally type the wrong thing in a dialog box, so you should do as much checking as possible. Before a procedure tries to use a value returned by a dialog box, it should check that the value is reasonable and of the right type (string or number). What a reasonable value is depends on what you are trying to get from the user. If you are trying to get a number, you can check its value to see whether it is in a range of reasonable numbers. If it is a string, you can see how many characters or words it contains. Again, though, what you check for depends on what you expect.

A good way to structure such checking is to combine a Do-Loop loop and a block If statement. The loop uses the flag OkFlag to determine whether the user needs to try again. The block If statement checks whether the string that the InputBox() function returns is reasonable. If not, the statement sets OkFlag to False so that the loop executes again. If the string is reasonable, OkFlag is set to True, the loop terminates, and the returned value is passed to the rest of the procedure.

With this structure you can easily add more tests by adding more ElseIf blocks to the block If structure. Usually you write negative logic tests, from which you conclude that a value is good if it fails all the tests. If you use positive logic, the first test to return True ends the testing.

In the AgeCalculator() procedure, the block If statement first checks for a string of blanks, or a blank within the string. A blank within a string indicates that the user typed more than one word, which is not reasonable for a first name. Next it checks for the default string, which indicates that the user simply pressed Enter without typing anything. If either of these situations occurs, one of the dialog boxes in figure 15.4 appears. If the name passes both of these tests, it is accepted.

Figure 15.4

The AgeCalculator() procedure displays one of these two dialog boxes when it finds an inconsistency in a name returned by the InputBox() function.

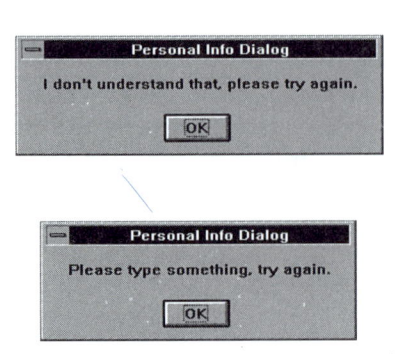

The second part of the procedure inserts the name from the first part into the prompt of the dialog box shown in figure 15.5. The procedure checks the result to see whether the user clicked the Cancel button, and then converts the string into a number and tests whether the number is of a reasonable size. For this testing, you use a Do-Loop, block If structure similar to that used in the first part of this procedure.

Figure 15.5

A dialog box created with the InputBox() function, requesting the user's age.

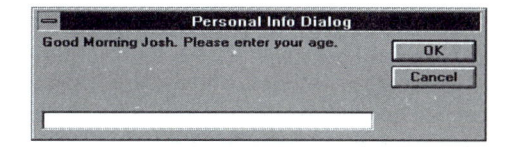

The structure consists of two tests. The first test is for missing numeric data, which indicates that the user typed text rather than a number. The second test is for the range of the number. If the number is greater than 120 or less than 1, the age is unlikely to be the valid age for a living person. If the procedure finds errors, it displays one of the two dialog boxes shown in figure 15.6. If the number seems reasonable, the age in days is calculated, converted to formatted text, and displayed in a dialog box as shown in figure 15.7.

Figure 15.6

The AgeCalculator() procedure displays one of these two dialog boxes when it finds an error the age returned by the InputBox() function.

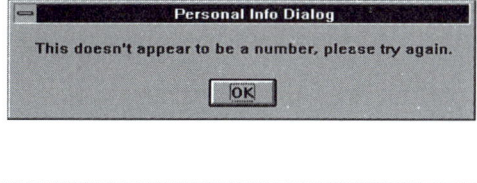

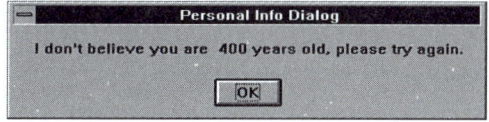

Figure 15.7

A message box displaying the calculated age in days of a 10 year old.

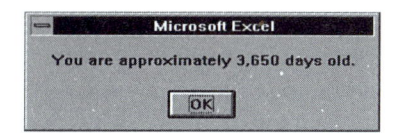

Using Other Built-In Dialog Boxes

Two other built-in dialog boxes are available in Visual Basic: GetOpenFilename and GetSaveAsFilename. Neither of these dialog boxes actually opens or saves a file, they only get the file name and the path. The commands that create these dialogs are not really statements, but methods applied to the Application object.

You use these two dialog boxes as follows:

```
theFileName = Application.GetOpenFilename(fileFilter, _
    filterIndex, title)

theFilename = Application.GetSaveAs Filename(initialFilename, _
    fileFilter, filterIndex, Title)
```

Both of these methods apply to the Application object and return a file name and path for the file that the user selects. The dialog boxes, which are the same as those that are displayed when you use the Excel commands File **O**pen and File Save **A**s, have an Open or Save button and a Cancel button. If you click the Cancel button, the methods return the value False.

The *fileFilter* argument determines which file filters are listed in the the dialog box's File Type drop-down list box. Only files that match the selected file filter appear in the dialog box's list of files. A file filter consists of two parts: a piece of text and a filter. The text is displayed in the File Type drop-down list, and the filter is used to select files for the list of files. For example, consider the following argument:

```
All Files (*.*), *.*
```

The text "All Files (*.*)" is displayed in the File Type drop-down list, and "*.*" is the actual filter, which in this case selects and lists all the directory's files.

Here's another example of a file filter:

```
All Files (*.*), *.*, Excel Workbooks (*.XLS), *.XLS
```

This file filter displays two optional entries in the File Type drop-down list: All Files and Excel Workbooks.

The *filterIndex* entry is an integer number that selects the default file filter from the File Type drop-down list. The *title* is the same as that used for the InputBox() function. Finally, the *initialFilename* argument specifies which initial, default file name to place in the text edit box.

Calling Application Dialog Boxes

A Visual Basic program can call all the dialog boxes available in Excel. However, they do not operate like the dialog boxes discussed so far in this chapter, which return a value to the Visual Basic program without affecting any underlying sheet or cell. If you call an Excel dialog box, it does not return a value to a Visual Basic program, but performs its normal function.

For example, if you execute the Format Number dialog box with some worksheet cells selected, the changes you make in the dialog box are applied to the cells and are not returned to the Visual Basic program.

> **Caution:** Because the application dialog boxes apply to the currently displayed object, you must be careful not to display a dialog box out of context, because the attempt will fail and cause a runtime error. For example, attempting to display the Format Number dialog box when a module sheet is active results in an error.

Visual Basic for Applications *By* EXAMPLE

To call an application dialog box, use the Dialogs collection of the Application object. The Dialogs collection takes an index number as an argument that selects the dialog box to display. All the index numbers have defined constants in Excel that name the dialog box they select. All the constants begin with xlDialog followed by the name of the dialog box. For example, the constant for the Format Number dialog box is xlDialogFormatNumber. To find the available dialog boxes and constants, use the Object Browser to search the Constants object of the Excel library for constants that begin with xlDialog.

For example, the following procedure displays the Format Number dialog box:

```
'
' Test dialog 2
' Display an Application dialog box
'
Sub TestDialog2()
    Application.Dialogs(xlDialogFormatNumber).Show
End Sub
```

To run this procedure, type it onto a module sheet, switch to a worksheet, select a cell, execute the **T**ools **M**acro command, select the TestDialog2 procedure, and then click the Run button. When you run the procedure, it displays the dialog box shown in figure 15.8. If you fail to select a worksheet cell before you run the procedure, the display of this dialog box results in an error.

Figure 15.8
An Excel dialog box displayed with the Show method.

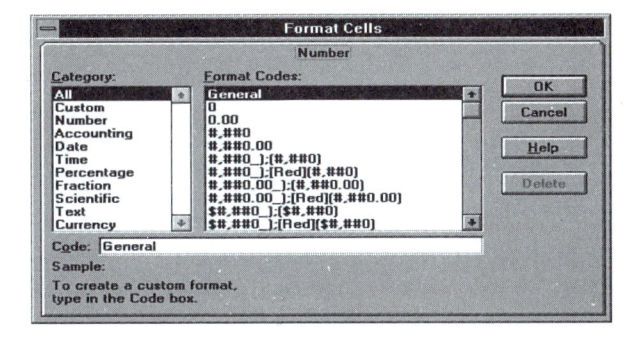

Summary

Dialog boxes are the primary media for transferring small amounts of data between a user and a running application. Two functions, MsgBox() and InputBox(), create built-in dialog boxes that can handle most simple data transactions. The GetOpenFilename() and GetSaveAsFilename() functions create dialog boxes that get file names for opening and saving files. Custom dialog boxes, which are discussed in Chapter 17, "Creating Custom Dialog Boxes," are also available.

Chapter 15 ◆ Using Built-In Dialog Boxes

In addition to the built-in Visual Basic dialog boxes, you can display any of the Excel program's dialog boxes, which perform their normal functions when displayed.

Review Questions

The answers to the review questions are in Appendix A.

1. What value does the MsgBox() function return if you click OK?
2. What code number would you use as an argument to add Yes and No buttons to a dialog box that you are creating with the MsgBox() function?
3. How do you display a number with the MsgBox() function?
4. How do you change the title of a dialog box?
5. Explain what a modal dialog box is.
6. Explain the difference between system modal and application modal.

Review Exercises

1. Write the list of constants that you must sum to include Abort, Retry, and Ignore buttons on a MsgBox() dialog box with Retry as the default button and with the Critical Message icon displayed on it. Then write a short procedure to display this dialog box with some appropriate text.
2. Write a procedure to display a dialog box with three buttons on it and to branch to three different routines depending on which buttons you press. In the three different routines, display a second dialog box that tells you which button you pressed.
3. Write a procedure that uses the InputBox() function to get an integer between 1 and 10 from the user. Be sure to test for a number in the correct range, and to try again if the user types something incorrect. Abort the procedure if the user clicks Cancel.
4. Write a procedure that uses the GetOpenFilename() function and displays the string returned by the function. Try the function on several different files to see what it returns in each case. Does it operate differently if the selected file is in the current directory?

CHAPTER 16

Using a Worksheet as a Data Form

In Excel, the primary data input and output medium is the worksheet. The worksheet is also useful as a data form for a Visual Basic program. You can also use Project worksheets as data forms; however, because Project worksheets are more specific than those of Excel, they are not as easily adapted to a Visual Basic program. Excel worksheets, on the other hand, are general purpose by design, making them much more adaptable as a data form.

In this chapter you learn how to do the following:

♦ Use an Excel worksheet as a front end to a Visual Basic program

♦ Define input ranges on a worksheet

♦ Put buttons and other objects on a worksheet

Defining Input Ranges

The first step in using an Excel worksheet as a data form is to determine how many input ranges you need and to define them on the worksheet. As you define them, keep in mind which ranges are to be changeable by the user and which are not. The running program accesses the data cells in the same manner that has been described previously in this book.

For example, try developing a front end for a contacts database. A contacts database keeps track of personal contacts, including contact information such as names and addresses, plus other information related to product usage that is important to your company. Additionally, you may want to keep personal data—

Chapter 16 ◆ Using a Worksheet as a Data Form

such as family status, likes, and dislikes—to help you minimize social blunders the next time you contact this person.

Depending on your business and the amount of time that you want to devote to maintaining your information, you might choose to include in your database any number of pieces of information about your personal contacts. Before proceeding, you usually should do a little cost-benefit analysis to balance the value of the information stored in your database and the cost of maintaining it.

For this example, store the name, address, phone, and e-mail address of each contact. Also include two fields, Referred By and Notes, to keep track of who gave you a particular lead and to note any follow-up. You can add any other fields the same way as you add these fields.

To create the data form, follow these steps:

1. Start with a blank worksheet, and rename it as ContactsIO with the Format Sheet **R**ename command.

2. Using figure 16.1 as a guide, type the titles, outline the cells, and adjust the column widths and line sizes of the data form.

3. Select cells B4:C14, choose the Format **C**ells command, select the Alignment tab, click the Left option button, and choose OK.

4. Select cell B11, choose the Format **C**ells command, select the Alignment tab, click the Right option button, and choose OK.

5. Name the cells according to the following table. You can select cells B4:C14 and use the Insert Names Create command first, then use the Insert Names Define command to change any cells that don't match the table.

Cell	Name
C4	Name
C5	Address
C6	City
C7	State
C8	Zip
C9	Phone
C10	E_Mail_Net
C11	E_Mail_Address
C12	Referral

Visual Basic for Applications By
EXAMPLE

Cell	Name
C13	Notes
C14	RecNo

6. Select cells C4:C13, choose the **F**ormat **C**ells command, select the Protection tab, uncheck the **L**ocked check box, and choose OK.

7. Select cells B1:C1, choose the **F**ormat **C**ells command, select the Alignment tab, select the Center **A**cross Selection option button, and choose OK.

8. Select cell C13, choose the **F**ormat **C**ells command, select the Alignment tab, check the **W**rap Text check box, and choose OK.

You've now created the data entry part of the worksheet form. Later you turn off the row and column headings and protect the sheet so that the user can change only those cells that you unlocked in step 6.

Figure 16.1

The layout for the cells on the worksheet data form for the personal contacts database.

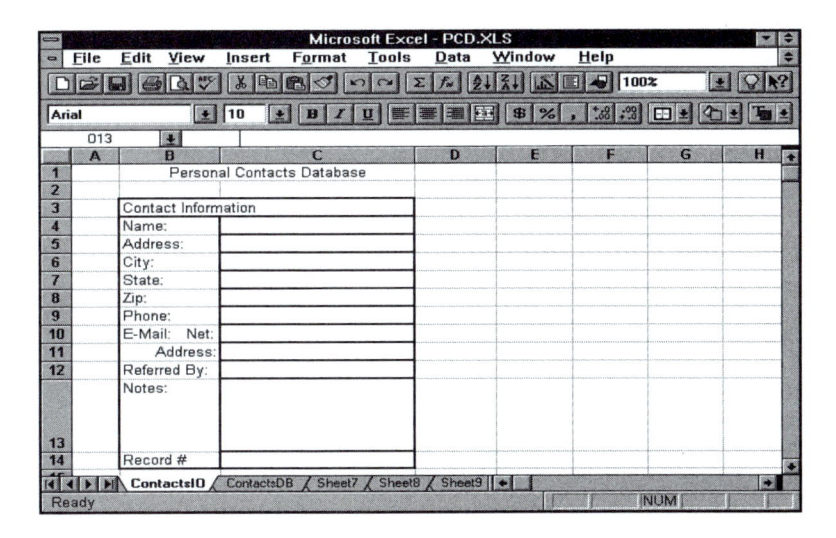

The next step is to gather data from the form and then store the data somewhere. There are several places that you can choose to store the data. You can store it in an internal data array, in an Excel database on another worksheet, in an external data file, or in an external database file. The different storage options offer different trade-offs between access speed and the size of the database. If you store the data in memory, either in an internal array or in another worksheet, it is available much faster than if you store it in a disk file. The trade-off is that you can store only a limited amount of data in memory, while you can store much more in a disk file. In

Chapter 16 ♦ Using a Worksheet as a Data Form

this first version of the personal contacts database, use an internal data array. Later chapters explore some of the other options.

For example, to extract and store the data from the ContactsIO worksheet, create the module, called ContactsDB, containing the code for the worksheet form version of the personal contacts database, as follows:

```
'
'   Contacts Database Program
'   Worksheet Form Version
'
Option Explicit 'Force all variables to be defined.
Option Base 1   'Make arrays start at 1.
Type DBEntry    'Define the structure of a single database entry.
  Name As String * 25
  Address As String * 25
  City As String * 15
  State As String * 2
  Zip As String * 10
  Phone As String * 20
  Net As String * 10
  NetAddr As String * 25
  Referral As String * 25
  Notes As String * 97
  RecNo As Integer
End Type    'Size of type is 256 bytes.
Dim theDB() As DBEntry     'The database array.
Dim numEntries As Integer  'Total number of entries.
Dim theEntryNum As Integer 'The currently displayed entry.
'
'   Initialize database
'
Sub InitializeIt()
  numEntries = 0
  ReDim theDB(1)
  theEntryNum = 0
End Sub
'
'   The Auto_Open procedure
'   runs whenever this workbook is opened.
'
Sub Auto_Open()
  InitializeIt    'Run the initialization procedure.
```

```vba
End Sub
'
' Transfer an entry to the database
'
Sub EntryToDB(anEntry As Integer)
  With Sheets("ContactsIO")
    theDB(anEntry).Name = .Range("Name").Value
    theDB(anEntry).Address = .Range("Address").Value
    theDB(anEntry).City = .Range("City").Value
    theDB(anEntry).State = .Range("State").Value
    theDB(anEntry).Zip = .Range("Zip").Value
    theDB(anEntry).Phone = .Range("Phone").Value
    theDB(anEntry).Net = .Range("E_Mail_Net").Value
    theDB(anEntry).NetAddr = .Range("E_Mail_Address").Value
    theDB(anEntry).Referral = .Range("Referral").Value
    theDB(anEntry).Notes = .Range("Notes").Value
    theDB(anEntry).RecNo = anEntry
  End With
End Sub
'
' Transfer a record to the form
'
Sub DBToEntry(anEntry As Integer)
  With Sheets("ContactsIO")
    .Range("Name").Value = theDB(anEntry).Name
    .Range("Address").Value = theDB(anEntry).Address
    .Range("City").Value = theDB(anEntry).City
    .Range("State").Value = theDB(anEntry).State
    .Range("Zip").Value = theDB(anEntry).Zip
    .Range("Phone").Value = theDB(anEntry).Phone
    .Range("E_Mail_Net").Value = theDB(anEntry).Net
    .Range("E_Mail_Address").Value = theDB(anEntry).NetAddr
    .Range("Referral").Value = theDB(anEntry).Referral
    .Range("Notes").Value = theDB(anEntry).Notes
    .Unprotect
    .Range("RecNo").Formula = theDB(anEntry).RecNo
    .Protect
  End With
End Sub
'
' Add a new entry
'
```

Chapter 16 ◆ Using a Worksheet as a Data Form

```
Sub NewEntry_Click()
  numEntries = numEntries + 1
  theEntryNum = numEntries
  ReDim Preserve theDB(numEntries) 'Expand the array.
  EntryToDB theEntryNum    'Write the entry to the array.
  DBToEntry theEntryNum    'Read the entry back to display theEntryNum.
End Sub
'
' Update an entry
'
Sub UpdateEntry_Click()
  If theEntryNum = 0 Then Exit Sub  'Exit if no entries are saved yet.
  EntryToDB theEntryNum   'Update the displayed entry.
End Sub
'
' Move forward one record
'
Sub Forward_Click()
  If numEntries = 0 Then Exit Sub  'No entries yet.
  theEntryNum = theEntryNum + 1
  'Test for an out of range entry number.
  If theEntryNum > numEntries Then theEntryNum = numEntries
  DBToEntry theEntryNum
End Sub
'
' Move backward one record
'
Sub Backward_Click()
  If numEntries = 0 Then Exit Sub  'No entries yet.
  theEntryNum = theEntryNum - 1
  'Test for an out of range entry number.
  If theEntryNum < 1 Then theEntryNum = 1
  DBToEntry theEntryNum
End Sub
'
' Delete a record
'
```

```
Sub DeleteEntry_Click()
  Dim I As Integer, buttons As Integer
  Dim theMsg As String
  If numEntries = 0 Then Exit Sub   'No entries yet.
  'Make sure the user really wants to do this.
  buttons = vbYesNo + vbDefaultButton2 + vbQuestion + _
      vbApplicationModal
  theMsg = "Are you sure you want to delete the current record?"
  If MsgBox(theMsg, buttons, "Delete Record") = vbNo Then Exit Sub
  'The user said yes, so delete the record and move the others down.
  If theEntryNum = numEntries Then   'It is the last entry.
    numEntries = numEntries - 1
    ReDim Preserve theDB(numEntries)
    theEntryNum = numEntries
  ElseIf theEntryNum = 0 Then   'No entry to delete.
    Exit Sub
  Else   'Shift everything down one.
    For I = theEntryNum + 1 To numEntries
      theDB(I - 1) = theDB(I)
      theDB(I - 1).RecNo = I - 1
    Next I
    numEntries = numEntries - 1
    ReDim Preserve theDB(numEntries)
  End If
  DBToEntry theEntryNum
End Sub
```

First, define some variables, including an array for storing the database data:

```
'
'    Contacts Database Program
'    Worksheet Form Version
'
Option Explicit   'Force all variables to be defined.
Option Base 1     'Make arrays start at 1.
Type DBEntry      'Define the structure of a single database entry.
  Name As String * 25
  Address As String * 25
  City As String * 15
  State As String * 2
  Zip As String * 10
```

Chapter 16 ♦ Using a Worksheet as a Data Form

```
    Phone As String * 20
    Net As String * 10
    NetAddr As String * 25
    Referral As String * 25
    Notes As String * 97
    RecNo As Integer
End Type    'Size of type is 256 bytes.
Dim theDB() As DBEntry     'The database array.
Dim numEntries As Integer  'Total number of entries.
Dim theEntryNum As Integer 'The currently displayed entry.
```

After the Option Explicit and Option Base 1 statements at the top of the module, a user-defined data type named DBEntry is defined to hold all the data from the worksheet. The strings are all defined with fixed lengths. Although you don't need to use fixed-length strings in this first version of the database, you will in later versions. For internally stored arrays, using fixed-length strings does not save more space than using variable-length strings. In fact, fixed-length strings probably use more space than variable-length strings, because they must store all the empty, unused spaces in the strings. The total size of the user-defined type is 256 bytes, a significant number that is explained in Chapter 19, "Saving Data in a Random Access File."

You declare the database array theDB() as a dynamic array with DBEntry type elements. You declare the array dynamically, without listing the number of elements, so that you can expand it later when you need storage space. Following the array declaration are a couple of other variable declarations. By declaring these variables at the top of the module, you make them available throughout the module.

The first procedure is an initialization procedure that initializes the global variables and the array to known values:

```
'
'   Initialize database
'
Sub InitializeIt()
  numEntries = 0
  ReDim theDB(1)
  theEntryNum = 0
End Sub
```

This procedure initializes everything to zero. You want to run this initialization procedure once, whenever you run the database program. You could run the procedure manually, by choosing the **T**ools **M**acro command each time that you run the database program, but you would likely forget to do so occasionally. To ensure that the routine runs each time that you run the database program, create an automatic macro that runs whenever you open the workbook:

```
'
' The Auto_Open procedure
' runs whenever this workbook is opened.
'
Sub Auto_Open()
  InitializeIt  'Run the initialization procedure.
End Sub
```

Any procedure named Auto_Open is automatically executed whenever you open the workbook that contains it. This Auto_Open procedure simply runs the initialization procedure.

Next, you need two procedures to transfer data from the worksheet to the internal array and from the internal array back to the worksheet. These two procedures aren't used directly, but are called by other procedures when they need to move the data.

```
'
' Transfer an entry to the database
'
Sub EntryToDB(anEntry As Integer)
  With Sheets("ContactsIO")
    theDB(anEntry).Name = .Range("Name").Value
    theDB(anEntry).Address = .Range("Address").Value
    theDB(anEntry).City = .Range("City").Value
    theDB(anEntry).State = .Range("State").Value
    theDB(anEntry).Zip = .Range("Zip").Value
    theDB(anEntry).Phone = .Range("Phone").Value
    theDB(anEntry).Net = .Range("E_Mail_Net").Value
    theDB(anEntry).NetAddr = .Range("E_Mail_Address").Value
    theDB(anEntry).Referral = .Range("Referral").Value
    theDB(anEntry).Notes = .Range("Notes").Value
    theDB(anEntry).RecNo = anEntry
  End With
End Sub
'
' Transfer a record to the form
'
Sub DBToEntry(anEntry As Integer)
  With Sheets("ContactsIO")
    .Range("Name").Value = theDB(anEntry).Name
    .Range("Address").Value = theDB(anEntry).Address
    .Range("City").Value = theDB(anEntry).City
    .Range("State").Value = theDB(anEntry).State
```

Chapter 16 ◆ Using a Worksheet as a Data Form

```
        .Range("Zip").Value = theDB(anEntry).Zip
        .Range("Phone").Value = theDB(anEntry).Phone
        .Range("E_Mail_Net").Value = theDB(anEntry).Net
        .Range("E_Mail_Address").Value = theDB(anEntry).NetAddr
        .Range("Referral").Value = theDB(anEntry).Referral
        .Range("Notes").Value = theDB(anEntry).Notes
        .Unprotect
        .Range("RecNo").Formula = theDB(anEntry).RecNo
        .Protect
    End With
End Sub
```

The first procedure, EntryToDB, moves an entry from the worksheet form to the data array. Using the With statement to name the worksheet that contains the data, the procedure then transfers the data into element anEntry of the global array theDB(). The second procedure, DBToEntry, performs just the opposite function.

The variable RecNo contains the element number in the data array that contains the data. The number is set by the procedure, not input by the user. Because you eventually will protect the data form, including this cell, the DBToEntry procedure must use the command Unprotect, change the value of RecNo (cell C14), and then use the command Protect to protect the sheet again.

Putting Buttons on a Worksheet

The next step is to add buttons to the worksheet and attach them to procedures that do the work of this program. Using buttons with attached procedures is much easier than having to use the Tools Macro command each time to run a procedure.

To attach a button, click the Drawing toolbar button to display the Drawing toolbar, click the Button tool button, and then draw the button on the worksheet. When you finish drawing the button, the Assign Macro dialog box appears automatically. Use that dialog box either to select a procedure to attach to the button, or to create a header for a new procedure.

> **Note:** It is common practice to name event procedures with the name of the event that triggers them. For example, to indicate that clicking the button named *buttonname* runs this procedure, name it *buttonname*_Click.

Add a procedure that copies new entries into the data array. This procedure creates a new entry in the data array that contains the data displayed on the worksheet. Add a related procedure that updates entries by replacing an entry in the data array with the data displayed on the worksheet.

Visual Basic for Applications *By* EXAMPLE

```
'
'   Add a new entry
'
Sub NewEntry_Click()
  numEntries = numEntries + 1
  theEntryNum = numEntries
  ReDim Preserve theDB(numEntries) 'Expand the array.
  EntryToDB theEntryNum    'Write the entry to the array.
  DBToEntry theEntryNum    'Read the entry back to display theEntryNum.
End Sub
'
'   Update an entry
'
Sub UpdateEntry_Click()
  If theEntryNum = 0 Then Exit Sub  'Exit if no entries are saved yet.
  EntryToDB theEntryNum    'Update the displayed entry.
End Sub
```

The NewEntry_Click procedure adds one to the number of entries, sets the current entry number to the number of the new entry, and redimensions the data array to hold that new entry. The procedure then copies the data from the worksheet to the entry, and then copies it back to ensure that everything is stored correctly and to update the entry number on the worksheet. The second procedure first tests to ensure that the entry is not the first one, and then simply inserts the data from the worksheet into the current entry.

To attach the procedures to buttons on the worksheet, follow these steps:

1. Switch to the worksheet.

2. Display the Drawing toolbar by choosing the **View Toolbars** command, checking the Drawing check box, and then selecting OK. Alternatively, you can click the Drawing button on the Standard toolbar.

3. Using figure 16.2 as a guide, select the Button tool button and then draw the New Entry button on the worksheet.

4. When the Attach Macro dialog box appears, select the NewEntry_Click procedure and then select OK.

5. Select the title on the top of the button and change it to **New Entry**.

6. Create the Update Entry button in the same manner as the first, attach it to the UpdateEntry_Click procedure, and change the button's name to **Update Entry**.

Chapter 16 ◆ Using a Worksheet as a Data Form

Figure 16.2

The layout of the buttons on the worksheet data form of the personal contacts database.

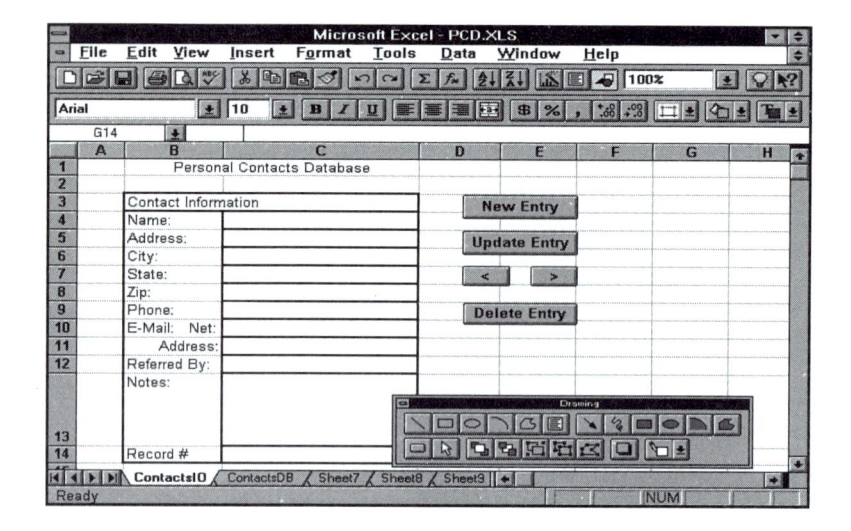

Note: While a button is selected, you can use the mouse to change its size and shape, and select and change the caption text on top of the button. If you click a button while it is unselected, you execute the attached procedure instead of selecting the button. To select a button or any object with an attached procedure without executing the attached procedure, use the selection tool that you turn on by clicking the Select button on the Drawing toolbar, or hold down the Ctrl key while selecting the button.

With the program as it currently exists, you can add or change data in your database, but you still have no way to move around in it. To enable users to move forward and backward in the database, you must add two more procedures:

```
'
' Move forward one record
'
Sub Forward_Click()
  If numEntries = 0 Then Exit Sub   'No entries yet.
  theEntryNum = theEntryNum + 1
  'Test for an out of range entry number.
  If theEntryNum > numEntries Then theEntryNum = numEntries
  DBToEntry theEntryNum
End Sub
'
' Move backward one record
'
```

220

```vba
Sub Backward_Click()
    If numEntries = 0 Then Exit Sub    'No entries yet.
    theEntryNum = theEntryNum - 1
    'Test for an out of range entry number.
    If theEntryNum < 1 Then theEntryNum = 1
    DBToEntry theEntryNum
End Sub
```

These two procedures increment or decrement the variable theEntryNum, test it to ensure that it is still in range, and finally display the selected entry. The following procedure deletes an entry:

```vba
'
' Delete a record
'
Sub DeleteEntry_Click()
    Dim I As Integer, buttons As Integer
    Dim theMsg As String
    If numEntries = 0 Then Exit Sub    'No entries yet.
    'Make sure the user really wants to do this.
    buttons = vbYesNo + vbDefaultButton2 + vbQuestion + _
        vbApplicationModal
    theMsg = "Are you sure you want to delete the current record?"
    If MsgBox(theMsg, buttons, "Delete Record") = vbNo Then Exit Sub
    'The user said yes, so delete the record and move the others down.
    If theEntryNum = numEntries Then    'It is the last entry.
        numEntries = numEntries - 1
        ReDim Preserve theDB(numEntries)
        theEntryNum = numEntries
    ElseIf theEntryNum = 0 Then     'No entry to delete.
        Exit Sub
    Else    'Shift everything down one.
        For I = theEntryNum + 1 To numEntries
            theDB(I - 1) = theDB(I)
            theDB(I - 1).RecNo = I - 1
        Next I
        numEntries = numEntries - 1
        ReDim Preserve theDB(numEntries)
    End If
    DBToEntry theEntryNum
End Sub
```

Chapter 16 ◆ Using a Worksheet as a Data Form

   This deletion procedure is more complicated than the other procedures, because it not only must delete an entry but also must move up all the entries after the deleted one to fill in the gap left by the deleted entry.
   The procedure first displays a dialog box that asks whether the user wants to delete the selected record. If the user answers No, the procedure is terminated immediately. The procedure has three main branches. The branch that handles the deletion depends on which entry in the array is to be deleted. If the entry to be deleted is the last one in the array, the procedure uses the first branch. The last entry is then simply deleted and the array size decreased. If the array has no entries (indicating that the user pressed the button by mistake), the procedure uses the second branch and thus does nothing. The procedure uses the last branch if the entry to be deleted is anything other than the last one. Before the procedure shortens the array by one entry, all the entries after the deleted one move up by one entry.
   Add three more buttons to the worksheet, as shown in figure 16.2, and then attach them to the three new procedures as previously described.

Locking the Worksheet

The next step is to clean up the layout of the worksheet data form, and to lock the worksheet so that users cannot inadvertently place data where they should not.
   To clean up and lock the data form, follow these steps:

1. Select the ContactsIO tab to display the worksheet data form.

2. Choose the **Tools Options** command, select the View tab, uncheck the Gridlines, Row & Column He**a**ders, Horizon**t**al Scroll Bar, **V**ertical Scroll Bar, and Sheet Ta**b**s check boxes, and then choose OK.

3. Adjust the height and width of the form window until the data form and the buttons are showing.

4. Choose the **Tools Protection Protect** Sheet command, and choose the OK button on the dialog box that appears.

   The worksheet should now look like figure 16.3, except without any data in the data form. You can try using the program now, by typing some data into the form and clicking the New Entry button to store it in the array. Don't put too much data in yet, because you have no way to save the data in this version of the program. Try clicking the two arrow buttons to move from one entry to the next. Also, try changing an entry and revising it with the Update Entry button and deleting an entry with the Delete Entry button.

Figure 16.3

The completed worksheet data form for the personal contacts database, with some data inserted.

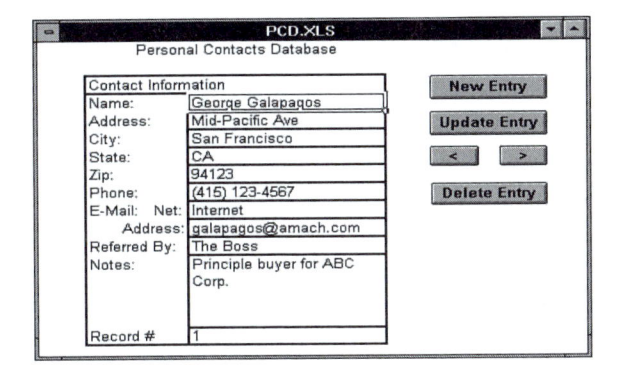

Summary

In this chapter, you learned how to use a worksheet as a data form. The cells on a worksheet are relatively straightforward to access, using the Sheets collection and Range objects. You can place buttons on a worksheet and attach them to procedures so that you can use them to manipulate the data on the worksheet.

In the next chapter, you develop a custom data form to perform the same function as the worksheet form that you developed in this chapter.

Review Questions

The answers to the review questions are in Appendix A.

1. Why should you name the cells on the worksheet and use the names in the Visual Basic procedures instead of simply using the cell references?

2. What is the trade-off at runtime between internal data storage in an array and external storage in a disk file?

3. What does the `Option Base 1` statement do?

4. What do you name a procedure that you want to run whenever a workbook is opened?

5. How do you select a button on a worksheet without executing the procedure attached to it?

Chapter 16 ◆ Using a Worksheet as a Data Form

Review Exercises

1. Add fast-forward and fast-backward buttons to the personal contacts database program to skip forward and backward 10 records at a time.

2. Write a variation of this program that stores the data on another worksheet rather than in a data array. Hint: You need to change only the array declarations and the DBToEntry and EntryToDB procedures.

3. Write a procedure that searches for a record that contains a specific name in the name field.

CHAPTER 17

Creating Custom Dialog Boxes

So far in this book, the primary input/output medium has been a worksheet cell, or the Immediate pane of the Debug window. Although good for experimenting with functions and values, the Immediate pane is not a good interface for a formal application. The worksheet is a good interface, but Visual Basic also enables you to use custom dialog boxes to create an elaborate user interface for an application.

In this chapter you learn about the following:

- ♦ How to use a dialog sheet to draw a dialog box
- ♦ The different input and output boxes and lists that you can attach to a dialog box
- ♦ How to attach procedures to custom dialog boxes

Opening a New Dialog Sheet

The capabilities of the dialog boxes that you have seen so far are fairly limited. You use such dialog boxes primarily to transfer single pieces of data between a program and the user. However, you often want to pass more than one piece of information, especially when the program receives information from the user.

An example of such a program is the personal contacts database that you developed in Chapter 16. This database uses a worksheet to create a data form so that the user can enter multiple pieces of input. To do this with the built-in dialog boxes, you could call the InputBox( ) function eight times, but that would be slow

Chapter 17 ◆ Creating Custom Dialog Boxes

and confusing for the user. Displaying an entry would also be a problem, because you would want to see the whole entry at one time.

For problems of this type, you use dialog sheets to create your own custom dialog boxes. A dialog sheet is quite different from anything else in Visual Basic, or Excel for that matter. A dialog sheet is a drawing environment in which you draw a dialog box, placing buttons, text, and edit fields where you want them.

To create a dialog box, you first open a dialog sheet with the **Insert Macro Dialog** command in Excel, or the **Tools Customize Forms** command in Project. Figure 17.1 shows the new dialog sheet that Excel then displays.

Figure 17.1
A new, blank dialog sheet created in Excel.

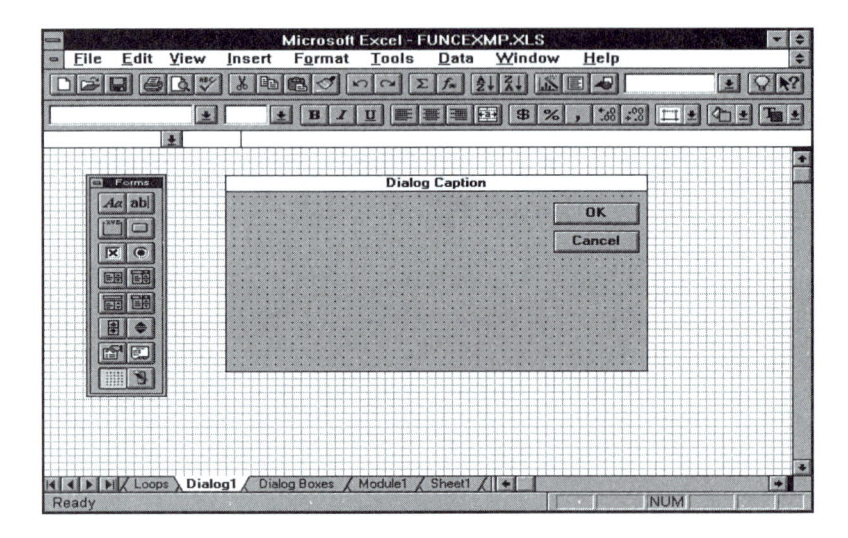

The new, blank *form*, as all windows are known in Visual Basic, is in the center of the screen, and the Forms toolbar is initially to the left. Each of the buttons on the toolbar enables you to draw different objects on the form to create your custom dialog box. Table 17.1 describes the function of each tool.

Table 17.1. The tools on the Forms toolbar.

Icon	Tool	Description
Aa	Label	Creates a text label
ab|	Edit Box	Creates a text box whose contents can be edited
	Group Box	Creates a visual grouping of buttons, and also defines a range for the option buttons

226

Icon	Tool	Description
	Create Button	Creates a command button
	Check Box	Creates a check box with a caption
	Option Button	Creates an option button with a caption for a set of exclusive options
	List Box	Creates a list box
	Drop-Down	Creates a drop-down list box
	Combination List Edit	Creates a combination list box and text edit box
	Combination Drop-Down Edit	Creates a combination drop-down list box and text edit box
	Scroll Bar	Creates a scroll bar
	Spinner	Creates a spinner

Running and Editing Option Buttons

Icon	Tool	Description
	Control Properties	Displays the properties of the selected object
	Edit Code	Displays the code attached to the selected object
	Toggle Grid	Turns the background grid on or off
	Run Dialog	Runs the dialog box just as if a running application were displaying it

In Project, the Dialog Editor opens with a blank form similar to that shown for Excel. Compared to Excel, Project offers a very limited choice of objects that you can place on a form. The only objects available on Project's toolbar are labels, text edit boxes, buttons, and groups.

Chapter 17 ♦ Creating Custom Dialog Boxes

Using Objects on a Form

To create a custom dialog box, select a tool for the object that you want, move to the form, and then click and drag a rectangle to hold the object. After placing objects on the form, you can move and reshape them. To move an object, select it and then drag its edge. To reshape an object, select and then drag its edit handle. *Edit handles* are the small black squares that appear around an object when you select it. Figure 17.2 shows examples of all the objects that you can attach to a form.

Figure 17.2

A custom form with examples of all the objects that you can draw on it.

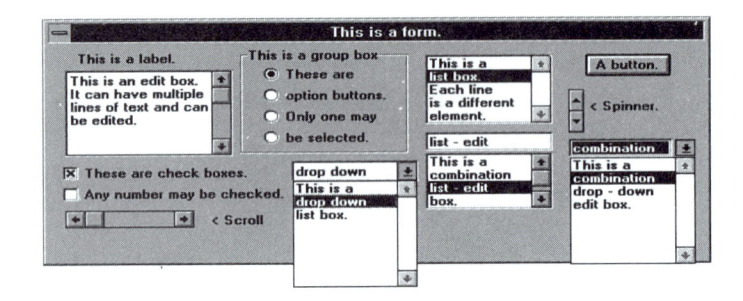

The Button Object

A new form, as shown in figure 17.1, already has an OK and Cancel button attached to it. To attach another button, click the Create Button button on the Forms toolbar. You can change the new button's caption by selecting it and then typing a new caption. However, to enable the button to do something, you must attach a procedure to it. To attach a procedure to a button, you select the button and then choose the **T**ools **A**ssign Macro command. In the Assign Macro dialog box that appears, select the procedure that you want to attach to the button or click New to create a new procedure header.

In addition to executing any procedures that you attach to them, buttons on dialog boxes have some special properties—Default, Cancel, Dismiss, and Help—that control what happens to the dialog box when the user presses them.

The Default property indicates which button is automatically clicked if the user presses the Enter key. Only one button on a form can have the Default property set. The Cancel property indicates which button is automatically clicked if the user presses the Esc key. Like the Default property, the Cancel property can be set for only one button on a form.

When you set the Dismiss property, the dialog box that the button is on is hidden when the procedure attached to the button completes. Also, control returns to the procedure that originally displayed the dialog box. (You can also explicitly hide the dialog box with the Hide method.) The Help property makes the button a help button. The user can press a help button to invoke the Help application.

Visual Basic for Applications By EXAMPLE

To change the properties of an object on a form, select the object, and then choose the **F**ormat Ob**j**ect command and the Control tab, or click the Control Properties button on the Forms toolbar. The dialog box that then appears displays only those properties that you can change at design time. For each of these objects, many properties are available that can change the object's appearance or operation. Check the online help for a complete list of the properties and methods for each object.

> **Note:** To access the objects on a dialog box, you must know each object's name. As you draw the objects on the dialog box, Visual Basic assigns default names like Label 2 and Button 3. When you select an object, its name appears in the Name box on the far-left side of the edit bar.
>
> To change an object's name, you can use the Name box or choose the **I**nsert **N**ame **D**efine command. For form objects, these two methods work slightly differently. When you select an object, type a name in the Name box, and then press Enter, you change the object's name from the default name that Visual Basic initially assigned to the object. The **I**nsert **N**ame **D**efine command creates a new name that refers to the default name, and the object is still named with the default name. Both methods give effectively the same results, but when the second method is used, Visual Basic must look up two names rather than one to locate the object referred to by a name.

The Label Object

A *label* is a simple string of text that the user cannot edit. You usually use a label to send a message to the user, or to supply more information about the other buttons and boxes on a form. Although an application's user cannot edit a label, a running application can change it.

To create a label, click the Label button, move to the form, and then click and drag a label of the appropriate size. Then select the label and type whatever text you want to display.

To use a running application to change the contents of a label, you change the label's Caption property. For example, the following procedure changes the contents of a label when the user presses a button:

```
'
' Button2_Click Macro
'
Sub Button2_Click()
  Sheets("Dialog1").Labels("Label 4").Caption = "Good Morning Matt"
End Sub
```

229

Chapter 17 ♦ Creating Custom Dialog Boxes

> **Note:** You can access all the objects on a form by using collections such as Labels( ) and EditBoxes( ). The argument to a collection is either the object's actual name or a number indicating which object in the collection to access. The number in the default object name (in the preceding example, the "4" in "Label 4") does *not* correspond to the object's place in the collection; rather it is the number of the object placed on the form (Label 4 is the fourth object placed on the form).

Assume that the Button2_Click procedure is attached to the ChangLabel button on the Dialog1 sheet. A label named Label 4 is drawn on the sheet. Initially the label's name is the same as its caption, as shown in figure 17.3. If you click the Run Dialog button on the Forms toolbar to run the dialog box, and then click the ChangLabel button on the dialog box, the label changes as shown on figure 17.4.

Figure 17.3
A dialog box with a label.

Figure 17.4
You change the contents of a label by changing the Caption property in a procedure.

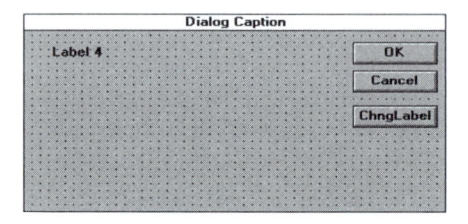

> **Note:** You can create the examples in this section by drawing the buttons and boxes on a form, attaching the code to a button, and then running the example by clicking the Run Dialog button on the Forms toolbar. You then execute the procedures by clicking the buttons to which the procedures are attached.

The Edit Box Object

An edit box is a framed box (see the upper-left corner of fig. 17.2) that contains text which the user can edit. An edit box is similar to a label, except that both a user and a running application can change its contents. To change the contents of an edit box, you use a procedure that is similar to the one for changing labels, but which uses the EditBoxes() collection rather than the Labels( ) collection, and uses the Text property rather than the Caption property.

An edit box has the MultiLine property. If you want the text in the edit box to word-wrap or to move down when the user presses Enter, you must set this property to True. An edit box also has the InputType property, which restricts the type of data that the user can type into the box. Set the value of InputType to one of the constant values: xlFormula, xlInteger, xlNumber, xlReference, or xlText. The default is xlText. You can set these properties in your code or by choosing the Format Object command.

The Group Box Object

The group box creates a visual grouping for other objects on a form. It also defines a group for a set of option buttons, as shown in the top-center of figure 17.2. To create a group box, click the group box button and then draw a group box on the form. Be sure to draw the group box before you draw any buttons that you want to include in the group. You use the Caption property of a group box to specify the string of text along its top edge.

The Check Box Object

A check box (see the left side of fig. 17.2) enables the user to select one or more options. The user can check any number of check boxes at any one time. When a check box is checked, its Value property is True; otherwise it is False. You access the Value property by using the CheckBoxes( ) collection, as in the following example:

```
isChecked = Sheets("Dialog1").CheckBoxes("Check Box 4").Value
```

The Caption property of a check box specifies the string of text to the right of the check box.

The Option Button Object

An option button enables the user to select one of a list of mutually exclusive options. Unlike check boxes, only one option button in a group can be selected at any one time, and selecting one button automatically unselects any other button that was previously selected. Option buttons are also known as radio buttons because of their similarity to the operation of the buttons on a car radio (for an older model car, anyway).

Chapter 17 ◆ Creating Custom Dialog Boxes

A group of option buttons consists of all option buttons drawn directly on a form. To have more than one group on a form, you first draw a group box, as shown in the top-center of figure 17.2, and then draw the option buttons on the group box. All the option buttons in the group box form one group.

As with a check box, an option button's Value property is True if the user presses it. You access the property just as you would for a check box, except that you use the OptionButtons( ) collection rather than the CheckBoxes( ) collection. The Caption property of an option button specifies the text to the right of the button.

> **Note:** Check boxes, option buttons, list boxes, scroll bars, and spinners all have a LinkedCell property that links the Value property of the control with the value in a worksheet cell. Changing either the Value of the control or the value in the cell changes the linked object.

The List Box Object

A list box provides the user with a list of values from which to select. The user cannot edit the contents of a list box, and can select only one element from the list. A list box is a little more difficult to implement than the other objects, because you cannot reliably add elements to a list at design time. Normally a running program adds elements to the lists in list boxes.

To add items to a list box, you have several options. The ListFillRange property of a list contains a reference to a worksheet range that contains the items to insert into the list. Setting this property to equal a string that contains a reference to some worksheet cells inserts the contents of those cells into the list. You can also set this property by choosing the Format Object command.

A more common method to fill a list is to use the List( ) property of the list box. The List( ) property behaves like an array of strings, with each element of the array containing an element from the list box. Changing any single element of List( ) changes the element in the list box, while equating List to an array replaces all the elements of the list box with the contents of the array. Using the List property in this way is useful, because it completely initializes a list, removing any old elements that might still remain in the list from the last time it was used.

Another common way to add items to a list is to use the AddItem method. This method takes two arguments: a string of text to insert into the list, and an index that specifies where to insert the item. If you omit the index, the new item is inserted at the end of the list.

Caution: If you initially load a list by using the ListFillRange property, changing an element by using the List( ) property breaks the connection between the list box and the worksheet range. Only those entries inserted with the List( ) property or the AddItem method are in the list. You can use the List( ) property to view the contents of the list box without breaking the connection.

For example, the following procedure first equates the List property to an array of names, which inserts those names into the list box. It then uses the AddItem method to insert the name Kyle at location 3 in the list. Figure 17.5 shows the result.

```
'
' Add items to a list.
'
Sub AddList_Click()
  Sheets("Dialog2").ListBoxes("List Box 4").List = _
    Array("Alec", "Adam", "Travis", "Corwin")
  Sheets("Dialog2").ListBoxes("List Box 4").AddItem "Kyle", 3
End Sub
```

Figure 17.5

Adding items to a list box using the List() property and the AddItem method.

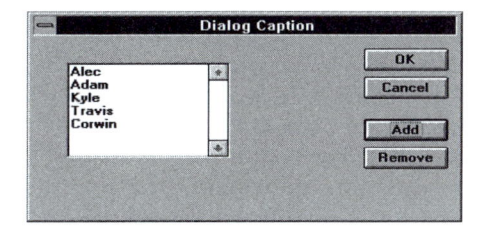

To remove items from the list, use the RemoveItem method, which takes two arguments: *index* and *count*. The *index* property is the first item in the list to remove, and *count* is the number of items to remove. The *count* argument defaults to 1 if you omit it. To remove all items in the list, use the RemoveAllItems method, or use the RemoveItem method with *index* equal to 1 and *count* greater than the number of items in the list.

For example, the following procedure removes the third item from the list box shown in figure 17.5. Figure 17.6 shows the resulting list, from which the name Kyle has been removed.

```
'
' Remove items from a list.
'
```

233

Chapter 17 ◆ Creating Custom Dialog Boxes

```
Sub RemoveList_Click()
  Sheets("Dialog2").ListBoxes("List Box 4").RemoveItem _
      Index:=3, Count:=1
End Sub
```

Figure 17.6
Removing the third item from a list box with the RemoveItem method.

To determine which item the user has selected from a list, use the ListIndex or Value properties of the list box. These properties contain the item number of the selected item in the list. To see the item itself, select the item from the List property by using the ListIndex property, as follows:

```
With Sheets("Dialog 2").ListBoxes("List Box 1")
  theContents = .List(.ListIndex)
End With
```

List Box 1 is then on dialog sheet Dialog 2, and theContents receives the text of the current selection in the list box. Note that the full specification of the list box object (`Sheets("Dialog 2").ListBoxes("List Box 1")`) applies to both the List and ListIndex properties. (Note the periods before each property. These periods link the properties to the argument of the With statement.)

The Drop-Down Object

A drop-down box is essentially the same as a list box, except that while the list box places the list in a scrollable window, the drop-down box places the list in a drop-down list. You access a drop-down box the same way as you access a list box, except that you use the DropDowns( ) collection rather than the ListBoxes( ) collection.

The Combination List-Edit Object

A combination list-edit box combines a list box and an edit box. The two boxes are linked so that if you select an item in the list box it appears in the edit box, where you can edit the item. In a combination list-edit box, the list box and the edit box are two separate boxes with different names and separate properties. You access the properties of each box independently, using the methods for accessing list boxes and edit boxes previously discussed.

The Combination Drop-Down Edit Object

A combination drop-down edit box is a drop-down list with an editable element. Although the box has the same capabilities of a combination list-edit box, it does not combine the two different objects. It is still a drop-down list, which you can access like any other drop-down list except that it now includes a Text property that gets the contents of the editable element.

If you select an item from the list, the Value and ListIndex properties contain the index to the selected item, and `.List(.ListIndex)` contains the text of the selected item. If you edit an item or type into the editable part of the box, the Value and ListIndex properties equal 0 and the text of the edited item is in the Text property.

> **Caution:** When an item in a combination drop-down edit box has been edited, don't try to get the value of `.List(.ListIndex)`. The ListIndex property has a value of 0 in this case, and `List(0)` results in an error because there is no element 0.

The Scroll Bar Object

The scroll bar button creates a vertical or horizontal scroll bar on the form. A scroll bar is actually just a sliding indicator. In its Value property it outputs a number that is determined by the location of the slider on the scroll bar. When you move the scroll bar's slider or thumb, the Value property changes proportionally. You can also use a scroll bar as an output indicator, because the slider moves proportionally when you change the value of the Value property. You can access the scroll bars by using the ScrollBars( ) collection.

The properties that control the range of values returned in the Value property, Min and Max, are accessible from the Format Object dialog box as well as in a program. Assign to these two properties the minimum and maximum values that you want the scroll bar's Value property to return. Set the LargeChange and SmallChange properties to the amount that you want the Value property to change when you click the body (page scroll) or the arrow (incremental scroll) of the scroll bar. All these properties are usually given integer values that are then converted to whatever range is needed in a program.

The Spinner Object

A spinner operates almost identically to a scroll bar, but without the slider to indicate where in the range the Value property is, and without the LargeChange property. It has Min, Max, and SmallChange properties that operate identically to those in a scroll bar. The Value property of a spinner is often linked to the Text property of an edit box so that the user can quickly change a small number by clicking the spinner. You access spinners by using the Spinners() collection.

Attaching Procedures to Custom Dialog Box Objects

Most of the controls on a form contain an OnAction property. The OnAction property contains the name of a procedure to execute when the control is changed. The buttons execute the procedure named in the OnAction property when they are clicked, list and drop-down boxes execute it when an item is selected, and text boxes execute it when the contents are changed in any way.

To set the OnAction property at design time, select the control, choose the **T**ools **A**ssign Macro command, and then in the Assign Macro dialog box select the procedure to attach to the control. Also, an executing application can set the OnAction property by equating the property to a text string that contains the name of the procedure to execute.

Displaying a Custom Dialog Box

To display a custom dialog box, you have several options, depending on your needs. From a dialog sheet, choosing the **T**ools **R**un **D**ialog command or clicking the Run Dialog button on the Forms toolbar activates the displayed form. This method is used primarily for debugging a dialog box and testing its operation. In Project, choose the **T**ools **C**ustomize **F**orms command to display a list of custom dialog boxes. From the list you can then select the one that you want to display.

From within a Visual Basic program, you can activate a custom dialog box by using its Show method. The syntax of the Show method is as follows:

```
object.Show
```

where *object* is a dialog sheet.

Execution of a Show method is similar to the calling of a procedure, in that control does not return to the statement following the one that contains the Show method until the dialog box is closed. To close a dialog box, set the Dismiss property of one of the command buttons to True or call the Hide method of the dialog sheet. The Hide method has the same syntax as the Show method.

In Project, use the Form or CustomForms statement to display a custom dialog box. The syntax of the Form statement is as follows:

```
Form(dialogName)
```

where *dialogName* is a string that contains the name of the custom dialog box to display. When the CustomForms statement has no arguments, and when it is executed, it displays the same dialog box as the **T**ools **C**ustomize **F**orms command. This dialog box enables you to select the dialog box to display.

Visual Basic for Applications **By EXAMPLE**

Adding a Custom Dialog Box to the Contacts Database

The personal contacts database that you developed in the last chapter uses a worksheet as the user interface. To demonstrate the use of the controls discussed in this chapter, you can change the user interface to a custom dialog box.

To create the custom dialog box, perform the following steps:

1. Open the PCD.XLS workbook. If you want to keep the previous version, copy the workbook before proceeding.

2. Choose the **Insert Macro Dialog** command to create a dialog sheet. Choose the **Format Sheet Rename** command (or double-click the sheet tab) to display a dialog box in which you change the name of the sheet to **ContactsDlog**. Select Dialog Caption and change it to **Personal Contacts Database**.

3. Select and delete the Cancel button, choose the OK button, and then change its caption to **Quit**.

4. Using figure 17.7 as a guide, draw, name, and add text to the following objects on the form. To change the name, select the object after you have drawn it on the form, select the object's name in the name box on the right of the edit bar, type the new name, and press Enter. To make the tab order correct, add the objects in the following order:

Control Type	Control Name	Text/Caption
Group Box Label		
Edit Box Label	DName	Contact Information Name:
Edit Box Label	DAddress	Address:
Edit Box Label	DCity	City:
Edit Box	DState	State
Edit Box Label	DZip	Zip:
Edit Box Label	DPhone	Phone:
Combination Drop-Down Edit Label	DE_Mail_Net	E-Mail: Net:
Edit Box Label	DE_Mail_Address	Address:
Edit Box Label	DReferral	Referred By:
Edit Box Label	DNotes / DRecNo	Notes: Record #:

Chapter 17 ♦ Creating Custom Dialog Boxes

> **Note:** The tab order determines which object on a form is selected whenever the user presses the Tab key. To simplify data input, you normally want the tab order to move logically from entry to entry. Initially, the tab order is the same order as you placed the objects on the form. To change the tab order, select an object and choose the **F**ormat **P**lacement command and then either the **B**ring to Front or **S**end to Back submenu command.

5. Select the Notes edit box, choose the **F**ormat **O**bject command, select the Control tab, check the **M**ultiline Edit and **V**ertical Scrollbar check boxes, and then choose OK.

6. Add the following buttons to the dialog box, change their captions as follows, and then use the **T**ools Assi**g**n Macro command to attach them to the indicated procedures.

Button Caption	Attached Procedure
New Entry	NewEntry_Click
Update Entry	UpdateEntry_Click
Delete Entry	DeleteEntry_Click
Find Name	FindName_Click

7. Attach a scroll bar on the form, name it ScrollEntry, and then attach to it the ScrollEntries_Click procedure (you'll create this procedure later; for now, simply type the name in the Assign Macro dialog box).

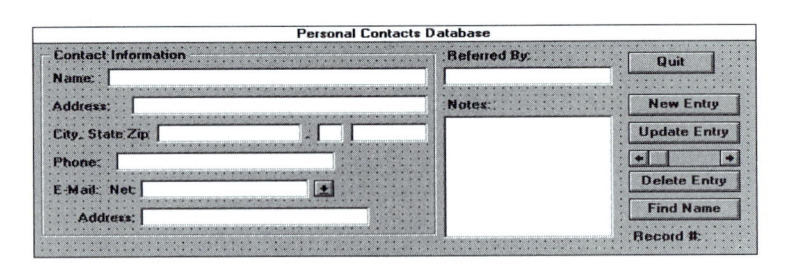

Figure 17.7
The layout of the custom form for the personal contacts database.

Now that you've finished designing the form, you must change the procedures to use the form rather than the worksheet. Because two procedures contain all the statements that access the user interface of the program, most of the changes are concentrated in those two procedures. You must modify the InitializeIt procedure slightly to display the new dialog box when the worksheet is opened and to initialize the scroll bar. To update the scroll bar range, you must modify the NewEntry_Click and the DeleteEntry_Click procedures. Also, two new procedures must handle the scroll bars and search for a name. All the other procedures are unchanged.

```
'
'   Contacts Database Program
'   Dialog Sheet Version
'
Option Explicit  'Force all variables to be defined.
Option Base 1    'Make arrays start at 1.
Type DBEntry     'Define the structure of a single database entry.
  Name As String * 25
  Address As String * 25
  City As String * 15
  State As String * 2
  Zip As String * 10
  Phone As String * 20
  Net As String * 10
  NetAddr As String * 25
  Referral As String * 25
  Notes As String * 97
  RecNo As Integer
End Type    'Size of type is 256 bytes.
Dim theDB() As DBEntry      'The database array.
Dim numEntries As Integer   'Total number of entries.
Dim theEntryNum As Integer  'The currently displayed entry.
'
'   Initialize database
'
Sub InitializeIt()
  numEntries = 0
  ReDim theDB(1)
  theEntryNum = 0
  Sheets("ContactsDlog").DropDowns("DE_Mail_Net").List = _
    Array("Compuserve", "Internet", "GEnie", "Prodigy")
  Sheets("ContactsDlog").ScrollBars("ScrollEntry").Min = 1
  Sheets("ContactsDlog").ScrollBars("ScrollEntry").Max = 1
  Sheets("ContactsDlog").Show
End Sub
'
' The Auto_Open procedure
' runs whenever this workbook is opened.
```

Chapter 17 ♦ Creating Custom Dialog Boxes

```
'
Sub Auto_Open()
  InitializeIt   'Run the initialization procedure.
End Sub
'
'  Add a new entry
'
Sub NewEntry_Click()
  numEntries = numEntries + 1
    Sheets("ContactsDlog").ScrollBars("ScrollEntry").Max =    numEntries
  theEntryNum = numEntries
  ReDim Preserve theDB(numEntries) 'Expand the array.
  EntryToDB theEntryNum   'Write the entry to the array.
    DBToEntry theEntryNum   'Read the entry back to display theEntryNum.
End Sub
'
'  Update an entry
'
Sub UpdateEntry_Click()
  If theEntryNum = 0 Then Exit Sub   'Exit if no entries are saved yet
.EntryToDB theEntryNum   'Update the displayed entry.
End Sub
'
' Transfer an entry to the database
'
Sub EntryToDB(anEntry As Integer)
  With Sheets("ContactsDlog")
    theDB(anEntry).Name = .EditBoxes("DName").Text
    theDB(anEntry).Address = .EditBoxes("DAddress").Text
    theDB(anEntry).City = .EditBoxes("DCity").Text
    theDB(anEntry).State = .EditBoxes("DState").Text
    theDB(anEntry).Zip = .EditBoxes("DZip").Text
    theDB(anEntry).Phone = .EditBoxes("DPhone").Text
    theDB(anEntry).Net = .DropDowns("DE_Mail_Net").Text
    theDB(anEntry).NetAddr = .EditBoxes("DE_Mail_Address").Text
    theDB(anEntry).Referral = .EditBoxes("DReferral").Text
    theDB(anEntry).Notes = .EditBoxes("DNotes").Text
    theDB(anEntry).RecNo = anEntry
  End With
```

```vba
End Sub
'
' Transfer a record to the form
'
Sub DBToEntry(anEntry As Integer)
  With Sheets("ContactsDlog")
    .EditBoxes("DName").Text = theDB(anEntry).Name
    .EditBoxes("DAddress").Text = theDB(anEntry).Address
    .EditBoxes("DCity").Text = theDB(anEntry).City
    .EditBoxes("DState").Text = theDB(anEntry).State
    .EditBoxes("DZip").Text = theDB(anEntry).Zip
    .EditBoxes("DPhone").Text = theDB(anEntry).Phone
    .DropDowns("DE_Mail_Net").Text = theDB(anEntry).Net
    .EditBoxes("DE_Mail_Address").Text = theDB(anEntry).NetAddr
    .EditBoxes("DReferral").Text = theDB(anEntry).Referral
    .EditBoxes("DNotes").Text = theDB(anEntry).Notes
    .Labels("DRecNo").Caption = "Record #: "theDB(anEntry).RecNo
    .ScrollBars("ScrollEntry").Value = anEntry
  End With
End Sub
'
' Scroll entries.
'
Sub ScrollEntries_Click()
  If numEntries = 0 Then Exit Sub 'No entries yet.
  theEntryNum = Sheets("ContactsDlog").ScrollBars("ScrollEntry").Value
  DBToEntry theEntryNum
End Sub
'
' Delete a record
'
Sub DeleteEntry_Click()
  Dim I As Integer, buttons As Integer
  Dim theMsg As String
  If numEntries = 0 Then Exit Sub  'No entries yet.
  'Make sure the user really wants to do this.
  buttons = vbYesNo + vbDefaultButton2 + vbQuestion _
      + vbApplicationModal
  theMsg = "Are you sure you want to delete the current record?"
  If MsgBox(theMsg, buttons, "Delete Record") = vbNo Then Exit Sub
```

Chapter 17 ◆ Creating Custom Dialog Boxes

```
      'The user said yes, so delete the record and move the others down.
      If theEntryNum = numEntries Then    'It is the last entry.
        numEntries = numEntries - 1
        ReDim Preserve theDB(numEntries)
        theEntryNum = numEntries
      ElseIf theEntryNum = 0 Then    'No entry to delete.
        Exit Sub
      Else    'Shift everything down one.
        For I = theEntryNum + 1 To numEntries
          theDB(I - 1) = theDB(I)
          theDB(I - 1).RecNo = I - 1
        Next I
        numEntries = numEntries - 1
        ReDim Preserve theDB(numEntries)
      End If
      Sheets("ContactsDlog").ScrollBars("ScrollEntry").Value = theEntryNum
      Sheets("ContactsDlog").ScrollBars("ScrollEntry").Max = numEntries
      DBToEntry theEntryNum
    End Sub
    '
    '   Find a name
    '
    Sub FindName_Click()
      Static theName As String
      Dim I As Integer
      Const TextComparison = 1
      If numEntries = 0 Then Exit Sub   'No entries yet.
      theName = InputBox("Input a name to search for.", "Find A Name", _
           theName)
      If theEntryNum <> numEntries Then
        For I = theEntryNum + 1 To numEntries
          If InStr(1, theDB(I).Name, theName, TextComparison) <> 0 Then
            'Found a matching entry
            theEntryNum = I
            DBToEntry theEntryNum
            Exit Sub
          End If
        Next I
```

```
    End If
    For I = 1 To theEntryNum
      If InStr(1, theDB(I).Name, theName, TextComparison) <> 0 Then
        'Found a matching entry
        theEntryNum = I
        DBToEntry theEntryNum
        Exit Sub
      End If
    Next I
    'No match found
    MsgBox "The name: " & theName & " was not found.", , "Find A Name"
End Sub
```

You change the InitializeIt procedure as follows, by adding the four lines in boldface to the previous version of the procedure:

```
'
'   Initialize database
'
Sub InitializeIt()
  numEntries = 0
  ReDim theDB(1)
  theEntryNum = 0
  Sheets("ContactsDlog").DropDowns("DE_Mail_Net").List = _
    Array("Compuserve", "Internet", "GEnie", "Prodigy")
  Sheets("ContactsDlog").ScrollBars("ScrollEntry").Min = 1
  Sheets("ContactsDlog").ScrollBars("ScrollEntry").Max = 1
  Sheets("ContactsDlog").Show
End Sub
```

The first new line loads the list in the combination drop-down edit box. The next two lines initialize the Min and Max properties of the scroll bar. The last line that you add uses the Show method to display the custom dialog box. To remove a dialog box, set the Dismiss property of a button on the dialog box to True (check it in the Format Object dialog box), and the dialog box closes when the button is pressed. Alternatively, you can use the Hide method, which you implement in the same way as the Show method.

Most of the connections to the user interface are in the EntryToDB and DBToEntry procedures. In each procedure, you change the references from the worksheet to the dialog sheet, as follows (again, the changes from the previous version of the procedure are indicated in boldface type):

```
'
' Transfer an entry to the database
'
```

Chapter 17 ♦ Creating Custom Dialog Boxes

```
Sub EntryToDB(anEntry As Integer)
  With Sheets("ContactsDlog")
    theDB(anEntry).Name = .EditBoxes("DName").Text
    theDB(anEntry).Address = .EditBoxes("DAddress").Text
    theDB(anEntry).City = .EditBoxes("DCity").Text
    theDB(anEntry).State = .EditBoxes("DState").Text
    theDB(anEntry).Zip = .EditBoxes("DZip").Text
    theDB(anEntry).Phone = .EditBoxes("DPhone").Text
    theDB(anEntry).Net = .DropDowns("DE_Mail_Net").Text
    theDB(anEntry).NetAddr = .EditBoxes("DE_Mail_Address").Text
    theDB(anEntry).Referral = .EditBoxes("DReferral").Text
    theDB(anEntry).Notes = .EditBoxes("DNotes").Text
    theDB(anEntry).RecNo = anEntry
  End With
End Sub
'
' Transfer a record to the form
'
Sub DBToEntry(anEntry As Integer)
  With Sheets("ContactsDlog")
    .EditBoxes("DName").Text = theDB(anEntry).Name
    .EditBoxes("DAddress").Text = theDB(anEntry).Address
    .EditBoxes("DCity").Text = theDB(anEntry).City
    .EditBoxes("DState").Text = theDB(anEntry).State
    .EditBoxes("DZip").Text = theDB(anEntry).Zip
    .EditBoxes("DPhone").Text = theDB(anEntry).Phone
    .DropDowns("DE_Mail_Net").Text = theDB(anEntry).Net
    .EditBoxes("DE_Mail_Address").Text = theDB(anEntry).NetAddr
    .EditBoxes("DReferral").Text = theDB(anEntry).Referral
    .EditBoxes("DNotes").Text = theDB(anEntry).Notes
    .Labels("DRecNo").Caption = "Record #:  &theDB(anEntry).RecNo
    .ScrollBars("ScrollEntry").Value = anEntry
  End With
End Sub
```

The NewEntry_Click and DeleteEntry_Click procedures both change the number of entries in the database. Therefore, you must add a statement to update the range of the scroll bar to the new range, as follows (the added lines are in boldface type):

```vb
'
'  Add a new entry
'
Sub NewEntry_Click()
   numEntries = numEntries + 1
   Sheets("ContactsDlog").ScrollBars("ScrollEntry").Max = numEntries
   theEntryNum = numEntries
   ReDim Preserve theDB(numEntries) 'Expand the array.
   EntryToDB theEntryNum    'Write the entry to the array.
   DBToEntry theEntryNum    'Read the entry back to displaytheEntryNum.
End Sub
'
' Delete a record
'
Sub DeleteEntry_Click()
   Dim I As Integer, buttons As Integer
   Dim theMsg As String
   If numEntries = 0 Then Exit Sub   'No entries yet.
   'Make sure the user really wants to do this.
   buttons = vbYesNo + vbDefaultButton2 + vbQuestion _
        + vbApplicationModal
   theMsg = "Are you sure you want to delete the current record?"
   If MsgBox(theMsg, buttons, "Delete Record") = vbNo Then Exit Sub
   'The user said yes, so delete the record and move the others down.
   If theEntryNum = numEntries Then    'It is the last entry.
      numEntries = numEntries - 1
      ReDim Preserve theDB(numEntries)
      theEntryNum = numEntries
   ElseIf theEntryNum = 0 Then    'No entry to delete.
      Exit Sub
   Else    'Shift everything down one.
      For I = theEntryNum + 1 To numEntries
         theDB(I - 1) = theDB(I)
         theDB(I - 1).RecNo = I - 1
      Next I
      numEntries = numEntries - 1
      ReDim Preserve theDB(numEntries)
   End If
   Sheets("ContactsDlog").ScrollBars("ScrollEntry").Value = theEntryNum
   Sheets("ContactsDlog").ScrollBars("ScrollEntry").Max = numEntries
   DBToEntry theEntryNum
End Sub
```

Chapter 17 ♦ Creating Custom Dialog Boxes

The new procedure, ScrollEntries_Click, handles the scroll bar. The procedure is similar to the Forward_Click and Backward_Click procedures, which it replaces. This procedure first checks for no entries, and then updates theEntryNum from the current value of the Value property of the scroll bar. You don't have to check for the minimum and maximum value of theEntryNum as you did for the buttons, because the scroll bar handles that automatically.

```
'
' Scroll entries.
'
Sub ScrollEntries_Click()
  If numEntries = 0 Then Exit Sub 'No entries yet.
  theEntryNum =  Sheets("ContactsDlog").ScrollBars("ScrollEntry").Value
  DBToEntry theEntryNum
End Sub
```

The following new procedure has been added to enable the user to search for a particular name in the database without having to step through each entry. The FindName_Click procedure displays an input box in which you type the name for which you are searching, and then searches for the first entry that includes the name.

```
'
'  Find a name
'
Sub FindName_Click()
   Static theName As String
   Dim I As Integer
   Const TextComparison = 1
   If numEntries = 0 Then Exit Sub   'No entries yet.
   theName = InputBox("Input a name to search for.", "Find A Name", _
       theName)
   If theEntryNum <> numEntries Then
     For I = theEntryNum + 1 To numEntries
       If InStr(1, theDB(I).Name, theName, TextComparison) <> 0 Then
         'Found a matching entry
         theEntryNum = I
         DBToEntry theEntryNum
         Exit Sub
       End If
```

```
    Next I
  End If
  For I = 1 To theEntryNum
    If InStr(1, theDB(I).Name, theName, TextComparison) <> 0 Then
      'Found a matching entry
      theEntryNum = I
      DBToEntry theEntryNum
      Exit Sub
    End If
  Next I
  'No match found
  MsgBox "The name: " & theName & " was not found.", , "Find A Name"
End Sub
```

This procedure has two parts: The first searches from the current position to the end of the database, and the second searches from the beginning of the database to the current position. In this way, consecutive searches locate the next entry with a matching name. If you use only one search that always starts at the beginning, you will always find the first occurrence of the name for which you are searching—for example, if your database includes the names John Smith, Jack Smith, and Harry Smith, and the name that you type in the input box is **smith**, you will always find John if you always start from the beginning of the database. However, by using the method implemented in this procedure, you find John on the first search, Jack on the second, and Harry on the third.

The first few lines of the procedure declare some variables. The variable theName is declared as Static so that it does not disappear between one call of the procedure and the next. The variable theName contains the string for which you are searching, and is also used as the default value in the InputBox() function. Because the FindName_Click procedure uses the variable in this way, each time you use the procedure, the previous string for which you searched is automatically inserted in the dialog box, so you don't have to retype the search string when doing multiple searches for the same string.

After the InputBox() function receives the string that it must search for, the current position in the database is tested. If it is not at the end, the first search loop is executed:

```
  For I = theEntryNum + 1 To numEntries
    If InStr(1, theDB(I).Name, theName, TextComparison) <> 0 Then
      'Found a matching entry
      theEntryNum = I
      DBToEntry theEntryNum
      Exit Sub
    End If
  Next I
```

Chapter 17 ◆ Creating Custom Dialog Boxes

This first search loop starts at one position beyond the current position in the database and extends to the end of the database. The InStr( ) function compares the string in theName to the string in the Name field of a database entry. Because the TextComparison option is used, the case of the text is ignored when the procedure compares the strings. If the string is found in the name field (InStr() <> 0), the procedure updates the current entry number to match this entry, displays the entry, and then ends. If the entry is not found, the procedure continues.

The second loop is executed if the search was unsuccessful in the first loop. The second loop operates identically to the first, except for the range of values of I used in the For statement. In the first loop, I ranged from one entry beyond the current location to the end of the database. In this second loop, I ranges from the beginning of the database back to the current location. If the second loop fails, the procedure calls the MsgBox( ) function to display a message reporting the failure, and then the procedure ends.

Save the workbook, and then run the personal contacts database. Use the **Tools Macro** command to run the InitializeIt procedure. If you close and then open this workbook, the procedure runs automatically, as shown in figure 17.8.

Figure 17.8

This custom dialog box is the user interface for the dialog box version of the personal contacts database.

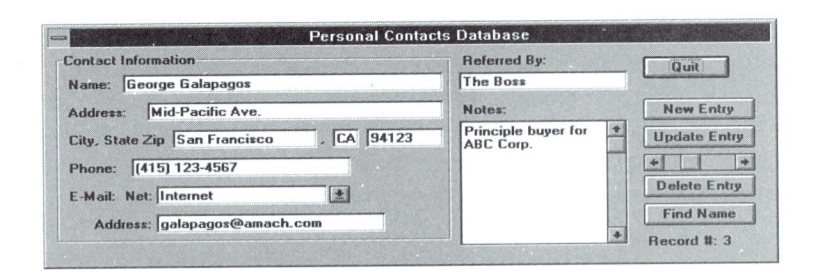

Using Dialog Box Objects on a Worksheet

All the dialog box objects except the edit box can be attached to a worksheet as well as to a dialog sheet. To do so, switch to the worksheet in which you want to place the controls, display the Forms toolbar, and draw the objects as you would on a dialog sheet. You access the objects just as you would if they were on a dialog sheet. Figure 17.9 shows the same controls (except the edit box) as figure 17.2 attached to a worksheet.

Figure 17.9

A worksheet with controls attached to it in the same manner as for a dialog sheet.

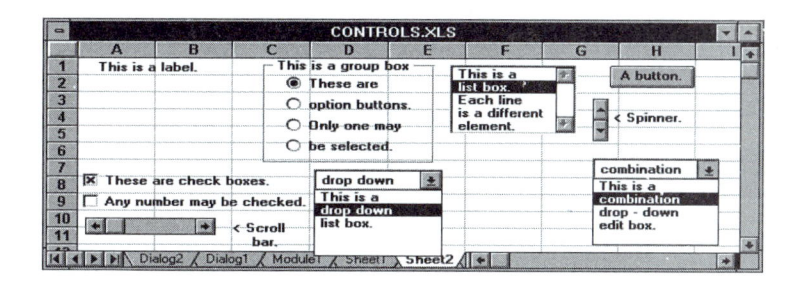

Summary

In this chapter, you learned to use dialog sheets to create the user interface of a custom application. Although you can use a worksheet as the interface, a custom dialog box provides a much more polished interface without all the clutter (cells, gridlines, row and column headings, and so forth) of a worksheet. You create custom dialog boxes on a dialog sheet, draw control objects on them, and then attach procedures to the objects. To display a custom dialog box, you use the Show method; to close the dialog box, you use the Hide method of the form or the Dismiss property of a control.

In the next chapter, you learn about disk files and how you can store data in them rather than in memory.

Review Questions

The answers to the review questions are in Appendix A.

1. How do you display a custom dialog box in Excel? In Project?
2. How do you open a new dialog sheet?
3. What two buttons are on a new blank dialog sheet form?
4. Explain the difference between a label and an edit box.
5. What is a group box for?
6. Explain the difference between option buttons and check boxes.
7. Explain the difference between scroll bars and spinners.
8. What is the Default property of a button? The Cancel property?
9. What is the tab order?

Chapter 17 ◆ Creating Custom Dialog Boxes

Review Exercises

1. Create a dialog box that gets your name and phone number, and then uses the MsgBox( ) function to display them.

2. Expand the FindName_Click procedure so that the user can select the field to search instead of only searching the Name field.

3. Add a new procedure that adds any new entries (those that are typed in the edit box and are not currently on the list) to the list in the combination drop-down edit box, and then attach the new procedure to the drop-down box.

4. Expand the FindName_Click procedure so that it uses a copy of the personal contacts database form to insert search strings into one or more fields. Add two search buttons: an And button that returns records only when all the fields match, and an Or button that returns records if any of the fields match.

CHAPTER 18

Saving Data in a Sequential Disk File

Up to this point, you have saved programs as part of an Excel or Project workbook, which included any data that happened to be on a worksheet. You have saved data in memory, but the data went away when you quit the application. In this and the next chapter, you learn to save your data in disk files so that you can use it again.

In this chapter you learn the following:

- ♦ How sequential and random files differ
- ♦ How to open sequential files
- ♦ How to save data in sequential files
- ♦ How to read data from sequential files

Sequential and Random Access Files

Visual Basic uses two main types of disk file: sequential and random access. (Actually, there are three types if you include worksheets, which Visual Basic can also use to store data. However, Visual Basic cannot read or write worksheet files directly; instead, it must write data into an open worksheet and then have Excel save it.)

The ways that sequential and random access files store data on a disk differ significantly. Sequential access files are read or written sequentially, from the beginning of the file to the end. Text files, such as the README files that come with many applications, are sequential access files. To reach any specific piece of information in a sequential file, you must start at the beginning and then read down the file until you find the information that you want.

Random access files are based on fixed-length records that are read or written randomly, in any order. A sequential file is either read or written, but a random access file can be both read and written at the same time.

Most database applications also use random access files, because such files enable the database to read any record in the file directly without having to read all the other records that precede it in the file. After reading a record, the database can change it and write it back into its original location on the disk without disturbing all the other records in the file. A similar application created with Visual Basic would use the same capability.

A limitation of random access files is that the length of a record is fixed. However, this limitation enables Visual Basic to locate quickly a record on the disk. For example, to read the eighth record in a file, Visual Basic moves down seven full records and then reads the next. If the records did not have a fixed length, you would have to maintain a separate index to determine where one record ends and the next begins.

Reading and Writing Sequential Files

The most common file type is the sequential file. Any file that you read into memory at one time should be a sequential file. Most unformatted text files are sequential files, as are most application files. Sequential access files in Visual Basic are text files, in that the data written to them is in the form of strings of ANSI text characters. If you open a Visual Basic sequential file with a word processor, you usually will see that it is readable.

Because the numbers are stored as text, sequential files do not provide the most efficient means of storing numeric values. However, sequential files do have definite advantages. For example, you can edit sequential files with a word processor, and you don't need a special application to display or modify them.

Opening A File

Before Visual Basic can do anything with a disk file, you must open the file and attach a file number to it. *File numbers* are small integer numbers that are associated with a file when you open it. The reading and writing commands use file numbers to specify which file to read or write.

To open a sequential file, use an Open statement with the following syntax:

```
Open filename For mode As filenumber
```

The argument *filename* is a string that contains the name and path of the file that you want to open. If the file is in the current directory, you need only supply the file name. If the file is not in the current directory, you must supply a complete path to the file. If you want the user to select which file to open, use the GetOpenFilename( ) function to display a standard File Open dialog box, as described in Chapter 15, "Using Built-In Dialog Boxes," in the section "Using Other Built-In Dialog Boxes." The string that the function returns contains the file name and path that you need to use in the Open statement.

The argument *mode* specifies the type of file that you want to open, and how you want to open it. The mode must be one of the literals Input, Output, or Append for sequential access files, or Random for a random access file. Binary mode access is also allowed for special situations. The Input mode opens a file to be read, and the Output mode opens a file to be written. Both of these modes open a sequential access file at the beginning. The Append mode opens a file at the end for writing, so that you can add to an existing file without having to rewrite the whole file first. Attempting to open a nonexistent file using the Input mode results in an error; however, if you open a nonexistent file using the Output or Append mode, the file is created.

The argument *filenumber* specifies the file number that you want to assign to the file. Usually you assign 1 to the first file that you open, 2 to the second, and so on. If a file is closed, you can reuse its file number, but you must not try to open a file using a file number that is already in use.

When you are unsure of which file numbers are available, use the FreeFile function to assign an available file number to a variable, and then use that variable in the Open statement and in any statements that read or write the file. For example, the following few lines open a sequential file for input:

```
FileNum1 = FreeFile
Open "myfile.txt" For Input As FileNum1
```

The file name is MYFILE.TXT, which is being opened at the beginning for reading, and the FreeFile function is used to select the next available file number.

Closing a File

When you're finished working with a file, close it with the Close statement. The Close statement takes a file number as an argument that tells it which file to close.

The syntax for the Close statement is as follows:

```
Close #fileNum
```

If you leave out the *fileNum* argument, Visual Basic closes all open files.

Chapter 18 ◆ Saving Data in a Sequential Disk File

Printing to a File

When a file is open for output, you can use the Print statement to write data to it. The data written by the Print statement generates text that is similar to that which is output to a printer.

For example, try executing the following statements in the Immediate pane of the Debug window:

```
Print "Hello World"
Hello World
Print 5
 5
a = 5
Print a
 5
```

Remember that when you use a Print statement in the Immediate pane, its output appears in the following line. If this same Print statement were printing to a disk file, only its output would appear in that file. As shown here, if you print some text, that text is written in the file. If you print a number, that number is placed in the file. If you print a variable, the value of that variable is placed in the file.

If you place multiple items on a line to be printed, they are spaced at the fixed tab stops every 14 characters, as in the following examples:

```
Print 1, 2, 3, 4
 1             2             3             4

Print "One","Two","Three","Four"
One           Two           Three         Four
```

However, if you use semicolons rather than commas, the printed items are printed without spacing:

```
Print 1; 2; 3; 4
 1  2  3  4

Print "One";"Two";"Three";"Four"
OneTwoThreeFour
```

> **Note:** When you enter semicolons between the numbers in a Print statement, the output seems to space each number at every third character space. This spacing results from the Print statement having to convert each number to a string of text. As the statement does this, it adds a leading and trailing blank space for each number, which results two blank spaces between each number.

254

Visual Basic for Applications

To control how you print things, use the Format( ) function. This function takes two arguments and returns a formatted string. The first is a variable that contains the number to be printed, and the second is a formatting string that shows how you want to print the number. This string is similar to that which you use to format the contents of cells in Excel. Pound signs (#) are number placeholders, commas (,) insert a comma every three characters, the period (.) marks the location of the decimal point, and a zero (0) marks a required character position. See the online reference for a complete list of the formatting characters.

The following statements executed in the Immediate pane of the Debug window demonstrate how the Format( ) function works:

```
a = 1234.567
print a
 1234.567
Print a, Format(a, "#,###.00"),Format(a, "#.0")
 1234.567    1,234.57      1234.6
a = 0.1234
Print a, Format(a, "#,###.00"),Format(a, "0.00"),Format(a,"00.00")
 0.1234       .12          0.12           00.12
a = 1234.
Print a, Format(a, "#,###.00"),Format(a, "0.00"),Format(a,"00.0")
 1234        1,234.00      1234.00        1234.0
```

First the variable a is loaded with a number, and then the variable is printed with different Format( ) functions. Note that the number is rounded if it does not fit in the formatting string. Also note that leading and trailing zeros are inserted to fill the required printing positions.

To print to a disk file rather than in the Immediate pane, follow the Print keyword with a pound sign, the file number, and a comma, as follows:

```
Print #fileNum, arglist
```

where *fileNum* is the file number that you used when you opened the file, and *arglist* is what you want to print.

For example, to print the preceding values into a file named SCRATCH.DAT using commands in the Immediate pane of the Debug window, you must first select a file number and then open the file for output, as follows:

```
Open "SCRATCH.DAT" For Output As 1
```

18 ♦ Saving Data in a Sequential Disk File

Next you print the data into the file and then close it:

```
Print #1, "Hello World"
Print #1, 5
a = 5
Print #1, a
Print #1, 1, 2, 3, 4
Print #1, 1; 2; 3; 4
Print #1, "One","Two","Three","Four"
Print #1, "One";"Two";"Three";"Four"
Print #1, a
Print #1, a, Format(a, "#,###.00"),Format(a, "#.0")
a = 0.1234
Print #1, a,Format(a, "#,###.00"),Format(a, "0.00"),Format(a, "00.00")
a = 1234.
Print #1, a, Format(a, "#,###.00"),Format(a, "0.00"),Format(a, "00.0")
Close #1
```

If you now use a word processor to open the file SCRATCH.DAT, as shown in figure 18.1, that the data is printed exactly as it was displayed previously in the Immediate pane.

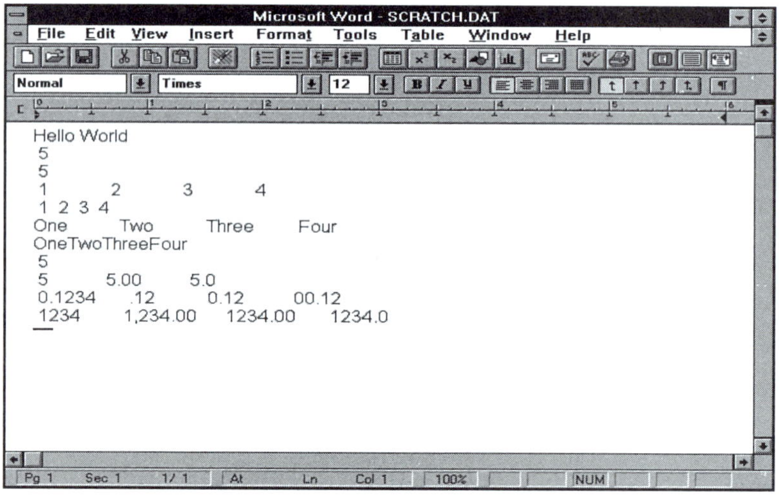

Figure 18.1

The SCRATCH.DAT file, created by a Print statement writing data to a disk file and viewed with a word processor such as Microsoft Word.

```
Hello World
5
5
1       2       3       4
1 2 3 4
One     Two     Three   Four
OneTwoThreeFour
5
5       5.00        5.0
0.1234  .12     0.12        00.12
1234    1,234.00 1234.00    1234.0
```

Writing to a File

When you use the Print statement, as the data is written into a disk file it is formatted nicely into a readable form that is suitable for a text document. However, if you intend to read that data back into a Visual Basic program, you should save the data using the Write statement rather than Print. The Write statement works much like the Print statement, but delimits the printed data with commas and quotation marks. These commas and quotation marks make it easier for Visual Basic to determine where one data item ends and the next begins. If you intend to store your data and then read it back later, use Write rather than Print.

You cannot examine the output of the Write statement in the Immediate pane, because the Write statement cannot print to the Immediate pane. However, you can do as you did in the last example for the Print statement, and simply write the data into a disk file named SCRATCH.DAT and then view that data with a word processor.

For example, the following statements executed in the Immediate pane write exactly the same data into the disk file as you used for the Print statement, but use the Write statement instead. After you execute these statements, view the disk file with a word processor as before.

```
FNum = FreeFile
Open "SCRATCH.DAT" For Output As FNum
Write #FNum, "Hello World"
Write #FNum, 5
a = 5
Write #FNum, a
Write #FNum, 1, 2, 3, 4
Write #FNum, 1; 2; 3; 4
Write #FNum, "One","Two","Three","Four"
Write #FNum, "One";"Two";"Three";"Four"
Write #FNum, a
Write #FNum, a, Format(a, "#,###.00"),Format(a, "#.0")
a = 0.1234
Write #FNum,a,Format(a,"#,###.00"),Format(a,"0.00"),Format(a,"00.00")
a = 1234.
Write #FNum,a,Format(a,"#,###.00"),Format(a,"0.00"),Format(a,"00.0")
Close #FNum
```

Note the differences between the results for the Write statement shown in figure 18.2 and the results for the Print statement shown in figure 18.1. The Write statement separates each data item with commas, and encloses each string with quotation marks. Because the Format( ) function returns a number as a string of text, such strings are also enclosed in quotation marks. Using the quotation marks and commas makes it much easier for the Input statement (discussed in the next section)

Chapter 18 ◆ Saving Data in a Sequential Disk File

to separate the different items that are printed in the file. Without the quotation marks and commas, you cannot tell where one printed item ends and the next begins.

Also note that instead of using an explicit file number as before, here the FreeFile function is used to select a file number. That file number is stored in the variable FNum, and the variable is used everywhere that the file number is needed.

Figure 18.2

The SCRATCH.DAT file, created by a Write statement writing data to a disk file and then viewed with a word processor.

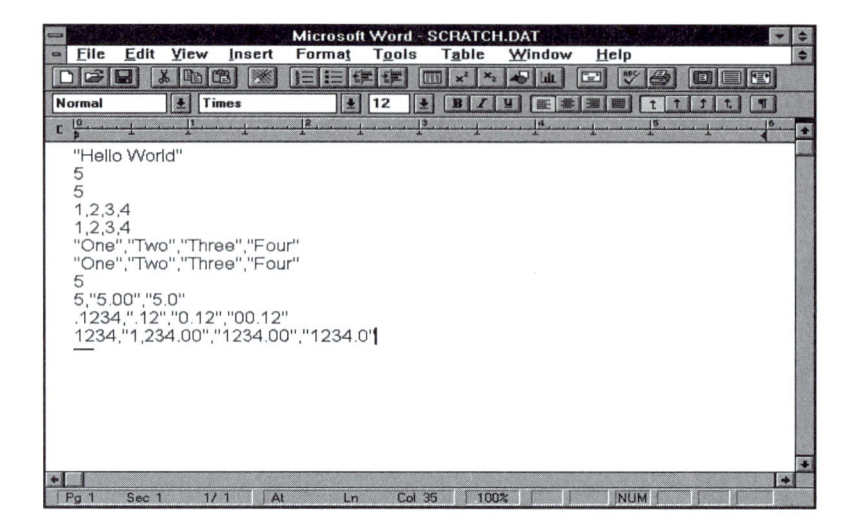

```
"Hello World"
5
5
1,2,3,4
1,2,3,4
"One","Two","Three","Four"
"One","Two","Three","Four"
5
5,"5.00","5.0"
.1234,".12","0.12","00.12"
1234,"1,234.00","1234.00","1234.0"
```

Inputting from a File

To read data from a file, use the Input and Line Input statements. The first argument for each consists of a pound sign, a file number, and a comma, to indicate which open file to read from. The arguments that follow the comma are variable names to be filled with data from the file.

For the Input statement, the variables that follow the comma determine which and how much data to read from the file. White space, such as spaces or tabs at the beginning of a line, is always ignored. If a variable is a numeric variable, Visual Basic tries to read a number from the file. The first nonblank character is assumed to be the start of the number, and Visual Basic continues reading until it encounters something that cannot be part of a number, such as a blank, a comma, an alphabetic character, or the end of the line. If the variable is a string variable, Visual Basic reads the first nonblank character into the string and stops reading if it encounters a comma or the end of the line. If the first nonblank character is a quotation mark, then the first character after the quotation mark is the first character read into the string, and all characters until the next quotation mark or the end of the line are part of the string, including commas.

As you can see from this description and the text in figure 18.2, the Write and Input statements are designed to work together to write data into a file and accurately retrieve it. The Print statement, on the other hand, is designed to create a text file that humans can read.

Complementing the Input statement is the Line Input statement. The Line Input statement stores in a single string argument all the characters found in a single line from the file. The string variable stores all the characters, including leading white space, commas, and quotation marks. The Line Input statement is used to read into a program an exact duplicate of the contents of a line in a file. The only characters not included in the Line Input statement are the carriage return and line feed pair at the end of the line.

For example, use Input and Line Input statements in the Immediate pane to read the contents of the file SCRATCH.TXT, shown in figure 18.3. You must first open the file and then read it with the Input and Line Input statements. The first line of the file is read with the statements shown here:

```
Open "SCRATCH.TXT" For Input As 100
Input #100, B$, C$, D$
Print B$
The number
Print C$
shown here
Print D$
is 12.643 more.
```

The first line opens the file and the second reads data from the first line into three separate string variables. The next lines print in the Immediate pane the contents of those string variables. The following is the first line of the file:

```
The number, shown here, is 12.643 more.
```

The first string variable gets the text from the beginning of the line to the first comma, the second gets the text from the first comma to the second, and the third variable gets the text from the second comma to the end of the line.

The second line in the file is as follows:

```
"The number, shown here, is 12.643 more."
```

Because this line is enclosed in quotation marks, you get the whole line when you read it into a single string variable and then print the contents of that variable in the Immediate pane:

```
Input #100, B$,
Print B$
The number, shown here, is 12.643 more.
```

Chapter 18 ◆ Saving Data in a Sequential Disk File

Figure 18.3

The contents of the text file SCRATCH.TXT.

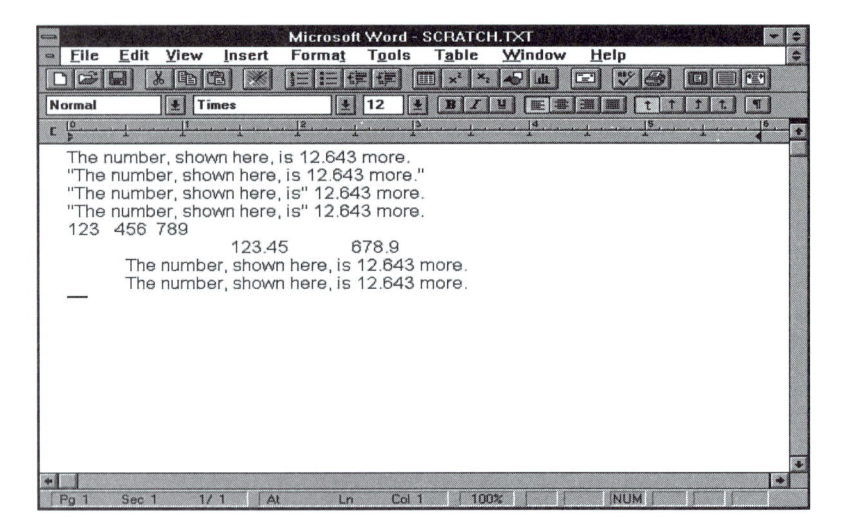

```
The number, shown here, is 12.643 more.
"The number, shown here, is 12.643 more."
"The number, shown here, is" 12.643 more.
"The number, shown here, is" 12.643 more.
 123  456 789
              123.45       678.9
      The number, shown here, is 12.643 more.
      The number, shown here, is 12.643 more.
___
```

Here's the next line in the file:

```
"The number, shown here, is" 12.643 more.
```

Note that the first half of the line is enclosed in quotation marks, but not the second half. In the Immediate pane, if you read this line into a string variable and a numeric variable, the string variable gets the data between the quotation marks, and the numeric variable gets the number. If you read from the file again with a string variable as an argument, the string variable gets the last part of the line.

```
Input #100, B$,a
Print B$
The number, shown here, is
Print a
 12.643
Input #100, B$
Print B$
more.
```

The next line is the same as the previous one. Reading it in the Immediate pane with the Line Input statement places the whole line in the string variable, including commas and quotation marks:

260

```
Line Input #100, B$
Print B$
"The number, shown here, is" 12.643 more.
```

Line 5 contains three numbers separated with spaces:

```
123   456   789
```

Reading this line in the Immediate pane with three numeric variables as arguments extracts the three numbers. The spaces between the numbers terminate one number and start the next:

```
Input #100, e, f, g
print e
 123
print f
 456
print g
 789
```

The next line in the file also contains numbers, but has a lot of white space at the beginning of the line and between the numbers:

```
              123.45         678.9
```

If this line is read in the Immediate pane with two numeric variables as arguments, the white space is ignored:

```
Input #100, e, f
print e
 123.45
print f
 678.9
```

The beginning of line 7 also contains white space:

```
         The number, shown here, is 12.643 more.
```

Read this line in the Immediate pane with a single string variable as an argument. The initial white space is ignored and the variable receives the text from the first nonblank character to the first comma. The Line Input statement is useful in such situations as when you want to read something from the beginning of a line but then want to skip over the rest to the next line. The Line Input statement reads into a string variable everything from the current position to the end of the line:

```
Input #100, B$
print B$
The number
```

Chapter 18 ♦ Saving Data in a Sequential Disk File

```
Line Input #100, B$
Print B$
  shown here, is 12.643 more.
```

The last line in the file is identical to the previous line. If you read it in the Immediate pane with a Line Input statement, you get the whole line, including all the white space at the beginning:

```
Line Input #100, B$
Print B$
            The number, shown here, is 12.643 more.
Close #100
```

Saving the Personal Contacts Database in a Sequential File

In the last chapter, when you exited the current version of the personal contacts database, you lost all its data because the program stores it in the computer's RAM memory. For this reason, the program is largely useless, because whenever you run it, you must retype all its data. To make it useful, you need a way to copy the database from RAM memory to a disk file when you are done with the program, and to copy it from the disk file and back into RAM memory when you restart the program later. The following example adds the capability to save data to the personal contacts database.

First, if you want to keep the current version of the program, save it with a different name. Then add two buttons to the form: one to save the database in a disk file, and another to open the disk file and load the data back into memory. Figure 18.4 shows these buttons added on the right side of the dialog box.

Figure 18.4
Layout of the sequential file version of the personal contacts database.

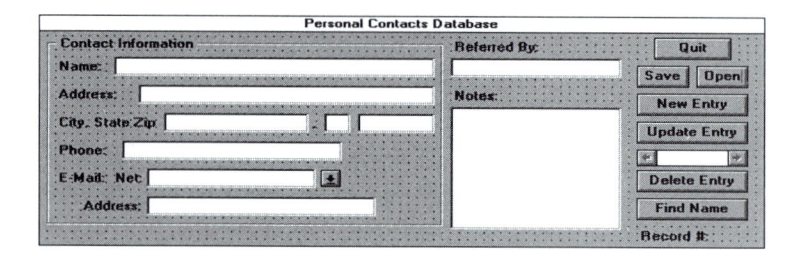

You then must attach to the two new buttons the code that saves the data into a file or reads it from a file. The following listing shows the modified contacts database program. Changes in the program from the previous version are highlighted with boldface type. The two new procedures, Save_Click and Open_Click, are attached to the Save and Open buttons on the form.

```
'
'   Personal Contacts Database Program
'   Sequential File Version
'
Option Explicit 'Force all variables to be defined.
Option Base 1   'Make arrays start at 1.
Type DBEntry    'Define the structure of a single database entry.
  Name As String * 25
  Address As String * 25
  City As String * 15
  State As String * 2
  Zip As String * 10
  Phone As String * 20
  Net As String * 10
  NetAddr As String * 25
  Referral As String * 25
  Notes As String * 97
  RecNo As Integer
End Type    'Size of type is 256 bytes.
Dim theDB( ) As DBEntry      'The database array.
Dim numEntries As Integer    'Total number of entries.
Dim theEntryNum As Integer   'The currently displayed entry.
Dim theFileName As String    'The current file name.
'
'   Initialize database
'
Sub InitializeIt( )
  numEntries = 0
  ReDim theDB(1)
  theEntryNum = 0
  Sheets("ContactsDlog").DropDowns("DE_Mail_Net").List = _
    Array("Compuserve", "Internet", "GEnie", "Prodigy")
  Sheets("ContactsDlog").Show
  Sheets("ContactsDlog").ScrollBars("ScrollEntry").Min = 1
  Sheets("ContactsDlog").ScrollBars("ScrollEntry").Max = 1
  theFileName = ""
  With Sheets("ContactsDlog")
    .EditBoxes("DName").Text = ""
    .EditBoxes("DAddress").Text = ""
    .EditBoxes("DCity").Text = ""
    .EditBoxes("DState").Text = ""
    .EditBoxes("DZip").Text = ""
```

Chapter 18 ◆ Saving Data in a Sequential Disk File

```
      .EditBoxes("DPhone").Text = ""
      .DropDowns("DE_Mail_Net").Text = ""
      .EditBoxes("DE_Mail_Address").Text = ""
      .EditBoxes("DReferral").Text = ""
      .EditBoxes("DNotes").Text = ""
      .Labels("DRecNo").Caption = "Record #: "
   End With
End Sub
'
' The Auto_Open procedure
' runs whenever this workbook is opened.
'
Sub Auto_Open( )
   InitializeIt   'Run the initialization procedure.
End Sub
'
'  Add a new entry
'
Sub NewEntry_Click( )
   numEntries = numEntries + 1
   Sheets("ContactsDlog").ScrollBars("ScrollEntry").Max = numEntries
   theEntryNum = numEntries
   ReDim Preserve theDB(numEntries) 'Expand the array.
   EntryToDB theEntryNum   'Write the entry to the array.
   DBToEntrytheEntryNum    'Read the entry back to display theEntryNum.
End Sub
'
'  Update an entry
'
Sub UpdateEntry_Click( )
   If theEntryNum = 0 Then Exit Sub   'Exit if no entries are saved yet.
   EntryToDB theEntryNum   'Update the displayed entry.
End Sub
'
' Transfer an entry to the database
'
Sub EntryToDB(anEntry As Integer)
   With Sheets("ContactsDlog")
```

```vb
      theDB(anEntry).Name = .EditBoxes("DName").Text
      theDB(anEntry).Address = .EditBoxes("DAddress").Text
      theDB(anEntry).City = .EditBoxes("DCity").Text
      theDB(anEntry).State = .EditBoxes("DState").Text
      theDB(anEntry).Zip = .EditBoxes("DZip").Text
      theDB(anEntry).Phone = .EditBoxes("DPhone").Text
      theDB(anEntry).Net = .DropDowns("DE_Mail_Net").Text
      theDB(anEntry).NetAddr = .EditBoxes("DE_Mail_Address").Text
      theDB(anEntry).Referral = .EditBoxes("DReferral").Text
      theDB(anEntry).Notes = .EditBoxes("DNotes").Text
      theDB(anEntry).RecNo = anEntry
  End With
End Sub
'
' Transfer a record to the form
'
Sub DBToEntry(anEntry As Integer)
  With Sheets("ContactsDlog")
    .EditBoxes("DName").Text = theDB(anEntry).Name
    .EditBoxes("DAddress").Text = theDB(anEntry).Address
    .EditBoxes("DCity").Text = theDB(anEntry).City
    .EditBoxes("DState").Text = theDB(anEntry).State
    .EditBoxes("DZip").Text = theDB(anEntry).Zip
    .EditBoxes("DPhone").Text = theDB(anEntry).Phone
    .DropDowns("DE_Mail_Net").Text = theDB(anEntry).Net
    .EditBoxes("DE_Mail_Address").Text = theDB(anEntry).NetAddr
    .EditBoxes("DReferral").Text = theDB(anEntry).Referral
    .EditBoxes("DNotes").Text = theDB(anEntry).Notes
    .Labels("DRecNo").Caption = "Record #: " & theDB(anEntry).RecNo
    .ScrollBars("ScrollEntry").Value = anEntry
  End With
End Sub
'
' Scroll entries
'
Sub ScrollEntries_Click( )
  If numEntries = 0 Then Exit Sub 'No entries yet.
  theEntryNum = Sheets("ContactsDlog").ScrollBars("ScrollEntry").Value
  DBToEntry theEntryNum
End Sub
```

Chapter 18 ◆ Saving Data in a Sequential Disk File

```
' Delete a record
'
Sub DeleteEntry_Click( )
  Dim I As Integer, buttons As Integer
  Dim theMsg As String
  If numEntries = 0 Then Exit Sub  'No entries yet.
  'Make sure the user really wants to do this.
  buttons = vbYesNo + vbDefaultButton2 + vbQuestion + _
      vbApplicationModal
  theMsg = "Are you sure you want to delete the current record?"
  If MsgBox(theMsg, buttons, "Delete Record") = vbNo Then Exit Sub
  'The user said yes, so delete the record and move the others down.
  If theEntryNum = numEntries Then   'It is the last entry.
    numEntries = numEntries - 1
    ReDim Preserve theDB(numEntries)
    theEntryNum = numEntries
  ElseIf theEntryNum = 0 Then   'No entry to delete.
    Exit Sub
  Else  'Shift everything down one.
    For I = theEntryNum + 1 To numEntries
      theDB(I - 1) = theDB(I)
      theDB(I - 1).RecNo = I - 1
    Next I
    numEntries = numEntries - 1
    ReDim Preserve theDB(numEntries)
  End If
  Sheets("ContactsDlog").ScrollBars("ScrollEntry").Value = theEntryNum
  Sheets("ContactsDlog").ScrollBars("ScrollEntry").Max = numEntries
  DBToEntry theEntryNum
End Sub
'
' Find a name
'
Sub FindName_Click( )
  Static theName As String
  Dim I As Integer
  Const TextComparison = 1
```

```
    If numEntries = 0 Then Exit Sub   'No entries yet.
    theName = InputBox("Input a name to search for.", _
        "Find A Name", theName)
    If theEntryNum <> numEntries Then
      For I = theEntryNum + 1 To numEntries
        If InStr(1, theDB(I).Name, theName, TextComparison) <> 0 Then
          'Found a matching entry
          theEntryNum = I
          DBToEntry theEntryNum
          Exit Sub
        End If
      Next I
    End If
    For I = 1 To theEntryNum
      If InStr(1, theDB(I).Name, theName, TextComparison) <> 0 Then
        'Found a matching entry
        theEntryNum = I
        DBToEntry theEntryNum
        Exit Sub
      End If
    Next I
    'No match found
    MsgBox "The name: " & theName & " was not found.", , "Find A Name"
End Sub
'
'Save the database.
'
Sub Save_Click( )
    Dim theFilter As String, Answer, theDot As Integer
    Dim fileNum As Integer, EntryNum As Integer
    If numEntries = 0 Then   'See whether there is something to save.
      MsgBox "You don't have anything to save.", , "PCD"
      Exit Sub
    End If
    'Get the file name for the data.
    theFilter = "PCD database (*.PCD),*.PCD"
    'theFileName is global, so it always defaults to the current name.
    Answer = Application.GetSaveAsFilename(theFileName, theFilter,1)
```

Chapter 18 ♦ Saving Data in a Sequential Disk File

```
    If Answer = False Then Exit Sub  'The user chose Cancel.
    theFileName = Trim(Answer)    'Remove any leading or trailing blanks.
    'Make sure the file name ends in .PCD.
    theDot = InStr(theFileName, ".")
    If theDot = 0 Then   'No extension typed; add one.
      theFileName = theFileName & ".PCD"
    Else  'Something was typed; delete it and add .PCD.
      theFileName = Left(theFileName, theDot - 1) & ".PCD"
    End If
    fileNum = FreeFile( )  'Get a file number and open the file.
    Open theFileName For Output As fileNum
    'First save the number of entries.
    Write #fileNum, numEntries
    'Now loop over each element of the database
    'and write all the components into the file.
    For EntryNum = 1 To numEntries
    With theDB(EntryNum)
      Write #fileNum, .Name
      Write #fileNum, .Address
      Write #fileNum, .City
      Write #fileNum, .State
      Write #fileNum, .Zip
      Write #fileNum, .Phone
      Write #fileNum, .Net
      Write #fileNum, .NetAddr
      Write #fileNum, .Referral
      Write #fileNum, .Notes
      Write #fileNum, .RecNo
    End With
    Next EntryNum
    Close #fileNum    'All done
    MsgBox "The database was saved in " & theFileName, , "PCD"
End Sub
'
'Open a database file.
'
Sub Open_Click( )
    Dim theFilter As String, Answer, theDot As Integer
    Dim fileNum As Integer, EntryNum As Integer
    Dim buttons As Integer, theMsg As String
    Dim Flag As Boolean
    If numEntries <> 0 Then   'See if there is something to save first.
```

```
      buttons = vbYesNoCancel + vbQuestion + vbApplicationModal
      theMsg = "Do you want to save the current data first?"
      Answer = MsgBox(theMsg, buttons, "PCD")
      If Answer = vbCancel Then   'Quit if the user chooses Cancel.
        Exit Sub
      ElseIf Answer = vbYes Then  'Call save if the user chooses Yes.
        Save_Click
      End If
    End If
    'Get the file name for the data.
    theFilter = "PCD database (*.PCD),*.PCD"
    Do
      Answer = Application.GetOpenFilename(theFilter, 1)
      If Answer = False Then Exit Sub 'The user chose Cancel.
      Answer = Trim(Answer)    'Remove any leading or trailing blanks.
      theDot = InStr(Answer, ".")
      If theDot = 0 Then   'Bad file name, no extension.
        MsgBox "You must choose a .PCD file.", , "PCD"
        Flag = False
      ElseIf Right(Answer, 4) <> ".PCD" Then   'Wrong extension.
        MsgBox "You must choose a .PCD file.", , "PCD"
        Flag = False
      Else   'Must be OK.
        Flag = True
      End If
    Loop Until Flag
    theFileName = Answer
    fileNum = FreeFile( )   'Get a file number and open the file.
    Open theFileName For Input As fileNum
    'First read the number of entries.
    Input #fileNum, numEntries
    'Now expand the database.
    ReDim theDB(numEntries)
    'Now loop over each element of the database
    'and read all the components into the file.
    For EntryNum = 1 To numEntries
    With theDB(EntryNum)
      Input #fileNum, .Name
      Input #fileNum, .Address
      Input #fileNum, .City
      Input #fileNum, .State
```

Chapter 18 ♦ Saving Data in a Sequential Disk File

```
      Input #fileNum, .Zip
      Input #fileNum, .Phone
      Input #fileNum, .Net
      Input #fileNum, .NetAddr
      Input #fileNum, .Referral
      Input #fileNum, .Notes
      Input #fileNum, .RecNo
   End With
   Next EntryNum
   Close #fileNum    'All done
   MsgBox theFileName & " was opened.", , "PCD"
   Sheets("ContactsDlog").ScrollBars("ScrollEntry").Max = numEntries
   theEntryNum = 1   'Insert the first entry into the form.
   DBToEntry theEntryNum
End Sub
```

The first change is at the module level, and defines theFileName as a global variable:

```
Dim theFileName As String    'The current file name.
```

The variable theFileName stores the name of the currently open file so that when you save the database, the program uses that file name as the default.

The next change is in the initialization procedure:

```
theFileName = ""
With Sheets("ContactsDlog")
   .EditBoxes("DName").Text = ""
   .EditBoxes("DAddress").Text = ""
   .EditBoxes("DCity").Text = ""
   .EditBoxes("DState").Text = ""
   .EditBoxes("DZip").Text = ""
   .EditBoxes("DPhone").Text = ""
   .DropDowns("DE_Mail_Net").Text = ""
   .EditBoxes("DE_Mail_Address").Text = ""
   .EditBoxes("DReferral").Text = ""
   .EditBoxes("DNotes").Text = ""
   .Labels("DRecNo").Caption = "Record #: "
End With
```

When the program first starts, no file is open, so the initialization procedure equates theFileName variable to an empty string. Additionally, the text boxes on the form must be cleared of any data from a previous run of the program.

Next come the two procedures that you attach to the Open and Save buttons. The first is the Save_Click procedure, which saves the database in a disk file.

> **Tip:** The Save_Click and Open_Click procedures are very similar, so when you create them you can use a shortcut to save yourself from having to type both. After typing the first procedure, simply select and copy it, paste it to the end of the module, and then edit the copy to create the second procedure.

The first block of the procedure declares the local variables and checks whether memory contains anything to save:

```
'
'Save the database.
'
Sub Save_Click( )
  Dim theFilter As String, Answer, theDot As Integer
  Dim fileNum As Integer, EntryNum As Integer
  If numEntries = 0 Then   'See whether there is something to save.
    MsgBox "You don't have anything to save.", , "PCD"
    Exit Sub
  End If
```

The variable Answer is declared variant because it must hold either the Boolean or String value returned by the GetSaveAsFilename method. If there is nothing in memory to save, the code displays the dialog box shown in figure 18.5 and quits the procedure.

Figure 18.5
The dialog box displayed when there is no data to save.

The next block of code gets the file name from the user:

```
'Get the file name for the data.
theFilter = "PCD database (*.PCD),*.PCD"
'theFileName is global, so it always defaults to the current name.
Answer = Application.GetSaveAsFilename(theFileName, theFilter, 1)
If Answer = False Then Exit Sub 'The user chose Cancel.
```

271

Chapter 18 ◆ Saving Data in a Sequential Disk File

```
theFileName= Trim(Answer)    'Remove any leading or trailing blanks.
'Make sure the file name ends in .PCD.
theDot = InStr(theFileName, ".")
If theDot = 0 Then   'No extension typed; add one.
  theFileName = theFileName & ".PCD"
Else  'Something was typed; delete it and add .PCD.
  theFileName = Left(theFileName, theDot - 1) & ".PCD"
End If
```

This code first prepares a filter for the dialog box displayed by the GetSaveAsFilename method that displays .PCD file names. This is where you need the global value of the file name, so that the program can use it as the default file name in the File Save As dialog box shown in figure 18.6. The Answer variable returns the file name that the user selects. The code immediately checks the variable for the logical value False, which indicates that the user chose the Cancel button. If the user chose the Cancel button, the procedure ends immediately. Next the procedure checks the file name's extension. If the user didn't type an extension, the code adds .PCD as the default extension; if the user included an extension, the code replaces it with .PCD. The procedure locates the extension by searching for the period that separates the file name from the extension.

At this point, you should have a good file name that you can use to open the file.

Figure 18.6

The File Save As dialog box created with the GetSaveAsFilename method.

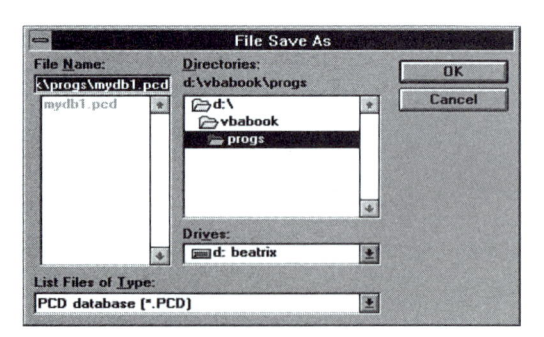

However, you first must save the number of entries, because when you later open the file to load it back into memory, the procedure must read this number first to know how many entries to read:

```
fileNum = FreeFile( )   'Get a file number and open the file.
Open theFileName For Output As fileNum
'First save the number of entries.
Write #fileNum, numEntries
```

> **Caution:** Before you begin reading data from a file, you first must know how much data the file contains. If you try to read more data than the file contains, you get an error. If you can't find out how much data the file contains, use the EOF( ) function to test the file each time before reading from it. If the EOF( ) function returns True, you are at the end of the file and should not try to read any more data from the file.

Next you add a loop over all the entries in the database and a block With structure that writes each of the elements of an entry into the disk file:

```
    'Now loop over each element of the database
    'and write all the components into the file.
    For EntryNum = 1 To numEntries
    With theDB(EntryNum)
      Write #fileNum, .Name
      Write #fileNum, .Address
      Write #fileNum, .City
      Write #fileNum, .State
      Write #fileNum, .Zip
      Write #fileNum, .Phone
      Write #fileNum, .Net
      Write #fileNum, .NetAddr
      Write #fileNum, .Referral
      Write #fileNum, .Notes
      Write #fileNum, .RecNo
    End With
    Next EntryNum
    Close #fileNum    'All done
    MsgBox "The database was saved in " & theFileName, , "PCD"
End Sub
```

When all the entries are written into the file, the file is closed and the dialog box shown in figure 18.7 appears.

Figure 18.7
The dialog box displayed when the database is successfully saved.

Chapter 18 ♦ Saving Data in a Sequential Disk File

The Open_Click procedure is almost identical to the Save_Click procedure, except that it reads the data from the file instead of putting the data into it:

```
'
'Open a database file.
'
Sub Open_Click( )
  Dim theFilter As String, Answer, theDot As Integer
  Dim fileNum As Integer, EntryNum As Integer
  Dim buttons As Integer, theMsg As String
  Dim Flag As Boolean
  If numEntries <> 0 Then   'See if there is something to save first.
    buttons = vbYesNoCancel + vbQuestion + vbApplicationModal
    theMsg = "Do you want to save the current data first?"
    Answer = MsgBox(theMsg, buttons, "PCD")
    If Answer = vbCancel Then   'Quit if the user chose Cancel.
      Exit Sub
    ElseIf Answer = vbYes Then   'Call save if the user chose Yes.
      Save_Click
    End If
  End If
```

The first block of the procedure declares the local variables as in the Save_Click procedure. The procedure then checks whether a file is already open and then displays the dialog box shown in figure 18.8. This dialog box gives the user a chance to save the data that is already in memory before loading a new file. The dialog box has three buttons: Yes, No, and Cancel. If the user chooses Cancel, the procedure ends immediately. If Yes is chosen, the Save_Click procedure is called to save the current data before opening another file. If the user chooses No, the procedure continues with its next block.

Figure 18.8
A dialog box that gives the user a chance to save the existing data before opening a new file.

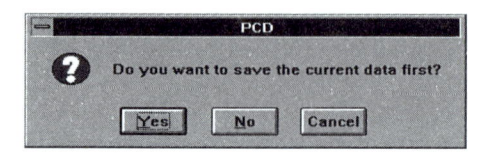

At this point, you know the user wants to open a file, so you set up the GetOpenFilename method to load a .PCD file:

```
'Get the file name for the data.
theFilter = "PCD database (*.PCD),*.PCD"
```

274

Visual Basic for Applications By EXAMPLE

```
Do
  Answer = Application.GetOpenFilename(theFilter, 1)
  If Answer = False Then Exit Sub 'The user chose Cancel.
  Answer = Trim(Answer)    'Remove any leading or trailing blanks.
  theDot = InStr(Answer, ".")
  If theDot = 0 Then   'Bad file name, no extension.
    MsgBox "You must choose a .PCD file.", , "PCD"
    Flag = False
  ElseIf Right(Answer, 4) <> ".PCD" Then   'Wrong extension
    MsgBox "You must choose a .PCD file.", , "PCD"
    Flag = False
  Else  'Must be OK.
    Flag = True
  End If
Loop Until Flag
theFileName = Answer
```

You use a Do-Loop structure to request a file name and then test whether it is valid. The tests primarily check for a .PCD extension before passing the file name on to the Open statement. Figure 18.9 shows the dialog box that the GetOpenFilename method creates.

Figure 18.9

The File Open dialog box created with the GetOpenFilename method.

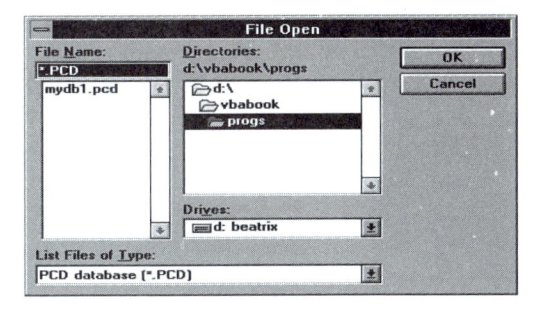

You now have a good file name, so you can open the file, read the number of entries, and then read the entries themselves:

```
fileNum = FreeFile( )   'Get a file number and open the file.
Open theFileName For Input As fileNum
'First read the number of entries.
Input #fileNum, numEntries
'Now expand the database.
ReDim theDB(numEntries)
'Now loop over each element of the database
'and read all the components into the file.
```

275

Chapter 18 ♦ Saving Data in a Sequential Disk File

```
    For EntryNum = 1 To numEntries
    With theDB(EntryNum)
      Input #fileNum, .Name
      Input #fileNum, .Address
      Input #fileNum, .City
      Input #fileNum, .State
      Input #fileNum, .Zip
      Input #fileNum, .Phone
      Input #fileNum, .Net
      Input #fileNum, .NetAddr
      Input #fileNum, .Referral
      Input #fileNum, .Notes
      Input #fileNum, .RecNo
    End With
    Next EntryNum
    Close #fileNum    'All done
    MsgBox theFileName & " was opened.", , "PCD"
    Sheets("ContactsDlog").ScrollBars("ScrollEntry").Max = numEntries
    theEntryNum = 1  'Insert the first entry into the form.
      DBToEntry theEntryNum
    End Sub
```

You can now see why the number of entries must be the first item stored in the file: because it is needed to redimension the array and to control the loop for reading the rest of the data into memory. When the procedure completes, the dialog box shown in figure 18.10 is displayed, the scroll bar is updated, and the first record is loaded into the form.

Figure 18.10
The PCD dialog box is displayed when a file is successfully opened and loaded into memory.

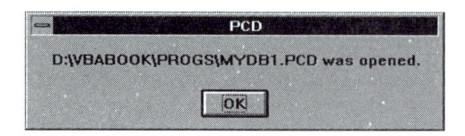

If you save this program, run it, insert some data as shown in figure 18.11, click the Save button, and then use a word processor to open the file in which the data was saved, you see the text-based data shown in figure 18.12.

Summary

In this chapter, you learned about sequential disk files. A sequential disk file is a text file that is read or written as a continuous stream of bytes from the beginning to the end. You open sequential files with the Open statement, read them with the Input

Visual Basic for Applications By EXAMPLE

and Line Input statements, and write them with the Print and Write statements. You use sequential files primarily for information that you want to load into memory or write to disk as a block. Programs that need to access parts of a file in random pieces should use the random access file type described in the next chapter.

Figure 18.11

The personal contacts database with some data stored on the custom form.

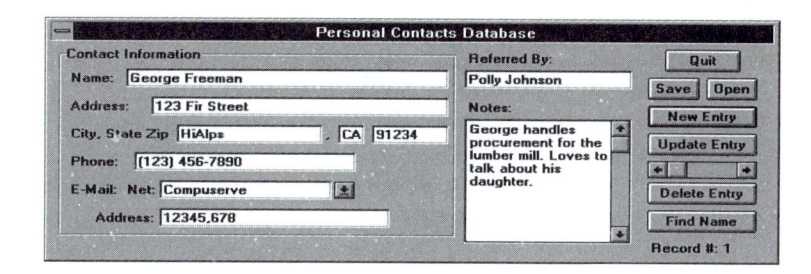

Figure 18.12

The data file created by storing the data shown in figure 18.11.

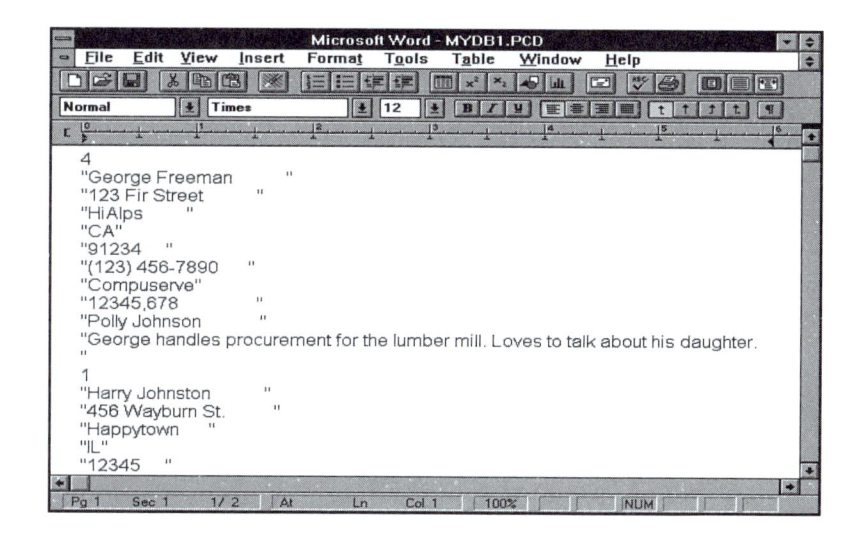

Review Questions

The answers to the review questions are in Appendix A.

1. What does the FreeFile function do?
2. How is data stored in a sequential file?
3. What does the Append qualifier of the *mode* argument of the Open statement do?
4. How do you open a file so that you can write data to it? Read data from it?
5. What must you do when you are done using a file?

Chapter 18 ◆ Saving Data in a Sequential Disk File

6. What is the difference between the Print and Write statements?
7. What is the difference between the Input and Line Input statements?
8. Explain the difference between sequential and random access files.

Review Exercises

1. Modify the Save_Click procedure in the personal contacts database program to display a warning dialog box whenever the user is about to overwrite an existing file. The dialog box should give you the option of canceling the save or of overwriting the file. Hint: Look up the Dir function.

2. Modify the Open_Click procedure so that it displays the dialog box shown in figure 18.8 only if the data in memory has been modified. Hint: Create a global flag that is initially False but changed to True by any procedure that changes the database.

3. Add to the personal contacts database a merge command that opens a file and combines its contents with the data that is already in memory.

4. Add or modify a procedure to check whether an entry was modified when you used the scroll bar to switch to another entry. If the entry was modified, have the procedure display a dialog box that asks whether you want to update the current entry before moving to the new entry.

CHAPTER 19

Saving Data in a Random Access File

Random access disk files differ significantly from sequential access files. A random access file treats a disk file as a list of equally sized records, any one of which may be read or written at any time and in any order.

In this chapter you learn how to do the following:

♦ Open random access files

♦ Save data in random access files

♦ Read data from random access files

Reading and Writing Random Access Files

Random access files are treated as sequences of fixed-length records, with each record being independent of all the others. The length of a record is specified in the Open statement, and a user-defined data type specifies the contents of the record. Data stored in a random access file generally is not stored as text, but as the binary representations of the numbers. Using binary numbers saves much space in a file compared to text representations of the same number. Additionally, binary numbers are loaded into memory much faster because they do not have to be translated from the text before they can be used.

Chapter 19 ◆ Saving Data in a Random Access File

Opening a File

Opening a random access file is much like opening a sequential access file with the Open statement, with two important differences: the mode argument is Random, and a `Len = RecLen` argument is placed at the end.

To open a random access file, use an Open statement as follows:

```
Open filename For Random As filenumber Len = RecLen
```

where `filename` is a string that contains the name and path to the file that you want to open, `filenumber` is the file number that you want to assign to the file, and `RecLen` is the length in bytes of a random access record.

> **Note:** The optimum record length to use is an integer fraction or multiple of a disk's sector size. Most disk drives use 512- or 1,024-byte sectors, making the optimum record lengths powers of 2, such as 32, 64, 128, 256, and so on. Such record lengths are optimum because of the way that a computer stores data on a disk drive. A computer stores data in sectors of equal length, and reads and writes one sector at a time. Even though you can read a disk file one byte at a time, the computer actually reads one or more sectors into a buffer in memory. When you read data from the disk file, you are actually reading from the buffer. Then when you reach the end of the buffer, the computer reads the next few sectors from the file into the buffer. Data is written to a disk file in much the same way: Initially data is written to the disk buffer in memory, and then after the buffer is full, the buffer is written to disk.
>
> To see why a power of 2 is an optimum length for a record, consider what happens if you have 512-byte sectors and a file with records that are 260 bytes long. With this record length, many of the records in this file require that two sectors be read from the disk file to fill one record. For example, record 2 uses bytes 261 through 512 of the first sector and bytes 1 through 8 of the second. Using a 256-byte record rather than a 260-byte record results in two complete records in each sector, so that only one sector must be read to load one record.
>
> Although you do not have to use record lengths that are a power of 2, you should do so unless it wastes much disk space or compromises the capabilities of your program.

For example, the following few lines open a random access file for input or output:

```
FileNum1 = FreeFile
Open "myfile.txt" For Random As FileNum1 Len = 256
```

This code opens a random access file named MYFILE.TXT with 256-byte records. FreeFile selects the file number.

> **Note:** Binary mode files are similar to Random mode files, except that the record length is fixed at one byte, and values written to disk are always placed in contiguous bytes.

Closing a Random Access File

As with sequential files, you close a random access file with the Close statement, as follows:

```
Close #fileNum
```

where *fileNum* is the file number with which you opened the file.

Using the Type Statement To Define a Record

The Type statement that you use to declare user-defined types is also used to declare the contents of a record variable used in a random access file. A Type statement that you use to declare a record variable is quite similar to that which you use to declare a user-defined type, except that when you declare a record variable you shouldn't use Variant types and you should require that any string variables have a fixed length. The maximum length of a record defined with a Type statement must be less than the length of the record declared in the Open statement. You can use types with a smaller length, but the difference in bytes between the type length and the record length is wasted for every record stored on a disk.

If you use a variable-length String type variable in a Type statement, an additional two bytes are added to the string to contain the length. If Variant types are used, they also have a two-byte value to define the type plus the bytes needed for the value being stored. If you use variable-length strings and variants in a type to be stored in a record, the total length of the type still must be less than the record length; otherwise you get an error. Because of the difficulties involved in ensuring that the total length of a record variable is less than the record length, you usually should declare the length of every variable in a type that is to be used as a record variable.

For example, the following Type statement from the personal contacts database program contains 256 bytes. Each string has a fixed length, which is not required in a normal Type statement.

```
Type DBEntry       'Define the structure of a single database entry.
    Name As String * 25      '25 bytes
    Address As String * 25   '25 bytes
```

Chapter 19 ◆ Saving Data in a Random Access File

```
    City As String * 15      '15 bytes
    State As String * 2      ' 2 bytes
    Zip As String * 10       '10 bytes
    Phone As String * 20     '20 bytes
    Net As String * 10       '10 bytes
    NetAddr As String * 25   '25 bytes
    Referral As String * 25  '25 bytes
    Notes As String * 97     '97 bytes
    RecNo As Integer         ' 2 bytes
End Type            'total is 256 bytes.
```

To determine the length of a user-defined type, you can either add up the variable sizes or declare a variable of that type and then apply the Len() function to it. For example, if you run the InitializeIt procedure in the personal contacts database with a breakpoint after the declaration of the array theDB(), and then use the Len() function in the Immediate pane of the Debug window, you get the following result:

```
? Len(theDB(1))
 256
```

Putting Data into a Record

Unlike sequential access files, random access files do not store data using Print or Write statements. Instead you use the Put statement. The Put statement takes three arguments: the file number, the record number, and a record variable.

```
Put #fileNum,RecNum,Variable
```

For example, the following Put statement stores the contents of theDB(1) in record 3 of the file opened with file number 1:

```
Put #1,3,theDB(1)
```

If you omit the record number from a Put statement, it uses the record that follows the one that the previous Get, Put, or Seek statement accessed.

Getting Data from a Record

To retrieve a record from a disk file and load it into a record variable, use the Get statement. The Get statement has exactly the same syntax as the Put statement. It also takes three arguments: the file number, the record number, and a record variable to receive the data from the record on disk.

```
Get #fileNum,RecNum,Variable
```

Reorganizing Data in Random Access Files

When you want to reorganize the data in a sequential file, you must read the data from the file and then write it back using the new organization. Random access files enable you to do this, but you can also choose to use an index and then reorganize the index rather than the file.

To use an index, you first create an array of integers, with each element of the array containing one record number for the random access file. Then when you want to access a record in the random access file, you use the array to supply the record number. File storage of this type is known as *indexed records*.

For example, if the variable I contains the record number that you want and RecVar is the record variable, you would normally access the random access file with the following Get statement:

```
Get #fileNum, I, RecVar
```

If the array theIndex() is the index array, you would change your access to the following:

```
Get #fileNum, theIndex(I), RecVar
```

Initially, each element of theIndex() contains the same number as the array element number, as follows:

```
theIndex(1) = 1
theIndex(2) = 2
theIndex(3) = 3
    .
    .
    .
```

The results of using this array to access the file records are identical to those of accessing the records directly. Suppose that you want to alphabetize the entries, and that to do so requires that you swap entry 3 with entry 2. You could actually swap the entries in the disk file, or you could simply change the values in the index array as follows:

```
theIndex(1) = 1
theIndex(2) = 3
theIndex(3) = 2
    .
    .
    .
```

As long as you use the index array to access the file, you get the records in your specified order and not in the order in which they were actually stored in the file.

Indexed records are also useful when you want to consolidate and reuse deleted records. When you delete a record, move its record number to the end of the index array and then move the other indexes down one. A second index number points to the boundary between free records and used records in the index. When you need a new record, first check whether the index array has any records available for reuse before you allocate a new one.

When working with indexed records, you must decide what to do with the index. You can store it in a separate sequential file, or allocate several records at the beginning of the random access file to hold it.

Saving the Personal Contacts Database in a Random Access File

As you might have guessed, you can easily adapt the personal contacts database to random access files. If your database is small and can fit into memory at one time, storing it in a sequential file is straightforward and makes access quite fast because everything is in memory. However, if your database becomes large, you should consider switching to a random access file and storing all the records on disk except for the single record that you are viewing.

To see how large your database is, multiply the size of a record by the number of records. For the personal contacts database, multiply 256 bytes by the number of records; if that number is greater than about a 100,000 (100K of RAM), you should use a random access file.

Changing the personal contacts database so that it can use random access files involves removing the array theDB() and replacing it with the theDB record variable, and opening the database file whenever data is to be loaded into the record variable. You no longer need the Save button, because the database is stored on disk and saved as you go. Instead, a New button replaces the Save button to create a new database file.

First, if you want to keep the previous version of the program, save it with a different name. Next, change the caption of the Save button to New, as shown in figure 19.1. Then assign the New button to the procedure New_Click, which you create from the Save_Click procedure. Attach the Quit button to the Quit_Click procedure, which you also will create shortly.

The next step is to change the program as shown in the following listing. The boldface type indicates changes made to the previous version of the personal contacts database.

Visual Basic for Applications By EXAMPLE

Figure 19.1
Layout of the random access file version of the personal contacts database.

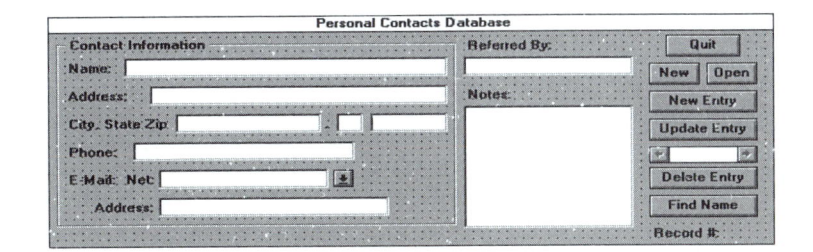

```
'
'   Personal Contacts Database Program
'   Random Access File Version
'
Option Explicit  'Force all variables to be defined.
Option Base 1    'Make arrays start at 1.
Type DBEntry     'Define the structure of a single database entry.
  Name As String * 25
  Address As String * 25
  City As String * 15
  State As String * 2
  Zip As String * 10
  Phone As String * 20
  Net As String * 10
  NetAddr As String * 25
  Referral As String * 25
  Notes As String * 97
  RecNo As Integer
End Type    'Size of type is 256 bytes.
Type FirstRecType  'Define a type for the first record
  numEntries As Integer
End Type    'Lots of space is left in this record for other stuff.
Dim FirstRec As FirstRecType  'A record variable for the first record.
Dim theDB As DBEntry          'The record variable.
Dim numEntries As Integer     'Total number of entries.
Dim theEntryNum As Integer    'The currently displayed entry.
Dim theFileName As String     'The current file name.
Dim fileNum As Integer        'The file number of the open file.
'
'   Initialize database
```

Chapter 19 ♦ Saving Data in a Random Access File

```
Sub InitializeIt()
  FirstRec.numEntries = 0
  theEntryNum = 0
  Sheets("ContactsDlog").DropDowns("DE_Mail_Net").List = _
    Array("Compuserve", "Internet", "GEnie", "Prodigy")
  Sheets("ContactsDlog").Show
  'The Min value is 2 because the first record contains
  'the number of records.
  Sheets("ContactsDlog").ScrollBars("ScrollEntry").Min = 2
  Sheets("ContactsDlog").ScrollBars("ScrollEntry").Max = 2
  theFileName = ""
  With Sheets("ContactsDlog")
    .EditBoxes("DName").Text = ""
    .EditBoxes("DAddress").Text = ""
    .EditBoxes("DCity").Text = ""
    .EditBoxes("DState").Text = ""
    .EditBoxes("DZip").Text = ""
    .EditBoxes("DPhone").Text = ""
    .DropDowns("DE_Mail_Net").Text = ""
    .EditBoxes("DE_Mail_Address").Text = ""
    .EditBoxes("DReferral").Text = ""
    .EditBoxes("DNotes").Text = ""
    .Labels("DRecNo").Caption = "Record #: "
  End With
End Sub
'
' The Auto_Open procedure
' runs whenever this workbook is opened.
'
Sub Auto_Open()
  InitializeIt  'Run the initialization procedure.
End Sub
'
'  Add a new entry
'
Sub NewEntry_Click()
  If FirstRec.numEntries = 0 Then 'See if a file is open.
    MsgBox "Open a file first.", , "PCD"
    Exit Sub
  End If
  FirstRec.numEntries = FirstRec.numEntries + 1
```

```vba
    Sheets("ContactsDlog").ScrollBars("ScrollEntry").Max = _
        FirstRec.numEntries
    theEntryNum = FirstRec.numEntries
    Put #fileNum, 1, FirstRec
    EntryToDB theEntryNum    'Write the entry to the file.
    DBToEntry theEntryNum    'Read the entry back to display theEntryNum.
End Sub
'
'  Update an entry
'
Sub UpdateEntry_Click()
    'Exit if no entries are saved yet.
    If FirstRec.numEntries < 2 Then Exit Sub
    EntryToDB theEntryNum    'Update the displayed entry.
End Sub
'
' Transfer an entry to the database
'
Sub EntryToDB(anEntry As Integer)
    With Sheets("ContactsDlog")
        theDB.Name = .EditBoxes("DName").Text
        theDB.Address = .EditBoxes("DAddress").Text
        theDB.City = .EditBoxes("DCity").Text
        theDB.State = .EditBoxes("DState").Text
        theDB.Zip = .EditBoxes("DZip").Text
        theDB.Phone = .EditBoxes("DPhone").Text
        theDB.Net = .DropDowns("DE_Mail_Net").Text
        theDB.NetAddr = .EditBoxes("DE_Mail_Address").Text
        theDB.Referral = .EditBoxes("DReferral").Text
        theDB.Notes = .EditBoxes("DNotes").Text
        theDB.RecNo = anEntry
    End With
    Put #fileNum, anEntry, theDB
End Sub
'
' Transfer a record to the form
'
Sub DBToEntry(anEntry As Integer)
    Get #fileNum, anEntry, theDB
    With Sheets("ContactsDlog")
        .EditBoxes("DName").Text = theDB.Name
        .EditBoxes("DAddress").Text = theDB.Address
```

Chapter 19 ♦ Saving Data in a Random Access File

```
        .EditBoxes("DCity").Text = theDB.City
        .EditBoxes("DState").Text = theDB.State
        .EditBoxes("DZip").Text = theDB.Zip
        .EditBoxes("DPhone").Text = theDB.Phone
        .DropDowns("DE_Mail_Net").Text = theDB.Net
        .EditBoxes("DE_Mail_Address").Text = theDB.NetAddr
        .EditBoxes("DReferral").Text = theDB.Referral
        .EditBoxes("DNotes").Text = theDB.Notes
        .Labels("DRecNo").Caption = "Record #: " & theDB.RecNo - 1
        .ScrollBars("ScrollEntry").Value = anEntry
    End With
End Sub
'
' Scroll entries.
'
Sub ScrollEntries_Click()
    If FirstRec.numEntries < 2 Then Exit Sub 'No entries yet.
    theEntryNum = Sheets("ContactsDlog").ScrollBars("ScrollEntry").Value
    DBToEntry theEntryNum
End Sub
'
' Delete a record
'
Sub DeleteEntry_Click()
    Dim I As Integer, buttons As Integer
    Dim theMsg As String
    If FirstRec.numEntries < 2 Then Exit Sub 'No entries yet.
    'Make sure the user really wants to do this.
    buttons = vbYesNo + vbDefaultButton2 + vbQuestion + _
        vbApplicationModal
    theMsg = "Are you sure you want to delete the current record?"
    If MsgBox(theMsg, buttons, "Delete Record") = vbNo Then Exit Sub
    'The user said yes, so delete the record and move the others down.
    If theEntryNum = FirstRec.numEntries Then   'It is the last entry.
        FirstRec.numEntries = FirstRec.numEntries - 1
        theEntryNum = FirstRec.numEntries
        Put #fileNum, 1, FirstRec
    ElseIf theEntryNum = 0 Then   'No entry to delete.
```

```
      Exit Sub
    Else  'Shift everything down one.
      For I = theEntryNum + 1 To FirstRec.numEntries
        Get #fileNum, I, theDB
        theDB.RecNo = I - 1
        Put #fileNum, I - 1, theDB
      Next I
      FirstRec.numEntries = FirstRec.numEntries - 1
      Put #fileNum, 1, FirstRec
    End If
    Sheets("ContactsDlog").ScrollBars("ScrollEntry").Value = theEntryNum
    Sheets("ContactsDlog").ScrollBars("ScrollEntry").Max = _
        FirstRec.numEntries
    DBToEntry theEntryNum
End Sub
'
'  Find a name
'
Sub FindName_Click()
    Static theName As String
    Dim I As Integer
    Const TextComparison = 1
    If FirstRec.numEntries < 2 Then Exit Sub 'No entries yet.
    theName = InputBox("Input a name to search for.", "Find A Name", _
        theName)
    If theEntryNum <> FirstRec.numEntries Then
      For I = theEntryNum + 1 To FirstRec.numEntries
        Get #fileNum, I, theDB
        If InStr(1, theDB.Name, theName, TextComparison) <> 0 Then
          'Found a matching entry
          theEntryNum = I
          DBToEntry theEntryNum
          Exit Sub
        End If
      Next I
    End If
    For I = 2 To theEntryNum
      Get #fileNum, I, theDB
      If InStr(1, theDB.Name, theName, TextComparison) <> 0 Then
        'Found a matching entry
```

Chapter 19 ◆ Saving Data in a Random Access File

```
        theEntryNum = I
        DBToEntry theEntryNum
        Exit Sub
      End If
   Next I
   'No match found
   MsgBox "The name: " & theName & " was not found.", , "Find A Name"
End Sub
'
'Create a new database.
'
Sub New_Click()
   Dim theFilter As String, Answer, theDot As Integer
   'Get the file name for the data.
   theFilter = "PCD database (*.PCD),*.PCD"
   'theFileName is global, so it always defaults to the current name.
   Answer = Application.GetSaveAsFilename(theFileName, theFilter, 1)
   If Answer = False Then Exit Sub 'The user chose Cancel.
   theFileName = Trim(Answer)    'Remove any leading or trailing blanks.
   'Make sure the file name ends in PCD.
   theDot = InStr(theFileName, ".")
   If theDot = 0 Then   'No extension typed; add one.
      theFileName = theFileName & ".PCD"
   Else  'Something was typed; delete it and add .PCD.
      theFileName = Left(theFileName, theDot - 1) & ".PCD"
   End If
   Close      'Close an existing file, if any.
' Open the data file
   fileNum = FreeFile()   'Get a file number and open the file.
   Open theFileName For Random As fileNum Len = 256
   FirstRec.numEntries = 1  'Mark the database as open but empty.
   theEntryNum = 0
   'Use record 1 to store the number of records.
   Put #fileNum, 1, FirstRec
   'Set to Min value.
   Sheets("ContactsDlog").ScrollBars("ScrollEntry").Max = 2
   'Clear the form.
   With Sheets("ContactsDlog")
```

```vb
      .EditBoxes("DName").Text = ""
      .EditBoxes("DAddress").Text = ""
      .EditBoxes("DCity").Text = ""
      .EditBoxes("DState").Text = ""
      .EditBoxes("DZip").Text = ""
      .EditBoxes("DPhone").Text = ""
      .DropDowns("DE_Mail_Net").Text = ""
      .EditBoxes("DE_Mail_Address").Text = ""
      .EditBoxes("DReferral").Text = ""
      .EditBoxes("DNotes").Text = ""
      .Labels("DRecNo").Caption = "Record #: "
   End With
   MsgBox "New database created: " & theFileName, , "PCD"
End Sub
'
'Open a database file.
'
Sub Open_Click()
   Dim theFilter As String, Answer, theDot As Integer
   Dim Flag As Boolean
   'Get the file name for the data.
   theFilter = "PCD database (*.PCD),*.PCD"
   Do
      Answer = Application.GetOpenFilename(theFilter, 1)
      If Answer = False Then Exit Sub 'The user chose Cancel.
      Answer = Trim(Answer)    'Remove any leading or trailing blanks.
      theDot = InStr(Answer, ".")
      If theDot = 0 Then   'Bad file name, no extension.
         MsgBox "You must choose a .PCD file.", , "PCD"
         Flag = False
      ElseIf Right(Answer, 4) <> ".PCD" Then   'Wrong extension
         MsgBox "You must choose a .PCD file.", , "PCD"
         Flag = False
      Else   'Must be OK.
         Flag = True
      End If
   Loop Until Flag
   theFileName = Answer
   Close   'Close the previous data file, if any.
   fileNum = FreeFile()   'Get a file number and open the file.
   Open theFileName For Random As fileNum Len = 256
```

Chapter 19 ◆ Saving Data in a Random Access File

```
    'Read the number of entries.
    Get #fileNum, 1, FirstRec
    MsgBox theFileName & " was opened.", , "PCD"
    Sheets("ContactsDlog").ScrollBars("ScrollEntry").Max = _
        FirstRec.numEntries
    If FirstRec.numEntries > 1 Then 'If there is an entry in the file.
      theEntryNum = 2   'Insert the first entry into the form.
      DBToEntry theEntryNum
    End If
End Sub
'
' The Quit procedure to end the program.
'
Sub Quit_Click()
    'You need to close any open data files here.
    Close
End Sub
```

> **Note:** In many of the following excerpts, the highlighted changes include lines that have been deleted from the previous version, which in this version have been changed to comment lines so that you can see all the changes that were made to create this version.

This program opens the data file in the New_Click or the Open_Click procedures and closes it in the Quit_Click procedure. An alternative approach is to keep the file closed and open it only when you must read or write a record. This second method is slightly slower because it must open the file each time it needs to access the file. However, the advantage of the method is that if the program crashes, the data file is unlikely to be open, and thus is unlikely to be damaged by a crash. To change to the alternative version, surround each Get and Put statement or block of statements with an Open and a Close statement.

Converting the version of the program that stores the data in an array to one that stores the data in a random access disk file requires many small changes to the program. Your first problem is to determine where to store the variable numEntries. This variable is not part of any record, so it does not fit directly into the record structure of the file. You can solve this problem by reserving the first record of the file for setup information and then putting the first data record in the second record of the file. To ensure that the first record is never displayed, however, you must make several small modifications throughout the program.

In the declarations section of the module, you replace the declaration for the array theDB() with a declaration of a theDB record variable. Throughout the program, you remove the parentheses from theDB and insert a Get statement to load theDB with the appropriate record. You define a new variable type that enables the first record of the database to store numEntries, and then define a record variable named FirstRec as the new variable type. Throughout the program, you replace numEntries with `FirstRec.numEntries`. Because the single variable does not come close to filling the first record, you can use the remaining space to hold other startup information, such as a database name. Also in the header is a global declaration of the variable fileNum, which holds the active file number.

```
'
'   Personal Contacts Database Program
'   Random Access File Version
'
Option Explicit 'Force all variables to be defined.
Option Base 1   'Make arrays start at 1.
Type DBEntry    'Define the structure of a single database entry.
  Name As String * 25
  Address As String * 25
  City As String * 15
  State As String * 2
  Zip As String * 10
  Phone As String * 20
  Net As String * 10
  NetAddr As String * 25
  Referral As String * 25
  Notes As String * 97
  RecNo As Integer
End Type    'Size of type is 256 bytes.
Type FirstRecType   'Define a type for the first record
  numEntries As Integer
End Type    'Lots of space is left in this record for other stuff.
Dim FirstRec As FirstRecType  'A record variable for the first record.
'Dim theDB() As DBEntry       'The database array.
Dim theDB As DBEntry          'The record variable.
'Dim numEntries As Integer    'Total number of entries.
Dim theEntryNum As Integer    'The currently displayed entry.
Dim theFileName As String     'The current file name.
Dim fileNum As Integer        'The file number of the open file.
```

Chapter 19 ♦ Saving Data in a Random Access File

In the InitializeIt procedure, you remove the ReDim statement because you no longer have an array. You also change the initial minimum and maximum values for the scroll bar value to 2 because record 2 is the first record that actually holds database information.

```
'
'  Initialize database
'
Sub InitializeIt()
  FirstRec.numEntries = 0
'  ReDim theDB(1)
  theEntryNum = 0
  Sheets("ContactsDlog").DropDowns("DE_Mail_Net").List = _
    Array("Compuserve", "Internet", "GEnie", "Prodigy")
  Sheets("ContactsDlog").Show
  'The Min value is 2 because the first record contains
  'the number of records.
  Sheets("ContactsDlog").ScrollBars("ScrollEntry").Min = 2
  Sheets("ContactsDlog").ScrollBars("ScrollEntry").Max = 2
  theFileName = ""
  With Sheets("ContactsDlog")
    .EditBoxes("DName").Text = ""
    .EditBoxes("DAddress").Text = ""
    .EditBoxes("DCity").Text = ""
    .EditBoxes("DState").Text = ""
    .EditBoxes("DZip").Text = ""
    .EditBoxes("DPhone").Text = ""
    .DropDowns("DE_Mail_Net").Text = ""
    .EditBoxes("DE_Mail_Address").Text = ""
    .EditBoxes("DReferral").Text = ""
    .EditBoxes("DNotes").Text = ""
    .Labels("DRecNo").Caption = "Record #: "
  End With
End Sub
'
' The Auto_Open procedure
' runs whenever this workbook is opened.
'
Sub Auto_Open()
  InitializeIt   'Run the initialization procedure.
End Sub
```

You make several changes to the NewEntry_Click procedure. Before you can insert a new entry, you first must check whether a file is open. If a file isn't open, you can't add a new entry. The variable numEntries is 0 until a file is opened, so you use it to test for an open file. Later in the procedure, you use a Put statement to update the number of entries and then store the number in the first record of the file.

```
'
'   Add a new entry
'
Sub NewEntry_Click()
  If FirstRec.numEntries = 0 Then 'See if a file is open.
    MsgBox "Open a file first.", , "PCD"
    Exit Sub
  End If
  FirstRec.numEntries = FirstRec.numEntries + 1
  Sheets("ContactsDlog").ScrollBars("ScrollEntry").Max = _
      FirstRec.numEntries
  theEntryNum = FirstRec.numEntries
'   ReDim Preserve theDB(numEntries) 'Expand the array.
  Put #fileNum, 1, FirstRec
  EntryToDB theEntryNum    'Write the entry to the file.
  DBToEntry theEntryNum    'Read the entry back to display
theEntryNum.
End Sub
```

The UpdateEntry_Click procedure also must check for an existing entry, because you can't update entries if they don't exist yet. The first entry is in record 2, so as long as numEntries is less than two, no record has yet been stored.

```
'
'   Update an entry
'
Sub UpdateEntry_Click()
  'Exit if no entries are saved yet.
  If FirstRec.numEntries < 2 Then Exit Sub
  EntryToDB theEntryNum    'Update the displayed entry.
End Sub
```

In both the EntryToDB and DBToEntry procedures, you change the array theDB() to the record variable theDB. Also, the EntryToDB procedure gets a Put statement to store the data in the file, and DBToEntry gets a Get statement to retrieve an entry from the file. In DBToEntry, you subtract one from the record number displayed on the form so that it indicates the number of the database record instead of the number of the file record.

Chapter 19 ◆ Saving Data in a Random Access File

```vb
'
' Transfer an entry to the database
'
Sub EntryToDB(anEntry As Integer)
  With Sheets("ContactsDlog")
    theDB.Name = .EditBoxes("DName").Text
    theDB.Address = .EditBoxes("DAddress").Text
    theDB.City = .EditBoxes("DCity").Text
    theDB.State = .EditBoxes("DState").Text
    theDB.Zip = .EditBoxes("DZip").Text
    theDB.Phone = .EditBoxes("DPhone").Text
    theDB.Net = .DropDowns("DE_Mail_Net").Text
    theDB.NetAddr = .EditBoxes("DE_Mail_Address").Text
    theDB.Referral = .EditBoxes("DReferral").Text
    theDB.Notes = .EditBoxes("DNotes").Text
    theDB.RecNo = anEntry
  End With
  Put #fileNum, anEntry, theDB
End Sub
'
' Transfer a record to the form
'
Sub DBToEntry(anEntry As Integer)
  Get #fileNum, anEntry, theDB
  With Sheets("ContactsDlog")
    .EditBoxes("DName").Text = theDB.Name
    .EditBoxes("DAddress").Text = theDB.Address
    .EditBoxes("DCity").Text = theDB.City
    .EditBoxes("DState").Text = theDB.State
    .EditBoxes("DZip").Text = theDB.Zip
    .EditBoxes("DPhone").Text = theDB.Phone
    .DropDowns("DE_Mail_Net").Text = theDB.Net
    .EditBoxes("DE_Mail_Address").Text = theDB.NetAddr
    .EditBoxes("DReferral").Text = theDB.Referral
    .EditBoxes("DNotes").Text = theDB.Notes
    .Labels("DRecNo").Caption = "Record #: " & theDB.RecNo - 1
    .ScrollBars("ScrollEntry").Value = anEntry
  End With
End Sub
```

Like the UpdateEntry_Click procedure, the ScrollEntries_Click procedure must now check for existing records, because you can't scroll records that don't exist yet.

```
'
' Scroll entries.
'
Sub ScrollEntries_Click()
    If FirstRec.numEntries < 2 Then Exit Sub 'No entries yet.
    theEntryNum = Sheets("ContactsDlog").ScrollBars("ScrollEntry").Value
    DBToEntry theEntryNum
End Sub
```

To the DeleteEntry procedure you add a check for existing entries. When the value of numEntries changes, a Put statement stores the new value in the first record. You also use Get and Put statements to shift all the records down one record, by doing a Get from one record and then doing a Put to the next lower record number.

```
'
' Delete a record
'
Sub DeleteEntry_Click()
    Dim I As Integer, buttons As Integer
    Dim theMsg As String
    If FirstRec.numEntries < 2 Then Exit Sub 'No entries yet.
    'Make sure the user really wants to do this.
    buttons = vbYesNo + vbDefaultButton2 + vbQuestion + _
        vbApplicationModal
    theMsg = "Are you sure you want to delete the current record?"
    If MsgBox(theMsg, buttons, "Delete Record") = vbNo Then Exit Sub
    'The user said yes, so delete the record and move the others down.
    If theEntryNum = FirstRec.numEntries Then   'It is the last entry.
        FirstRec.numEntries = FirstRec.numEntries - 1
'       ReDim Preserve theDB(numEntries)
        theEntryNum = FirstRec.numEntries
        Put #fileNum, 1, FirstRec
    ElseIf theEntryNum = 0 Then    'No entry to delete.
        Exit Sub
    Else   'Shift everything down one.
```

Chapter 19 ◆ Saving Data in a Random Access File

```
    For I = theEntryNum + 1 To FirstRec.numEntries
      Get #fileNum, I, theDB
      theDB.RecNo = I - 1
      Put #fileNum, I - 1, theDB
'     theDB(I - 1) = theDB(I)
    Next I
    FirstRec.numEntries = FirstRec.numEntries - 1
'   ReDim Preserve theDB(numEntries)
    Put #fileNum, 1, FirstRec
  End If
  Sheets("ContactsDlog").ScrollBars("ScrollEntry").Value = theEntryNum
  Sheets("ContactsDlog").ScrollBars("ScrollEntry").Max = _
      FirstRec.numEntries
  DBToEntry theEntryNum
End Sub
```

The FindName_Click procedure now must check whether there are any entries. You also insert a Get statement to load a record that the procedure can search for the search string.

```
'
'   Find a name
'
Sub FindName_Click()
  Static theName As String
  Dim I As Integer
  Const TextComparison = 1
  If FirstRec.numEntries < 2 Then Exit Sub 'No entries yet.
  theName = InputBox("Input a name to search for.", _
      "Find A Name", theName)
  If theEntryNum <> FirstRec.numEntries Then
    For I = theEntryNum + 1 To FirstRec.numEntries
      Get #fileNum, I, theDB
      If InStr(1, theDB.Name, theName, TextComparison) <> 0 Then
        'Found a matching entry
        theEntryNum = I
        DBToEntry theEntryNum
        Exit Sub
      End If
    Next I
  End If
```

```
  For I = 2 To theEntryNum
    Get #fileNum, I, theDB
    If InStr(1, theDB.Name, theName, TextComparison) <> 0 Then
      'Found a matching entry
      theEntryNum = I
      DBToEntry theEntryNum
      Exit Sub
    End If
  Next I
  'No match found
  MsgBox "The name: " & theName & " was not found.", , "Find A Name"
End Sub
```

To create a new database file, you change the Save_Click procedure into the New_Click procedure:

```
'
'Create a new database.
'
Sub New_Click()
' Sub Save_Click()
  Dim theFilter As String, Answer, theDot As Integer
'   Dim fileNum As Integer, EntryNum As Integer
'   If numEntries = 0 Then  'See if there is something to save.
'     MsgBox "You don't have anything to save.", , "PCD"
'     Exit Sub
'   End If
  'Get the file name for the data.
  theFilter = "PCD database (*.PCD),*.PCD"
  'theFileName is global, so it always defaults to the current name.
  Answer = Application.GetSaveAsFilename(theFileName, theFilter, 1)
  If Answer = False Then Exit Sub 'The user chose Cancel.
  theFileName = Trim(Answer)    'Remove any leading or trailing blanks.
  'Make sure the file name ends in PCD.
  theDot = InStr(theFileName, ".")
  If theDot = 0 Then   'No extension typed; add one.
    theFileName = theFileName & ".PCD"
  Else  'Something was typed; delete it and add .PCD.
    theFileName = Left(theFileName, theDot - 1) & ".PCD"
  End If
```

299

Chapter 19 ◆ Saving Data in a Random Access File

```
    Close     ' Close an existing file, if any.
' Open the data file
    fileNum = FreeFile()   'Get a file number and open the file.
    Open theFileName For Random As fileNum Len = 256
    FirstRec.numEntries = 1  'Mark the database as open but empty.
    theEntryNum = 0
    'Use record 1 to store the number of records.
    Put #fileNum, 1, FirstRec
    'Set to Min value.
    Sheets("ContactsDlog").ScrollBars("ScrollEntry").Max = 2
    'Clear the form.
    With Sheets("ContactsDlog")
      .EditBoxes("DName").Text = ""
      .EditBoxes("DAddress").Text = ""
      .EditBoxes("DCity").Text = ""
      .EditBoxes("DState").Text = ""
      .EditBoxes("DZip").Text = ""
      .EditBoxes("DPhone").Text = ""
      .DropDowns("DE_Mail_Net").Text = ""
      .EditBoxes("DE_Mail_Address").Text = ""
      .EditBoxes("DReferral").Text = ""
      .EditBoxes("DNotes").Text = ""
      .Labels("DRecNo").Caption = "Record #: "
    End With
'   'First save the number of entries.
'   Write #fileNum, numEntries
'   'Now loop over each element of the database
'   'and write all the components into the file.
'   For EntryNum = 1 To numEntries
'   With theDB(EntryNum)
'     Write #fileNum, .Name
'     Write #fileNum, .Address
'     Write #fileNum, .City
'     Write #fileNum, .State
'     Write #fileNum, .Zip
'     Write #fileNum, .Phone
'     Write #fileNum, .Net
'     Write #fileNum, .NetAddr
'     Write #fileNum, .Referral
'     Write #fileNum, .Notes
'     Write #fileNum, .RecNo
'   End With
```

```
'    Next EntryNum
'    Close #fileNum    'All done
     MsgBox "New database created: " & theFileName, , "PCD"
End Sub
```

The first half of the procedure works largely the same as before, and gets a file name to use for the new file. The procedure no longer has to check for an existing file that must be saved, because this version of the program saves the data as you go. The second half of the procedure opens the file, initializes the first record, and clears the form. The program also no longer needs the code to save the database because it is saved as you go.

> **Note:** The code that clears the form can be copied from the InitializeIt procedure. If you needed to clear the form more often, you could put this code in a separate procedure and call it whenever you needed to clear a form.

The Open_Click procedure works much like the previous version:

```
'
'Open a database file.
'
Sub Open_Click()
    Dim theFilter As String, Answer, theDot As Integer
'   Dim fileNum As Integer, EntryNum As Integer
'   Dim buttons As Integer, theMsg As String
    Dim Flag As Boolean
'   If numEntries <> 0 Then   'See if there is something to save first.
'       buttons = vbYesNoCancel + vbQuestion + vbApplicationModal
'       theMsg = "Do you want to save the current data first?"
'       Answer = MsgBox(theMsg, buttons, "PCD")
'       If Answer = vbCancel Then    'Quit if the user chose Cancel.
'           Exit Sub
'       ElseIf Answer = vbYes Then   'Call save if the user chose Yes.
'           Save_Click
'       End If
'   End If
    'Get the file name for the data.
    theFilter = "PCD database (*.PCD),*.PCD"
```

Chapter 19 ♦ Saving Data in a Random Access File

```
    Do
      Answer = Application.GetOpenFilename(theFilter, 1)
      If Answer = False Then Exit Sub 'The user chose Cancel.
      Answer = Trim(Answer)    'Remove any leading or trailing blanks.
      theDot = InStr(Answer, ".")
      If theDot = 0 Then  'Bad file name, no extension.
        MsgBox "You must choose a .PCD file.", , "PCD"
        Flag = False
      ElseIf Right(Answer, 4) <> ".PCD" Then  'Wrong extension
        MsgBox "You must choose a .PCD file.", , "PCD"
        Flag = False
      Else  'Must be OK.
        Flag = True
      End If
    Loop Until Flag
    theFileName = Answer
    Close   'Close the previous data file, if any.
    fileNum = FreeFile()  'Get a file number and open the file.
    Open theFileName For Random As fileNum Len = 256
    'Read the number of entries.
    Get #fileNum, 1, FirstRec
'   'Now expand the database.
'   ReDim theDB(numEntries)
'   'Now loop over each element of the database
'   'and read all the components into the file.
'   For EntryNum = 1 To numEntries
'     With theDB(EntryNum)
'       Input #fileNum, .Name
'       Input #fileNum, .Address
'       Input #fileNum, .City
'       Input #fileNum, .State
'       Input #fileNum, .Zip
'       Input #fileNum, .Phone
'       Input #fileNum, .Net
'       Input #fileNum, .NetAddr
'       Input #fileNum, .Referral
'       Input #fileNum, .Notes
'       Input #fileNum, .RecNo
'     End With
'   Next EntryNum
'   Close #fileNum    'All done
```

```
    MsgBox theFileName & " was opened.", , "PCD"
    Sheets("ContactsDlog").ScrollBars("ScrollEntry").Max = _
        FirstRec.numEntries
    If FirstRec.numEntries > 1 Then 'If there is an entry in the file.
      theEntryNum = 2   'Insert the first entry into the form.
      DBToEntry theEntryNum
    End If
End Sub
```

The first half of the procedure gets and validates the file name. You don't have to check for unsaved data because now all data is saved as you go. The second half of the procedure opens the file and loads numEntries by reading the first record of the file into the FirstRec record variable. You can now create a file that has no entries, so before you display the first entry you must check whether it exists.

Quit_Click is a new procedure that closes the data file when the user chooses the Quit button. Without this procedure, the file would be left open, which could cause errors.

```
'
' The Quit procedure to end the program.
'
Sub Quit_Click()
  'You need to close any open data files here.
  Close
End Sub
```

> **Note:** If you get "File already open" type errors while working with this program, the program most likely crashed with a file open. When you run the program again, it tries to open the already open file and gets an error. To fix this, you can close all open files by executing a Close command in the Immediate pane of the Debug window.

This completes the review of the modifications you must make to the personal contacts database program to enable it to use random access files. Save the workbook and then run the procedure to see how it works. Don't forget to create a file before entering any data on the form.

Chapter 19 ◆ Saving Data in a Random Access File

Summary

In this chapter, you learned to use random access disk files to store record-based data. Random access files differ significantly from sequential files. As you recall from Chapter 18, sequential files handle data as a continuous stream from the beginning of the file to the end. However, random access files handle data in independent blocks called records that can be stored or retrieved from the disk file in any order. You use a file mode of Random to open random access files, and a Len = *reclen* qualifier to specify the record length. To read and write data to the file, you use the Get and Put statements.

In the next chapter, you learn about storing data in worksheet files.

Review Questions

The answers to the review questions are in Appendix A.

1. How do you open a random access file?
2. When opening a random access file, what does the Len = specifier specify?
3. Which two statements do you use to read and write random access files?
4. If you read a record from a random access file, must you store it back in the same place?
5. What is a record variable? How does it differ from a normal variable?
6. What is an indexed record?

Review Exercises

1. In the personal contacts database program, extract the code that clears the form and make it a separate procedure. Then call that procedure from the two places from which you extracted the code.
2. To the NewEntry_Click, UpdateEntry_Click, ScrollEntries_Click, DeleteEntry_Click, and FindName_Click procedures, add messages that tell the user why the control is doing nothing when no data is available. Currently, the control does nothing when there is no data.
3. Add procedures that monitor the number of characters typed into the fields on the form, and have the program beep if the user types more characters than are allowed in the field.

4. Write a procedure that ensures that the state field consists of all uppercase letters, no matter what the user types. Automatically change any lowercase text to uppercase.

5. Change the state field to a drop-down list that contains all the state abbreviations.

6. Change the storage method so that it uses indexed records, and move the index to the end of the index array instead of moving the contents of the records when records are deleted. Also, use deleted records before adding new ones to the file.

7. Write a procedure that alphabetizes the records according to last name. Before you can alphabetize the records, you must extract the rightmost word from the name field.

CHAPTER 20

Saving Data in Other Places

Sequential and random access disk files are the primary storage media for Visual Basic applications. However, you can store data on disk in other places, such as in the worksheets of an open workbook or in external database files. You access worksheet files using the same methods that you have already seen several times. To access an external database, you must use the Microsoft Access engine.

In this chapter you will learn how to do the following:

- ♦ Save data in worksheets
- ♦ Create, open, and save worksheets remotely
- ♦ Access external database files

Saving Data in a Worksheet

Worksheets are available to any Visual Basic program running in Excel. They also are available in Project, although they are not as flexible in Project as they are in Excel. To use a worksheet as a data storage location, use the techniques described earlier in this book for accessing cells and storing data. Visual Basic also has access to all of Excel's commands to open and save worksheets and workbooks.

Opening or Creating a Worksheet or Workbook

Creating a new worksheet or workbook is straightforward: You use the Add method of the Worksheets or Workbooks collections.

Chapter 20 ♦ Saving Data in Other Places

For example, to add a new worksheet to the Book2 workbook and name it ContactsData, use the following:

```
Sub addWorksheet()
  Workbooks("Book2").Worksheets.Add
  ActiveSheet.Name = "ContactsData"
End Sub
```

The Add method contains several options that enable you to control where you insert a worksheet in a workbook. For a complete list of these options, see the on-line help. To add the worksheet to the current workbook, you would use the ActiveWorkbook object rather than the Workbooks collection.

For example, to create a new workbook, save it with a specified name, rename the first worksheet, and then save the changes, you would write a subroutine similar to the following:

```
Sub addWorkbook()
  Workbooks.Add
  ActiveWorkbook.SaveAs "PCDDATA.XLS"
  Worksheets(1).Name = "ContactsData"
  ActiveWorkbook.Save
End Sub
```

To open an existing workbook and select the ContactsData worksheet, you would write the following subroutine:

```
Sub getWorkbook()
  Workbooks.Open "PCDDATA.XLS"
  Worksheets("ContactsData").Select
End Sub
```

To open a specific workbook, you could use the GetOpenFilename method. However, when you are working with workbooks and worksheets, it's easier to call Excel's Open dialog box and let it handle the selecting and opening of the file. To display Excel's Open dialog box, you would write the following subroutine:

```
Sub openWorkbook()
  Application.Dialogs(xlDialogOpen).Show
End Sub
```

Whichever file the user selects and opens from the dialog box then becomes the active workbook. To find out which file the user opened, examine the Name property of the ActiveWorkbook object. Just in case the user chose Cancel, you need to check whether the value that the Show method returned equals False.

To use the Save As dialog box to save an open workbook, replace the built-in constant with xlDialogSaveAs as shown in the following procedure:

```
Sub saveWorkbook()
  Application.Dialogs(xlDialogSaveAs).Show
End Sub
```

Writing Data to Worksheet Ranges

You have already seen how to write data to worksheet cells. However, as a quick review, use the Range object to select a cell. To select cells in order, use the Cells method. This method takes two integer arguments: *row* and *column*. Note that the Cells method applies to the current Range object, not the worksheet, so Cells(1,1) is not necessarily cell A1. For example, if the current Range object is cell B5, then Cells(1,1) refers to B5 and Cells(2,3) refers to D6.

When writing to a single known cell, name the cell on the worksheet and use that name with the Range method to select the cell. When writing to a range of cells, name the cell in the upper-left corner of the range, use that name with the Range method to select that cell as a Range object, and then access the rest of the range by applying the Cells method to the Range object.

For example, if numEntries is the name of a cell on a worksheet named ContactsData, you can access its value by using the following:

```
Sheets("ContactsData").Range("numEntries").Value
```

If DBTop is the upper-left cell of a range of cells on the same worksheet, you can access the rest of the range with the following:

```
Sheets("ContactsData").Range("DBTop").Cells(I, J).Value
```

where I and J are the row and column number of the cell measured down and to the right from DBTop.

Caution: The worksheet attempts to interpret some values when you insert them into worksheet cells. For example, if numbers have leading zeros, the worksheet removes them, and if strings look like formulas, the worksheet calculates them or treats them as dates. Therefore, you may have to format some values as text to ensure that you get back the correct values. Or, you can add a single quotation mark to the beginning of the string before you place it in the worksheet cell, because this character forces the value to be a string.

Chapter 20 ◆ Saving Data in Other Places

Storing the Personal Contacts Database on a Worksheet

The following version of the personal contacts database uses a worksheet to store its data. Once again, the new and changed lines are highlighted with boldface type. The worksheet is part of the workbook that contains the database application, and is opened when the workbook is opened and saved when the workbook is saved. An obvious benefit of this scheme is that the data is now part of a worksheet, so you can use Excel's Data commands to search and sort the data.

```
'
' Personal Contacts Database Program
' Worksheet Storage Version
'
Option Explicit 'Force all variables to be defined.
Option Base 1   'Make arrays start at 1.
Const pcdName = 2, pcdAddress = 3, pcdCity = 4
Const pcdState = 5, pcdZip = 6, pcdPhone = 7
Const pcdNet = 8, pcdNetAddr = 9, pcdReferral = 10
Const pcdNotes = 11, pcdRecNo = 1
Const pcdNumFields = 11 'Number of fields in the database.
Dim numEntries As Integer  'Total number of entries.
Dim theEntryNum As Integer 'The currently displayed entry.
'
' Initialize database
'
Sub InitializeIt()
  Dim theMaxVal As Integer
  numEntries = Sheets("ContactsData").Range("numEntries").Value
  If numEntries = 0 Then
    theEntryNum = 0
    theMaxVal = 1
    ClrFrm
  Else
    theEntryNum = 1
    theMaxVal = numEntries
    DBToEntry theEntryNum
  End If
  Sheets("ContactsDlog").DropDowns("DE_Mail_Net").List = _
    Array("Compuserve", "Internet", "GEnie", "Prodigy")
  Sheets("ContactsDlog").ScrollBars("ScrollEntry").Min = 1
  Sheets("ContactsDlog").ScrollBars("ScrollEntry").Max = theMaxVal
```

```vb
    Sheets("ContactsDlog").Show
End Sub
'
'   Clear the form.
'
Sub ClrFrm()
  With Sheets("ContactsDlog")
    .EditBoxes("DName").Text = ""
    .EditBoxes("DAddress").Text = ""
    .EditBoxes("DCity").Text = ""
    .EditBoxes("DState").Text = ""
    .EditBoxes("DZip").Text = ""
    .EditBoxes("DPhone").Text = ""
    .DropDowns("DE_Mail_Net").Text = ""
    .EditBoxes("DE_Mail_Address").Text = ""
    .EditBoxes("DReferral").Text = ""
    .EditBoxes("DNotes").Text = ""
    .Labels("DRecNo").Caption = "Record #: "
  End With
End Sub
'
' The Auto_Open procedure
' runs whenever this workbook is opened.
'
Sub Auto_Open()
  InitializeIt  'Run the initialization procedure.
End Sub
'
'   Add a new entry
'
Sub NewEntry_Click()
  numEntries = numEntries + 1
  Sheets("ContactsData").Range("numEntries").Value = numEntries
  Sheets("ContactsDlog").ScrollBars("ScrollEntry").Max = numEntries
  theEntryNum = numEntries
  EntryToDB theEntryNum    'Write the entry to the array.
  DBToEntry theEntryNum    'Read the entry back to display theEntryNum.
End Sub
'
'   Update an entry
'
```

Chapter 20 ♦ Saving Data in Other Places

```vb
Sub UpdateEntry_Click()
  If theEntryNum = 0 Then Exit Sub  'Exit if no entries are saved yet.
  EntryToDB theEntryNum  'Update the displayed entry.
End Sub
'
' Transfer an entry to the database
'
Sub EntryToDB(anEntry As Integer)
  Dim theRow
  Set theRow = Sheets("ContactsData").Range("DBTop").Cells(anEntry, 1)
  With Sheets("ContactsDlog")
    theRow.Cells(1, pcdName).Value = .EditBoxes("DName").Text
    theRow.Cells(1, pcdAddress).Value = .EditBoxes("DAddress").Text
    theRow.Cells(1, pcdCity).Value = .EditBoxes("DCity").Text
    theRow.Cells(1, pcdState).Value = .EditBoxes("DState").Text
    theRow.Cells(1, pcdZip).Value = .EditBoxes("DZip").Text
    theRow.Cells(1, pcdPhone).Value = .EditBoxes("DPhone").Text
    theRow.Cells(1, pcdNet).Value = .DropDowns("DE_Mail_Net").Text
    theRow.Cells(1, pcdNetAddr).Value = .EditBoxes("DE_Mail_Address").Text
    theRow.Cells(1, pcdReferral).Value = _
        .EditBoxes("DReferral").Text
    theRow.Cells(1, pcdNotes).Value = .EditBoxes("DNotes").Text
    theRow.Cells(1, pcdRecNo).Value = anEntry
  End With
End Sub
'
' Transfer a record to the form
'
Sub DBToEntry(anEntry As Integer)
  Dim theRow
  Set theRow = Sheets("ContactsData").Range("DBTop").Cells(anEntry, 1)
  With Sheets("ContactsDlog")
    .EditBoxes("DName").Text = theRow.Cells(1, pcdName).Value
    .EditBoxes("DAddress").Text = theRow.Cells(1, pcdAddress).Value
    .EditBoxes("DCity").Text = theRow.Cells(1, pcdCity).Value
    .EditBoxes("DState").Text = theRow.Cells(1, pcdState).Value
    .EditBoxes("DZip").Text = _
        Format(theRow.Cells(1, pcdZip).Value,"00000")
```

```
        .EditBoxes("DPhone").Text = theRow.Cells(1, pcdPhone).Value
        .DropDowns("DE_Mail_Net").Text = theRow.Cells(1, pcdNet).Value
        .EditBoxes("DE_Mail_Address").Text = _
            theRow.Cells(1, pcdNetAddr).Value
        .EditBoxes("DReferral").Text = theRow.Cells(1, pcdReferral).Value
        .EditBoxes("DNotes").Text = theRow.Cells(1, pcdNotes).Value
        .Labels("DRecNo").Caption = "Record #: " & _
            theRow.Cells(1, pcdRecNo).Value
        .ScrollBars("ScrollEntry").Value = anEntry
    End With
End Sub
'
' Scroll entries.
'
Sub ScrollEntries_Click()
    If numEntries = 0 Then Exit Sub 'No entries yet.
    theEntryNum = Sheets("ContactsDlog").ScrollBars("ScrollEntry").Value
    DBToEntry theEntryNum
End Sub
'
' Delete a record
'
Sub DeleteEntry_Click()
    Dim I As Integer, buttons As Integer, J As Integer
    Dim theMsg As String, theRow
    If numEntries = 0 Then Exit Sub   'No entries yet.
    'Make sure the user really wants to do this.
    buttons = vbYesNo + vbDefaultButton2 + vbQuestion + _
        vbApplicationModal
    theMsg = "Are you sure you want to delete the current record?"
    If MsgBox(theMsg, buttons, "Delete Record") = vbNo Then Exit Sub
    'The user said yes, so delete the record and move the others down.
    If theEntryNum = numEntries Then  'It is the last entry.
        numEntries = numEntries - 1
        Sheets("ContactsData").Range("numEntries").Value = numEntries
        theEntryNum = numEntries
    ElseIf theEntryNum = 0 Then   'No entry to delete.
        Exit Sub
    Else  'Shift everything down one.
```

Chapter 20 ♦ Saving Data in Other Places

```
      For I = theEntryNum + 1 To numEntries     'Loop over the rows.
        Set theRow = Sheets("ContactsData").Range("DBTop").Cells(I, 1)
        For J = 1 To pcdNumfields     'Loop over the columns
          theRow.Cells(1, J).Value = theRow.Cells(2, J).Value
        Next J
        theRow.Cells(1, pcdRecNo).Value = I - 1
      Next I
      numEntries = numEntries - 1
      Sheets("ContactsData").Range("numEntries").Value = numEntries
    End If
    Sheets("ContactsDlog").ScrollBars("ScrollEntry").Value = theEntryNum
    Sheets("ContactsDlog").ScrollBars("ScrollEntry").Max = numEntries
    DBToEntry theEntryNum
End Sub
'
' Find a name
'
Sub FindName_Click()
    Static theName As String
    Dim I As Integer, theRow
    Const TextComparison = 1
    If numEntries = 0 Then Exit Sub   'No entries yet.
    theName = InputBox("Input a name to search for.", _
        "Find A Name", theName)
    If theEntryNum <> numEntries Then
      For I = theEntryNum + 1 To numEntries
        Set theRow = Sheets("ContactsData").Range("DBTop").Cells(I, 1)
        If InStr(1, theRow.Cells(1, pcdName).Value, _
            theName, TextComparison) <> 0 Then
          'Found a matching entry
          theEntryNum = I
          DBToEntry theEntryNum
          Exit Sub
        End If
      Next I
    End If
    For I = 1 To theEntryNum
      Set theRow = Sheets("ContactsData").Range("DBTop").Cells(I, 1)
      If InStr(1, theRow.Cells(1, pcdName).Value, _
          theName, TextComparison) <> 0 Then
        'Found a matching entry
        theEntryNum = I
        DBToEntry theEntryNum
```

```
        Exit Sub
     End If
   Next I
   'No match found
   MsgBox "The name: " & theName & " was not found.", , "Find A Name"
End Sub
```

To produce the worksheet version of the personal contacts database program, you follow these steps:

1. Start with a copy of the sequential file version of the program that you developed in Chapter 18. This is the same version of the program that served as the starting point for the random access file version that you created in Chapter 19.

2. Delete the Open and Save buttons, because the worksheet version of the database is automatically opened and saved with the workbook.

3. Select an unused worksheet and change its name to **ContactsData**.

4. Place the following list of labels in the indicated cells as shown in figure 20.1.

Cell	Label
A1	numEntries =
A2	Database
A3	RecNo
B3	Name
C3	Address
D3	City
E3	State
F3	Zip
G3	Phone
H3	Net
I3	NetAddress
J3	Referral
K3	Notes

Chapter 20 ◆ Saving Data in Other Places

Figure 20.1
Layout of the worksheet that holds the data for the worksheet storage version of the personal contacts database.

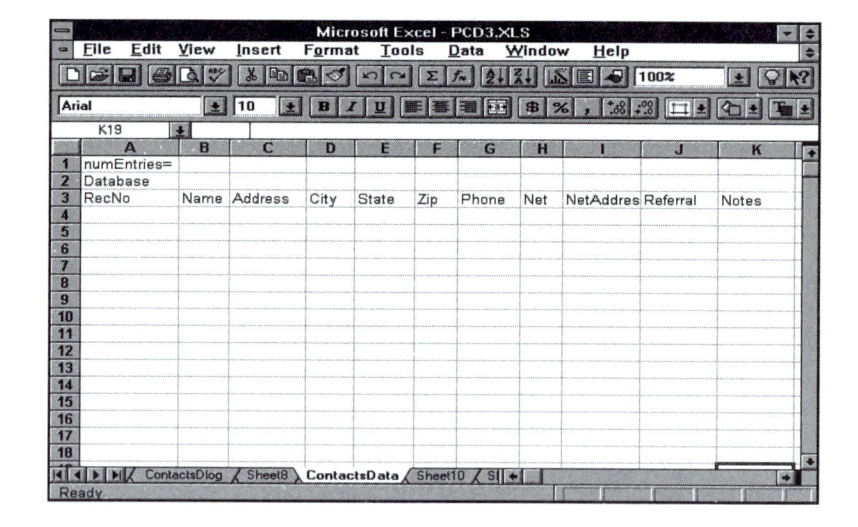

5. Name cell B1 as numEntries and cell A4 as DBTop.

6. Change the code in the module as indicated in the preceding listing. The following descriptions make it easier to determine which lines to delete or change.

In the following descriptions, new and changed lines are highlighted in boldface type, and the deleted lines are commented out (that is, a single quotation mark appears at the beginning of the line) and in boldface type.

In the module heading, the user-defined type and the array variables are deleted because they are not needed. A series of constants are defined that contain the column number for the named database fields. Using these constants makes the program more readable.

```
'
'   Personal Contacts Database Program
'   Worksheet Storage Version
'
Option Explicit  'Force all variables to be defined.
Option Base 1    'Make arrays start at 1.
'Type DBEntry    'Define the structure of a single database entry.
'   Name As String * 25
'   Address As String * 25
'   City As String * 15
'   State As String * 2
'   Zip As String * 10
```

Visual Basic for Applications By EXAMPLE

```
'    Phone As String * 20
'    Net As String * 10
'    NetAddr As String * 25
'    Referral As String * 25
'    Notes As String * 97
'    RecNo As Integer
'End Type      'Size of type is 256 bytes.
'Dim theDB() As DBEntry       'The database array.
Const pcdName = 2, pcdAddress = 3, pcdCity = 4
Const pcdState = 5, pcdZip = 6, pcdPhone = 7
Const pcdNet = 8, pcdNetAddr = 9, pcdReferral = 10
Const pcdNotes = 11, pcdRecNo = 1
Const pcdNumFields = 11 'Number of fields in the database.
Dim numEntries As Integer   'Total number of entries.
Dim theEntryNum As Integer 'The currently displayed entry.
'   Dim theFileName As String   'The current file name.
```

The InitializeIt procedure does not zero out the database as in the previous versions, but connects to the worksheet that contains the data and then loads the first record. The procedure first loads the number of entries from the worksheet and then checks whether the worksheet contains any entries. If there are no entries yet, InitializeIt clears the form; if there are entries, the procedure loads the first one onto the form. Also, to make the procedure more readable, the code to clear the form has been removed and made a separate procedure.

```
'
'    Initialize database
'
Sub InitializeIt()
  Dim theMaxVal As Integer
'   numEntries = 0
  numEntries = Sheets("ContactsData").Range("numEntries").Value
'   ReDim theDB(1)
  If numEntries = 0 Then
    theEntryNum = 0
    theMaxVal = 1
    ClrFrm
  Else
    theEntryNum = 1
    theMaxVal = numEntries
    DBToEntry theEntryNum
  End If
```

317

Chapter 20 ♦ Saving Data in Other Places

```
    Sheets("ContactsDlog").DropDowns("DE_Mail_Net").List = _
      Array("Compuserve", "Internet", "GEnie", "Prodigy")
    Sheets("ContactsDlog").ScrollBars("ScrollEntry").Min = 1
    Sheets("ContactsDlog").ScrollBars("ScrollEntry").Max = theMaxVal
    Sheets("ContactsDlog").Show
'   theFileName = ""
End Sub
'
'   Clear the form.
'
Sub ClrFrm()
  With Sheets("ContactsDlog")
    .EditBoxes("DName").Text = ""
    .EditBoxes("DAddress").Text = ""
    .EditBoxes("DCity").Text = ""
    .EditBoxes("DState").Text = ""
    .EditBoxes("DZip").Text = ""
    .EditBoxes("DPhone").Text = ""
    .DropDowns("DE_Mail_Net").Text = ""
    .EditBoxes("DE_Mail_Address").Text = ""
    .EditBoxes("DReferral").Text = ""
    .EditBoxes("DNotes").Text = ""
    .Labels("DRecNo").Caption = "Record #: "
  End With
End Sub
```

The Auto_Open and UpdateEntry_Click procedures do not change. However, in the NewEntry_Click procedure you remove the reference to theDB and insert a statement that changes the value of the cell named numEntries on the worksheet after the variable numEntries increases by one.

```
'
'   Add a new entry
'
Sub NewEntry_Click()
  numEntries = numEntries + 1
  Sheets("ContactsData").Range("numEntries").Value = numEntries
  Sheets("ContactsDlog").ScrollBars("ScrollEntry").Max = numEntries
  theEntryNum = numEntries
'  ReDim Preserve theDB(numEntries) 'Expand the array.
  EntryToDB theEntryNum      'Write the entry to the array.
  DBToEntry theEntryNum      'Read the entry back to display theEntryNum.
End Sub
```

The EntryToDB and DBToEntry procedures must change significantly to convert from saving the data in the theDB array to saving the data on the worksheet:

```vba
'
' Transfer an entry to the database
'
Sub EntryToDB(anEntry As Integer)
   Dim theRow
   Set theRow = Sheets("ContactsData").Range("DBTop").Cells(anEntry, 1)
   With Sheets("ContactsDlog")
      theRow.Cells(1, pcdName).Value = .EditBoxes("DName").Text
      theRow.Cells(1, pcdAddress).Value = .EditBoxes("DAddress").Text
      theRow.Cells(1, pcdCity).Value = .EditBoxes("DCity").Text
      theRow.Cells(1, pcdState).Value = .EditBoxes("DState").Text
      theRow.Cells(1, pcdZip).Value = .EditBoxes("DZip").Text
      theRow.Cells(1, pcdPhone).Value = .EditBoxes("DPhone").Text
      theRow.Cells(1, pcdNet).Value = .DropDowns("DE_Mail_Net").Text
      theRow.Cells(1, pcdNetAddr).Value = _
         .EditBoxes("DE_Mail_Address").Text
      theRow.Cells(1, pcdReferral).Value = .EditBoxes("DReferral").Text
      theRow.Cells(1, pcdNotes).Value = .EditBoxes("DNotes").Text
      theRow.Cells(1, pcdRecNo).Value = anEntry
   End With
End Sub
'
' Transfer a record to the form
'
Sub DBToEntry(anEntry As Integer)
   Dim theRow
   Set theRow = Sheets("ContactsData").Range("DBTop").Cells(anEntry, 1)
   With Sheets("ContactsDlog")
      .EditBoxes("DName").Text = theRow.Cells(1, pcdName).Value
      .EditBoxes("DAddress").Text = theRow.Cells(1, pcdAddress).Value
      .EditBoxes("DCity").Text = theRow.Cells(1, pcdCity).Value
      .EditBoxes("DState").Text = theRow.Cells(1, pcdState).Value
      .EditBoxes("DZip").Text = _
         Format(theRow.Cells(1, pcdZip).Value,"00000")
      .EditBoxes("DPhone").Text = theRow.Cells(1, pcdPhone).Value
```

Chapter 20 ♦ Saving Data in Other Places

```
        .DropDowns("DE_Mail_Net").Text = theRow.Cells(1, pcdNet).Value
        .EditBoxes("DE_Mail_Address").Text = _
            theRow.Cells(1, pcdNetAddr).Value
        .EditBoxes("DReferral").Text = theRow.Cells(1, pcdReferral).Value
        .EditBoxes("DNotes").Text = theRow.Cells(1, pcdNotes).Value
        .Labels("DRecNo").Caption = "Record #: " & _
            theRow.Cells(1, pcdRecNo).Value
        .ScrollBars("ScrollEntry").Value = anEntry
    End With
End Sub
```

To shorten the entries in the block With structure, the object variable theRow is defined as a range reference to the first cell in the row where the data is to be stored. DBTop is a named cell on the worksheet at the upper-left corner of the range in which the data is to be stored. The Cells method is used to move down from DBTop to the row in which the procedure will store the data.

The procedure stores the data in the worksheet with the statements in the block With structure. The object variable theRow selects the row in which the data is to be stored, and the Cells method is used a second time to move along that row to the column in which the data item is to be stored. To select the columns, use the constants, such as pcdName, that were defined in the module header. The DBToEntry procedure works the same way, except that it retrieves the values from the worksheet instead of passing them to it. The zip code entry uses a Format statement to return any leading zeros that the worksheet removes.

The ScrollEntries_Click procedure is unchanged. However, the DeleteEntry_Click procedure gets changes similar to those of the EntryToDB procedure, to enable the procedure to transfer data from one entry in the database to another. The procedure accomplishes this data transfer by using two loops: one that loops over the rows and one that loops over the columns in the worksheet. Also, the value of numEntries is updated on the worksheet after it is reduced by one.

```
'
' Delete a record
'
Sub DeleteEntry_Click()
    Dim I As Integer, buttons As Integer, J As Integer
    Dim theMsg As String, theRow
    If numEntries = 0 Then Exit Sub    'No entries yet.
```

```
    'Make sure the user really wants to do this.
    buttons = vbYesNo + vbDefaultButton2 + vbQuestion + _
        vbApplicationModal
    theMsg = "Are you sure you want to delete the current record?"
    If MsgBox(theMsg, buttons, "Delete Record") = vbNo Then Exit Sub
    'The user said yes, so delete the record and move the others down.
    If theEntryNum = numEntries Then    'It is the last entry.
      numEntries = numEntries - 1
      Sheets("ContactsData").Range("numEntries").Value = numEntries
'     ReDim Preserve theDB(numEntries)
      theEntryNum = numEntries
    ElseIf theEntryNum = 0 Then  'No entry to delete.
      Exit Sub
    Else  'Shift everything down one.
      For I = theEntryNum + 1 To numEntries    'Loop over the rows.
        Set theRow = Sheets("ContactsData").Range("DBTop").Cells(I, 1)
        For J = 1 To pcdNumfields    'Loop over the columns
          theRow.Cells(1, J).Value = theRow.Cells(2, J).Value
        Next J
        theRow.Cells(1, pcdRecNo).Value = I - 1
'       theDB(I - 1) = theDB(I)
'       theDB(I - 1).RecNo = I - 1
      Next I
      numEntries = numEntries - 1
'     ReDim Preserve theDB(numEntries)
      Sheets("ContactsData").Range("numEntries").Value = numEntries
    End If
    Sheets("ContactsDlog").ScrollBars("ScrollEntry").Value = theEntryNum
    Sheets("ContactsDlog").ScrollBars("ScrollEntry").Max = numEntries
    DBToEntry theEntryNum
End Sub
```

The FindName_Click procedure gets a change similar to that of the DBToEntry procedure, to extract the contents of the name field in the worksheet and make it available for comparison to the search string:

```
'
' Find a name
'
Sub FindName_Click()
  Static theName As String
```

Chapter 20 ◆ Saving Data in Other Places

```
Dim I As Integer, theRow
Const TextComparison = 1
If numEntries = 0 Then Exit Sub  'No entries yet.
theName = InputBox("Input a name to search for.", _
    "Find A Name", theName)
If theEntryNum <> numEntries Then
  For I = theEntryNum + 1 To numEntries
    Set theRow = Sheets("ContactsData").Range("DBTop").Cells(I, 1)
    If InStr(1, theRow.Cells(1, pcdName).Value, _
        theName, TextComparison) <> 0 Then
      'Found a matching entry
      theEntryNum = I
      DBToEntry theEntryNum
      Exit Sub
    End If
  Next I
End If
For I = 1 To theEntryNum
  Set theRow = Sheets("ContactsData").Range("DBTop").Cells(I, 1)
  If InStr(1, theRow.Cells(1, pcdName).Value, _
      theName, TextComparison) <> 0 Then
    'Found a matching entry
    theEntryNum = I
    DBToEntry theEntryNum
    Exit Sub
  End If
Next I
'No match found
MsgBox "The name: " & theName & " was not found.", , "Find A Name"
End Sub
```

When you run the procedure, it places data on the worksheet as shown in figure 20.2. Each row in the worksheet is a record that contains the data from one form, and each column contains the data from a field on the form. After the data is on the worksheet, you can use the **Data** **S**ort command to sort the records, or the **Data** **F**orm command to search the database.

Saving Data in an External Database

You can use Visual Basic to access a database file that was created with a database application. If you do so, you can use both Visual Basic's and the database application's capabilities to examine and change the database file.

Figure 20.2

The data in the worksheet storage version of the personal contacts database is stored on the ContactsData worksheet.

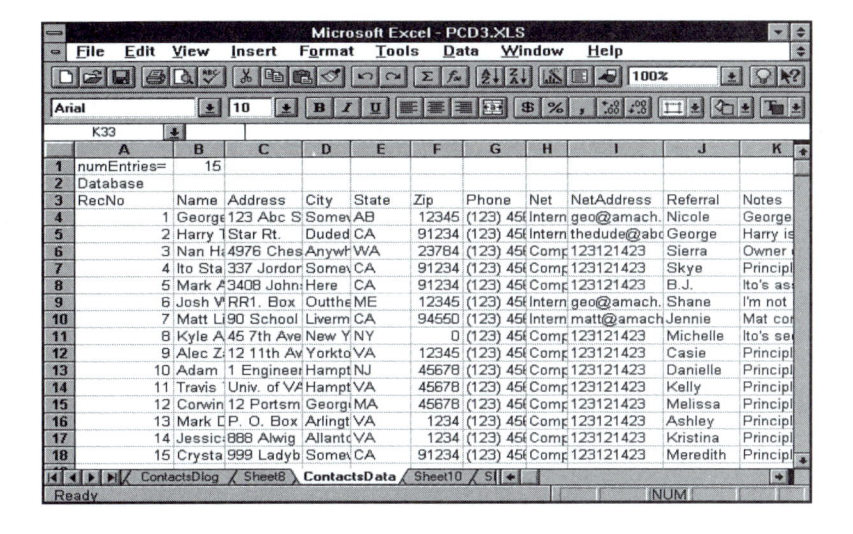

To control an external database from within a Visual Basic program requires knowledge of the database language SQL (Structured Query Language). This section does not describe the SQL database language, but does describe the Visual Basic extensions that enable you to connect to an external database.

To access an external database file, the ODBC (Open Database Connectivity) add-in must be installed in Excel. To install this feature, choose the **T**ools Add-**I**ns command, and then in the **A**dd-Ins Available drop-down list, check the ODBC Add-In option as shown in figure 20.3. When the add-in is attached, use the **T**ools Re**f**erence command to establish a reference to the add-in, and then check the XLODBC.XLA library. Then you can execute the Visual Basic functions contained in XLODBC.XLA. See the online help for more information on installing ODBC drivers and add-ins.

Figure 20.3

The Add-Ins dialog box that you use to attach the ODBC add-in.

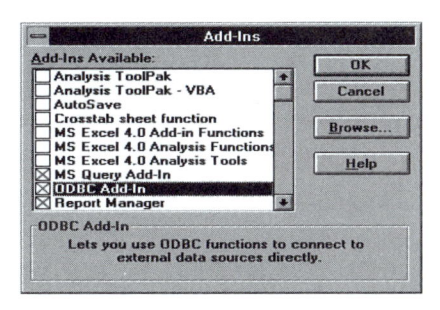

After you install and reference the ODBC add-in, you can execute from Visual Basic the functions stored in the add-in file. Table 20.1 lists the available functions.

323

Table 20.1. The ODBC functions available in the XLODBC.XLA add-in.

Function	Description
SQLOpen	Opens a connection to an external data source and returns a connection ID that is similar to a file number.
SQLBind	Specifies where to send the results received from the external data source. The location is a worksheet range.
SQLClose	Closes a connection to an external data source.
SQLError	Returns detailed error information about a failed ODBC function call.
SQLExecQuery	Sends a query to the open external data source in the SQL language.
SQLGetSchema	Requests information about the structure of the external data source.
SQLRequest	Opens a connection to an external data source, sends it a query, receives the result, and closes the connection.
SQLRetrieve	Gets the results of the previous query and places them on a worksheet.
SQLRetrieveToFile	Gets the results of the previous query and places them in a file.

The type of database that you are accessing—such as dBASE or FoxPro—determines the actual arguments that you use with these add-in functions. To determine your driver's required arguments, see your driver's documentation and the online help provided for the drivers. Again, to access an external database, you must know the SQL language.

> **Note:** ODBC conspicuously lacks the capability to create new databases and tables from within Excel or Visual Basic. Although the add-in enables you to add or delete records, you can create or modify the structure of the database file only with a database application.

> **Tip:** If you don't want to learn the SQL language, you can use Microsoft Query, which is included with Excel. Query handles all database manipulations in a point-and-click environment. You can call Query from a worksheet to embed the results of the query in the worksheet.

Summary

In this chapter, you learned how to store data on an Excel worksheet. Using the Range object and the Range and Cells methods, you can easily access cell ranges for storing or retrieving data. Data stored on a worksheet is automatically stored or opened when the workbook to which the sheet is attached is stored or opened.

You also learned about the capability to access external database files. To use this capability, you need to know how to use SQL, the standard database language. An easier proposition is to use the Microsoft Query program, which is included with Excel.

This completes Part VI of this book. In Part VII, you learn about error trapping and debugging.

Review Questions

The answers to the review questions are in Appendix A.

1. How do you add a new worksheet to the active workbook?
2. How do you rename a worksheet?
3. How do you open an existing worksheet when you know its name?
4. How do you open an existing worksheet when the user knows its name?
5. If the active range object points to cell K13, to which cell does the `Cells(5,7)` method point when applied to that object?

Review Exercises

1. Insert several entries to the personal contacts database. Then exit the program and switch to the ContactsData form, select the database, including the field names in row 3, and then choose the **D**ata **F**orm command. Work with the form to search and display different parts of the database.

Chapter 20 ◆ Saving Data in Other Places

2. Run Microsoft Query, open one of the example databases, and then experiment with searching and displaying records. Open Query from within Excel and return a selection of records to a worksheet range.

3. Add a button to the ContactsDlog form of the personal contacts database program that sorts the database using Excel's worksheet functions.

4. Rewrite the DeleteEntry_Click procedure so that it uses the worksheet's **Edit Copy** and **Edit Paste** commands to select the database range beyond the deleted row and move it up as a block.

5. Rewrite the DeleteEntry_Click procedure again, this time so that it uses the worksheet's **Edit Delete** command to delete the row to be removed.

6. Rewrite the FindEntry_Click procedure so that it conducts a search using the worksheet's **Edit Find** command.

Part VII

Debugging a Procedure

CHAPTER 21

What To Do When Your Code Crashes

Part VII of this book covers debugging and error trapping with Visual Basic. Chapters 21 and 22 deal with examining your code to locate problems using the built-in debugging tools. Chapter 23 deals with trapping program errors so that your program can handle them instead of crashing.

Suppose that you run your latest and greatest program (the one that is going to make you rich and famous), press the OK button, and then a dialog box pops up telling you that your program has just crashed. What do you do now? Do you cry? (Remember not to get tears in your keyboard—tears conduct electricity.) Do you kick your computer? (This may be very gratifying in the short term, but is generally hard on your pocket book in the long term. It may also cause your hard drive to forget your new program completely, which may make you cry even more.) In this chapter you learn to search actively for the problems that make your program crash. In the next chapter you learn what to do when your program does not run as you planned.

In this chapter, you learn how to do the following:

- ♦ Use the debugging tools on the Debug window
- ♦ Examine the value of variables
- ♦ See how your program got to where it is
- ♦ Experiment with problem code using the Immediate pane

Chapter 21 ◆ What To Do When Your Code Crashes

What Is Debugging?

Next to program design, debugging is the second most fun part of computer programming. Debugging is the art of finding and removing bugs. Computer bugs aren't small, living creatures that crawl around inside your computer causing problems (although that has been known to happen). They are simply errors in your programming that cause your programs to crash or work improperly. You can cause such errors simply by misplacing a comma or misspelling a word, or they can result from complex program design errors.

Debugging is an art rather than a science because there is no fixed set of steps for you to take each time you encounter a bug. If there were, you could write a program to handle debugging for you. Instead, locating and fixing a bug requires the use of all your knowledge, experience, and intuition. Debugging is also where all those hours of typing comment statements and carefully block-structuring your code finally pay off. Actually, fixing the bug is usually relatively easy after you have found it—it's finding the bug that takes time. On any reasonably sized coding project, debugging can easily take more than half the time necessary to develop the application.

Essentially three kinds of bugs plague computer programs: syntax errors, runtime errors, and logical errors.

Syntax errors occur when you mistype a statement, omit a required argument, or use an argument of the incorrect type. Normally the Visual Basic interpreter discovers syntax errors for you automatically. Syntax errors that involve the syntax of a statement or keyword are usually discovered while you edit your program. As soon as you finish editing a statement and move to another, the Visual Basic interpreter examines the statement and tries to make sense of what you have typed. If some punctuation, like a comma or parenthesis, is missing or out of place, the interpreter immediately displays a dialog box indicating what is wrong.

The interpreter also finds any syntax errors when you first run a program after editing it. At that time, the interpreter compiles the program into p-code and locates any block-level errors. Block-level syntax errors involve more than one statement, so the interpreter cannot discover them until you finish creating the blocks. Block-level syntax errors are caused by the use of the wrong argument type in a statement or the omission of a closing statement for a loop or block If statement.

> **Note:** A Visual Basic program is not compiled to machine code, but to an intermediate code known as p-code. Machine codes are those commands that the microprocessor knows how to execute directly. P-code is a machine-independent command code that an interpreter executes. The p-code interpreter is much more efficient than traditional BASIC interpreters, because the compiler has already done all the parsing and syntax checking.

A *runtime error* occurs when a value is used incorrectly, such as when using zero as the denominator of a fraction or when taking the square root of a negative number. These errors cannot be found until the code is actually running and the values are calculated. When runtime errors occur, your program displays a dialog box that lists the error number and a short description. Every runtime error has an error number associated with it to make it easy for a program to identify an error. Appendix C lists all of Visual Basic's error numbers.

A *logical error* is an error in the actual logic of the program rather than in the syntax of the code itself. When a logical error occurs, your program still runs, apparently without problem, but gives the wrong results. Logical errors are the hardest to find, because your computer does exactly what you told it to do—it's just that this doesn't happen to be what you wanted it to do. Logical errors may also manifest themselves as syntax errors when the calculated values reach a point where they are no longer valid in a calculation. The source of a logical error can be within a line or two of the line that causes a runtime error, or it may be far away from the location of the runtime error. Therefore, locating logical errors is where your knowledge and experience come into play, as you attempt to discover why the numbers are wrong and how they got that way.

When Your Code Crashes

To access the main debugging tools of Visual Basic, you use the Debug window. You have already used the Debug window several times in this book to examine the operation of different functions and methods. In those cases, you opened the Debug window explicitly by choosing the **View Debug Window** command. When a program crashes, the Macro Error dialog box appears. This dialog box lets you choose whether to quit the program, continue, jump to the offending line of code, open the Debug window, or get help.

For example, running the following procedure causes the Macro Error dialog box shown in figure 21.1 to appear:

```
Sub testBugs()
    A = 1
    B = 0
    C = A / B
End Sub
```

Choosing the **End** button simply ends the program. Use it if you want to quit without performing any debugging of the active program, or if you know where the error is and want to go there manually. The **Continue** button is not available for most errors, because they leave the code in a condition that cannot be continued. The **Goto** button opens the macro sheet and selects the statement that has the problem. Choose this button when you know what the error is and want to edit the offending statement or one near it. The **Help** option displays the help topic that explains the error.

Chapter 21 ◆ What To Do When Your Code Crashes

Figure 21.1
The Macro Error dialog box, reporting a division-by-zero error.

The **D**ebug button is the most useful for locating bugs in an operating program. When you choose the **D**ebug button, the Debug window appears as shown in figure 21.2.

Figure 21.2
The Debug window with code displayed in the code pane.

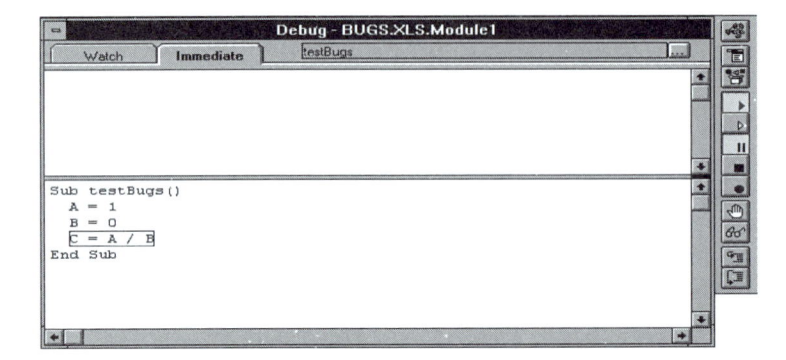

The bottom of the Debug window is the code pane, which displays the statement that caused the error as well as a few adjacent statements. The code pane highlights the offending statement by drawing a box around it. If you examine the code of the procedure testBugs that is displayed in the code pane, it's obvious how the divide-by-zero calculation that caused the error occurred. In most situations, though, the cause of the error isn't so obvious. Above the code pane are the Immediate and Watch panes, which you access by selecting their respective tabs, and the Procedure box, which displays the active procedure.

Examining and Changing Variables in the Immediate Pane

You have already used the Immediate pane several times in this book. You can execute almost any Visual Basic command in the Immediate pane, and the results are then printed just below the statements that caused the printing. Any printing caused by `Debug.Print` statements in your code appear in the Immediate pane. In addition, you can print the value of any variable in the list of active procedures, calculate a simple formula using those variables, or change the value of a variable and later continue the program using that value.

> **Caution:** Usually you should not change the value of a variable in a running application. If possible, fix the application and then rerun it.

For example, figure 21.3 shows the Immediate pane with the values of A and B displayed, a statement to change the value of B, and a simple formula that prints the value of A/B. At this point, the calculation of A/B no longer gives an error, so you can continue executing the program from the point at which it crashed, either by choosing the **R**un Con**t**inue command or by clicking the Resume Macro button on the Visual Basic toolbar.

> **Note:** Typing **?** or **Print** in the Immediate pane causes the values to be printed.

Figure 21.3
Printing values and manipulating variables in the Immediate pane.

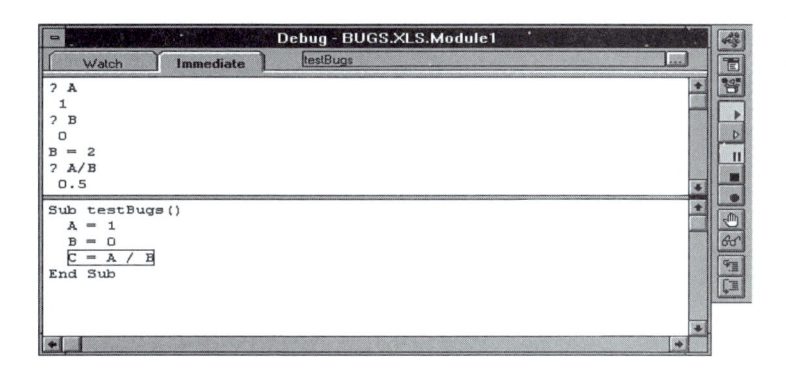

```
? A
 1
? B
 0
B = 2
? A/B
 0.5

Sub testBugs()
    A = 1
    B = 0
    C = A / B
End Sub
```

Use the Immediate pane to examine variables and calculate expressions to determine the source of your program's problem. If the crash occurred in a complex formula, try calculating parts of the formula separately until you determine which part caused the problem. When you know which variable contains the erroneous value, try tracing it back through the procedures to see where the variable got the bad value.

Examining a Variable with Instant Watch

Another way to determine where your program went wrong is to use the Instant Watch feature. This feature enables you to examine the values of different variables and expressions, just as you do when you use the Immediate pane. Using the Instant Watch feature is simpler than using the Immediate pane if the variable or formula you want to display is visible in the code pane, which is often the case. However, one disadvantage of the feature is that it does not create a printed record of previous values as the Immediate pane does.

Chapter 21 ◆ What To Do When Your Code Crashes

Select the variable in the code pane and then choose the **T**ools Instant **W**atch command or click the Instant Watch button on the Visual Basic toolbar. When you do so, the Instant Watch dialog box appears, displaying the variable and its value as shown in figure 21.4.

Figure 21.4
The Instant Watch dialog box displaying the current value of the variable A.

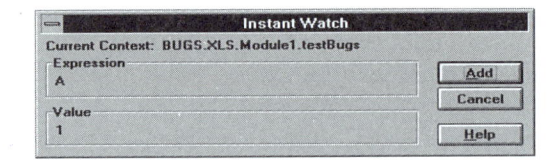

The Instant Watch dialog box can display short expressions as well as single values. For example, if you select the formula A/B and choose the **T**ools Instant **W**atch command, the Instant Watch dialog box appears as shown in figure 21.5.

Figure 21.5
The Instant Watch dialog box displaying the current value of the expression A/B.

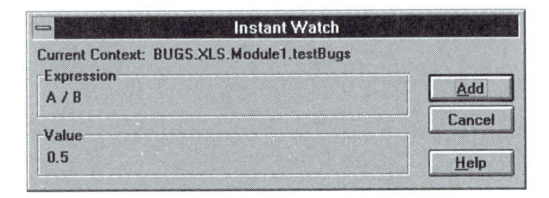

Examining Variables in the Watch Pane

The Instant Watch dialog box shown in figures 21.4 and 21.5 has an **A**dd button on the right side. If you click the **A**dd button or select a variable or expression and then choose the **T**ools **A**dd Watch command, you change the selection into a watch variable and display it on the Watch pane of the Debug window. The Instant Watch dialog box shows you the current value of an expression, but you must close that dialog box before you can continue debugging. However, you do not have to remove a watch variable on the Watch pane before you can continue debugging, and the watch variable continuously displays an expression's current value, as shown in figure 21.6. Whenever a watch variable's value changes, the watch variable on the Watch pane displays that new value.

The Context column on the right side of the Watch pane lists the procedure that provided the variable's value. If two variables are in two different procedures, only the one listed in the Context column is displayed. Of course, to see the current value of both variables, you could place both variables on the Watch pane.

334

Visual Basic for Applications By
EXAMPLE

Figure 21.6

The Watch pane of the Debug dialog box shows the current values of selected variables or expressions.

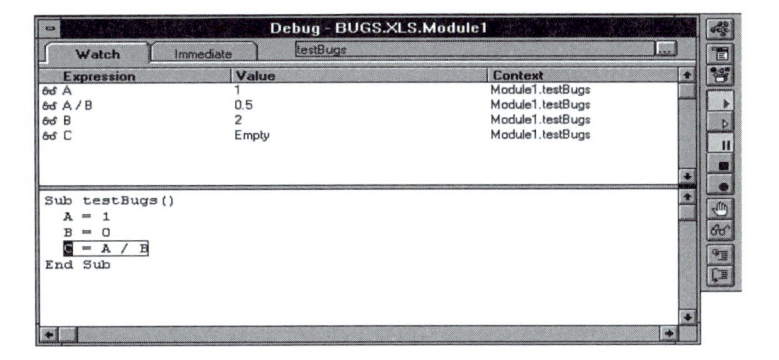

Expression	Value	Context
A	1	Module1.testBugs
A / B	0.5	Module1.testBugs
B	2	Module1.testBugs
C	Empty	Module1.testBugs

```
Sub testBugs()
    A = 1
    B = 0
    C = A / B
End Sub
```

> **Note:** If the procedure shown in the Context column is not in the active call chain, the value shown in the Watch pane is indicated as out of context. If a procedure is not in the active call chain, none of its variables are in the active context of the program, and thus have no values yet. The *active call chain* is a list that includes the procedure that was active when the program stopped executing as well as all the procedures that have not completed executing because they are waiting for the return of a called subprocedure. This list is called a call chain because one procedure calls the next, which calls the next, and so forth, until the active procedure is reached. Figure 21.8 shows a call chain displayed in the Calls dialog box.

Listing Procedures in the Calls Dialog Box

The Procedure box at the top of the Debug window displays the current active procedure. Clicking the button on the right side of the Procedure box displays the Calls dialog box, which contains the current active call chain. In most cases, the current procedure is the only one in the list. The Calls dialog box is useful because it tells you how you got to the procedure, by listing the procedure that called it, the procedure that called the calling procedure, and so forth. If the Calls dialog box lists only the current procedure, then the current procedure was started directly, either by executing the **R**un **S**tart command or the **T**ools **M**acro command or by clicking a control that has the current procedure attached.

Chapter 21 ◆ What To Do When Your Code Crashes

For example, the following three procedures form a call chain when you run testBugs2:

```
Sub testBugs2()
    A = 1
    testProc2 A
End Sub
'
Sub testProc2(A)
    testProc3 A
End Sub
'
Sub testProc3(A)
    B = 0
    C = A / B
End Sub
```

The procedure testBugs2 defines the variable A and passes its value to testProc2, which passes it to testProc3. The procedure testProc3 defines the variable B as zero and then calculates the expression A/B, which results in a divide-by-zero error. Figure 21.7 shows the Debug dialog box that is displayed in this situation, with several different variables and expressions displayed in the Watch pane. Note the context of the different variables and the values that the variables return. Note particularly the value of A in the testBugs procedure, which is not in the active call chain, and C, which is in the active procedure but has no value yet because the calculation of A/B results in an error.

Figure 21.7
The Debug window showing the statement that caused the error, and the values of the variables at the time the error occurred.

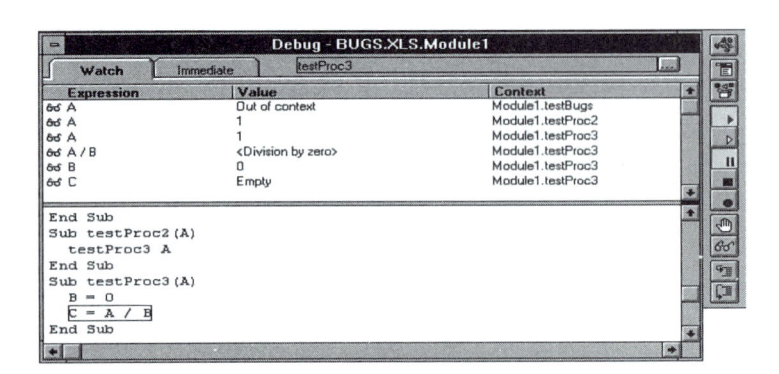

The Procedure box at the top of the Debug dialog box indicates that the current procedure is testProc3, as expected. Clicking the button to the right of the box displays the Calls dialog box shown in figure 21.8. The Calls dialog box lists the procedures, in order, that were called to get to the current procedure.

Figure 21.8

The Calls dialog box showing the call chain that resulted in the execution of the testProc3 procedure.

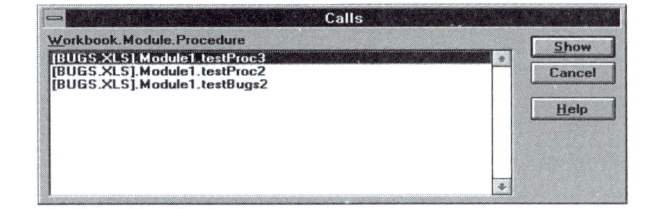

Use the Calls dialog box to determine how your program got to where it is. If you are unsure of how a procedure called the current one, select it and click the Show button to move to the statement that called the procedure in which you are interested. Then try to determine what went wrong with your procedure in that statement by examining the values of the variables and expressions passed to the next procedure.

Summary

In this chapter, you learned what happens when your program encounters an error, and how to use the Debug window to track the value of variables and expressions. The values of these variables and expressions should indicate where you can find the source of the error.

In the next chapter, you learn how to continue tracking the values of variables and expressions while continuing to execute your program.

Review Questions

The answers to the review questions are in Appendix A.

1. What is a syntax error? When does it occur?
2. What is a runtime error? When does it occur?
3. What is a logical error? When does it occur?
4. What is debugging?
5. What does the Procedure box display?
6. Explain the difference between an instant watch variable and a watch variable.

Chapter 21 ◆ What To Do When Your Code Crashes

Review Exercise

1. Try causing other errors and then see which dialog boxes appear, and how the values in your procedures change. Try the following, for example:

   Calculate the square root of –1

   Pass a Variant to a procedure that wants a Single type value

   Pass a String to a procedure that expects a number

   Read beyond the end of a file

   Calculate with a really big number

CHAPTER 22

Using Breakpoints and Watch Points

In the last chapter, you stopped a running program by inserting an invalid calculation. There are much easier ways to make a program stop than intentionally inserting an error. In this chapter, you learn to start and stop an executing application so that you can examine how the variables change their values.

In this chapter you learn about the following:

- Break mode
- Using breakpoints to enter break mode
- Using watch points to enter break mode
- Single-stepping through an application

Understanding Break Mode

When a program encounters an error, stops execution, and displays the Macro Error dialog box, that program is in *break mode*. Unlike ending a program, which stops execution and clears the values of all the variables, break mode is simply a pause in the execution of a program. When a program enters break mode, all variables retain their values at the point that the program entered break mode. Additionally, the program remembers which statement to execute next if the program is continued. Break mode is also known as *wait mode*.

Chapter 22 ◆ Using Breakpoints and Watch Points

You continue execution of a program that is in break mode either by choosing the **R**un **Continue** command or clicking the Resume Macro button on the Visual Basic toolbar. A continued program should run no differently from a program that was not placed in break mode unless you change the values of some of the variables while the program is in break mode.

You can put an executing program into break mode in several ways. There is one restriction, though: The program must be actually executing Visual Basic code, and not be a dialog box waiting for you to choose a button. In the last chapter, you saw that encountering an error causes a program to go into break mode. Other occurrences that cause a program to stop executing and go into break mode include Ctrl-Break being pressed, a Stop statement being encountered, a breakpoint being encountered, or a watch point being tripped.

Breaking a Program with Ctrl-Break or a Stop Statement

The simplest way to put a program into break mode is to press Ctrl-Break. If you do so while some Visual Basic code is executing, the Macro Error dialog box appears as shown in figure 22.1. Note that the dialog box includes a message that explains why the dialog box is being displayed. If the user pressed Ctrl-Break, the message says that the program has been interrupted.

From the Macro Error dialog box, you can proceed as before. You can choose the **E**nd button to end the program, **C**ontinue to continue execution, **D**ebug to go to the Debug window, **G**oto to go to the statement that was to be executed when the program was stopped, or **H**elp to access the online help.

Figure 22.1
The Macro Error dialog box appears when you press Ctrl-Break.

When you choose **D**ebug, the Debug window opens and the next statement to be executed in the program is marked with a box.

For example, the following program calculates all the different ways that you can make a dollar in change, and inserts the number of each type of coin in a row of worksheet cells:

340

Visual Basic for Applications *By* EXAMPLE

```
Option Explicit
Option Base 1
'
' Find all combinations that make 1.00
'
Sub findCoins()
  Dim Row As Integer, halves As Integer
  Dim quarters As Integer, dimes As Integer
  Dim nickels As Integer, theSum As Integer
  Row = 1
  For halves = 2 To 0 Step -1
    For quarters = 4 To 0 Step -1
      For dimes = 10 To 0 Step -1
        For nickels = 20 To 0 Step -1
          theSum = halves * 50 + quarters * 25 + dimes _
              * 10 + nickels * 5
          If theSum = 100 Then
            With Worksheets("Sheet1").Range("A4")
              .Cells(Row, 1).Value = Row
              .Cells(Row, 2).Value = halves
              .Cells(Row, 3).Value = quarters
              .Cells(Row, 4).Value = dimes
              .Cells(Row, 5).Value = nickels
              .Cells(Row, 6).Value = theSum
            End With
            Row = Row + 1
          End If
        Next nickels
      Next dimes
    Next quarters
  Next halves
End Sub
```

The program works by looping over all possible numbers of coins and displaying on the worksheet only those combinations that add up to 100. Figure 22.2 shows the Debug window that opens for this program. Note that the program was about to execute the statement `.Cells(Row, 2).Value = halves` when Ctrl-Break was pressed. The End If statement is the next one to be executed.

Chapter 22 ◆ Using Breakpoints and Watch Points

Figure 22.2

The Debug window that opens after Ctrl-Break is pressed and the Debug button is chosen.

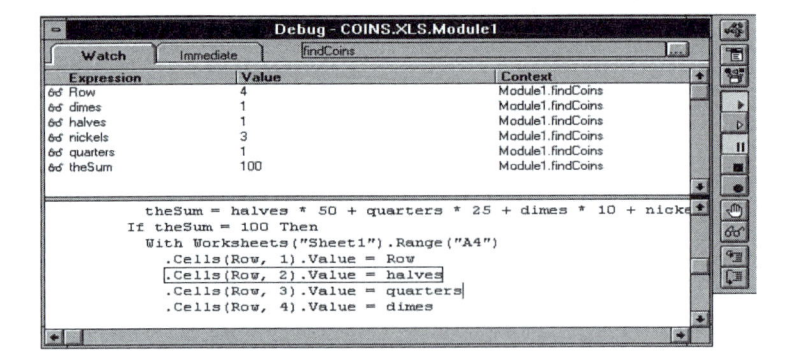

```
                      Debug - COINS.XLS.Module1
   Watch    Immediate       findCoins
  Expression          Value              Context
  66 Row              4                  Module1.findCoins
  66 dimes            1                  Module1.findCoins
  66 halves           1                  Module1.findCoins
  66 nickels          3                  Module1.findCoins
  66 quarters         1                  Module1.findCoins
  66 theSum           100                Module1.findCoins

           theSum = halves * 50 + quarters * 25 + dimes * 10 + nicke
        If theSum = 100 Then
           With Worksheets("Sheet1").Range("A4")
              .Cells(Row, 1).Value = Row
              .Cells(Row, 2).Value = halves
              .Cells(Row, 3).Value = quarters
              .Cells(Row, 4).Value = dimes
```

At this point, you can create watch variables or watch expressions to examine the values of the variables, as shown in the Watch pane in figure 22.2. A watch expression is like a watch variable, but consists of a formula rather than a value of a variable. The formula's value is displayed in the Watch pane.

The effect of using a Stop statement in a program is much like that of pressing Ctrl-Break, except that when the program encounters the statement, the Debug window is displayed directly rather than the Macro Error dialog box. A problem with using the Stop statement is that you must quit your program and manually remove the Stop statement before you can run your program without having it stop every time it encounters the statement. A better way to break programs is to use breakpoints.

Setting and Removing Breakpoints

Breakpoints are markers placed in a program that cause it to go into break mode when they are encountered. Unlike the Stop statement, breakpoints can be added or deleted without ending a program. Also, unlike a Stop statement, breakpoints are not saved with a program, but go away when you quit the program and close its workbook.

To place a breakpoint in a program, select the statement at which you want the program to stop and then choose the **R**un Toggle **B**reakpoint command, press F9, or click the Toggle Breakpoint button on the Visual Basic toolbar. To remove the breakpoint, choose the **R**un Toggle **B**reakpoint command or press F9 again; to remove all breakpoints that are set in a program, choose the **R**un **C**lear All Breakpoints command. Note that you do not have to remove all breakpoints before ending or saving a program, because they are not saved with the program. The breakpoint is set just before the selected statement, so it becomes the next statement to be executed in the program.

Visual Basic for Applications By EXAMPLE

1 2 For example, in the findCoins procedure, select the If statement and then choose the **R**un Toggle **B**reakpoint command. The background of the statement is then colored red, as shown in figure 22.3, to indicate that the statement contains a breakpoint.

Figure 22.3

The findCoins procedure with a breakpoint set on the If statement. On a color monitor, the statement that contains a breakpoint has a red background.

```
Row = 1
For halves = 2 To 0 Step -1
  For quarters = 4 To 0 Step -1
    For dimes = 10 To 0 Step -1
      For nickels = 20 To 0 Step -1
        theSum = halves * 50 + quarters * 25 + dimes * 10 + nickels * 5
        If theSum = 100 Then
          With Worksheets("Sheet1").Range("A4")
            .Cells(Row, 1).Value = Row
            .Cells(Row, 2).Value = halves
            .Cells(Row, 3).Value = quarters
            .Cells(Row, 4).Value = dimes
            .Cells(Row, 5).Value = nickels
            .Cells(Row, 6).Value = theSum
          End With
          Row = Row + 1
        End If
      Next nickels
    Next dimes
  Next quarters
```

When you run the program by choosing the **R**un **S**tart command or clicking the Run Macro button on the Visual Basic toolbar, the program executes until it reaches the breakpoint. The program then goes into break mode and displays the Debug dialog box as shown in figure 22.4. You can then examine the values of variables and expressions as before.

Figure 22.4

The Debug dialog box with the findCoins procedure stopped at a breakpoint.

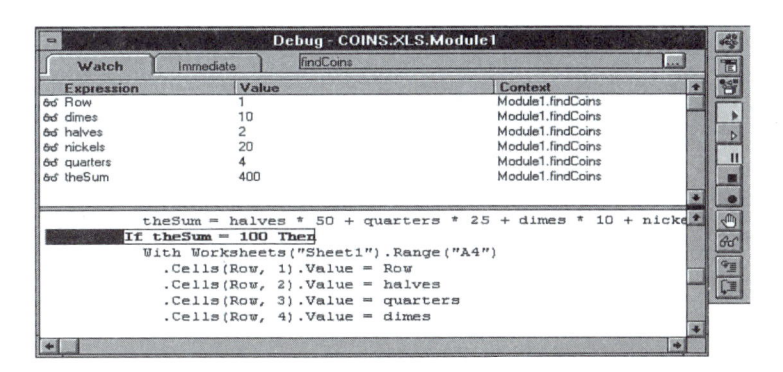

Expression	Value	Context
Row	1	Module1.findCoins
dimes	10	Module1.findCoins
halves	2	Module1.findCoins
nickels	20	Module1.findCoins
quarters	4	Module1.findCoins
theSum	400	Module1.findCoins

```
        theSum = halves * 50 + quarters * 25 + dimes * 10 + nickels
        If theSum = 100 Then
          With Worksheets("Sheet1").Range("A4")
            .Cells(Row, 1).Value = Row
            .Cells(Row, 2).Value = halves
            .Cells(Row, 3).Value = quarters
            .Cells(Row, 4).Value = dimes
```

343

Chapter 22 ◆ Using Breakpoints and Watch Points

Running a Program after a Breakpoint

If you choose the **Run** Continue command or click the Resume Macro button on the Visual Basic toolbar, the procedure continues from where it was and executes until it reaches the breakpoint again, as shown in figure 22.5. Note that the value of `nickels`, the loop variable for the inner loop, is reduced by one, as you would expect for a downward-stepping loop. The value of `theSum` has also decreased, by five.

Figure 22.5

The Debug dialog box for the findCoins procedure stopped a second time at the breakpoint.

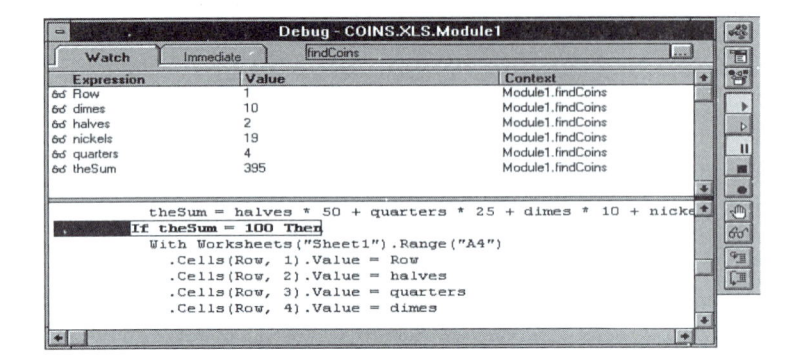

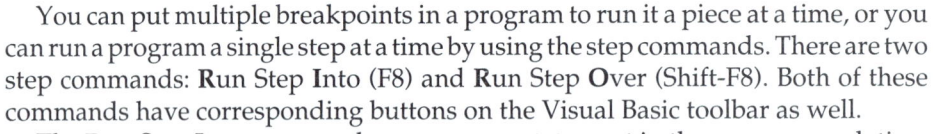

```
                    Debug - COINS.XLS.Module1
    Watch    Immediate    findCoins
    Expression          Value           Context
    66 Row              1               Module1.findCoins
    66 dimes            10              Module1.findCoins
    66 halves           2               Module1.findCoins
    66 nickels          19              Module1.findCoins
    66 quarters         4               Module1.findCoins
    66 theSum           395             Module1.findCoins

            theSum = halves * 50 + quarters * 25 + dimes * 10 + nicke
            If theSum = 100 Then
                With Worksheets("Sheet1").Range("A4")
                    .Cells(Row, 1).Value = Row
                    .Cells(Row, 2).Value = halves
                    .Cells(Row, 3).Value = quarters
                    .Cells(Row, 4).Value = dimes
```

You can put multiple breakpoints in a program to run it a piece at a time, or you can run a program a single step at a time by using the step commands. There are two step commands: **R**un Step **I**nto (F8) and **R**un Step **O**ver (Shift-F8). Both of these commands have corresponding buttons on the Visual Basic toolbar as well.

The **R**un Step **I**nto command executes one statement in the program each time it is selected, and then returns to break mode. If a procedure calls another procedure, the **R**un Step **I**nto command moves to that other procedure and executes it one step at a time.

The **R**un Step **O**ver command works much the same as the **R**un Step **I**nto command, but if another procedure is called, the **R**un Step **O**ver command calculates all the statements in the other procedure and does not stop until it returns to the first procedure. Thus the command appears to step over procedure calls, even though it is actually executing them.

For example, choosing either step command for the procedure shown in figure 22.5 gives you the procedure shown in figure 22.6, with the execution point moved down to the End If statement. The execution point moved to that statement because the argument of the If statement was False, causing the contents of the block If statement to be skipped. If you choose a step command again, you get the results shown in figure 22.7, in which the execution point has moved down one more line.

Figure 22.6

The Debug dialog box for the findCoins procedure after you click the Step Into button on the Visual Basic toolbar. The execution point moves to the end of the block If statement.

Figure 22.7

The Debug dialog box for the findCoins procedure after you click the Step Into button a second time. The execution point moves down one line.

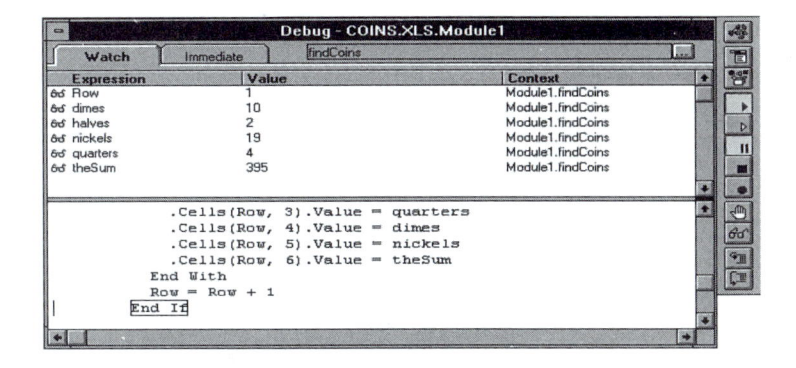

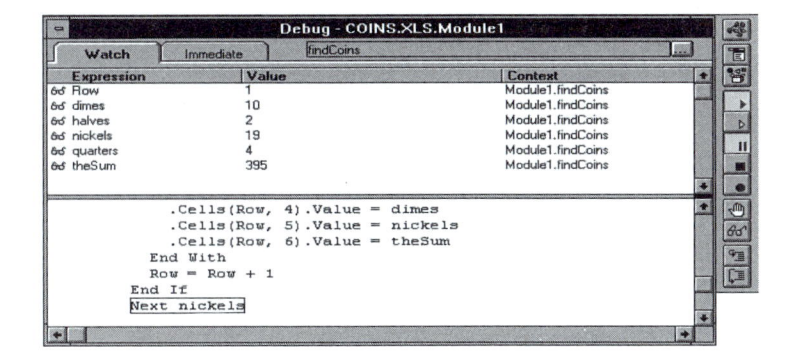

Thus you can use breakpoints to move up close to the point in a program that is causing problems, and then use the step commands to step carefully through the problem region, checking the values of the variables as you go, to determine the cause of the problem.

Setting Watch Points

In the previous section, you set the breakpoint within the loops and then ran the code. As soon as the loops were executed for the first time, the program stopped at the breakpoint so that you could examine the variables. To execute the loop again, you continued the program, which then stopped at the breakpoint a second time. If you wanted to see what would happen during the third or fourth time through the loop, you could simply choose the **R**un Con**t**inue command three or four times. But what if you are interested in the value of the variables after the 1,000th iteration of the loops, or the 10,000th iteration? You most likely haven't the time to sit around choosing the **R**un Con**t**inue command 10,000 times.

Chapter 22 ◆ Using Breakpoints and Watch Points

To handle problems of this type, use a watch point instead of a breakpoint. A combination of a watch expression and a breakpoint, a *watch point* watches the value of a variable or expression and then triggers a break in a program when a specified change occurs. Two situations trigger a watch point: the expression changing to True, and the expression making any change at all.

To insert a watch point, select in the procedure the variable that you want to watch and then choose the **Tools Add** Watch command. The **Tools Add** Watch command displays the Add Watch dialog box, as shown in figure 22.8. This dialog box enables you to select the watch point and its options.

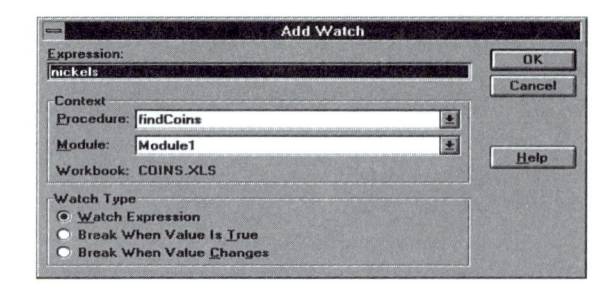

Figure 22.8
The Add Watch dialog box.

For example, say that you want to break the findCoins procedure when the number of nickels is three and the number of quarters is one. You would then fill in the dialog box as shown in figure 22.9. In the Watch Type section, be sure to turn on the Break When Value Is **T**rue radio button. Then continue running the program by choosing OK and the **R**un Con**t**inue command.

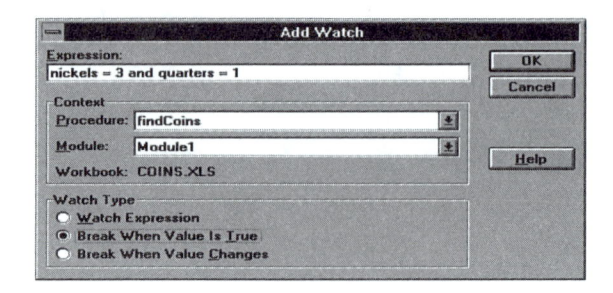

Figure 22.9
The Add Watch dialog box set up to stop when nickels = 3 and quarters = 1.

Oops, you forgot to turn off the breakpoint on the If statement, so the procedure stopped there again. Choose the **R**un Toggle **B**reakpoint command to turn off the breakpoint. Now choose the **R**un Con**t**inue command again. In a few moments, the Debug window shown in figure 22.10 appears.

346

Figure 22.10

The Debug window for findCoins stopped by a watch point.

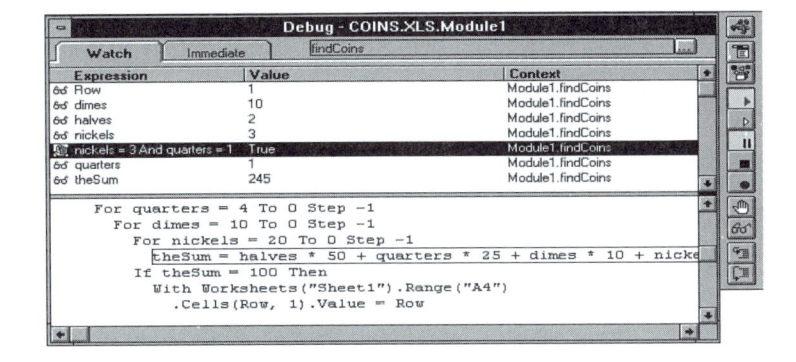

[Screenshot of Debug - COINS.XLS.Module1 window showing Watch and Immediate tabs. Watch pane shows:
Expression | Value | Context
66 Row | 1 | Module1.findCoins
66 dimes | 10 | Module1.findCoins
66 halves | 2 | Module1.findCoins
66 nickels | 3 | Module1.findCoins
nickels = 3 And quarters = 1 | True | Module1.findCoins
66 quarters | 1 | Module1.findCoins
66 theSum | 245 | Module1.findCoins

Code pane shows:
```
     For quarters = 4 To 0 Step -1
        For dimes = 10 To 0 Step -1
           For nickels = 20 To 0 Step -1
              theSum = halves * 50 + quarters * 25 + dimes * 10 + nicke
              If theSum = 100 Then
                 With Worksheets("Sheet1").Range("A4")
                    .Cells(Row, 1).Value = Row
```
]

Note that the values of nickels and quarters now equal the values specified in the Add Watch dialog box. Note also that the watch point is highlighted in the Watch pane to indicate what caused the program to go into break mode.

> **Note:** Unlike breakpoints, watch points are not set on statements, but are set on procedures. Wherever the execution point is in the procedure when the watch expression becomes True is where the procedure goes into break mode. In figure 22.10, the marked line in the code pane is the one following the For statement that changes the value of nickels. Thus when nickels changes to the required value, the procedure stops.

As before, you can now check the values of the variables and step through the procedure to determine where a problem is.

Using Debug.Print To Track Changes in Values

Sometimes you want to watch the value of a variable or variables evolve as a program runs. Instead of stopping the program at each step and checking the value, insert a Debug.Print statement into your code to print a value in the Immediate pane of the Debug window.

Debugging code like this Print statement is usually inserted within a block If statement. The argument of the block If statement is a global debugging variable. You can turn off the debugging code by changing the debugging variable's value to False. Otherwise, to turn off the debugging you must manually remove the code or change it to comment lines.

Chapter 22 ♦ Using Breakpoints and Watch Points

For example, the variable DebugIsOn is a global Boolean variable that controls the execution of the following block:

```
If DebugIsOn Then
  Debug.Print "At point 1"
..Debug.Print "The value of A is: ";A
End If
```

The value of DebugIsOn is set to True in the initialization code while the program is being tested. When testing is complete, simply change the value of DebugIsOn to False and the debugging code is no longer active.

When inserting more than one Debug.Print statement, be sure to insert text that indicates which statement is being executed. You can also use such statements to create a log of where the thread of execution is going in a complex program, by printing a message as the thread passes each important branch.

Using Beep To Track the Progress of a Program

Often, you don't really want to stop a program, you just want to know which part of the program is executing. Use the Beep statement to emit one or more system beeps whenever you reach an important place. You must add a short pause following the Beep statement, or the beeps all run together so that you can't tell one from another.

For example, the following procedure takes a single integer argument that indicates how many beeps the procedure is to emit. Call the procedure whenever you need to know where you are in a program.

```
'
' doBeeps
'
Sub doBeeps(numBeeps As Integer)
  Dim I As Integer, J As Integer
  For I = 1 To numBeeps
    Beep
    For J = 1 To 5000   'Short pause.
    Next J
  Next I
  For J = 1 To 1000   'Longer pause at end.
  Next J
End Sub
```

The first J loop creates a short pause so that multiple beeps do not run together. The second J loop places a longer pause at the end. You may need to change the upper limits of the loops, depending on the speed of the machine that you are using. You want the pause to be as short as possible, but not so short that you can't count the beeps.

Summary

In this chapter, you learned how to examine the variables in a running program so that you can track the changes that lead to a failure. Using breakpoints, watch points, and the step commands, you can stop a program and step through it a line at a time. Using the Debug.Print and Beep statements, you can dynamically examine a program's execution.

In the next chapter, you learn how to trap errors so that your code can handle them instead of causing your program to crash.

Review Questions

The answers to the review questions are in Appendix A.

1. What is break mode?
2. What is a breakpoint?
3. What is the difference between a watch expression and a watch point?
4. What does the Stop statement do?
5. How many different ways can you make change for a dollar?
6. How do you remove a breakpoint? All breakpoints?
7. What is the difference between the Step Into and Step Over commands?

Review Exercises

1. Insert into findCoins a call to doBeeps so that the procedure beeps each time the value of Row changes.
2. Insert breakpoints into the personal contacts database program and track the changes in some of the variables.
3. Insert into findCoins a watch point that breaks the program whenever the variable `dimes` equals two. Then add a watch point that breaks the program whenever the number of dimes changes.
4. Insert Debug.Print statements into findCoins so that the procedure prints the combinations of coins that are not printed on the worksheet.

CHAPTER 23

Using Error Trapping To Handle Unforeseen Events

When a program encounters an error, the Visual Basic error handler is invoked. The error handler stops the program and displays the Macro Error dialog box, the error number, and the error description. At this point, the user usually has no choice but to quit the program and lose any unsaved information. This is not something you want to force the users of your latest and greatest application to do. As the programmer, you might be able to switch to the Debug window and save the data, but you can't expect the user of your program to be able to do so. So what can you do to handle such unforeseen events and either fix the problem or at least enable the user to exit the program gracefully? Set traps!

In this chapter you learn about the following:

- ♦ How to set traps for errors
- ♦ How to create an error handler
- ♦ The error handler hierarchy

What Is an Error Trap?

An *error trap* captures errors before the Visual Basic error handler displays an error message. Actually, error traps are part of the Visual Basic error handler. When an error occurs, the Visual Basic error handler gets control of the user's program. It gets

Chapter 23 ◆ Using Error Trapping To Handle Unforeseen Events

the error number from the system and checks for an enabled error trap in the user's program. If an error trap is enabled, control passes to the program's error handler. If an error handler isn't enabled, the Visual Basic error handler brings up the Macro Error dialog box to display the error number and message for the user.

Thus, to set an error trap, you need two things: an error handler and an error trap enabler. The *error handler* contains the code to handle the error, and the *error trap enabler* is a statement that turns on the error trap and identifies the error handler routine.

Why Trap Errors?

Why trap errors when the Visual Basic error handler can handle them for you? In many cases, the Visual Basic error handler works just fine: When your code crashes for some reason, you simply restart the program and try again. But consider the sequential file version of the personal contacts database program. That program stores the database in memory until you choose the Save button to save it on disk. What if you had just typed in 100 new entries and started to save them on a floppy disk that was not in the drive? With the drive empty, you get a "drive not ready" error and your code crashes. If you choose the End button on the Macro Error dialog box, you lose all the entries in memory. Although you could start over and retype the 100 entries, an easier solution is to let an error handler take control, tell you to insert a disk, and then return to the point at which the error occurred so that the code can continue.

Procedures that access disk files are the most common locations for error handlers. When a procedure attempts to access a disk, many unexpected problems can occur: You might read beyond the end of the file, or pop the floppy disk from the drive as the program is starting to write to it, or the floppy disk could be locked, full, or missing from the drive. Therefore, such procedures almost always need a general-purpose error handler. You could have the procedure try to check for every conceivable error before accessing a disk, but often the act of checking causes an error. Besides, your application's users not only are likely to commit every error that you can think of, but also a few hundred more that you won't anticipate.

The second most common location for error traps is in number-crunching procedures, especially procedures that perform iterative calculations. *Iterative calculations* are numerical methods that repeatedly calculate the same formula, using the result of the previous calculation as the input for the next. One example of such a procedure is the method of successive approximations for finding the roots of an equation. Iterative procedures occasionally produce results that diverge and cause numeric overflow or underflow. Also, if you are performing calculations that may divide by zero or take the square root of minus one, you need an error handler that can capture and correct such errors so that your program doesn't crash.

Enabling the Trap

Visual Basic's error trap enabler is the On Error statement, which has the following syntax:

```
On Error GoTo label
```

You place this statement in your code wherever you want to turn on error trapping, and set the `label` equal to the label at the beginning of your error handler. This statement does not execute the error handler, but enables a trap to execute the error handler if an error occurs in the program.

A restriction on error trap enablers and error handlers is that they must both be in the same procedure. Therefore, the following is a common layout for procedures with error handlers:

```
Sub aProc()
  On Error GoTo theErrorHandler   'Turn on the trap.
  '
  ' Balance of the procedure goes here.
  '
  Exit Sub  'This is the end of the normal procedure.
  theErrorHandler:   'Start of the error handler.
  '
  ' The error handler code goes here.
  '
  Resume   'The end of the error handler.
End Sub
```

You don't have to use this layout, but it does separate the error handler code from the normal code in the procedure with an Exit Sub statement so that a normally executing procedure cannot accidentally start executing the code in the error handler. The layout for a function procedure is identical, except that you replace the Exit Sub statement with an Exit Function statement.

Error traps are disabled when the procedure that contains them ends. To turn off or disable an error trap within the procedure that contains it, use the following statement:

```
On Error GoTo 0
```

Only one error handler in a procedure may be active at any one time. If you have different error handlers for different blocks of code, you must disable an enabled handler before you enable a different one.

Chapter 23 ◆ Using Error Trapping To Handle Unforeseen Events

Which Trap Responds?

In a single procedure, only one error handler is active at any one time. However, other procedures in the active call chain may also have active error handlers, forming a hierarchy of error handlers (see fig. 23.1). Remember that the active call chain is the list of active procedures in the order that they were called to reach the currently executing procedure.

Figure 23.1
A hierarchy of error handlers in two active call chains. The active call chains are procedures A and B, and procedures A, C, D, and E.

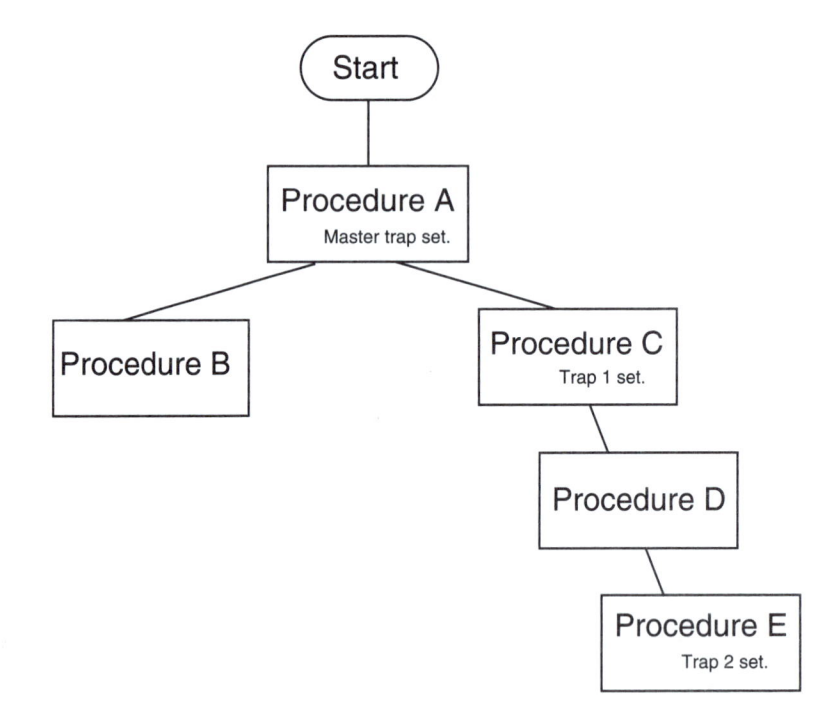

```
                    Start
                      │
                 Procedure A
                 Master trap set.
                 ┌────┴────┐
          Procedure B   Procedure C
                        Trap 1 set.
                             │
                        Procedure D
                             │
                        Procedure E
                        Trap 2 set.
```

When the Visual Basic error handler gets control of an application, it first looks in the currently active procedure for an active error handler. If it does not find one, it switches to the procedure that called the procedure that had the error and looks there. If no active error handler is in that procedure, the Visual Basic error handler backs up one more procedure and looks again. It continues this process until it reaches the start of the call chain. If at this point the Visual Basic error handler has not found an active error handler, it handles the error itself and displays the Macro Error dialog box.

Because of the way that Visual Basic searches for error handlers, every procedure does not have to include code that can handle all possible errors. More general errors can be handled at the beginning of the call chain, with more specific errors handled in the procedures most likely to have them.

For example, in figure 23.1, the hierarchy includes two active call chains. If procedure B is the active procedure, procedures A and B form the active call chain. Because only procedure A has an error trap, that trap handles any errors in procedures A or B.

If procedure E is the active procedure, then the call chain consists of procedures A, C, D, and E. If an error occurs in procedure E, it is first passed to Trap 2 in procedure E. If Trap 2 cannot handle the error and passes it back to the system, the system checks procedure D for an active error trap. Finding none in procedure D, the system checks procedure C for an active error trap, finds Trap 1, and passes the error to it. If Trap 1 cannot handle the error, it again passes the error back to the system, which checks procedure A for an active error handler, finds the master trap, and passes the error to it. Finally, if the master trap cannot handle the error and passes it back to the system again, the system then displays the Macro Error dialog box.

Creating the Error Handler

In general, the structure of an error handler consists of a header, the handler body, and a footer. The header consists of a label at the beginning of the handler. The On Error statement points to this label. The handler body contains the code that actually handles the error, and the footer contains a Resume statement that returns to the existing program.

> **Note:** In a Visual Basic program, a label consists of a word or number at the beginning of a line, followed by a colon. Additional code may appear on the line with the label or more commonly on the next line.

While the error handler is operating, error trapping by that handler is disabled. If your error handler causes an error, control returns to the Visual Basic error handler, which looks for a different error handler to process the error or displays the Macro Error dialog box. When the Resume statement executes at the end of the error handler, the error trap is reenabled.

Usually an error handler first finds out which error occurred, so that it can determine what it must do to handle it. The Err function returns the error number of the most recent error. See Appendix C for a list of the Visual Basic error codes. With the error number as an argument, the Error() function returns a string that contains the same description of the error as the Macro Error dialog box presents.

The body of the handler usually consists of a Select Case or block If statement with the error number used to select the correct block of code to handle the specific error.

Chapter 23 ♦ Using Error Trapping To Handle Unforeseen Events

For example, a file-opening procedure might have an error handler like the following:

```
'
' Get a file name and open the file.
'
Sub OpenAFile(filenum As Integer, filename)
  Const errBadFileNameOrNumber = 52
  Const errFileNotFound = 53
  Const errBadFileMode = 54
  Const errFileAlreadyOpen = 55
  Const errDeviceIOError = 57
  Const errTooManyFiles = 67
  Const errDeviceUnavailable = 68
  Const errPermissionDenied = 70
  Const errDiskNotReady = 71
  Const errPathFileAccessError = 75
  Const errPathNotFound = 76

' These file errors are not valid in an Open procedure.
'   Const errFileAlreadyExists = 58
'   Const errDiskFull = 61
'   Const errInternalError = 51
'   Const errBadRecordLength = 59
'   Const errBadRecordNumber = 63
'   Const errCantRenameWithDifferentDrive = 74
'   Const errInputPastEndOfFile = 62
'
' Enable the error handler.
  On Error GoTo DiskErrorHandler
  filenum = FreeFile()
TryAgain:
  filename = InputBox("Input filename")
  If filename = "" Then Exit Sub   'The user chose Cancel.
  Open filename For Input As filenum
Exit Sub  'End of the normal procedure.
'
'The start of the handler.
DiskErrorHandler:
  Select Case Err
    Case errBadFileNameOrNumber
      MsgBox "Bad file name, try again."
      Resume TryAgain
```

```
        Case errFileNotFound
            MsgBox "No such file, try again."
            Resume TryAgain
        Case errBadFileMode
            MsgBox "Can't open that file for input, try again."
            Resume TryAgain
        Case errFileAlreadyOpen
            MsgBox "That file is already open, try again."
            Resume TryAgain
        Case errDeviceIOError
            MsgBox "I/O Error, try again."
            Resume TryAgain
        Case errTooManyFiles
            MsgBox "Too many files open, close some first."
            Resume Next
        Case errDeviceUnavailable
            MsgBox "The drive specified is not available, try again."
            Resume TryAgain
        Case errPermissionDenied
            MsgBox "Permission denied, try again."
            Resume TryAgain
        Case errDiskNotReady
            MsgBox "Insert a disk and press Enter."
            Resume
        Case errPathFileAccessError
            MsgBox "That file is inaccessible, try again."
            Resume TryAgain
        Case errPathNotFound
            MsgBox "No such path, try again."
            Resume TryAgain
        Case Else    'Cannot handle this error, pass back to system.
            Error Err
    End Select
End Sub
```

This procedure merely passes control back to the input box so that the user can try again. A more complex error handler would give the user the choice of trying again, quitting, saving and quitting, or continuing.

An example of a numerical error handler, the following function procedure calculates the Sin(x)/x and then uses an error trap to trap the divide-by-zero error when x equals 0. Then the procedure replaces the value with 1, the correct value for Sin(0)/0. If the error is not a divide-by-zero error, the error handler displays a dialog box and returns the error to the Visual Basic error handler.

Chapter 23 ♦ Using Error Trapping To Handle Unforeseen Events

```
'
' Calculate Sin(x)/x
'
Function SinXOverX(X As Double) As Double
Const errDivideByZero = 11
On Error GoTo FixIt
  SinXOverX = Sin(X) / X
Exit Function
FixIt:
  If Err = errDivideByZero Then
    SinXOverX = 1
    Resume Next
  Else
    MsgBox "Unexpected error " & Err & ", " & Error(Err) & _
      ", in Sin(x)/x function."
    Error Err
  End If
End Function
```

Returning from the Error Handler

An error handler must end with an Exit Sub, Resume, or Error statement.

The Exit Sub (or Exit Function) statement disables the error trap and returns control to the procedure that called the procedure that had the error. Of course, before returning control to the calling procedure, you should fix the problem that caused the error.

The Resume statement reenables the error trap and returns control to the current procedure. This is the normal way to return from an error handler, when the handler is in the procedure that had the error. The Resume statement has three different forms:

```
Resume
Resume Next
Resume label
```

The first form returns control to the statement that caused the error so that the statement can try again to perform the action that caused the error. Use this form after you have fixed whatever caused the error and want to try again.

The second form passes control to the statement that follows the one that caused the error, and the third form passes control to the statement with the specified label. If the error trap is not in the procedure that caused the error, you can use only the last form of the Resume statement, because the first two yield unpredictable results.

The OpenAFile procedure in the preceding section primarily uses the third form of the Resume statement, because most of the errors require the user to select another file name before trying the Open statement again. If you got a new file name in the error handler, you could return control to the Open statement using the first form of the Resume statement.

The Error statement, which differs from the Error() function, takes an error number as an argument and simulates an error. That error then causes control to return to the Visual Basic error handler. Use this statement to return an error to the system for it to handle.

Handling Unexpected Errors

What do you do if your error handler traps an error that it does not know how to handle? The simplest thing to do is to pass the error back to the system and let the system handle it. Alternatively, you can create a catch-all procedure that performs an orderly termination of your program, saving data and closing files. Whether you handle the error yourself or pass it back to the system, you normally implement this catch-all error code in a Case Else block of a Select Case statement or an Else block of a block If statement.

To return control to the Visual Basic error handler, use the Error statement with the Err function as its argument, as follows:

```
Error Err
```

This statement simulates the error that caused the initial error, passing the error back to the system. The Visual Basic error handler must either find another error handler or handle the error itself, because the error handler in this procedure is already in use and the trap is disabled. Use this statement to pass an error down the active call chain to error handlers in the procedures that called this one.

Using the hierarchy of error handlers in this way, you place your orderly termination error handler in the first procedure of a call chain. When an error occurs in another procedure later in the call chain, that procedure either handles the error or passes it back down the chain. If the error makes it all the way to the first procedure without being handled, the orderly termination procedure takes over and ends the program.

Creating User-Defined Errors

Instead of returning the original error number to a calling procedure, you can create and return a user-defined error. Error numbers range from 1 to 65,535, but Visual Basic uses only the first few thousand. You can use any of the unused error numbers to create your own program-specific errors.

Chapter 23 ♦ Using Error Trapping To Handle Unforeseen Events

> **Tip:** Although Visual Basic currently uses only the first few thousand error numbers, you never know which error numbers future versions might use. Because the existing list of error numbers is likely to increase, you should avoid using the lower numbers for your user-defined errors. Start at 20,000 or 30,000 and work up from there, or start at the top, 65,535, and work down. Then you should have few conflicts with future versions of Visual Basic.

Use a user-defined error when you must return an error to an earlier error handler but cannot use the original error number. For example, a divide-by-zero error might require some major changes at the beginning of a program, but if you pass the divide-by-zero error down the call chain, an earlier error handler might simply correct it instead of passing the error back to the beginning of the program.

Passing Error Values in Variables

In addition to interrupting a program with a user-defined error and using that interruption to pass an error to the calling procedure, you can give a variable an error value and then return that value to the calling procedure using a procedure's arguments or a function's return value. You can return two types of error values in a variable: Excel error values and user-defined error values. In both cases, the variable must be the Variant type so that it can contain an error value rather than a number.

Using Excel's Error Values

In Chapter 10, "Using Select Case," you used Excel's error values to return errors to a worksheet from a user-defined function. You can pass the same values to another procedure and use them to detect errors in that procedure. You create the error values with the CVErr() function, which takes an error number as an argument. Table 23.2 lists the built-in constants that cause this function to return Excel errors.

An alternative to using the CVErr() function is to enclose the error value in square brackets. This technique yields the same result as the function. For example, the following two statements give identical results:

```
theResult = CVErr(xlErrRef)
theResult = [#REF!]
```

Table 23.1. The constants that cause the CVErr() function to return Excel error values.

Constant	Value	Error Value
xlErrDiv0	2007	#DIV/0!
xlErrNA	2042	#N/A
xlErrName	2029	#NAME?
xlErrNull	2000	#NULL!
xlErrNum	2036	#NUM!
xlErrRef	2023	#REF!
xlErrValue	2015	#VALUE!

To test variables for an error value, use the IsError() function, which returns True if the argument is an error and False if it is not. Any calculation that you perform with a variable that contains an error value results in the same error value. Be sure that any variables that might contain error values are of the Variant type.

Passing User-Defined Errors in Variables

In addition to the seven Excel error values listed in table 23.1, you can use any other number to create a user-defined error value. The error numbers must be in the range 1 to 65,535, and are created using the CVErr() function in the same manner as the Excel error values. Again, the variables must be of the Variant type, and you use the IsError() function to detect an error value.

> **Caution:** If you write a logical expression to determine which error value is stored in a variable, be sure to compare it to another error value created with the CVErr() function and not to the error number itself.

Trapping User Interrupts

When the user presses Ctrl-Break to stop an operation, the program stops and displays the Macro Error dialog box. Even if an error handler is enabled, the program ignores it after you press Ctrl-Break. At this point the only real options that the user has are to continue or quit. (You could switch to the Debug window if you know how, but that is unlikely for most users.) When users press Ctrl-Break, they usually do not want to end the program, but want only to stop the current operation and return to a situation in which the program is essentially doing nothing but waiting for a command.

The error handler manages such situations exactly the same as any other error. The difference here is that the EnableCancelKey property of the Application object must be set to the xlErrorHandler constant value. When this is done, pressing Ctrl-Break is treated exactly the same as any error, and Err returns an error number of 18. At this point, you create an error handler that terminates the program in a more controlled way than simply ending it. To reset the EnableCancelKey property, equate it to the constant xlInterrupt. The EnableCancelKey property is also reset when the procedure that changed it terminates.

In addition to enabling the trapping of user interrupts, you can disable interrupts completely by equating the EnableCancelKey property to xlDisabled. When you disable interrupts, be careful not to create a procedure that never returns to the user. If the procedure gets stuck in an infinite loop and you have disabled interrupts, the only way to end the procedure is to reset your computer.

Delayed Error Processing

Occasionally the procedure that you are executing is time-critical, so you don't want to have to stop it to handle an error right in the middle of processing. For these types of time-critical procedures—such as timing operations and communications procedures—you can delay handling the error until the procedure or operation is complete. To do this, use the following statement to enable error trapping:

```
On Error Resume Next
```

This error trap simply skips the problem statement and goes on to the next. When the time-critical operation is complete, check the value of Err to see whether an error has occurred, and then handle any that has.

> **Caution:** This technique entails some risk, because the value of Err contains the error number of only the last error that occurred. If multiple errors occur between the times that you enable the error trap and check the value of Err, all but the last error are lost. Use this statement with care.

Using an Error Handler To Count Array Dimensions

When you pass arrays to a procedure, especially from a worksheet, you cannot get the number of dimensions in the array. Although you can use the UBounds() and LBounds() functions to get the number of elements in any one dimension, you can't get the number of dimensions directly. Indirectly, though, you can get the number of dimensions by enabling an error trap and accessing a dimension. If the dimension does not exist, you get an error; if you don't get an error, the dimension exists.

The following procedure uses an error trap to determine how many dimensions an array has. If it gets any other error, it returns the Excel error value #VALUE!.

```
'
' Get the number of dimensions
'
Function GetDimensions(theArray)
  Dim dummy, I As Integer
  Const errSubscriptOutOfRange = 9
  On Error GoTo trapDim
    For I = 1 To 100
      dummy = UBound(theArray, I)
    Next I
    GetDimensions = CVErr(xlErrValue)
  Exit Function
trapDim:
  If Err = errSubscriptOutOfRange Then
    GetDimensions = I - 1
  Else  'Unexpected error.
    GetDimensions = CVErr(xlErrValue)
  End If
End Function
```

Adding an Error Handler to the Personal Contacts Database

The sequential access version of the personal contacts database program has two places that could make use of an error trap: the Open_Click procedure and the FindName_Click search procedure. The Open_Click procedure must trap errors associated with opening a file not created with the program. For example, opening a file from the random access file version of the program causes errors.

Chapter 23 ♦ Using Error Trapping To Handle Unforeseen Events

If the database is large, the FindName_Click procedure may take a long time to find a record. The user may want to interrupt the procedure and do something else instead of waiting for the results. Therefore, the program must trap the Ctrl-Break keystroke and use it to terminate the FindName_Click procedure, but not the whole application.

To create this example, start with a copy of the sequential file version of the personal contacts database program that you created in Chapter 18, "Saving Data in a Sequential Disk File." Then change the code in the procedures as shown in the following listing. Changes in the procedures are highlighted in boldface type. The form does not change.

```
'
'  Personal Contacts Database Program
'  Sequential File Version
'  With error traps.
'
Option Explicit 'Force all variables to be defined.
Option Base 1   'Make arrays start at 1.
Type DBEntry    'Define the structure of a single database entry.
  Name As String * 25
  Address As String * 25
  City As String * 15
  State As String * 2
  Zip As String * 10
  Phone As String * 20
  Net As String * 10
  NetAddr As String * 25
  Referral As String * 25
  Notes As String * 97
  RecNo As Integer
End Type    'Size of type is 256 bytes.
Dim theDB() As DBEntry     'The database array.
Dim numEntries As Integer  'Total number of entries.
Dim theEntryNum As Integer 'The currently displayed entry.
Dim theFileName As String  'The current file name.
'
'  Initialize database
'
Sub InitializeIt()
  numEntries = 0
  ReDim theDB(1)
  theEntryNum = 0
```

```
    Sheets("ContactsDlog").DropDowns("DE_Mail_Net").List = _
      Array("Compuserve", "Internet", "GEnie", "Prodigy")
    Sheets("ContactsDlog").ScrollBars("ScrollEntry").Min = 1
    Sheets("ContactsDlog").ScrollBars("ScrollEntry").Max = 1
    theFileName = ""
    ClearEntries
    Sheets("ContactsDlog").Show
End Sub
'
'   Clear the dialog box.
'
Sub ClearEntries()
  With Sheets("ContactsDlog")
    .EditBoxes("DName").Text = ""
    .EditBoxes("DAddress").Text = ""
    .EditBoxes("DCity").Text = ""
    .EditBoxes("DState").Text = ""
    .EditBoxes("DZip").Text = ""
    .EditBoxes("DPhone").Text = ""
    .DropDowns("DE_Mail_Net").Text = ""
    .EditBoxes("DE_Mail_Address").Text = ""
    .EditBoxes("DReferral").Text = ""
    .EditBoxes("DNotes").Text = ""
    .Labels("DRecNo").Caption = "Record #: "
  End With
End Sub
'
' The Auto_Open procedure
' runs whenever this workbook is opened.
'
Sub Auto_Open()
  InitializeIt   'Run the initialization procedure.
End Sub
'
'   Add a new entry
'
Sub NewEntry_Click()
  numEntries = numEntries + 1
  Sheets("ContactsDlog").ScrollBars("ScrollEntry").Max = numEntries
  theEntryNum = numEntries
```

Chapter 23 ◆ Using Error Trapping To Handle Unforeseen Events

```
    ReDim Preserve theDB(numEntries) 'Expand the array.
    EntryToDB theEntryNum    'Write the entry to the array.
    DBToEntry theEntryNum    'Read the entry back to display theEntryNum.
End Sub
'
'  Update an entry
'
Sub UpdateEntry_Click()
  If theEntryNum = 0 Then Exit Sub  'Exit if no entries are saved yet.
  EntryToDB theEntryNum   'Update the displayed entry.
End Sub
'
' Transfer an entry to the database
'
Sub EntryToDB(anEntry As Integer)
  With Sheets("ContactsDlog")
    theDB(anEntry).Name = .EditBoxes("DName").Text
    theDB(anEntry).Address = .EditBoxes("DAddress").Text
    theDB(anEntry).City = .EditBoxes("DCity").Text
    theDB(anEntry).State = .EditBoxes("DState").Text
    theDB(anEntry).Zip = .EditBoxes("DZip").Text
    theDB(anEntry).Phone = .EditBoxes("DPhone").Text
    theDB(anEntry).Net = .DropDowns("DE_Mail_Net").Text
    theDB(anEntry).NetAddr = .EditBoxes("DE_Mail_Address").Text
    theDB(anEntry).Referral = .EditBoxes("DReferral").Text
    theDB(anEntry).Notes = .EditBoxes("DNotes").Text
    theDB(anEntry).RecNo = anEntry
  End With
End Sub
'
' Transfer a record to the form
'
Sub DBToEntry(anEntry As Integer)
  With Sheets("ContactsDlog")
    .EditBoxes("DName").Text = theDB(anEntry).Name
    .EditBoxes("DAddress").Text = theDB(anEntry).Address
    .EditBoxes("DCity").Text = theDB(anEntry).City
    .EditBoxes("DState").Text = theDB(anEntry).State
    .EditBoxes("DZip").Text = theDB(anEntry).Zip
    .EditBoxes("DPhone").Text = theDB(anEntry).Phone
```

```vb
      .DropDowns("DE_Mail_Net").Text = theDB(anEntry).Net
      .EditBoxes("DE_Mail_Address").Text = theDB(anEntry).NetAddr
      .EditBoxes("DReferral").Text = theDB(anEntry).Referral
      .EditBoxes("DNotes").Text = theDB(anEntry).Notes
      .Labels("DRecNo").Caption = "Record #: " & theDB(anEntry).RecNo
      .ScrollBars("ScrollEntry").Value = anEntry
  End With
End Sub
'
' Scroll entries.
'
Sub ScrollEntries_Click()
  If numEntries = 0 Then Exit Sub 'No entries yet.
  theEntryNum = Sheets("ContactsDlog").ScrollBars("ScrollEntry").Value
  DBToEntry theEntryNum
End Sub
'
' Delete a record
'
Sub DeleteEntry_Click()
  Dim I As Integer, buttons As Integer
  Dim theMsg As String
  If numEntries = 0 Then Exit Sub  'No entries yet.
  'Make sure the user really wants to do this.
  buttons = vbYesNo + vbDefaultButton2 + vbQuestion + _
      vbApplicationModal
  theMsg = "Are you sure you want to delete the current record?"
  If MsgBox(theMsg, buttons, "Delete Record") = vbNo Then Exit Sub
  'The user said yes, so delete the record and move the others down.
  If theEntryNum = numEntries Then   'It is the last entry.
    numEntries = numEntries - 1
    ReDim Preserve theDB(numEntries)
    theEntryNum = numEntries
  ElseIf theEntryNum = 0 Then   'No entry to delete.
    Exit Sub
  Else   'Shift everything down one.
    For I = theEntryNum + 1 To numEntries
```

Chapter 23 ◆ Using Error Trapping To Handle Unforeseen Events

```
        theDB(I - 1) = theDB(I)
        theDB(I - 1).RecNo = I - 1
    Next I
    numEntries = numEntries - 1
    ReDim Preserve theDB(numEntries)
  End If
  Sheets("ContactsDlog").ScrollBars("ScrollEntry").Value = theEntryNum
  Sheets("ContactsDlog").ScrollBars("ScrollEntry").Max = numEntries
  DBToEntry theEntryNum
End Sub
'
'  Find a name
'
Sub FindName_Click()
  Static theName As String
  Dim I As Integer
  Const TextComparison = 1
  Const errUserInterrupt = 18
' Enable user interrupts.
  Application.EnableCancelKey = xlErrorHandler
  On Error GoTo HandleInterrupt   'Enable trapping the interrupt.
  If numEntries = 0 Then Exit Sub  'No entries yet.
  theName = InputBox("Input a name to search for.", "Find A Name", _
      theName)
  If theEntryNum <> numEntries Then
    For I = theEntryNum + 1 To numEntries
      If InStr(1, theDB(I).Name, theName, TextComparison) <> 0 Then
        'Found a matching entry
        On Error GoTo 0  'Turn off trap.
        Application.EnableCancelKey = xlDisabled  'Disable interrupts.
        theEntryNum = I
        DBToEntry theEntryNum
        Exit Sub
      End If
    Next I
  End If
  For I = 1 To theEntryNum
```

```vb
      If InStr(1, theDB(I).Name, theName, TextComparison) <> 0 Then
        'Found a matching entry
        On Error GoTo 0  'Turn off trap.
        Application.EnableCancelKey = xlDisabled   'Disable interrupts.
        theEntryNum = I
        DBToEntry theEntryNum
        Exit Sub
      End If
    Next I
    On Error GoTo 0 'Turn off trap.
' Turn normal interrupts back on.
    Application.EnableCancelKey = xlInterrupt
    'No match found.
    MsgBox "The name: " & theName & " was not found.", , "Find A Name"
Exit Sub
HandleInterrupt:  'Handle user interrupts here.
' If it was an interrupt, exit the procedure.
    If err = errUserInterrupt Then
      Exit Sub
    Else   'If it was not an interrupt, then give it back to the system.
'     Turn normal interrupts back on.
      Application.EnableCancelKey = xlInterrupt
      Error err
    End If
End Sub
'
'Save the database.
'
Sub Save_Click()
  Dim theFilter As String, Answer, theDot As Integer
  Dim fileNum As Integer, EntryNum As Integer
  If numEntries = 0 Then   'See if there is something to save.
    MsgBox "You don't have anything to save.", , "PCD"
    Exit Sub
  End If
  'Get the file name for the data.
  theFilter = "PCD database (*.PCD),*.PCD"
  'theFileName is global, so it always defaults to the current name.
```

Chapter 23 ♦ Using Error Trapping To Handle Unforeseen Events

```
    Answer = Application.GetSaveAsFilename(theFileName, theFilter, 1)
    If Answer = False Then Exit Sub 'The user chose Cancel.
    theFileName = Trim(Answer)    'Remove any leading or trailing blanks.
    'Make sure the file name ends in .PCD.
    theDot = InStr(theFileName, ".")
    If theDot = 0 Then  'No extension typed; add one.
      theFileName = theFileName & ".PCD"
    Else  'Something was typed; delete it and add .PCD.
      theFileName = Left(theFileName, theDot - 1) & ".PCD"
    End If
    fileNum = FreeFile()  'Get a file number and open the file.
    Open theFileName For Output As fileNum
    'First save the number of entries.
    Write #fileNum, numEntries
    'Now loop over each element of the database
    'and write all the components into the file.
    For EntryNum = 1 To numEntries
    With theDB(EntryNum)
      Write #fileNum, .Name
      Write #fileNum, .Address
      Write #fileNum, .City
      Write #fileNum, .State
      Write #fileNum, .Zip
      Write #fileNum, .Phone
      Write #fileNum, .Net
      Write #fileNum, .NetAddr
      Write #fileNum, .Referral
      Write #fileNum, .Notes
      Write #fileNum, .RecNo
    End With
    Next EntryNum
    Close #fileNum    'All done
    MsgBox "The database was saved in " & theFileName, , "PCD"
End Sub
'
'Open a database file.
'
Sub Open_Click()
    Dim theFilter As String, Answer, theDot As Integer
    Dim fileNum As Integer, EntryNum As Integer
```

```vba
Dim buttons As Integer, theMsg As String
Dim Flag As Boolean
Const errInputPastEndOfFile = 62
Const errSubscriptOutOfRange = 9
If numEntries <> 0 Then    'See if there is something to save first.
  buttons = vbYesNoCancel + vbQuestion + vbApplicationModal
  theMsg = "Do you want to save the current data first?"
  Answer = MsgBox(theMsg, buttons, "PCD")
  If Answer = vbCancel Then    'Quit if the user chose Cancel.
    Exit Sub
  ElseIf Answer = vbYes Then    'Call save if the user chose Yes.
    Save_Click
  End If
End If
'Get the file name for the data.
theFilter = "PCD database (*.PCD),*.PCD"
Do
  Answer = Application.GetOpenFilename(theFilter, 1)
  If Answer = False Then Exit Sub 'The user chose Cancel.
  Answer = Trim(Answer)    'Remove any leading or trailing blanks.
  theDot = InStr(Answer, ".")
  If theDot = 0 Then    'Bad file name, no extension.
    MsgBox "You must choose a .PCD file.", , "PCD"
    Flag = False
  ElseIf Right(Answer, 4) <> ".PCD" Then    'Wrong extension.
    MsgBox "You must choose a .PCD file.", , "PCD"
    Flag = False
  Else    'Must be OK.
    Flag = True
  End If
Loop Until Flag
theFileName = Answer
fileNum = FreeFile()    'Get a file number and open the file.
On Error GoTo FixBadFile    'Turn on the error trap.
Open theFileName For Input As fileNum
'First read the number of entries.
Input #fileNum, numEntries
'Now expand the database.
ReDim theDB(numEntries)
```

Chapter 23 ◆ Using Error Trapping To Handle Unforeseen Events

```
    'Now loop over each element of the database
    'and read all the components into the file.
    For EntryNum = 1 To numEntries
    With theDB(EntryNum)
      Input #fileNum, .Name
      Input #fileNum, .Address
      Input #fileNum, .City
      Input #fileNum, .State
      Input #fileNum, .Zip
      Input #fileNum, .Phone
      Input #fileNum, .Net
      Input #fileNum, .NetAddr
      Input #fileNum, .Referral
      Input #fileNum, .Notes
      Input #fileNum, .RecNo
    End With
    Next EntryNum
    Close #fileNum    'All done
    On Error GoTo 0  'Turn off the error trap after closing the file.
    MsgBox theFileName & " was opened.", , "PCD"
    Sheets("ContactsDlog").ScrollBars("ScrollEntry").Max = numEntries
    theEntryNum = 1  'Insert the first entry into the form.
    DBToEntry theEntryNum
Exit Sub
FixBadFile:   'The error handler.
    Select Case Err
      Case errInputPastEndOfFile   'The file length is bad.
        MsgBox "Input Passed End Of File" & Chr(13) & _
          "Bad file, check file name and try again.", , "PCD Error"
      Case errSubscriptOutOfRange  'Number of records is bad.
        MsgBox "Subscript Out Of Range" & Chr(13) & _
          "Bad file, check file name and try again.", , "PCD Error"
      Case Else   'Anything else.
        MsgBox "Unexpected error. " & Chr(13) & "Error number: " & _
          Err & Chr(13) & "Description: " & Error(Err), , "PCD Error"
    End Select
    Close
    theFileName = ""
    theEntryNum = 0
    numEntries = 0
    ClearEntries
End Sub
```

First, you remove the block of code from the InitializeIt procedure that clears the form, and then change it into a separate procedure named ClearEntries. You must clear the form in several places, so it makes sense to convert this code to a separate procedure and simply call it when you need it.

```
'
'   Clear the dialog box.
'
Sub ClearEntries()
  With Sheets("ContactsDlog")
    .EditBoxes("DName").Text = ""
    .EditBoxes("DAddress").Text = ""
    .EditBoxes("DCity").Text = ""
    .EditBoxes("DState").Text = ""
    .EditBoxes("DZip").Text = ""
    .EditBoxes("DPhone").Text = ""
    .DropDowns("DE_Mail_Net").Text = ""
    .EditBoxes("DE_Mail_Address").Text = ""
    .EditBoxes("DReferral").Text = ""
    .EditBoxes("DNotes").Text = ""
    .Labels("DRecNo").Caption = "Record #: "
  End With
End Sub
```

In the FindName_Click procedure, enable user interrupts and the error trap, and then add the error handler at the end, as follows:

```
'
'   Find a name
'
Sub FindName_Click()
  Static theName As String
  Dim I As Integer
  Const TextComparison = 1
  Const errUserInterrupt = 18
'  Enable user interrupts.
  Application.EnableCancelKey = xlErrorHandler
  On Error GoTo HandleInterrupt   'Enable trapping the interrupt.
  If numEntries = 0 Then Exit Sub   'No entries yet.
  theName = InputBox("Input a name to search for.", "Find A Name", _
      theName)
  If theEntryNum <> numEntries Then
    For I = theEntryNum + 1 To numEntries
```

```
      If InStr(1, theDB(I).Name, theName, TextComparison) <> 0 Then
        'Found a matching entry
        On Error GoTo 0  'Turn off trap.
        Application.EnableCancelKey = xlDisabled   'Disable interrupts.
        theEntryNum = I
        DBToEntry theEntryNum
        Exit Sub
      End If
    Next I
  End If
  For I = 1 To theEntryNum
    If InStr(1, theDB(I).Name, theName, TextComparison) <> 0 Then
      'Found a matching entry
      On Error GoTo 0  'Turn off trap.
      Application.EnableCancelKey = xlDisabled   'Disable interrupts.
      theEntryNum = I
      DBToEntry theEntryNum
      Exit Sub
    End If
  Next I
  On Error GoTo 0 'Turn off trap.
  Application.EnableCancelKey = xlInterrupt   'Turn interrupts back on.
  'No match found.
  MsgBox "The name: " & theName & " was not found.", , "Find A Name"
Exit Sub
HandleInterrupt:  'Handle user interrupts here.
' If it was an interrupt, exit the procedure.
  If Err = errUserInterrupt Then
    Exit Sub
  Else   'If it was not an interrupt, then give it back to the system.
'   Turn interrupts back on.
    Application.EnableCancelKey = xlInterrupt
    Error Err
  End If
End Sub
```

When the search part of the procedure finishes, turn off the error trap and disable interrupts until the form is updated. Otherwise the user might press Ctrl-Break while the form is being updated and accidentally end the program.

The interrupt handler simply ends the procedure if Err is an interrupt. Anything else is passed back to the Visual Basic error handler.

In the Open_Click procedure, you turn on the error trap just before you open the file and turn off the trap after you close the file. Put the error handler at the end of the procedure, as follows:

```vba
'
'Open a database file.
'
Sub Open_Click()
  Dim theFilter As String, Answer, theDot As Integer
  Dim fileNum As Integer, EntryNum As Integer
  Dim buttons As Integer, theMsg As String
  Dim Flag As Boolean
  Const errInputPastEndOfFile = 62
  Const errSubscriptOutOfRange = 9
  If numEntries <> 0 Then   'See if there is something to save first.
    buttons = vbYesNoCancel + vbQuestion + vbApplicationModal
    theMsg = "Do you want to save the current data first?"
    Answer = MsgBox(theMsg, buttons, "PCD")
    If Answer = vbCancel Then   'Quit if the user chose Cancel.
      Exit Sub
    ElseIf Answer = vbYes Then   'Call save if the user chose Yes.
      Save_Click
    End If
  End If
  'Get the file name for the data.
  theFilter = "PCD database (*.PCD),*.PCD"
  Do
    Answer = Application.GetOpenFilename(theFilter, 1)
    If Answer = False Then Exit Sub 'The user chose Cancel.
    Answer = Trim(Answer)    'Remove any leading or trailing blanks.
    theDot = InStr(Answer, ".")
    If theDot = 0 Then   'Bad file name, no extension.
      MsgBox "You must choose a .PCD file.", , "PCD"
      Flag = False
    ElseIf Right(Answer, 4) <> ".PCD" Then   'Wrong type,
                                             'wrong extension.
```

Chapter 23 ♦ Using Error Trapping To Handle Unforeseen Events

```
      MsgBox "You must choose a .PCD file.", , "PCD"
      Flag = False
    Else  'Must be OK.
      Flag = True
    End If
  Loop Until Flag
  theFileName = Answer
  fileNum = FreeFile()  'Get a file number and open the file.
  On Error GoTo FixBadFile  'Turn on the error trap.
  Open theFileName For Input As fileNum
  'First read the number of entries.
  Input #fileNum, numEntries
  'Now expand the database.
  ReDim theDB(numEntries)
  'Now loop over each element of the database
  'and read all the components into the file.
  For EntryNum = 1 To numEntries
  With theDB(EntryNum)
    Input #fileNum, .Name
    Input #fileNum, .Address
    Input #fileNum, .City
    Input #fileNum, .State
    Input #fileNum, .Zip
    Input #fileNum, .Phone
    Input #fileNum, .Net
    Input #fileNum, .NetAddr
    Input #fileNum, .Referral
    Input #fileNum, .Notes
    Input #fileNum, .RecNo
  End With
  Next EntryNum
  Close #fileNum    'All done
  On Error GoTo 0  'Turn off the error trap after closing the file.
  MsgBox theFileName & " was opened.", , "PCD"
  Sheets("ContactsDlog").ScrollBars("ScrollEntry").Max = numEntries
  theEntryNum = 1  'Insert the first entry into the form.
  DBToEntry theEntryNum
Exit Sub
FixBadFile:  'The error handler.
```

```
  Select Case Err
    Case errInputPastEndOfFile   'The file length is bad.
      MsgBox "Input Passed End Of File" & Chr(13) & _
        "Bad file, check file name and try again.", , "PCD Error"
    Case errSubscriptOutOfRange  'Number of records is bad.
      MsgBox "Subscript Out Of Range" & Chr(13) & _
        "Bad file, check file name and try again.", , "PCD Error"
    Case Else  'Anything else.
      MsgBox "Unexpected error. " & Chr(13) & "Error number: " & _
        Err & Chr(13) & "Description: " & Error(Err), , "PCD Error"
  End Select
  Close
  theFileName = ""
  theEntryNum = 0
  numEntries = 0
  ClearEntries
End Sub
```

The handler looks for two errors: Input Passed End Of File and Subscript Out Of Range. Both of these errors indicate that the program has opened a file other than a sequential .PCD database file. After testing for the two expected errors, the error handler displays the dialog boxes shown in figures 23.2 and 23.3. Any other errors get the dialog box shown in figure 23.4, which explains that the error is unexpected and gives the error number and the error text. In figure 23.4, for example, the dialog box reports the Out of memory error (error number 7). If you choose OK in any of these three dialog boxes, the file is closed and the form cleared.

Figure 23.2
The dialog box displayed when the Input Passed End Of File error occurs.

Figure 23.3
The dialog box displayed when the Subscript Out Of Range error occurs.

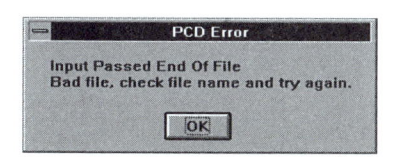

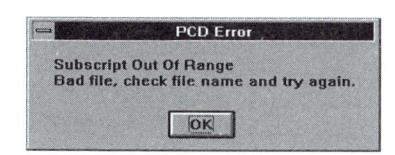

Figure 23.4
The dialog box displayed when the Case Else clause of the error handler is triggered.

> **Note:** You don't have to check for file name, device, and path type errors (error numbers 51 through 76), because the GetOpenFilename method ensures that your file name and path are good. The same is true in the Save_Click procedure, in which you use the GetSaveAsFilename method. If you are working in a shared environment, you might want to check for file access errors, and in the Save_Click procedure you may want to check for the disk full and media not ready errors.

Summary

In this chapter, you learned how to trap errors with the On Error GoTo statement. Error trapping enables your program to handle unexpected errors in a logical and controlled way, instead of letting the system simply crash your program. Error trapping is especially important in procedures that access the file system, because many potential problems can occur during file access.

This completes Part VII, "Debugging a Procedure." Part VIII introduces some of the more advanced features of the Visual Basic language.

Review Questions

The answers to the review questions are in Appendix A.

1. How do you enable an error trap in a procedure?
2. What are the three parts of an error handler?
3. What two functions do you use to find out about an error?
4. Why do you place an Exit Sub or Exit Function statement between the normal procedure and the error handler?
5. How do you pass an error back to the system so that it can handle the error?

6. What three things turn off an error trap?

7. How do you disable user interrupts with Ctrl-Break?

Review Exercises

1. Add an error trap and handler to the Open_Click procedure of the personal contacts database.

2. Add error traps and handlers to the random access file version of the personal contacts database.

3. Write a procedure that prints all the error numbers and descriptions in the Immediate pane of the Debug window. Print only Visual Basic errors and not the user-defined errors.

4. Place error traps in the DBToEntry and EntryToDB procedures of the random access file version of the personal contacts database.

5. Write a procedure that calls a procedure that calls a procedure. Place error traps in each procedure, and then use the Error statement to simulate different errors. In the Debug window, follow the program's progress by using the step commands to step through the procedures. Try different locations for the error and different enabled and disabled error traps. Place Error Err statements in the error handlers to pass on the error each time so that you can see where control moves in a program during an error event.

Part VIII

Advanced Language Features

CHAPTER 24

Creating Custom Menus and Toolbars

In Part VIII of this book, you learn about some of Visual Basic's more advanced features. In upcoming chapters, you learn about such features as Dynamic Data Exchange (DDE) and Object Linking and Embedding (OLE), while in this chapter you learn how to create custom menus and toolbars.

Most Windows programs feature a drop-down menu structure that simplifies access to the program's commands and controls. A more recent innovation, toolbars, provides even simpler access to the program's more commonly used commands. In Visual Basic, you can create your own menus and toolbars to use with your applications.

In this chapter you learn how to do the following:

- Add commands to existing menus
- Create custom menus
- Add tools to existing toolbars
- Create custom toolbars

The Layout of a Menu Bar

Figure 24.1 shows the layout of a typical menu. A menu is attached to a menu bar, and each menu has one or more menu items. Some of the menu items are commands, and others are submenus. Submenus have menu items just like menus.

Chapter 24 ♦ Creating Custom Menus and Toolbars

Figure 24.1
The layout of a menu.

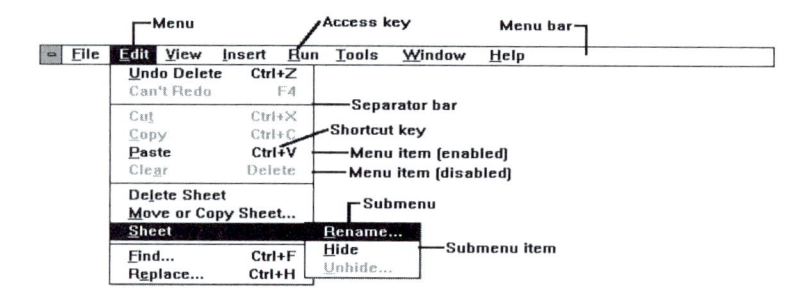

[Figure showing menu layout with labels: Menu, Access key, Menu bar, Undo Delete (Ctrl+Z), Can't Redo (F4), Separator bar, Cut (Ctrl+X), Copy (Ctrl+C), Shortcut key, Paste (Ctrl+V), Menu item (enabled), Clear (Delete), Menu item (disabled), Delete Sheet, Move or Copy Sheet..., Submenu, Sheet, Rename..., Hide, Submenu item, Find... (Ctrl+F), Unhide..., Replace... (Ctrl+H)]

Excel provides nine built-in menu bars as well as three shortcut menus, each of which is listed in table 24.1 along with the name of the Excel constant that you use to invoke the menu.

Table 24.1. Excel's built-in and shortcut menus.

Menu Bar	Constant	Description
Worksheet	xlWorksheet	Displayed when a worksheet, macro sheet, or dialog sheet is active.
Chart	xlChart	Displayed when a chart is active.
No Documents	xlNoDocuments	Displayed when no documents are open.
Visual Basic Module	xlModule	Displayed when a Visual Basic module sheet is active.
Shortcut Menus 1		Displayed for a cell, column, row, toolbar, or toolbar button.
Shortcut Menus 2		Displayed for a drawing object, button, or text box.
Shortcut Menus 3		Displayed for a chart, chart series, chart text, plot area, axis, gridline, floor, or legend.
Info	xlInfo	Displayed when the Info window is active.
Short Worksheet	xlWorksheetShort	The same as the Excel 3 short menus worksheet menu.

Menu Bar	Constant	Description
Short Chart menus chart menu.	xlChartShort	The same as the Excel 3 short
XL4 Worksheet	xlWorksheet4	The Excel 4 worksheet menu.
XL4 Chart	xlChart4	The Excel 4 chart menu.

The built-in menu bars are displayed only when a specific type of sheet is currently active. Thus, the worksheet menu bar is displayed only when a worksheet is the active sheet, and the chart menu bar is displayed only when a chart sheet is active. Remember this as you design additions to the built-in menuing system.

The three Shortcut Menus menu bars contain menus that are displayed when the user clicks the right mouse button and a specific object is selected. Each object has a different shortcut menu. The last four menu bars are included for compatibility with macros written to work with versions 3 and 4 of Excel. In addition to these built-in menu bars, you can create up to 15 custom menu bars.

Attached to each menu bar are the menus. The number of menus that you can attach to a single menu bar depends on the length of a menu name and the type of monitor that you have available. A single menu bar often includes seven to ten menus. If you need more menus, group them together as submenus on a single menu.

Each menu has menu items that are either linked to a command or are the header for a submenu. Submenu heads are marked with a small black arrow on the right side of the item's name. Menu items that open a dialog box instead of directly invoking a command are marked with an ellipsis (...) at the end of the item's name. In addition to commands and submenu heads, separator bars are also menu items. Separator bars do not invoke any commands, but simply separate the menu items visually.

Menus and menu items can be enabled or disabled. A disabled menu item is grayed, and cannot be selected. Also, menu items can be checked or not checked. A checked menu item has a check mark to the left of the item's name. You can use check marks to signify anything, but they are usually used with menu items that toggle options. When the option is enabled, check the menu item; when it is disabled, uncheck the menu item. For example, Excel's View menu has check marks next to the Formula Bar and Status Bar items when those bars are displayed.

Most menus and menu items have access keys, which are underlined in the menu's or menu item's name. You use an access key to choose a menu or menu item with the keyboard rather than a mouse. To choose a menu, you press Alt and then the access key for the desired menu. To choose a menu item from the active menu, you press the access key for the desired menu item.

Chapter 24 ♦ Creating Custom Menus and Toolbars

Some of the built-in menu items also have shortcut keys, which are listed to the right of the items' names. Pressing a shortcut key directly executes the command associated with the item. Shortcut keys are not automatically added to user-defined menu items, although you can add them manually.

Creating Menus with the Menu Editor

There are two ways to add menus, menu bars, and menu items to an Excel program: with the Menu Editor or with Visual Basic code. Using the Menu Editor is by far the easiest method. However, menus that you create with code are more portable, because menus created with code are recreated whenever you run that code. In contrast, menus that you create with the Menu Editor are attached to the workbook in which they were created, and do not go with the code if you copy it to another workbook.

There is actually a third way to attach commands to a menu bar: The **Tools Macro Options** command enables you to attach procedures to the bottom of the **Tools** menu. However, that command is limited to placing menu items at that one location.

To activate the Menu Editor, switch to a module and choose the **Tools Menu Editor** command. This displays the Menu Editor dialog box, in which you can select a menu for editing. The dialog box shown in figure 24.2 shows the Edit menu on the Visual Basic Module toolbar selected for editing. It is the same menu that is displayed in figure 24.1, with the same items selected.

Figure 24.2

The Menu Editor dialog box with the Edit menu displayed for editing. This is the same menu as shown in figure 24.1.

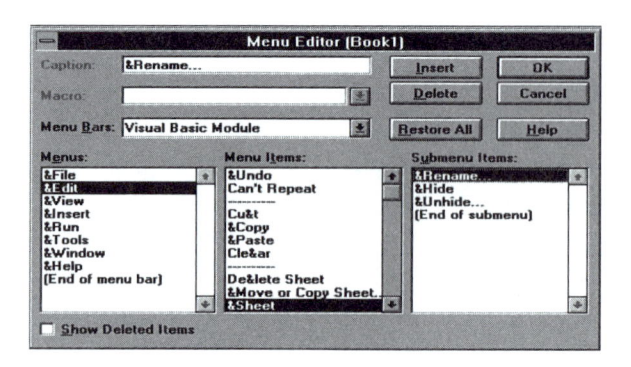

At the top of the Macro Editor dialog box are two edit boxes in which you insert the caption and the name of a macro that you want to attach to the currently selected menu item. To edit a specific menu item, select the menu bar from the Menu **B**ars drop-down list, the menu from the M**e**nus list, the item from the Menu Items list, and, if the item is a submenu, the submenu item from the S**u**bmenu Items list. Then you can edit or delete the item. If you are editing a built-in menu, the **R**estore All button changes everything in the current menu back to its default value.

Adding a Menu Item to an Existing Menu

In most cases, you need to add only one or two commands to a menu for a Visual Basic application, so it is appropriate to add those commands to an existing menu. When writing a Visual Basic program that augments Excel, you should use the built-in menus so that when users activate the specific sheet in which they need the commands, the program automatically makes the commands available. Otherwise you must attach to a sheet's OnSheetActivate property some code that replaces the default menu bar with yours.

To add a menu item to an existing menu, follow these steps:

1. Open or switch to a module and choose the **T**ools Menu **E**ditor command.

2. In the Menu **B**ars drop-down list and the **M**enus list, select a menu bar and menu from the lists of existing menu bars and menus.

3. Select in the Menu **I**tems list the location where you want to place the custom item. Then choose the **I**nsert button. As shown in figure 24.3, the item list opens a space in which you can insert your new item. If you don't select a location, your new item goes at the end of the list.

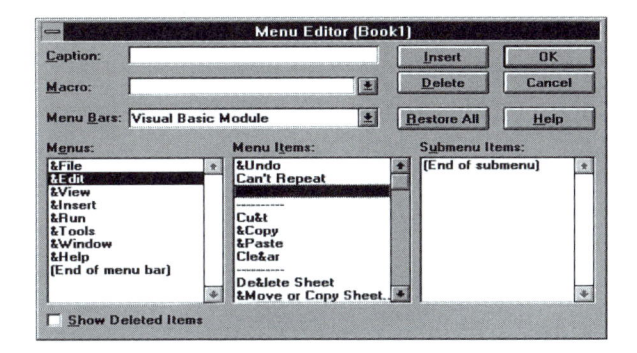

Figure 24.3
The Menu Editor dialog box after you choose the Insert button.

4. Type a caption in the **C**aption box. Place an ampersand (&) before the letter that is to be the access key. The ampersand does not appear in the item's name, but the letter following it is underlined.

> **Caution:** When you select a letter to use as an access key, be sure to pick one that is not already in use in the menu. If you have two menu items with the same access key, the user can use that key to select only the first item on the menu with that access key. To select the second item with that key, the user would have to use the arrow keys to space down to it and press the Enter key. This caution also applies to menu access keys on the menu bar.

Chapter 24 ♦ Creating Custom Menus and Toolbars

5. If your new menu item is to be a command, select from the **M**acro list box the procedure to attach to the item, or type the name of a procedure that you are going to create for this item, as shown in figure 24.4. If the item is to be a submenu head, click the location of your choice in the **S**ubmenu Items list, choose the **I**nsert button, and then type the submenu item's caption and macro.

Figure 24.4
The Menu Editor dialog box with a new menu item inserted and attached to a procedure.

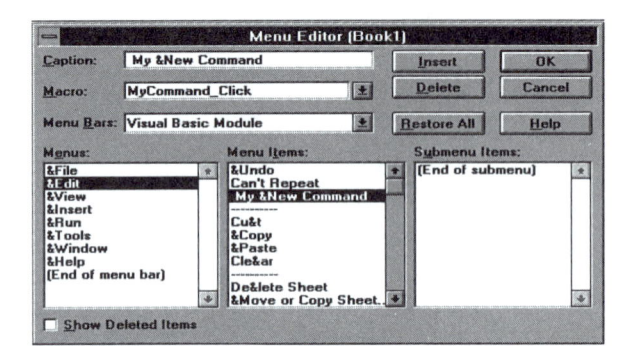

6. Choose OK. The new menu item is then inserted. Now when you choose the menu, you see the new item listed in the menu.

Figure 24.5 shows the menu that results after you enter in the Menu Editor dialog box the specifications shown in figure 24.4. Note in figure 24.5 that the letter "N" in "New" is underlined because in the dialog box shown in figure 24.4, you defined the letter as the access key by typing an ampersand before the letter.

Figure 24.5
The new menu item, My New Command, attached to the existing Edit menu.

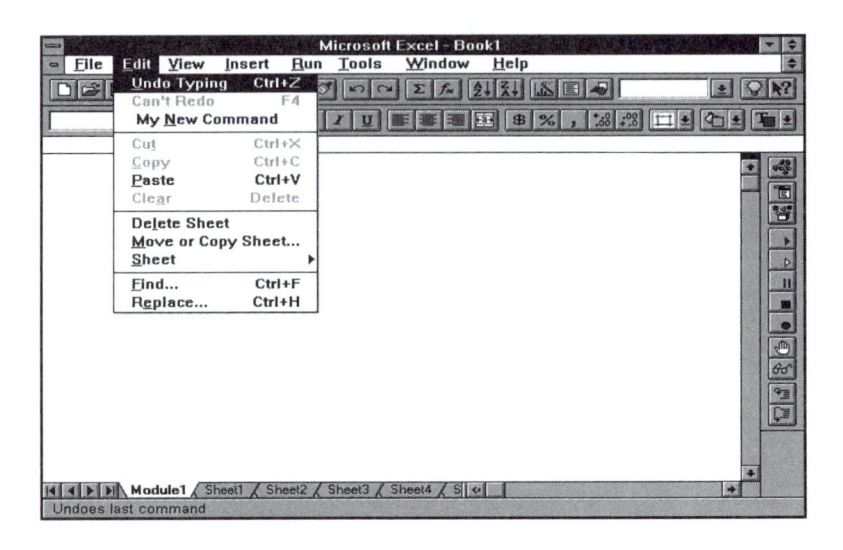

388

> **Note:** Keep in mind that the built-in menu bars change as you change from a worksheet to a chart sheet or module sheet. If you want your new menu command to be available to all these sheets, you must add it to the menus on all three menu bars. If you want it to be on the shortcut menus, you must attach it to each shortcut menu for each item for which you want the command to appear.

To add an item to a submenu or to one of the shortcut menus, use exactly the same set of steps that you use to create a menu item, except choose the submenu or shortcut menu before you choose the Insert button.

Adding a Menu to an Existing Menu Bar

In addition to adding new menu items to an existing menu, you can add a new menu to an existing menu bar. You proceed in much the same way as you do when adding an item to a menu.

To add a menu to an existing menu bar, follow these steps:

1. Create or switch to a module and choose the Tools Menu Editor command.

2. In the Menu Bars drop-down list, select one of the existing menu bars.

3. In the Menus list, click the location at which you want to place the custom menu. Make sure that you click a location in the Menus list, not in the Menu Items list; otherwise you create a new menu item rather than a new menu. As with menu items, if you don't select a location, your new menu goes at the end of the list, which is on the right side of the menu bar, to the left of the Help menu. The Help menu is always the rightmost menu, no matter where you place a new menu.

4. Choose the Insert button. The list of menus opens a space in which you can insert a new menu.

5. Type a caption in the Caption box. Type an ampersand (&) before the letter that you want to specify as the access key. For example, in figure 24.6, an ampersand was typed before "C," which makes "C" the command's access key. You do not attach a procedure to a menu.

6. Choose OK. The new menu item is then inserted, as shown in figure 24.7.

After attaching a new menu, you must add to it menu items and submenus as described in the previous section. You can add menu items and submenus before you choose OK in step 6. Keep in mind the same restriction as for adding menu items to the built-in menus: Different menu bars are displayed when different sheets are active. Placing a menu on one built-in menu bar does not automatically place it on any of the others.

Chapter 24 ◆ Creating Custom Menus and Toolbars

Figure 24.6
The Menu Editor dialog box with a new menu inserted.

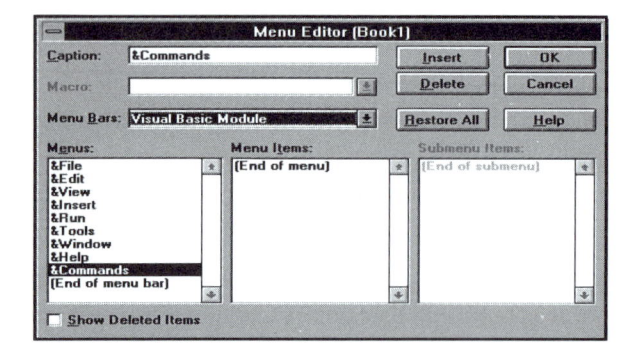

Figure 24.7
The new menu, Commands, attached to the existing Module menu bar.

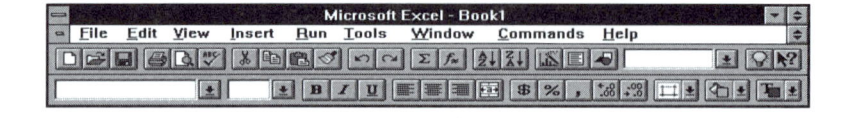

Adding a New Menu Bar

If you are creating a custom application with many menus, you should create a custom menu bar that includes only those commands to which you want the user to have access. You add a new menu bar the same way that you add new menus or menu items.

To create a new menu bar, follow these steps:

1. Create or switch to a module and choose the Tools Menu Editor command.

2. In the Menu Bars drop-down list, select any of the listed menu bars. This unselects items in the Menus and Menu Items lists. If you don't unselect these items, you create a new menu or menu item rather than a new menu bar. It doesn't matter which menu bar you select, because new menus are always added to the end of the list of menus.

3. Choose the Insert button. Then type a name for the new menu bar in the Caption box, as shown in figure 24.8. This name is only used to select the menu bar and is not displayed.

4. Add any menus, menu items, and submenus to your new menu bar as previously described. Then choose OK.

After you choose OK, your new menu bar is not displayed, because it is not one of the built-in menu bars that are automatically displayed.

390

Figure 24.8
The Menu Editor dialog box with a new menu bar, MyBar1, inserted.

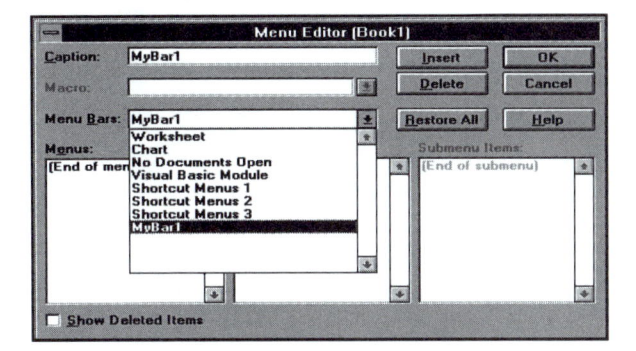

Displaying a Custom Menu Bar

To display a custom menu bar, you must activate it using the Activate method of the MenuBar object. Common places to attach such a procedure include the initialization procedure of your application or the OnSheetActivate property of the sheet to which your code applies.

For example, the following short procedure selects and then activates the MyBar1 menu bar from the MenuBars collection:

```
'
' Display a custom menu bar
'
Sub DisplayMenu()
  Application.MenuBars("MyBar1").Activate
End Sub
```

The menu bar MyBar1 consists of one menu, named Commands. Running this procedure displays that menu bar as shown in figure 24.9. Custom menu bars do not change automatically when you change the active sheet. After a custom menu bar is activated, you can change to worksheets, charts, and so on, and the custom menu bar is still displayed. Thus, when a custom menu bar is displayed, you must activate one of the built-in menu bars to reenable automatic menu bar switching.

Removing a Custom Menu Bar

Removing a custom menu bar is not quite as easy as displaying it. To remove a custom menu bar and display the built-in menus again, you must activate one of the built-in menus. However, you must activate the right one. Excel displays specific menu bars, depending on which kind of a sheet is active. Trying to activate the wrong one causes an error. If you are certain of which kind of a sheet is active, then simply apply the Activate method to the specific built-in menu bar. To determine which kind of sheet is active, apply the TypeName() function to the ActiveSheet property.

Chapter 24 ◆ Creating Custom Menus and Toolbars

Figure 24.9
The new menu bar consists of a single menu named Commands.

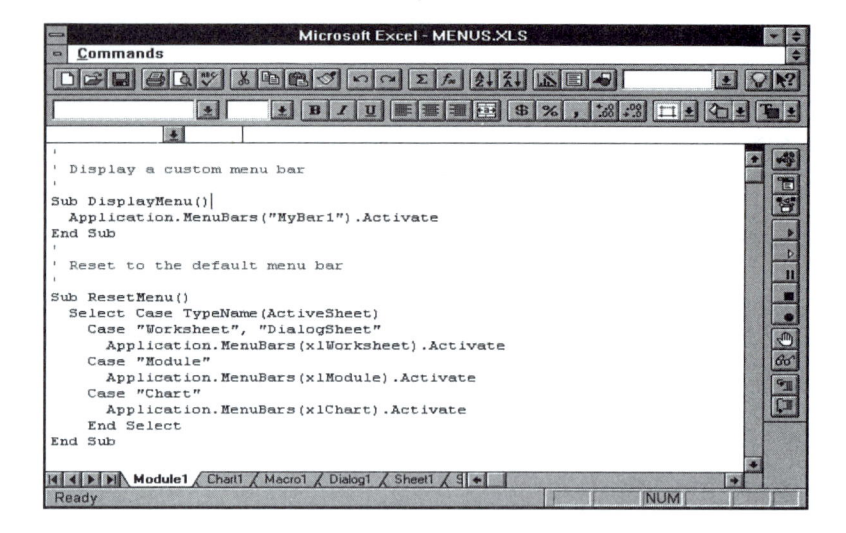

[Screenshot: Microsoft Excel - MENUS.XLS window showing a Commands menu bar with the following code:]

```
' Display a custom menu bar

Sub DisplayMenu()
  Application.MenuBars("MyBar1").Activate
End Sub

' Reset to the default menu bar

Sub ResetMenu()
  Select Case TypeName(ActiveSheet)
    Case "Worksheet", "DialogSheet"
      Application.MenuBars(xlWorksheet).Activate
    Case "Module"
      Application.MenuBars(xlModule).Activate
    Case "Chart"
      Application.MenuBars(xlChart).Activate
  End Select
End Sub
```

For example, the following procedure determines the kind of sheet that the active sheet is, and then activates the corresponding menu bar using the built-in constants from table 24.1:

```
'
' Reset to the default menu bar
'
Sub ResetMenu()
  Select Case TypeName(ActiveSheet)
    Case "Worksheet", "DialogSheet"
      Application.MenuBars(xlWorksheet).Activate
    Case "Module"
      Application.MenuBars(xlModule).Activate
    Case "Chart"
      Application.MenuBars(xlChart).Activate
  End Select
End Sub
```

Procedures that deactivate a custom menu bar are commonly placed in one of the following types of procedures:

◆ The exit procedure that executes when your application finishes

◆ A procedure attached to a sheet's OnSheetDeactivate property, to remove the custom menu when the sheet to which it applies is no longer active

392

Creating Menus with Code

In addition to creating menus with the Menu Editor, you can create them with code. Although using code is not as visual as using the Menu Editor, the results are the same. As previously mentioned, menus created with code are more portable than those created with the Menu Editor. When you use code, you can create the same menus in another application simply by copying the code to the other application.

Accessing Menu Bars, Menus, and Menu Items

A menu item is part of the MenuItems collection of a menu, and a menu is part of the Menus collection of a menu bar, which is part of the MenuBars collection of the Application object. Now, if you didn't get lost following that chain of collections, you would see that you access a menu bar as follows:

```
Application.MenuBars(BarName)
```

And you access a menu using the following syntax:

```
Application.MenuBars(BarName).Menus(MenuName)
```

Finally, you access a menu item as follows:

```
Application.MenuBars(BarName).Menus(MenuName).MenuItems(ItemName)
```

Normally you can omit the Application object, but you cannot omit the collections if you want to ensure that you get the correct menu item. The *BarName*, *MenuName*, and *ItemName* are either a string that contains the name of the menu bar, menu, or menu item, or the index number of the menu bar, menu, or menu item in the respective collection.

The index numbers for the built-in Excel menu bars are available as Excel constants, which are listed in table 24.1. The index numbers of the menus are in the same order as the menus are displayed onscreen when the menu bar is active. The first menu on the left (usually **F**ile) is index number 1, the one on its right is number 2, and so on. The menu items are listed from the top down, with the topmost menu item as number 1, the next below it as number 2, and so on. The separator bars are counted as individual menu items. To be more readable, your code should use the name of the menu whenever possible.

Adding a Menu Item to an Existing Menu

To add menu items to an existing menu, you use the Add method. The Add method has several arguments that you use to set some of the new menu item's properties with a single statement. Alternatively, you can set each of the properties separately, first using the Add method to add the new menu item and then accessing each of the new menu item's properties.

When you apply the Add method to a menu item, the named arguments are `caption`, `onAction`, `shortcutKey`, `before`, and `restore`.

The `caption` argument sets the Caption property of the menu item. Equate it to a string that contains the name of the menu item. Include an ampersand (&) in the string before the character that is to be the access key, and use a single hyphen (–) to create a separator bar.

The `onAction` argument sets the `OnAction` property of the menu item. Set it equal to a string that contains the name of the procedure to run when the item is selected.

The `shortcutKey` argument specifies a shortcut key for the menu item, but this argument is only for future use on the Macintosh computer.

The `before` argument specifies where the new item is to be inserted in the list of items. The item currently in that location is moved down to make room for the new item. This argument can be either an index number, or a string that contains the name of the item currently in the desired location. If you omit this argument, the new menu item is placed at the bottom of the menu.

The `restore` argument restores a previously deleted menu item from one of the built-in menus. You place the name of the item to be restored in the `caption` argument, and set the `restore` argument to True. Adding a menu item with the same name as a deleted built-in menu item without setting `restore` to True does not restore the functionality of the deleted item, but creates a user-defined item with the same name as the deleted item.

For example, the menu item shown in figure 24.5, which you previously added with the Menu Editor, can also be added with the following code:

```
'
' Add a menu item.
'
Sub AddMenuItem()
  MenuBars(xlModule).Menus("Edit").MenuItems.Add _
    Caption:="My &New Command", _
    OnAction:="MyCommand", _
    before:=3
End Sub
```

This code selects the menu bar with the built-in constant xlModule, and selects the Edit menu with the Menus collection. The caption argument is set to My &New Command, with the N in New set as the access key. The procedure MyCommand is set as the procedure to run when the item is selected, and the menu is inserted at location 3 on the menu. You must set the location with an index number because the third item on the existing menu is a separator bar and has no name.

To remove this menu item, apply the Delete method to it.

For example, the following procedure deletes the menu item inserted in the previous example:

```
'
' Delete a menu item
'
Sub DeleteMenuItem()
    MenuBars(xlModule).Menus("Edit").MenuItems("My New Command").Delete
End Sub
```

Note that when you the item to the menu, the menu caption that selects the menu item does not contain the ampersand that defines the access key.

Adding a Menu to an Existing Menu Bar

You add a menu to a menu bar the same way that you add a menu item to a menu. To add a menu to the menu bar, you apply the Add method to the Menus collection of that menu bar. You cannot apply the `OnAction` argument to a menu, although you can apply the other arguments. The `reset` argument resets the indicated menu to the default.

For example, the following procedure adds the menu Commands to the Module menu bar as shown in figure 24.7:

```
'
' Display a custom menu
'
Sub DisplayMenu()
    MenuBars(xlModule).Menus.Add _
        Caption:="&Commands", _
        before:="Help"
End Sub
```

To delete the Commands menu, use the following procedure:

```
'
' Delete a menu
'
Sub DeleteMenu()
    MenuBars(xlModule).Menus("Commands").Delete
End Sub
```

Adding a New Menu Bar

Adding a new menu bar is similar to adding new menus and menu items. The only argument allowed to the Add method is the Name argument, which sets the name of the new menu bar in the same manner as the `caption` argument sets the name of a menu or menu item.

Chapter 24 ♦ Creating Custom Menus and Toolbars

For example, the following procedure creates and displays the menu bar shown in figure 24.9:

```
'
' Create a custom menu bar
'
Sub CreateBar()
  MenuBars.Add Name:="MyBar2"
  MenuBars("MyBar2").Menus.Add Caption:="&Commands"
  Application.MenuBars("MyBar2").Activate
End Sub
```

To delete a custom menu bar, first run the preceding ResetMenu procedure or a similar procedure to display a different menu bar, and then apply the Delete method to the MenuBars collection. If the menu that you want to delete from the collection is currently displayed, you must change the menu first, because you cannot delete a menu that is being displayed. Also, if you try to use the Add method to create a new menu bar, and a menu bar with the same name already exists, the Add method will fail. Instead, apply the Delete method first, to delete the named menu bar, and then apply the Add method, to create a new bar with the same name.

For example, the following procedure deletes the MyBar2 menu bar from the MenuBars collection. For this procedure to work, MyBar2 must not be displayed.

```
'
' Delete a custom menu bar
'
Sub DeleteBar()
  MenuBars("MyBar2").Delete
End Sub
```

Changing the Properties of Menus and Menu Items

Menus and menu items have several properties that control how they look and are accessed. Both menus and menu items have a Caption property, which contains the menu's or the item's name as displayed onscreen. You can change the name of a menu or command at any time by changing this property.

Menu items have a Checked property, which if True places a check mark to the left of the item on the menu. When menu items represent options, use the Checked property to indicate whether the item is selected or not.

Both menus and menu items have an Enabled property. If the Enabled property is True, the menu or menu item behaves like normal. If Enabled is False, the menu or menu item is grayed and disabled so that the user cannot select it. When a menu is disabled, the user cannot access any of the menu items for that menu.

Adding a Shortcut Key to a Menu Command

For a user-defined menu item, Visual Basic does not automatically support shortcut keys as it does for the built-in menu items. To add a shortcut key, you must add the key name to the Caption property of the menu item. Normally, you place the menu item's name on the left, followed by the shortcut key on the right.

To enable the shortcut key, you must execute the OnKey method, which takes two arguments. The first is a string that contains the key combination to assign to the procedure, and the second is a string that contains the procedure name to execute when the user presses the key combination.

> **Caution:** Disabling the menu item by setting its Enabled property to False does not disable the shortcut key. You disable the shortcut key by reexecuting the OnKey method without a second argument.

Table 24.2 lists the codes for the special keys, along with modifier keys.

Table 24.2. Key codes for use with the OnKey method.

Key	Code
Backspace	{BACKSPACE}, {BS}
Break	{BREAK}
CapsLock	{CAPSLOCK}
Clear	{CLEAR}
Delete or Del	{DELETE}, {DEL}
Down Arrow	{DOWN}
End	{END}
Enter (keypad)	{ENTER}
Enter (keyboard)	~
Esc	{ESCAPE}, {ESC}
Help	{HELP}
Home	{HOME}
Insert or Ins	{INSERT}

continues

Table 24.2. Continued

Key	Code
Left arrow	{LEFT}
Num Lock	{NUMLOCK}
Page Down	{PGDN}
Page Up	{PGUP}
Return	{RETURN}
Right arrow	{RIGHT}
Scroll Lock	{SCROLLLOCK}
Tab	{TAB}
Up arrow	{UP}
F1 through F15	{F1} through {F15}

Modifier Codes

Key	Code
Shift	+ (plus sign)
Ctrl	^ (caret)
Alt or Option	% (percent sign)

> **Note:** To use the modifier codes ~, +, ^, and % in a string, you must enclose them in braces (as in {~}).

For example, the following three procedures create a menu item with a shortcut key, disable the item and the key, and then reenable the item and the key:

```
' Create a shortcut key.
```

```
Sub CreateShortcut()
  MenuBars(xlModule).Menus("Edit").MenuItems.Add _
    Caption:="DoIt  Ctrl-a", _
    OnAction:="DoItProc", _
    before:=3
  Application.OnKey "^a", "DoItProc"   'Attach Ctrl-a to DoItProc
End Sub
'
' Disable an item and key.
'
Sub DisableShortcut()
  MenuBars(xlModule).Menus("Edit").MenuItems("DoIt  Ctrl-a") .Enabled _
      = False
  Application.OnKey "^a", ""    'Reset Ctrl-a to nothing.
End Sub
'
' Enable a shortcut key.
'
Sub EnableShortcut()
  MenuBars(xlModule).Menus("Edit").MenuItems("DoIt  Ctrl-a").Enabled _
      = True
  Application.OnKey "^a", "DoItProc"
End Sub
```

Modifying Shortcut Menus

Shortcut menus work much like regular menus, except that they are not attached to a visible toolbar. Shortcut menus drop down when you click an object with the right mouse button. The object that you click determines which menu drops down.

To change the menu items in a shortcut menu, you can use the Menu Editor or you can use the ShortcutMenus collection in your code. The ShortcutMenus collection takes a single Excel constant and returns the selected menu. The constant determines which menu is accessed, and is named after the object that selects the menu. Table 24.3 lists the constants. After selecting a menu, you can change it by using the commands for adding and deleting menu items.

Table 24.3. The constants that select the different shortcut menus, and the object that the user clicks to display the menu.

Constant	Object
xlAxis	Chart axis
xlButton	Button
xlChartSeries	Chart series
xlChartTitles	Chart titles
xlColumnHeader	Column
xlDebugCodePane	Debug code pane
xlDesktop	Desktop
xlDialogSheet	Dialog sheet
xlDrawingObject	Drawing object
xlEntireChart	Entire chart
xlFloor	Chart floor
xlGridline	Chart gridline
xlImmediatePane	Immediate pane
xlLegend	Chart legend
xlMacrosheetCell	Macro sheet cell
xlModule	Module
xlPlotArea	Chart plot area
xlRowHeader	Row
xlTextBox	Text box
xlTitleBar	Title bar
xlToolbar	Toolbar
xlToolbarButton	Toolbar button
xlWatchPane	Watch pane
xlWorkbookTab	Workbook tab
xlWorksheetCell	Worksheet cell

Accessing Toolbars

You display and delete toolbars much like menus. To access a toolbar, use the Toolbars collection. You access the built-in toolbars by using the names listed in table 24.4 as arguments to the Toolbars collection. For toolbars you should use names rather than numbers, because the members and ordering of the Toolbars collection can change, which in turn changes the numbering. To make an existing toolbar visible, set its Visible property to True, because setting Visible to False hides the toolbar.

Table 24.4. The names of the built-in toolbars.

Name	Contents
Standard	Tools for accessing files, cutting and pasting, and printing. It is normally visible at the top of the screen.
Formatting	Tools for formatting cells. It is normally visible below the Standard toolbar.
Query and Pivot	Tools for using query and pivot tables.
Chart	Tools for changing chart types and editing charts.
Drawing	Tools for drawing lines, squares, buttons, and other graphic objects.
TipWizard	Tools for accessing the tip wizard.
Forms	Tools for drawing controls on forms.
Stop Recording	The button that stops the Macro Recorder.
Visual Basic	Tools for starting and stopping programs, and for using the debugging tools.
Auditing	Tools for locating the sources of information to check the validity of calculations.
WorkGroup	Tools for locating files and sending mail.
Microsoft	Tools to switch to other Microsoft applications.
Full Screen	A button that switches between full-screen and normal display of a worksheet.

Chapter 24 ◆ Creating Custom Menus and Toolbars

1 For example, the first of the following procedures turns on the Microsoft toolbar, and the second turns it off:

```
'
' Display a toolbar.
'
Sub DisplayToolbar()
  Application.Toolbars("Microsoft").Visible = True
End Sub
'
' Hide a toolbar.
'
Sub HideToolbar()
  Application.Toolbars("Microsoft").Visible = False
End Sub
```

Adding Buttons to a Toolbar

The simplest way to add buttons to a toolbar is to use the Customize dialog box. Display the toolbar to which you want to add a button, and then choose the View Toolbars command and the Customize button. The Customize dialog box appears as shown in figure 24.10. Note in figure 24.10 that the Save button is selected, so its function is described at the bottom of the dialog box.

Figure 24.10
The Customize dialog box for adding buttons to toolbars.

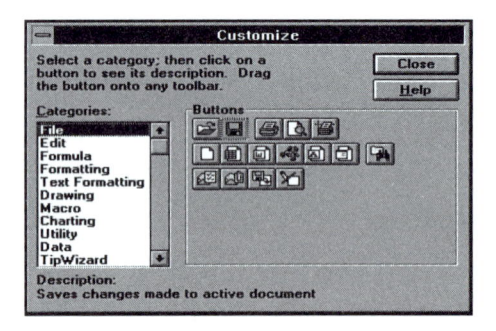

In the Categories box, select the category in which you are interested and then click the buttons displayed in the dialog box to see what they do. Then click a button that you want to add to your toolbar and then drag the button to the displayed toolbar.

To attach to a toolbar buttons that activate Visual Basic procedures, select Custom in the Categories box of the Customize dialog box. All the buttons in this category, as shown in figure 24.11, are not attached to any procedure. If you drag

402

one of these buttons to a toolbar, the Assign Macro dialog box appears so you can assign a procedure to that toolbar button.

Figure 24.11
The Customize dialog box showing the Custom buttons available for attachment to Visual Basic procedures.

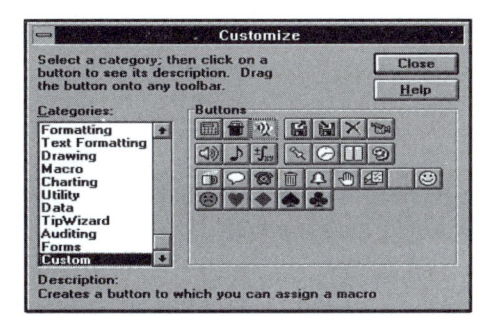

Creating Custom Toolbars

To create a new toolbar, choose the **V**iew **T**oolbars command to display the Toolbars dialog box as shown in figure 24.12. Then, in the Tool**b**ar Name window, type a name. Choose the **N**ew button, and the new toolbar and the Customize dialog box appear. Drag to the new toolbar any tools that you want, and the toolbar expands so that the new tools fit (see fig. 24.13). If you drag to the toolbar a custom button, the Assign Macro dialog box appears to enable you to attach a procedure to the button.

Figure 24.12
The Toolbars dialog box ready to create a custom toolbar.

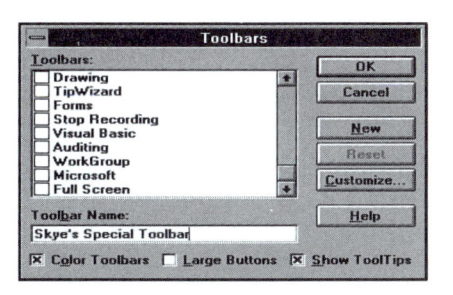

Figure 24.13
The custom toolbar with some buttons attached.

403

Chapter 24 ◆ Creating Custom Menus and Toolbars

Creating Buttons with the Button Image Editor

Say that you have just created a custom toolbar, but you dislike an image that is displayed on one of the toolbar's buttons. For example, note the image displayed on the rightmost button of the toolbar shown in figure 24.13. You might prefer to present a more uplifting image than this frowning face. To change the image on a button, you use the Button Image Editor. This editor is difficult to locate, because there is no normal menu command that you can use to start it. It's available only on the Buttons shortcut menu.

To access the Button Image Editor and edit a button, follow these steps:

1. Make certain that the button that you want to edit is on a toolbar and is visible onscreen.

2. Choose the View Toolbars Customize command to display the Customize dialog box.

3. While displaying both the Customize dialog box and the toolbar that contains the button that you want to edit, click the right mouse button while pointing to the button that you want to edit. This displays the Buttons shortcut menu.

4. Choose the Edit Button Image command from the shortcut menu. The Button Editor dialog box then appears as shown in figure 24.14.

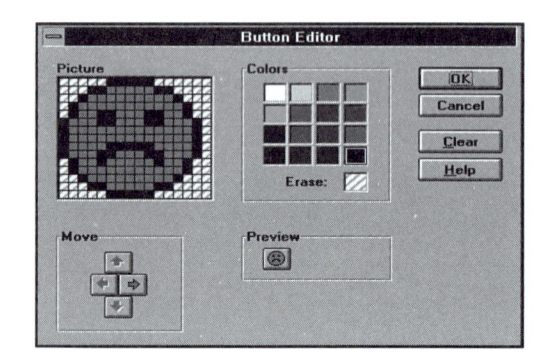

Figure 24.14

The Button Editor dialog box displaying a button image that you want to change.

5. To edit the image on the button, click the color first, then click the area of the button image where you want to change the color.

6. When you have completed converting the image (as shown in fig. 24.15, for example), choose OK. The new button image then replaces your old one on the toolbar.

Figure 24.15
The Button Editor dialog box with the edited button image.

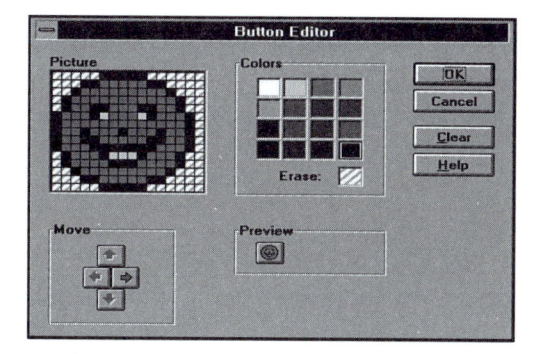

Attaching a Toolbar to a Workbook

Toolbars that you create with the Toolbars and Customize dialog boxes are attached to Excel, and not to the workbook that was open when you created the toolbars. However, you can attach a custom toolbar to a workbook so that the toolbar is available whenever the user opens the workbook.

To attach a custom toolbar to a workbook, follow these steps:

1. Choose the Tools Attach Toolbars command to display the Attach Toolbars dialog box, which lists all the custom toolbars in the Custom Toolbars box.

2. Select one of the listed toolbars and then choose Copy. The toolbar then moves to the Toolbars in Workbook box, as shown in figure 24.16.

3. Choose OK to attach the custom toolbar to the currently active workbook.

Figure 24.16
A custom toolbar and the Attach Toolbars dialog box, which enables you to attach the custom toolbar to a workbook.

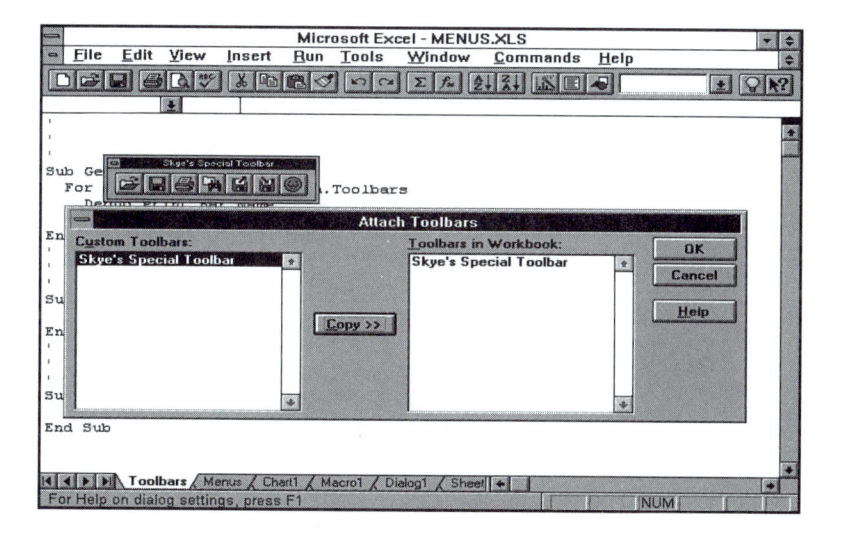

Chapter 24 ◆ Creating Custom Menus and Toolbars

Using Code To Control Toolbars and Toolbar Buttons

Toolbars and toolbar buttons are very difficult to control with code. Although the commands are the same as those that you use with menus, the buttons are numbered and it's difficult to find out what the numbers are. The best way to use code to create a toolbar is to turn on the Macro Recorder and record the creation of the toolbar with the Toolbars and Customize dialog boxes.

You create new toolbars by applying the Add method to the Toolbars collection. The method requires only one argument: the new name of the toolbar. If you don't name the toolbar, Visual Basic assigns a default name of Toolbar 1, Toolbar 2, and so forth.

To add a button to a toolbar, use the Add method with the ToolbarButtons collection. The Add method here has six arguments: `button`, `before`, `onAction`, `enabled`, and `pushed`.

The `button` argument sets the number of the button to attach to the toolbar. The number is stored in the button's ID property.

The `before` argument gets a number that controls the location of the button, counting from left to right and from top to bottom. This argument works the same as for menus and menu items.

The `onAction` argument gets the name of a procedure to run when the user presses the button.

The `enabled` argument sets the Enabled property of the button to either True or False, indicating whether the button is usable or not.

The `pushed` argument sets the Pushed property to either True or False, indicating whether the button looks pushed or not. A pushed button has the shadows on the top and left instead of on the bottom and right, and the button is slightly lighter in color.

For example, the following code creates the custom toolbar shown in figure 24.17. This code was simply recorded with the Macro Recorder as the toolbar was created, moving the toolbar, editing a button, and attaching the toolbar to the worksheet.

```
'
' Record creating a toolbar.
'
Sub RecordToolbar()
    Toolbars.Add Name:="Shane's Tools"
    Toolbars(21).Visible = True
    With Application
        .ShowToolTips = True
        .LargeButtons = False
        .ColorButtons = True
    End With
```

```
        Toolbars("Shane's Tools").ToolbarButtons.Add Button:=76, Before:=1
        Toolbars("Shane's Tools").ToolbarButtons.Add Button:=77, Before:=2
        Toolbars("Shane's Tools").ToolbarButtons.Add Button:=78, Before:=3
        Toolbars("Shane's Tools").ToolbarButtons.Add Button:=215, _
            Before:=4
        Toolbars("Shane's Tools").ToolbarButtons(4).OnAction = "DoItProc"
        With Toolbars("Shane's Tools")
            .Left = 25
            .Top = 162
        End With
        Toolbars("Shane's Tools").ToolbarButtons(4).Edit
    End Sub
```

Figure 24.17

A custom toolbar created with the Macro Recorder running.

Examining this code piece by piece reveals the actions of the different commands and dialog boxes. The first statement uses the Add method to create a new toolbar, the second statement makes the toolbar visible, and the following block of five statements sets some default properties:

```
Toolbars.Add Name:="Shane's Tools"
Toolbars(21).Visible = True
With Application
    .ShowToolTips = True
    .LargeButtons = False
    .ColorButtons = True
End With
```

Only the first two statements are actually necessary to create the new toolbar. The other statements result from creating a new toolbar with the Toolbars dialog box. In the second statement, the number 21, which the Macro Recorder used to select the toolbar, should be replaced with the name of the toolbar, because the number of the toolbar may change.

The following block of four statements results from using the Customize dialog box to add the four buttons to the toolbar. The fifth statement occurs when the Assign Macro dialog box appears and the DoItProc procedure is attached to the fourth button.

Chapter 24 ◆ Creating Custom Menus and Toolbars

```
Toolbars("Shane's Tools").ToolbarButtons.Add Button:=76, Before:=1
Toolbars("Shane's Tools").ToolbarButtons.Add Button:=77, Before:=2
Toolbars("Shane's Tools").ToolbarButtons.Add Button:=78, Before:=3
Toolbars("Shane's Tools").ToolbarButtons.Add Button:=215, _
    Before:=4
Toolbars("Shane's Tools").ToolbarButtons(4).OnAction = "DoItProc"
```

The next four statements result from dragging the toolbar half way down the left side of the screen. These statements change the value of the toolbar's Left and Top properties.

```
With Toolbars("Shane's Tools")
    .Left = 25
    .Top = 162
End With
```

> **Note:** Most controls and drawing objects have Top and Left properties that locate the objects on the screen. The values of these properties are the measurement in points of the top-left corner of the object to the top-left corner of the object's container. Points are equal to 1/72 inch, and an object's container is the object to which it is attached or in which it is located. For example, for a button on a form, the button's container is the form; for a toolbar displayed onscreen, the toolbar's container is the worksheet area. Because you can use code to manipulate these properties, you can move buttons and objects onscreen to create special effects.

The next line results from running the Button Editor:

```
Toolbars("Shane's Tools").ToolbarButtons(4).Edit
```

This line only displays the editor; however, the changes made to the fourth button are not included in the recording. Also, the toolbar is not attached to the workbook. These actions cannot be done with code, but must be done by hand.

Summary

In this chapter, you learned to edit or create menus, menu bars, and menu items. You handle most of these tasks by using the Add method to create new objects or the Delete method to remove them. In addition to menus, you learned to create and edit toolbars and toolbar buttons.

In the next chapter, you learn how to create custom objects with Visual Basic.

Review Questions

The answers to the review questions are in Appendix A.

1. What are the three objects that make up a menu?
2. Can you attach a procedure to a menu?
3. What is a shortcut menu?
4. How do you invoke the Button Image Editor?
5. How do you create and display a custom menu bar?

Review Exercises

1. Create a custom menu bar that is modeled after the Visual Basic Module menu bar, and include menus and menu items that are modeled after the File and Edit menus. Attach the items to dummy procedures.
2. Create a custom toolbar that includes all your favorite commands.
3. Write a procedure that checks and unchecks a menu item each time that the user chooses the menu item.
4. Write a procedure that disables another menu when the menu that you created in exercise 2 is checked.
5. Write a procedure to make a button jump whenever the user clicks it. Use a pair of random numbers to select a location for the button to jump to.
6. Write a procedure that displays the ID numbers for any buttons dropped on a custom toolbar.

CHAPTER 25

Creating Custom Objects

Although Visual Basic is well suited for manipulating objects, it is not fully capable of creating new objects using only code resources. However, it can closely imitate the functionality of an object.

In this chapter you learn the following:

- ♦ How Visual Basic imitates objects
- ♦ How to create custom property procedures
- ♦ How to create custom methods

Defining the Custom Object

A custom code object in Visual Basic is tied to a module. The module's name is the object's name, and you use this name to access the object's properties. For standard objects, you start with an object class and then, using a generating function such as the Add method, you create objects from the class. In Visual Basic, you can't create a class, so you must construct a custom object from scratch. However, after you construct the object, you access it much like any other object. Perhaps future versions of Visual Basic for Applications will enable you to create a class structure, but unfortunately the current version does not do so.

Because you create Visual Basic objects from modules, the objects are attached to the currently open workbook. However, you rarely need to include the Workbooks collection when accessing them, because they are created as a series of procedures in a module, and Visual Basic already knows how to locate procedures.

Chapter 25 ◆ Creating Custom Objects

To create a custom object, start with a new module. Don't use an existing module, because combining normal procedures and a custom object will confuse things. Use the **Edit Sheet Rename** command or double-click the module's tab to rename the module so that its name matches that of the custom object you want to create. In the module header, use the Private statement, rather than the Dim statement, to declare the global variables for the module as private variables. This protects all the object's data from being accessed by any outside procedures. The only access to the data stored in a module is through its properties and methods. Any other procedures stored in the module should be only for the use of other procedures in the module, and should be private as well.

You could also insert in the procedure header an Option Private Module statement, which makes the properties and methods available only within the current project, and not to any modules and procedures outside of the project. A *project* consists of all the modules in a workbook, and any workbooks that you attach to the workbook using the **Tools References** command.

Creating the Custom Properties

You create properties with Property procedures. There are three types of property procedures: Property Let, Property Get, and Property Set. The Property Let procedures control the input of data into the object—that is, they define the properties that receive data. These procedures appear on the left side of a formula. The Property Get procedures control the output of data from an object, and appear on the right side of a formula. Property Let and Property Get procedures can share the same name, in which case the procedure that is used depends on the direction in which data is being passed.

The Property Set procedures work much like Property Let procedures, except that Property Set procedures pass objects rather than values. To pass objects out of the custom object, use a Property Get procedure with its result declared as an Object.

The Property Let Procedures

The Property Let procedures control how the values of properties are set. These procedures create properties that can receive data and store it. Thus, properties that the Property Let procedures declare always appear on the left side of a formula so that they receive the value calculated by the formula.

The declaration of a Property Let procedure is nearly identical to that of a subprocedure, except that you use the keywords Property Let rather than Sub. The following is the basic syntax of a Property Let procedure:

```
Property Let propname(arguments)
'   Some statements.
    Exit Property
```

```
    '  More statements.
    End Property
```

The name of the procedure, *propname*, is the name of the property, and its container is the name of the module that contains the procedure. The argument list must contain at least one argument to receive the value passed to the property. If you have more than one argument, the rightmost one receives the value that is passed to the property. Any other arguments to be passed are enclosed in parentheses and attached to the property name. Depending on your needs, this procedure's syntax can be much more complex; see the online help for details.

For example, the following procedure, which is in a module named BankAccount, declares a property named Deposit:

```
Property Let Deposit(ByVal Received As Currency)
    Index = Index + 1
    theDeposit(Index) = Received
End Property
```

To use this property in another procedure, use it in a statement as follows:

```
BankAccount.Deposit = 250
```

When this statement is executed, the value 250 is passed to the Deposit procedure and stored in the variable Received. Note that these properties do not require that you use literal values such as 250; instead, you can use any variable or formula that evaluates to an appropriate value. Note also that the argument is declared as ByVal so that the data passed to the procedure is copied, which protects the variable in the calling procedure from change. The procedure then increments a global variable Index and stores the deposit in a global array named theDeposit.

To change the value of a previous deposit, you must create another procedure to pass an index to indicate which deposit to change along with the new value. You could write such a procedure as follows:

```
Property Let Deposits(anIndex As Long, ByVal Received As Currency)
    theDeposit(anIndex) = Received
End Property
```

You could use this property in a statement such as the following:

```
BankAccount.Deposits(10) = 250
```

This statement passes the value 10 to the variable anIndex, and 250 is passed to the variable Received. These two variables are then used to change the value of the tenth element of theDeposit().

Chapter 25 ♦ Creating Custom Objects

The Property Get Procedures

The complement of the Property Let procedures is the Property Get procedures. The Property Get procedures pass data out of an object. The syntax of the Property Get procedures is nearly identical to that of a Function procedure, in that data is passed out of the procedure in a variable with the procedure's name.

The syntax of the procedure is as follows:

```
Property Get propname(arguments) As type
'   Some statements.
    Exit Property
'   More statements.
End Property
```

The *arguments* and *type* are the same as in a Function procedure. As with a function, a statement in the body of the procedure must pass a value to a variable with the same name as the procedure. This is the value that the procedure passes back to the calling program. Note that the arguments are passed to the procedure and that the result is passed back as the property.

For example, the following is a procedure that returns the account balance from the CheckBook object:

```
Property Get Balance() As Currency
Balance = theBalance
End Property
```

To access this procedure from another, you would use the following statement:

```
CashAvail = CheckBook.Balance
```

When the Balance property procedure is called, the current balance is placed in the procedure name and passed to the variable CashAvail in the calling program.

Property Let and Property Get procedures can have the same name to form a complementary pair of procedures that transfer data in both directions. Because the value of the Balance property is usually a calculated value, the property has only a Property Get procedure, making it a read-only property. The Deposits property can be read or changed, and should have the following Property Get procedure as well as the preceding Property Let procedure:

```
Property Get Deposits(anIndex As Long) As Currency
Deposits = theDeposit(anIndex)
End Property
```

You would use this property in a statement such as the following:

```
aDeposit = BankAccount.Deposits(10)
```

414

This statement gets the value of the tenth deposit and returns it to the variable aDeposit.

You can use both the Property Let and Property Get procedures in the same formula. When you do so, Visual Basic determines which procedure the formula is calling by examining the direction in which the data flows. For example, you could add 125 to the 27th deposit by writing the following statement:

```
BankAccount.Deposits(27) = BankAccount.Deposits(27) + 125
```

This statement first calls the Property Get procedure to get the old value of the deposit, and then adds 125 to the value. The statement then passes the new value to the Property Let procedure, which stores the value in the BankAccount object.

The Property Set Procedure

The Property Set procedure is almost identical to the Property Let procedure, except that it passes objects rather than values. The syntax of the Property Set procedure is as follows:

```
Property Set propname(arguments)
'   Some statements.
    Exit Property
'   More statements.
End Property
```

The argument list is the same as that of the Property Let procedure. The rightmost argument receives the object from the calling procedure and must be a Variant type or declared As Object. Any other arguments are passed directly to the procedure.

For example, the CheckBook object might have the capability to display a list of transactions on a worksheet. To do so, the object first must be passed the number of transactions to be listed and then an object reference to a cell range for the table. To prepare for printing this list, you might write a procedure such as the following:

```
Property Set PrintRange(startIndex As Long, numTrans As Long, _
    aPrintRange As Object)
theStartIndex = startIndex
theNumTrans = numTrans
Set thePrintRange = aPrintRange
End Property
```

Note the use of the Set statement, which stores in the variable thePrintRange the object in aPrintRange.

This procedure could actually create the list, or you could create a method to create the list using the data that is passed to this procedure.

Chapter 25 ◆ Creating Custom Objects

To call this procedure, you write a statement such as the following:

```
CheckBook.PrintRange(12,10) = Sheets("Sheet1").Range("B5")
```

Here, the number 12 is passed to startIndex, 10 is passed to numTrans, and a range reference to cell B5 on Sheet1 is passed to aPrintRange. Within the Property Set procedure, these three values are stored in global variables.

To pass an object back to the calling program, use the Property Get procedure with the returned value set to the Object type.

Creating the Custom Methods

The custom methods are the easiest part of the object to implement, as they are simply public Sub procedures in the module with the property procedures. The Sub procedure has access to all the global variables in the module, which are the private data of the object.

Using a Custom Object

As an example of using a custom object, consider a comparison of two investments to determine which is more lucrative. First, create an object called InvTable to calculate an investment table for the two investments and then display the table on a worksheet. The following are the two investments that you want to compare:

- Leave the cash in a savings account with interest compounded monthly.

- Lend the money at interest compounded and paid in yearly installments, and then invest the cash that you receive in the same savings account as investment 1.

The following program calculates the future value of these two investments so that you can see which generates the most income. Store this program in a module named InvTable. To test the object, you need a second procedure in another module to load the following program's properties and call its method.

```
'
' Create a custom procedure.
'
' Properties are:
'    PresentValue = The present value of the investment.
'    Years = The total number of years of the two investments.
'    Rate1 = The interest rate of the first investment.
'    Rate2 = The interest rate of the second investment.
'    TLCell = A reference to the top-left cell of the table.
'    Assume there are monthly payments for both investments.
```

```vb
'   Methods are:
'      DrawTable = Draw the table.
'
Option Private Module 'Limit access to the current project.
Option Explicit      'Force declaration of all variables.
Private thePresVal As Currency 'Hide everything but property calls.
Private theYears As Single
Private theRate1 As Single
Private theRate2 As Single
Private theTLCell As Object
Private DataFlags(5) As Boolean  'An array of flags indicating
                                 'which variables are declared.
Const dtPresVal = 1    'Constants identifying the elements of the
Const dtYears = 2      'array DataFlags.
Const dtRate1 = 3
Const dtRate2 = 4
Const dtTLCell = 5
'
'   Begin the definition of the property procedures.
'
'  Input the present value.
'
Property Let PresentValue(ByVal data As Currency)
  If IsNumeric(data) Then
    thePresVal = data
    DataFlags(dtPresVal) = True
  Else
    MsgBox "PresentValue must be a number.", , "Draw Table Error"
  End If
End Property
'
'  Output the present value.
'
Property Get PresentValue() As Currency
  PresentValue = thePresVal
End Property
'
'  Input the years.
'
Property Let Years(ByVal data As Single)
```

```
    If IsNumeric(data) Then
      theYears = data
      DataFlags(dtYears) = True
    Else
      MsgBox "Years must be a number.", , "Draw Table Error"
    End If
End Property
'
' Output the years.
'
Property Get Years() As Single
  PresentValue = theYears
End Property
'
' Input rate1.
'
Property Let Rate1(ByVal data As Single)
    If IsNumeric(data) Then
      theRate1 = data
      DataFlags(dtRate1) = True
    Else
      MsgBox "Rate1 must be a number.", , "Draw Table Error"
    End If
End Property
'
' Output rate1.
'
Property Get Rate1() As Single
  PresentValue = theRate1
End Property
'
' Input rate2.
'
Property Let Rate2(ByVal data As Single)
    If IsNumeric(data) Then
      theRate2 = data
      DataFlags(dtRate2) = True
    Else
      MsgBox "Rate2 must be a number.", , "Draw Table Error"
    End If
End Property
```

```vb
'
'Output rate2.
'
Property Get Rate2() As Single
  PresentValue = theRate2
End Property
'
' Input TLCell.
'
Property Set TLCell(data As Object)
  If TypeName(data) = "Range" Then
    Set theTLCell = data
    DataFlags(dtTLCell) = True
  Else
    MsgBox "TLCell must be a Range reference", , "Draw Table Error"
  End If
End Property
'
' Output TLCell.
'
Property Get TLCell() As Object
  Set TLCell = theTLCell
End Property
'
'  Begin definition of the methods.
'
' Create a method.
'   Draw the table.
'
Sub DrawTable()
' Fake a method with a property.
' See whether all data is available.
  If Not DataFlags(dtTLCell) Then
    MsgBox "Cell range, TLCell, not defined.", , "Draw Table Error"
  ElseIf Not DataFlags(dtPresVal) Then
    'No present value defined.
    MsgBox "Present value not defined.", , "Draw Table Error"
  ElseIf Not DataFlags(dtYears) Then
    'No years defined.
    MsgBox "Years not defined.", , "Draw Table Error"
```

Chapter 25 ♦ Creating Custom Objects

```
    ElseIf Not DataFlags(dtRate1) Then
      'No rate1 defined, use default.
      MsgBox "Rate1 not defined.", , "Draw Table Error"
    ElseIf Not DataFlags(dtRate2) Then
      'No rate2 defined, use default.
      MsgBox "Rate2 not defined.", , "Draw Table Error"
    Else  'Data is okay, draw the table'
      MakeTable
    End If
End Sub
'
'  Begin definition of private supporting procedures.
'  These procedures are not accessible outside of this module.
'
'  Draw the table
'
Private Sub MakeTable()
  Dim thePmt As Currency
  With theTLCell
    .FormulaR1C1 = "Compare Investments"
    .Columns("A:A").ColumnWidth = 18
    .Range("A2").FormulaR1C1 = "1. Monthly."
    .Range("A3").FormulaR1C1 = "2. Yearly."
    .Range("B1").FormulaR1C1 = "Present Val"
    .Range("C1").FormulaR1C1 = "Rate"
    .Range("D1").FormulaR1C1 = "Years"
    .Range("E1").FormulaR1C1 = "Payment"
    .Range("F1").FormulaR1C1 = "Future Value"
    .Columns("F:F").ColumnWidth = 11
    .Columns("F:F").ColumnWidth = 11
    .Columns("B:B").ColumnWidth = 12
    With .Range("A1:F3")
      .Borders(xlLeft).Weight = xlThin
      .Borders(xlRight).Weight = xlThin
      .Borders(xlTop).Weight = xlThin
      .Borders(xlBottom).Weight = xlThin
      .BorderAround Weight:=xlMedium, ColorIndex:=xlAutomatic
    End With
    With .Range("B2:F3")
        .Borders(xlLeft).Weight = xlThin
        .Borders(xlTop).Weight = xlThin
        .BorderAround Weight:=xlMedium, ColorIndex:=xlAutomatic
    End With
```

```
        .Range("E2:F3").NumberFormat = "$#,##0.00_);($#,##0.00)"
        .Range("B2:B3").NumberFormat = "$#,##0.00_);($#,##0.00)"
        .Range("C2:C3").NumberFormat = "0.00%"
     With .Range("E2").Interior
         .ColorIndex = 0
         .Pattern = 17
         .PatternColorIndex = xlAutomatic
     End With
     'Insert the data in the cells.
     .Range("B2").Formula = thePresVal
     .Range("B3").Formula = 0
     .Range("C2").Formula = theRate1
     .Range("C3").Formula = theRate2
     .Range("D2:D3").Formula = theYears
     'This is the formula for the money put in the bank at interest
     'paid once a month.
     .Range("F2").Formula = Application.Fv(theRate1 / 12, _
         theYears * 12, 0, -thePresVal)
     'This is the formula for the loan being paid back with interest
     'paid once per year and then put in the bank.
     thePmt = Application.Pmt(theRate2, theYears, -thePresVal)
     .Range("E3").Formula = thePmt
     .Range("F3").Formula = Application.Fv(theRate1, _
         theYears, -thePmt, 0)
   End With
End Sub
```

First, look at the module header:

```
'
'   Create a custom procedure.
'
'   Properties are:
'     PresentValue = The present value of the investment.
'     Years = The total number of years of the two investments.
'     Rate1 = The interest rate of the first investment.
'     Rate2 = The interest rate of the second investment.
'     TLCell = A reference to the top-left cell of the table.
'     Assume there are monthly payments for both investments.
'   Methods are:
'     DrawTable = Draw the table.
```

Chapter 25 ♦ Creating Custom Objects

```
'
Option Private Module 'Limit access to the current project.
Option Explicit    'Force declaration of all variables.
Private thePresVal As Currency 'Hide everything but property calls.
Private theYears As Single
Private theRate1 As Single
Private theRate2 As Single
Private theTLCell As Object
Private DataFlags(5) As Boolean   'An array of flags indicating
                                  'which variables are declared.
Const dtPresVal = 1      'Constants identifying the elements of the
Const dtYears = 2        'array DataFlags.
Const dtRate1 = 3
Const dtRate2 = 4
Const dtTLCell = 5
```

In this header, the module is declared as private, and all the global variables are private to this module. Therefore, no procedure outside of this module has access to any of the data within the module. The only way to access the data is with the properties.

Next come the property procedures:

```
'
'  Begin the definition of the property procedures.
'
' Input the present value
'
Property Let PresentValue(ByVal data As Currency)
  If IsNumeric(data) Then
    thePresVal = data
    DataFlags(dtPresVal) = True
  Else
    MsgBox "PresentValue must be a number.", , "Draw Table Error"
  End If
End Property
'
' Output the present value.
'
Property Get PresentValue() As Currency
  PresentValue = thePresVal
End Property
```

```
'
' Input the years.
'
Property Let Years(ByVal data As Single)
  If IsNumeric(data) Then
    theYears = data
    DataFlags(dtYears) = True
  Else
    MsgBox "Years must be a number.", , "Draw Table Error"
  End If
End Property
'
' Output the years.
'
Property Get Years() As Single
  PresentValue = theYears
End Property
'
' Input rate1.
'
Property Let Rate1(ByVal data As Single)
  If IsNumeric(data) Then
    theRate1 = data
    DataFlags(dtRate1) = True
  Else
    MsgBox "Rate1 must be a number.", , "Draw Table Error"
  End If
End Property
'
' Output rate1.
'
Property Get Rate1() As Single
  PresentValue = theRate1
End Property
'
' Input rate2.
'
Property Let Rate2(ByVal data As Single)
  If IsNumeric(data) Then
    theRate2 = data
    DataFlags(dtRate2) = True
```

Chapter 25 ♦ Creating Custom Objects

```
      Else
        MsgBox "Rate2 must be a number.", , "Draw Table Error"
      End If
    End Property
    '
    ' Output rate2.
    '
    Property Get Rate2() As Single
      PresentValue = theRate2
    End Property
    '
    ' Input TLCell.
    '
    Property Set TLCell(data As Object)
      If TypeName(data) = "Range" Then
        Set theTLCell = data
        DataFlags(dtTLCell) = True
      Else
        MsgBox "TLCell must be a Range reference", , "Draw Table Error"
      End If
    End Property
    '
    ' Output TLCell.
    '
    Property Get TLCell() As Object
      Set TLCell = theTLCell
    End Property
```

For each property, there are two procedures: one to receive the data into the object, and one to pass the data out of the object. The procedures that receive the data have some work to do, to ensure that the values passed to the procedure are of the correct type and range. If not, these procedures can generate a runtime error with the Error() statement, or display a dialog box that indicates what the problem is. In either case, they should refuse to change the value of the property. These procedures simply display a dialog box and then quit.

There is one pair of procedures for each of the five properties, PresentValue, Years, Rate1, Rate2, and TLCell. The first four properties are checked to ensure that they are numbers. If the numbers are strange, the results are going to be strange, but the procedures don't check for that. If you have specific ranges for the properties, you could check for them as well. The property TLCell (Top Left Cell) is a range reference, so it is checked to ensure that it is a range.

Whenever a good value is passed to a property procedure, the procedure sets an element of the array DataFlags to True. The constants defined in the module header select the correct element of the array for each of the procedures. When all the elements of the array are set to True, the table can be drawn on a worksheet.

Following the property procedures is the one method in this object, DrawTable:

```
'
'   Begin definition of the methods.
'
'  Create a method.
'   Draw the table.
'
Sub DrawTable()
'  Fake a method with a property.
'  See whether all data is available.
   If Not DataFlags(dtTLCell) Then
      MsgBox "Cell range, TLCell, not defined.", , "Draw Table Error"
   ElseIf Not DataFlags(dtPresVal) Then
      'No present value defined.
      MsgBox "Present value not defined.", , "Draw Table Error"
   ElseIf Not DataFlags(dtYears) Then
      'No years defined.
      MsgBox "Years not defined.", , "Draw Table Error"
   ElseIf Not DataFlags(dtRate1) Then
      'No rate1 defined, use default.
      MsgBox "Rate1 not defined.", , "Draw Table Error"
   ElseIf Not DataFlags(dtRate2) Then
      'No rate2 defined, use default.
      MsgBox "Rate2 not defined.", , "Draw Table Error"
   Else  'Data is okay, draw the table'
      MakeTable
   End If
End Sub
```

The DrawTable method first checks whether all the data has been input, by checking whether all the elements of the DataFlags array are True. If not, the method displays an error message; otherwise it calls the MakeTable procedure to draw the table on the worksheet.

The MakeTable procedure is next:

```vb
'
'   Begin definition of private supporting procedures.
'   These procedures are not accessible outside of this module.
'
'   Draw the table
'
Private Sub MakeTable()
  Dim thePmt As Currency
  With theTLCell
    .FormulaR1C1 = "Compare Investments"
    .Columns("A:A").ColumnWidth = 18
    .Range("A2").FormulaR1C1 = "1. Monthly."
    .Range("A3").FormulaR1C1 = "2. Yearly."
    .Range("B1").FormulaR1C1 = "Present Val"
    .Range("C1").FormulaR1C1 = "Rate"
    .Range("D1").FormulaR1C1 = "Years"
    .Range("E1").FormulaR1C1 = "Payment"
    .Range("F1").FormulaR1C1 = "Future Value"
    .Columns("F:F").ColumnWidth = 11
    .Columns("F:F").ColumnWidth = 11
    .Columns("B:B").ColumnWidth = 12
    With .Range("A1:F3")
      .Borders(xlLeft).Weight = xlThin
      .Borders(xlRight).Weight = xlThin
      .Borders(xlTop).Weight = xlThin
      .Borders(xlBottom).Weight = xlThin
      .BorderAround Weight:=xlMedium, ColorIndex:=xlAutomatic
    End With
    With .Range("B2:F3")
        .Borders(xlLeft).Weight = xlThin
        .Borders(xlTop).Weight = xlThin
        .BorderAround Weight:=xlMedium, ColorIndex:=xlAutomatic
    End With
    .Range("E2:F3").NumberFormat = "$#,##0.00_);($#,##0.00)"
    .Range("B2:B3").NumberFormat = "$#,##0.00_);($#,##0.00)"
    .Range("C2:C3").NumberFormat = "0.00%"
    With .Range("E2").Interior
        .ColorIndex = 0
        .Pattern = 17
        .PatternColorIndex = xlAutomatic
    End With
```

```
    'Insert the data in the cells.
    .Range("B2").Formula = thePresVal
    .Range("B3").Formula = 0

    .Range("C2").Formula = theRate1
    .Range("C3").Formula = theRate2
    .Range("D2:D3").Formula = theYears
    'This is the formula for the money put in the bank at interest
    'paid once a month.
    .Range("F2").Formula = Application.Fv(theRate1 / 12, _
        theYears * 12, 0, -thePresVal)
    'This is the formula for the loan being paid back with interest
    'paid once per year and then put in the bank.
    thePmt = Application.Pmt(theRate2, theYears, -thePresVal)
    .Range("E3").Formula = thePmt
    .Range("F3").Formula = Application.Fv(theRate1, _
        theYears, -thePmt, 0)
  End With
End Sub
```

The MakeTable procedure is a supporting routine, so it is marked as a Private procedure and is available only to the other procedures in this module. The procedure first fills in all the headings, changes the column widths, and formats the cells. To create this part of the procedure, the Macro Recorder was used to record the creation of a table, and then the recorded statements were edited to produce the procedure. You could create this part of the procedure by hand, but it is much easier to do it with the Macro Recorder because you can see what the table looks like while you create it.

The last half of the procedure calculates the values to be placed in the cells. It uses worksheet functions to calculate the future value for the first investment and the payment for the second. The payment for the second investment is inserted into a calculation to determine the future value of the investment assuming the payments received from the second investment were placed in a savings account.

Note that the references used in this procedure are relative to cell A1. When you apply these range references to the range reference passed to the procedure in theTLCell, Visual Basic translates the table's location so that it corresponds to the location specified by theTLCell, which in this case is the upper-left corner. Therefore, if theTLCell is a range reference to cell B7, then a reference to A1 is translated to refer to cell B7, a reference to B2 is translated to C8, and so forth.

To test the new object, place the following procedure in another module and then run it:

Chapter 25 ♦ Creating Custom Objects

```
'
' Test the new object
'
Sub testIt()
  InvTable.PresentValue = 10000#    '$10,000
  InvTable.Rate1 = 0.1        '10%
  InvTable.Rate2 = 0.11       '11%
  InvTable.Years = 10         '10 years
  Set InvTable.TLCell = Sheets("Sheet1").Range("B7")
  InvTable.DrawTable
End Sub
```

When this procedure executes, it first stores values in all the properties and then calls the DrawTable method. If you run this procedure and switch to Sheet1, you see the table shown in figure 25.1. Note that the second of these two investments generates the most income. The button on the worksheet is attached to the TestIt procedure to make it easy to run that procedure and test the custom object.

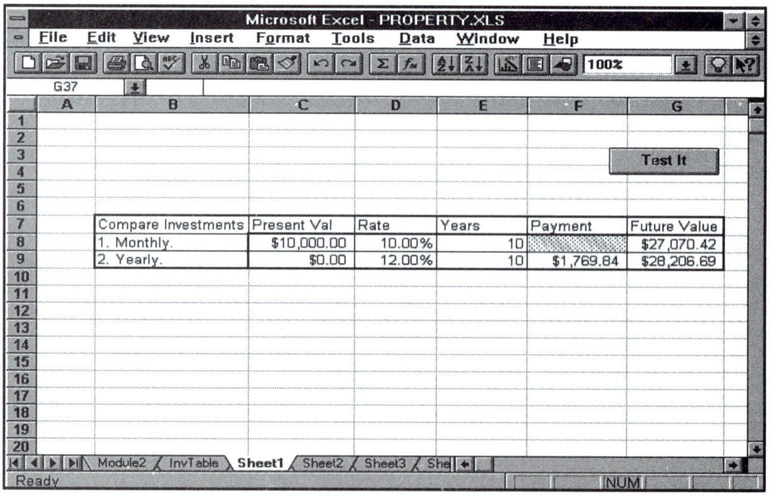

Figure 25.1

The investment comparison table created by the InvTable object.

![Screenshot of Microsoft Excel - PROPERTY.XLS showing the investment comparison table with columns: Compare Investments, Present Val, Rate, Years, Payment, Future Value. Row 8: "1. Monthly.", $10,000.00, 10.00%, 10, (blank), $27,070.42. Row 9: "2. Yearly.", $0.00, 12.00%, 10, $1,769.84, $28,206.69. A "Test It" button is visible.]

To test the error checking in the Property procedures, try commenting out some of the statements in the testIt procedure, and run it again.

Summary

In this chapter, you learned how to create custom objects with Visual Basic. Although custom objects in Visual Basic are not true objects as defined by the precepts of object-oriented programming, they mimic most of an object's functionality. This functionality makes this structure useful for programming in an object-oriented environment.

In the next chapter, you learn how to use Dynamic Data Exchange (DDE) and Object Linking and Embedding (OLE) to communicate with other applications.

Review Questions

The answers to the review questions are in Appendix A.

1. Where does a custom object reside?
2. What does a Property Let procedure do?
3. What does a Property Get procedure do?
4. What does a Property Set procedure do?
5. How do you return an object reference to an outside procedure?
6. How do you create a method for a custom object?

Review Exercises

1. Create a custom object named Stephanie that contains the properties Birthdate, Birthplace, and Age. Make the Age property read-only, and have it return the current age calculated from the Birthdate and the current date obtained from the system.

2. Complete the CheckBook object that you started to create in this chapter. Add procedures that get check numbers, input data from checks, input deposits, retrieve the balance, and so forth. Do consistency checks on the data input to the object.

CHAPTER 26

Interapplication Communications

Modern applications programs can link themselves together and pass information among themselves. The range of communication possibilities extends from passing keystrokes or transferring data with Dynamic Data Exchange (DDE), to creating fully embedded applications with Object Linking and Embedding (OLE).

In this chapter you learn how to do the following:

- ♦ Initiate a DDE link
- ♦ Transfer information and commands with DDE
- ♦ Initiate an OLE session
- ♦ Control objects in another application
- ♦ Pass keystrokes to another application

What Is Interapplication Communication?

Interapplication communication is exactly what the name implies—communication between two applications. What they communicate is a different matter, and depends largely on the capabilities of the two applications. Two standard methods of interapplication communication are built into most mainline applications: Dynamic Data Exchange (DDE) and Object Linking and Embedding (OLE). In addition to these standards, the Windows operating system allows the simple passing of keystrokes to most Windows applications.

Chapter 26 ♦ Interapplication Communications

The older standard is DDE, which creates a simple data channel between two applications. Usually the *data channel* handles text, but some applications can also pass binary data and the type of data used to create graphics. Visual Basic for Applications can handle only text or numbers in a DDE channel. DDE is useful when you want to pass small amounts of data from one application to another.

OLE, the more modern standard, can be used only with object-oriented applications. Instead of passing data from one application to another, an OLE communication link passes objects. If you pass data between two applications, both applications must know how to handle that data, how to operate on it, and how to display it. When objects are passed between applications, the receiving application doesn't need to know anything about the data contained in the object. The object knows all about the data, and handles all the manipulation and display. Thus you can edit an Excel worksheet embedded in a Word document (as shown in fig. 26.1) just as you would in Excel. Word does not need to know how to edit worksheets, it needs only to make room for the worksheet to reside, and to pass requests to it.

Figure 26.1

An Excel worksheet embedded in a Word document using OLE.

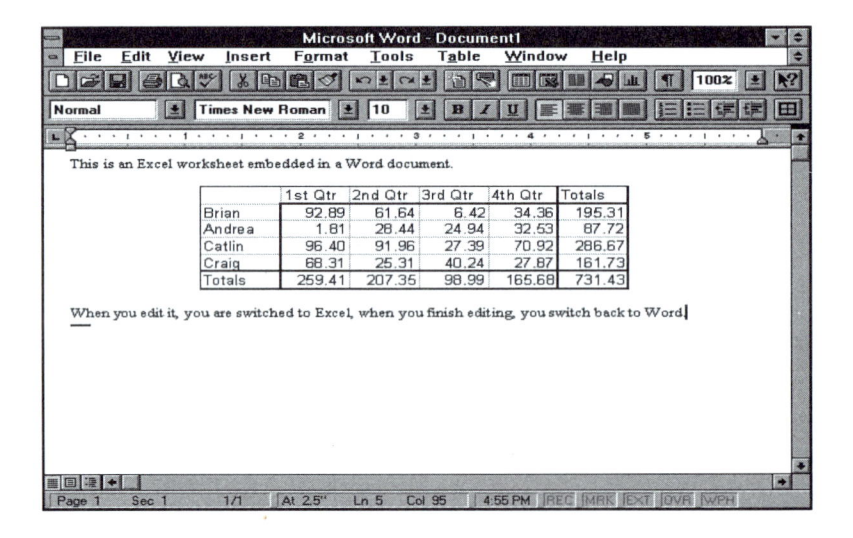

Usually you initiate interapplication communications by copying an object in one application and pasting a link to that object in another. Thus, if you embed an Excel worksheet in a Word document, Word handles the communications process. This is by far the simplest method of establishing such a communication path. On the other hand, for special applications, Visual Basic can initiate and control the communications process.

What Is DDE?

Dynamic Data Exchange, or DDE, is a simple message channel between two applications controlled by the Windows operating system. A DDE channel is a link or pipeline through which information can pass. Usually the channel passes text, but some applications can also pass graphics. In Visual Basic for Applications, however, a DDE channel can pass only text or numbers.

All DDE communications involve two applications: the DDE server and the DDE client. The DDE server is the application that has the data that the client application wants. The client application initiates a DDE communications exchange by requesting data from the server. Usually information flows from the server to the client, but there are DDE commands to send data from the client to the server. Additionally, the data sent to the server can be commands that instruct the server to do other things, such as open files.

> **Caution:** To establish two-way communications, a program can be both a server and a client. However, be careful not to create a circular connection by making the same object on both ends of the connection both a server and a client. If you then have the server automatically update the client whenever the data in the server changes, one server will update a second server, which will then update the first server again, and so on. Your system is then locked into a circle of continuous updating.

DDE links come in two "temperatures": hot and cold. Hot DDE links automatically update the client's data whenever the linked data in the server changes. Cold links update the data only when the server sends a DDERequest command. Visual Basic for Applications can automatically handle only cold links. Hot links must be implemented with code.

Using Dynamic Data Exchange

To use DDE, you must first establish a communications channel between two applications. To establish that channel and specify what to communicate between the two applications, you need three pieces of information: the application, the topic, and the item. The meaning of these three terms depends on the application with which you are trying to communicate, and how that application handles data.

The *application* is the name of the server application with which you want to communicate. Applications that support DDE have registered their application name with the Windows system. The application name is not necessarily the name of the application displayed in the Program Manager. Table 26.1 lists some applications and the name that they have registered with the system.

Table 26.1. The DDE-registered application names for some Windows programs.

Windows Application	DDE-Registered Name
Word for Windows	WinWord
Excel	Excel
Project	Project
Access	MSAccess
FoxPro	FoxPro
Windows Program Manager	ProgMan
Visual Basic for Windows	*progname*[*]

[*]*For an interpreted program,* progname *is the name of the program's Project window; for a compiled program,* progname *consists of the name of the executable file without the extension .EXE.*

The *topic* is almost always the name of the document that contains the data of interest, and the *item* is some logical element of that document. For Excel, the *topic* is the document, and the *item* is a cell range. For a Visual Basic for Windows application, the *topic* is the form name, and the *item* is the control on the form that has the data. For Word, the *topic* is the document, and the *item* is either a bookmark or a Word Basic selector, such as \StartOfDoc, that points to the beginning of the document. (Word Basic is the BASIC programming capability that is built into the current version of Word.) For a list of available topics and items, see the documentation for the program that you want to control, or the program's online help.

Opening a DDE Communication Channel

To open a DDE channel with another application, the other application must first be running. Use the Shell or AppActivate statements to start the application. Be careful when using Shell; because the command starts programs asynchronously, the next statement in your program may execute before the other application is operating. After the Shell command you may need a pause to wait for the application to initialize and start working.

Use the DDEInitiate function to initiate a link between two running applications. The DDEInitiate function has the following syntax:

```
channel = DDEInitiate(application,topic)
```

The *application* and *topic* arguments are strings. To find out which application and topic to use for an application, check the application's documentation. The function returns a channel number that you use with other Visual Basic commands to identify which channel to use when communicating with the other application. When this function is executed, a DDE connection is established between Visual Basic for Applications and some other application.

Closing a DDE Channel

When you finish working with a DDE channel, close it with the DDETerminate statement. The syntax of the DDETerminate statement is as follows:

```
DDETerminate(channel)
```

Again, *channel* is the channel number obtained with the DDEInitiate function.

Getting Information from a Server

To request data from the server when a communication channel is open, use the DDERequest function. This function has the following syntax:

```
variable = DDERequest(channel, item)
```

The *channel* argument is the channel number returned by the DDEInitiate function, and the *item* points to the specific piece of data that you want. The *variable* argument receives the data, and must be of the Variant type.

For example, create a dialog sheet in Excel that uses DDE to request a line of text from Word. In Word, select a sentence, choose the **Edit B**ookmark command, and name the bookmark BookMark1. Then switch to Excel and type the following three procedures into a module. Change the procedures' references to document 26VBAOR.DOC so that they reference one of your own documents.

```
Option Explicit
Dim ChannelNum As Integer
Dim Result
'
' Establish a DDE link
' to Word and get a sentence.
'
Sub OpenChannel()
  'Start Word and open the document 26VBAOR.DOC.
  'Change the document and path to one of your own.
  ChannelNum = DDEInitiate("WinWord","D:\VBABOOK\DOCS\26VBAOR.DOC")
  'Display the channel number in the dialog box.
  DialogSheets("DDEDialog").EditBoxes("DDEChannelBox").Text = _
      ChannelNum

End Sub
```

Chapter 26 ♦ Interapplication Communications

```
'
' Get the data.
'
Sub GetData()
  Result = DDERequest(ChannelNum, "BookMark1") 'Request the data.
  'Display the data in the dialog box.
  DialogSheets("DDEDialog").EditBoxes("DDEDataBox").Text = Result
End Sub
'
' Close the link.
'
Sub CloseChannel()
  DDETerminate (ChannelNum)
End Sub
```

Insert a dialog sheet named DDEDialog, and add three buttons, two labels, and two text boxes, as shown in figure 26.2. Name the text box below the Result label as DDEDataBox and the other text box as DDEChannelBox. Use the **T**ools **A**ssi**gn** Macro command to attach the Open DDE button to the OpenChannel procedure, the Get Data button to the GetData procedure, and the Close DDE button to the CloseChannel procedure.

Figure 26.2
Layout of the DDE Tester dialog box.

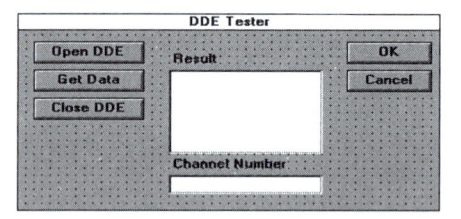

Click the Run Dialog button on the Visual Basic toolbar and click the Open DDE button on the form. Clicking the Open DDE button executes the OpenChannel procedure, which opens a channel to Word for Windows (WinWord), requests the document 26VBAOR.DOC, and displays the channel number in the DDEChannelBox.

Clicking the Get Data button executes the GetData procedure, which requests the contents of the BookMark1 bookmark. The DDEData edit box then displays whatever text is found in the bookmark, as shown in figure 26.3.

Figure 26.3
The DDE tester dialog box after retrieving the contents of the BookMark1 bookmark.

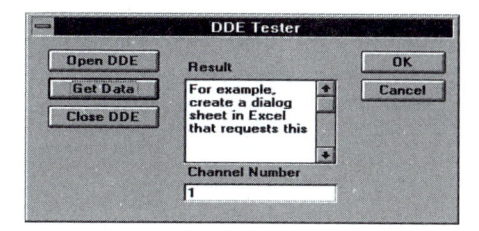

To terminate the DDE channel, click the Close DDE button.

Sending Information to a Server

To send information to the server, use the DDEPoke method. This method has the following syntax:

```
DDEPoke(channel, item, data)
```

The *item* argument selects the text to be replaced in the server, while the *data* argument specifies what is to replace that text. One problem with this command is that the *data* argument cannot be a simple string, but must be a worksheet range. Future versions of Excel may correct this problem.

For example, add a procedure that sends some text to Word to replace the text marked with the BookMark1 bookmark. First add a button named Poke Data to the form, as shown in figure 26.4. Then attach the button to the following procedure:

```
'
' Poke some data.
'
Sub PokeChannel()
  'Copy the data from the dialog box to a worksheet cell.
  Sheets("Sheet1").Cells(1, 1).Formula = _
      DialogSheets("DDEDialog").EditBoxes("DDEDataBox").Text
  'Create a reference to the worksheet cell.
  Set Result = Sheets("Sheet1").Cells(1, 1)
  'Send the reference to the cell to the linked application,
  'to replace the text marked with BookMark1.
  Application.DDEPoke ChannelNum, "BookMark1", Result
End Sub
```

Chapter 26 ♦ Interapplication Communications

Figure 26.4
The DDE Tester dialog box with the Poke button attached.

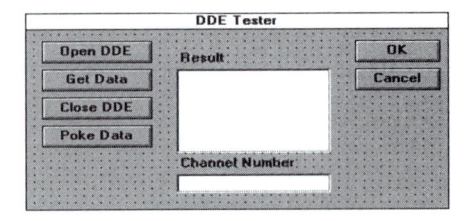

Run this procedure by clicking the Run Dialog button on the Visual Basic toolbar. Then click the Open DDE button to attach the procedure to Word, and click the Get Data button to copy the current value of BookMark1 into the text box as shown in figure 26.5. At the top of the screen is Word for Windows, showing the line of text labeled BookMark1. At the bottom of the screen is Excel and the DDE Tester dialog box, with the text from the Word document copied into the Result text box of the DDE Tester dialog box.

Figure 26.5
Using the DDE Tester program to get the text labeled with BookMark1 from Word for Windows.

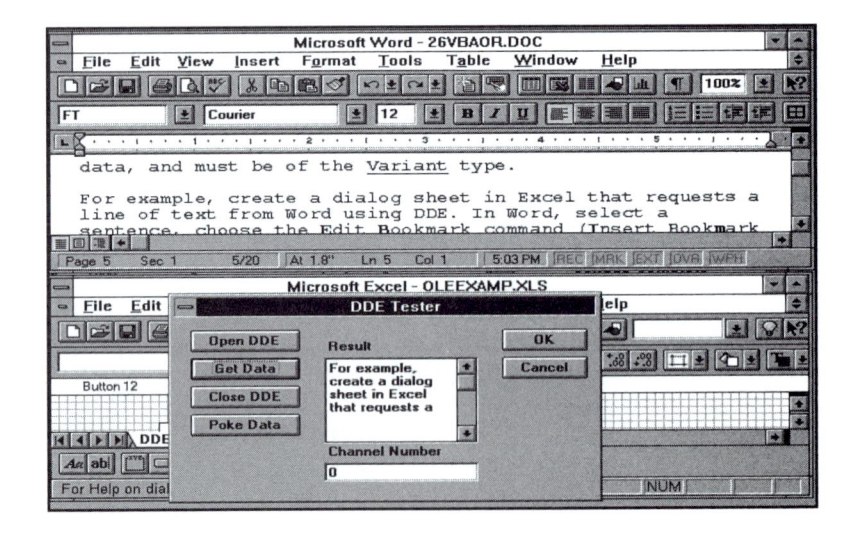

You can now edit the text in the Result text box. To have the edited text replace the text labeled BookMark1 as shown in figure 26.6, click t he Poke Data button.

The PokeChannel procedure first copies the contents of the text box to cell A1 on Sheet1. The procedure then loads that value as an object into the variable Result. Remember, the DDEPoke method must have a range reference as an argument rather than a simple string, so this odd step is required to change the text into a range reference that contains text. The DDEPoke method then sends that text to Word, which replaces the text currently selected as BookMark1. To close the link, click the ⁻Close DDE button.

Visual Basic for Applications By EXAMPLE

Figure 26.6

Replacing the text in the Word for Windows document with text from the Result box in Excel's DDE Tester dialog box.

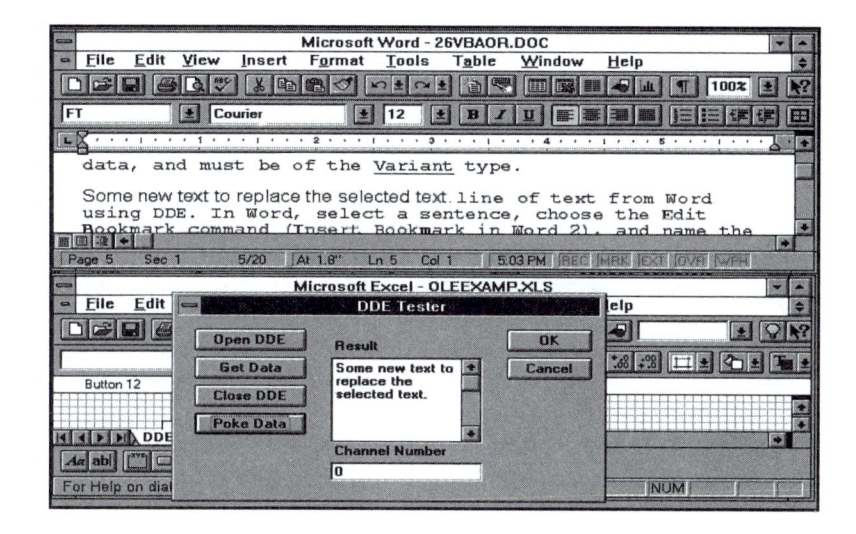

Sending Commands to a Server

In addition to using a DDE link to send data to an application, you can send commands to the application. The commands that you send must be in the command language of the application with which you are communicating.

To send commands to the attached application, you use the DDEExecute method, which has the following syntax:

```
DDEExecute(channel, CommandString)
```

Again, *channel* is the DDE channel number and *CommandString* is a string that contains the commands for the remote procedure to execute.

For example, send the print preview command to Word for Windows. Add a Print Preview button to the DDE Tester dialog box and attach the following procedure to the button:

```
'
' Turn on Print Preview.
'
Sub PreviewIt()
  'Send the print preview command to the linked application.
  DDEExecute ChannelNum, "[FilePrintPreview]"
End Sub
```

Note that the FilePrintPreview command is enclosed in square brackets. If you omit the square brackets, Word inserts the command as text at the insertion point instead of executing it as a command.

439

Chapter 26 ♦ Interapplication Communications

Using Object Linking and Embedding

Object Linking and Embedding (OLE) is much more advanced than DDE. Where DDE simply passes data between applications, OLE passes objects. There are two different types of OLE: Linking and Embedding, and OLE Automation.

With Linking and Embedding, you embed one application's objects into another application's documents. Figure 26.1 shows an example of embedding an Excel worksheet in a Word document. You create embedded objects by copying the object in one application and then pasting a link to the object into the other application. After you have thus linked an embedded object, you can edit it in its native application. The application displaying the embedded object does not have to know anything about how the embedded object is created or updated, it needs only to display it.

OLE Automation enables one object to control another application by accessing its objects and methods. Using OLE automation, an attached application's objects and methods become an extension of the Visual Basic language.

Using OLE Automation

Before you can use the objects and methods in another application, it is useful to know what those objects are. If the other application has an object library that it registers with the system and makes available, you can use the Object Browser to examine the objects and methods in that library. If the other application does not make the library available, you must use the other application's documentation to see which objects and methods are available.

To examine an application's objects with the Object Browser, you must register the application with Excel. First, choose the **T**ools **R**eferences command to display the References dialog box. Then check the other application's check box in the **A**vailable References list box, as shown in figure 26.7. After you register an application, all of its objects are available to Visual Basic.

Figure 26.7

Registering another application's objects in the References dialog box.

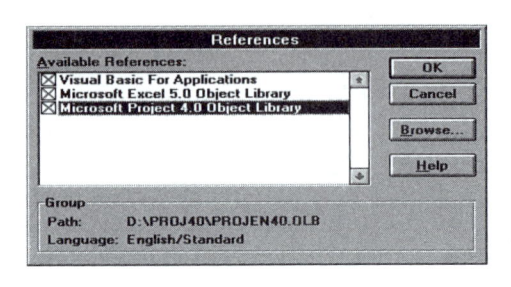

You can now use the Object Browser to examine the other application's objects, as shown in figure 26.8. The Object Browser also displays the name under which the other application is registered. In figure 26.8, Project, for example, is registered as MSProject.

Figure 26.8

Using the Object Browser to view another application's objects and the name under which the application is registered.

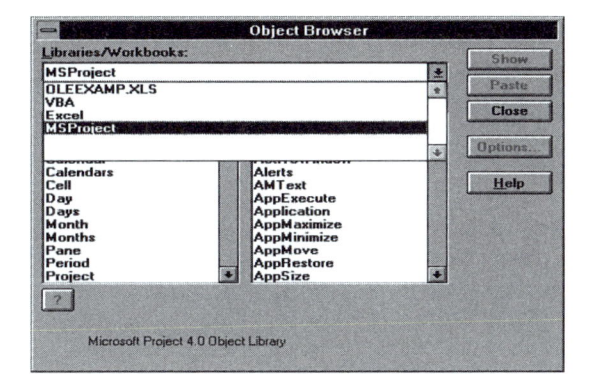

Caution: The name an application uses to register itself for OLE communications differs from the name used with DDE. This is because DDE communicates with an application while OLE accesses objects in an object library.

For example, the following procedure uses objects from both Project and Excel. The procedure first uses Project objects to start Project, open a file, and copy the value of the Name field of the first Task. It then uses Excel objects to insert that name into cell A1 on Sheet3. Finally, it uses a Project method to close the current project and end the Project application. If you want to try this, be sure to substitute one of your own project files for the one in the example.

```
'
' OLE Automation Example
'
Sub GetTask()
  Dim msProj As Object, aTask As String
   'Start Project and open a file.
  MSProject.Application.FileOpen Name:="D:\VBABOOK\PROGS\BOOKPLAN.MPP"
   'Store the name of the first task in a variable.
  aTask = MSProject.Application.Projects(1).Tasks(1).Name
   'Display the task name in a worksheet cell.
  Sheets("Sheet3").Range("A1").Value = aTask
   'Close the file and end Project.
  MSProject.Application.FileExit
End Sub
```

Objects can have the same name in different applications, so be sure to use fully qualified object names when accessing another application's objects. For example, if you are running Visual Basic in Excel and execute the statement

```
Application.Name
```

you get the name Excel. However, if you are in Excel and execute the statement

```
MSProject.Application.Name
```

you get the name Project.

When accessing any objects outside of the current application, use fully qualified object references, not only to ensure that you get the right object, but also to make your code more readable.

> **Note:** Many applications are invisible when you start them with OLE Automation. Such applications also are not displayed in the Task List, so you cannot switch to them and view any open documents. To make an application visible when you start it with OLE, set the application's Visible property to True. For example, to make Project visible and display it in the Task List so that you can switch to it, you would use the following statement:
>
> ```
> MSProject.Application.Visible = True
> ```

Creating and Opening Objects

Two methods are available for creating new objects, or for opening an existing object in an application being controlled with OLE Automation: CreateObject() and GetObject(). In general, the objects that you access with these methods are documents of the accessed application. For fully OLE-compliant applications, such as Project and Excel, open or create new files using methods from the linked objects rather than using the CreateObject and GetObject methods. For partially OLE-compliant applications, like Word, you must use CreateObject and GetObject to create links to documents.

The syntax of CreateObject is as follows:

```
Set ObjectVariable = CreateObject(class)
```

where *ObjectVariable* is any variable declared as Object or Variant, and *class* is the object class to create. The *class* argument consists of two parts separated by a period:

```
RegisteredName.Object
```

where *RegisteredName* is the name with which an application is registered to the system, such as Excel, MSProject, or Word, and the *Object* is the object type to create. For Excel, the object type can be Application, Sheet, or Chart. For Project, the object type is `Project`; for Word, the object type is `Basic`.

For example, the following statement starts Excel and creates a new worksheet object:

```
Set XLSheet = CreateObject("Excel.Sheet")
```

If Excel is already running and a workbook is open, this statement adds a new worksheet to the open workbook. If Excel isn't running, the statement starts Excel with a new workbook.

The following statement starts Project with a new blank project sheet:

```
Set ProjSheet = CreateObject("MSProject.Project")
```

The next statement starts Word and returns an object that references Word Basic:

```
Set WordSheet = CreateObject("Word.Basic")
```

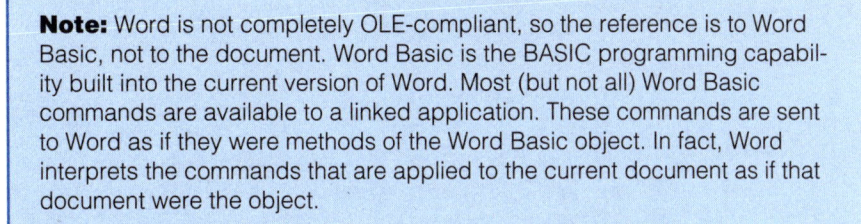

> **Note:** Word is not completely OLE-compliant, so the reference is to Word Basic, not to the document. Word Basic is the BASIC programming capability built into the current version of Word. Most (but not all) Word Basic commands are available to a linked application. These commands are sent to Word as if they were methods of the Word Basic object. In fact, Word interprets the commands that are applied to the current document as if that document were the object.

The GetObject function opens an existing object, and has the following syntax:

```
Set ObjectVariable = GetObject(filename, class)
```

where *ObjectVariable* and *class* are the same as for the CreateObject function. The *filename* argument contains the file name and path to the object to open. This argument is normally the file name of an application's document. You can omit the *class* argument if the file name's extension enables you to determine object's class. For example, if the file name has an .XLC extension, you know that such an extension indicates that the file is an Excel chart sheet. GetObject does not start an application if it is not currently running.

For example, the following statement opens the COSTS.XLS worksheet in the PROJ3 directory on the D drive:

```
Set XLSheet = GetObject("D:\PROJ3\COSTS.XLS", "Excel.Sheet")
```

Embedding an Object with Code

The simplest method for embedding one object in another is to copy the object manually in one application and then paste a link to that object in another application. However, you can do the same thing with Visual Basic code.

Chapter 26 ♦ Interapplication Communications

For example, the following code embeds the Excel worksheet into the Word document as shown in figure 26.1. For this procedure to link to Word, you must have a table on Sheet2 in cells A1:F6. Much of this example was created by turning on the Macro Recorder in both Excel and Word, recording the linking process, and then copying and editing the recorded macros.

```
'
' Paste a linked worksheet.
'
Sub LinkToWord()
  Dim WordObj As Object, ChannelNum As Integer
  'Select and copy the table in Excel.
  Sheets("Sheet2").Select
  Range("A1:F6").Select
  Selection.Copy
  'Start Word, make it active, and open a new document.
  Set WordObj = CreateObject("Word.Basic")
  AppActivate "Microsoft Word"
  WordObj.FileNew
  'Use DDE to send the EditPasteSpecial command to Word,
  'to paste and link the table copied from Excel.
  ChannelNum = Application.DDEInitiate("WinWord", "System")
  DDEExecute ChannelNum, "[EditPasteSpecial .Link = 1, _
      .Class = ""Excel.Sheet.5"", .DataType = ""Object""]"
  DDETerminate ChannelNum
End Sub
```

Unfortunately, this code isn't as simple as it could be, because of a "feature" of Word that I hope will change in the next release. That "feature" is that the EditPasteSpecial command is not accessible with OLE. The first few lines select the table on Sheet2 in cells A1:F6 and then copy the table onto the clipboard. The Set statement uses the CreateObject function to start Word and return it as an object. The AppActivate statement brings Word to the front and puts it in the Task List. If you don't include this statement, the Word program ends when this procedure ends.

The next statement uses the FileNew command to create a new document. You should follow the FileNew command with an EditPasteSpecial command, which is the Word Basic command that pastes an OLE link into a document. Unfortunately, Word Basic is not object-oriented, and only some of the Word Basic commands are available to OLE applications outside of Word. In the current version (6), the EditPasteSpecial command is not available to OLE applications. The EditPaste command is available, but it pastes only the numbers and not the link. To work around this problem, open a DDE link and send the EditPasteSpecial command with the DDEExecute command. The arguments of the EditPasteSpecial command declare this a link to an Excel worksheet.

Visual Basic for Applications By EXAMPLE

The easiest way to examine the commands and options in Word or another application is to turn on the Macro Recorder in Word and record the actions. You can then move those commands to a module sheet in Excel, append the Word Basic object to them, and treat them as standard objects. Most commands work this way, except for those like EditPasteSpecial, which are not available to OLE applications. When you execute statements that don't work, Visual Basic returns error codes that tell you which methods are unavailable.

> **Note:** In the LinkToWord procedure, notice the pairs of double quotation marks and the square brackets. Each double quotation mark (" ") evaluates to a single double quotation mark (") in the string sent to Word. This is how you place double quotation marks in a literal string. Without this capability, the double quotation marks would end the string instead of being included in it. The square brackets tell Word that this is a command to execute, not a string to insert in a document. The square brackets also prevent Visual Basic from trying to evaluate the contents of a Word Basic command, which might cause syntax errors or make your code operate incorrectly.

When you run the procedure, the results look similar to figure 26.9, with the table on the Excel worksheet copied and linked to the document in Word.

Figure 26.9
A table on an Excel worksheet in the background, copied and linked to a Word document in the foreground.

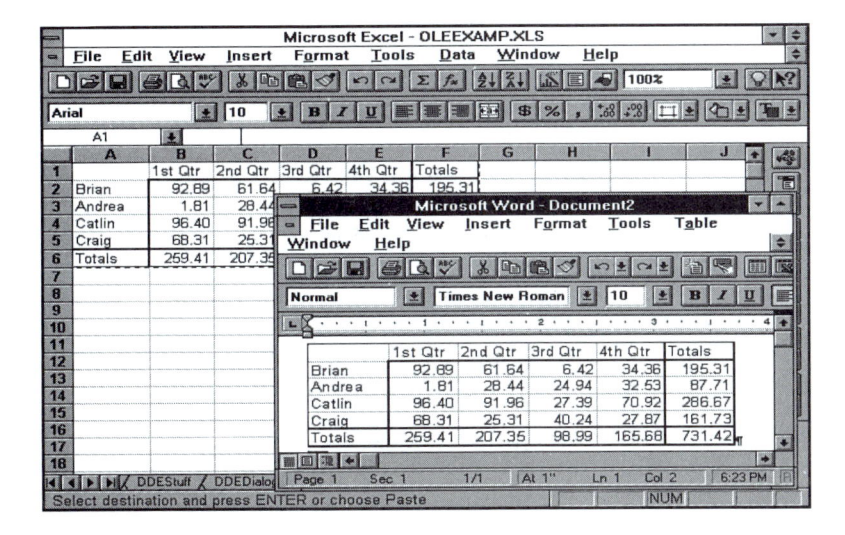

445

Chapter 26 ♦ Interapplication Communications

> **Note:** One problem you that may encounter while experimenting with OLE objects and code is a mangled system. When you test new code, it tends to crash a lot until you get the bugs out. Each of these crashes can leave a link in place that isn't being used, or that goes nowhere. After a while, the OLE handlers in Windows get confused and nothing works anymore. When things that used to work don't seem to work anymore, you may have to end Windows and restart it to clear away the confusion.

> **Note:** Because OLE links are prone to errors, you will find that error-trapping procedures are necessary for preventing OLE link errors from crashing your program (see Chapter 23, "Using Error Trapping To Handle Unforeseen Events"). Your error procedure could try the link again or could quit the procedure, depending on which command caused the error. If you try the link again, be sure to use a counter so that after some number of tries (10, for example), the procedure gives up and exits. Otherwise it may run forever, trying to establish a damaged link.

Passing Keystrokes to Windows Applications

One last way to send information to other applications is by sending keystrokes. You should use keystrokes to pass information only if you cannot use either DDE or OLE. You cannot send keystrokes to an application running in a DOS window.

The SendKeys statement sends the characters in its argument to whichever application has the active window, so activate the application before sending keystrokes to it.

To activate a running application, use the AppActivate command followed by the caption text of the application's window that you want to bring into the foreground. If the application isn't running, use the Shell command to start it. The following is the syntax of the AppActivate command:

```
AppActivate WindowCaption
```

where `WindowCaption` is the text of the caption of the application's window. If you have an object reference to an application, you can use that reference to get the caption. For example, to activate Project, you could use the following:

```
AppActivate MSProject.Application.Caption
```

If you don't have an object reference, you must use text, and you must know what text the application's window uses. For example, for Word the caption is "Microsoft Word-" followed by the name of the currently open document. Therefore, if you use the statement

```
AppActivate "Microsoft Word"
```

the system activates the first instance of Word that it finds running, no matter which document is open. If only one copy of Word is running, this is no problem, but if more than one copy of Word is running at one time, you have to be more explicit to get the correct copy. This is because the AppActivate statement matches the text in its argument to the names of the open windows and activates the first one that matches. To match the argument string, an application's window caption can have more characters than the argument string, but not less.

The following is the syntax of the Shell command:

```
windowID = Shell(path,windowStyle)
```

The *path* argument is a string that contains the path and file name of the program to run. The *windowStyle* argument is optional, and specifies how to open the application's window. Table 26.2 lists the options for *windowStyle*.

Table 26.2. The allowed values for the *windowStyle* argument of the Shell command.

Code	Description
1, 5, 9	Normal with focus
2	Minimized with focus
3	Maximized with focus
4, 8	Normal without focus
6, 7	Minimized without focus

When the Shell command starts the application, it returns a window number that can be used in place of the window name as an argument to the AppActivate statement. For example, the following starts Word in a maximized window in the foreground:

```
hWind = Shell("D:\WINWORD\WINWORD.EXE", 3)
```

Finally, the syntax of the SendKeys function is as follows:

```
SendKeys string,wait
```

Chapter 26 ♦ Interapplication Communications

The *string* argument contains the keystrokes that you want to send to the application, and the *wait* argument controls when the keystrokes are sent. If you omit the *wait* argument or set it to False, your keystrokes are placed in a buffer and your program continues. The contents of the buffer are not sent to the active application until your program is idle or the DoEvents statement is executed. If *wait* is True, the keystrokes are sent immediately. An application is idle while waiting for the user to click a button or choose a menu command. The DoEvents command causes your Visual Basic code to pause for a moment and pass control to the system so that it can handle any necessary business, including sending your keystrokes to another application. The key codes for the nonprinting keys are the same as the codes used with the OnKey command, and are listed in table 24.2.

For example, the following procedure starts Word, activates it, and sends it some keystrokes. This is not how you would normally access Word, because Word can use DDE and OLE, which are much more efficient and easier to control.

```
Option Explicit
'
' Sending keystrokes.
'
Sub SendText()
  Dim hWind
  Const normalFocus = 1
  hWind = Shell("D:\WINWORD6\WINWORD.EXE", normalFocus) 'Run Word.
  Application.Wait Now + TimeValue("00:00:05") 'Pause five seconds.
  AppActivate hWind   'Make Word the active window.
  SendKeys "Good Morning World {ENTER}" 'Send Word some keystrokes.
End Sub
```

The Shell command starts Word, and the Wait command inserts a short pause so that Word can start up before the AppActivate command tries to activate it. If you try to activate a nonexistent window, you get an error. When the application is activated, the SendKeys statement sends the characters followed by the Enter key. You send the Enter key using the code {ENTER}, as indicated in table 24.2. When this procedure completes, the screen looks like figure 26.10.

Figure 26.10
The Word program started with Shell and sent the keystrokes "Good Morning World" and the Enter key.

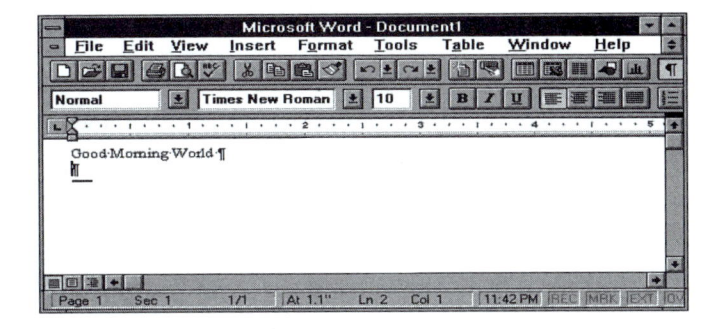

Summary

In this chapter you learned about interapplication communications. Visual Basic offers you three methods of interapplication communications: using DDE, using OLE, and sending keystrokes. OLE, or Object Linking and Embedding, is the most powerful method for communicating with another application. With OLE you can embed one application's objects in another application. When you embed another application's objects in your application, it does not need to know how to manipulate and display the objects, because the source application handles all those activities. With OLE Automation, your Visual Basic program can use another program's objects as if they were part of Visual Basic itself.

DDE, or Dynamic Data Exchange, is an older method for communicating with another application. DDE simply communicates data from one application to the other. Unlike OLE, DDE passes only data, and requires that both applications know how to manipulate and display that data.

Sending keystrokes is the simplest communication method. It is one-directional, and simply mimics the user typing at the keyboard.

Congratulations for making it this far! You have reached the end of the book. I hope that you find this book is useful and that you can now delight in being able to take control of your computer and make it do what you want it to.

Review Questions

The answers to the review questions are in Appendix A.

1. Explain the difference between DDE and OLE.
2. What kind of data do you pass in a DDE link?
3. What kind of data do you pass in an OLE link?

Chapter 26 ♦ Interapplication Communications

4. What function do you use to send data through a DDE channel?
5. What function do you use to send commands through a DDE channel?
6. What function do you use to send commands through an OLE channel?
7. Name an application in which you must use CreateObject or GetObject to create an OLE object that refers to a document?
8. What is the difference between pasting a worksheet table into a Word document and embedding a worksheet table into a Word document?

Review Exercises

1. Write an OLE procedure that embeds a Project task list in an Excel worksheet.
2. Write a DDE procedure that starts Word, opens a short document, and copies the contents of that document into a worksheet.
3. Write a DDE procedure that starts Project, and updates some fields using data from some cells on an Excel worksheet.
4. Using the SendKeys statement, create a procedure that demonstrates another application, such as Word. Have the procedure start Word or another application, open a file, edit it, and then close the file and quit the application. You must use the keyboard commands to select menu items and move around the document, because you cannot use the mouse.
5. Write an OLE procedure that inserts into a Word document a picture of a Project schedule and a picture of an Excel worksheet table.
6. Write an OLE procedure that embeds a Project schedule and an Excel table into a Word document.

APPENDIX A

Answers to the Review Questions

Chapter 1 Answers

1. Visual Basic's continuation character for continuing a statement on the next line is the underscore, preceded by a space.

2. A new macro can be stored in the current workbook, in some other workbook, and in the global module.

3. Absolute cell references always refer to the same cell, no matter where the formula containing them is copied or moved. Relative cell references point to a cell at a location that is relative to the cell containing the reference. When a formula that contains a relative cell reference is copied into another cell, it points to a cell in the same relative location to the copy of the formula as the original cell was to the original formula. For example, if a formula in cell C5 contains a relative reference to F7 (two rows down and three columns right), and that formula is copied into cell B2, the relative reference changes to E4 (again, two rows down and three columns right).

Appendix A ◆ Answers to the Review Questions

Chapter 2 Answers

1. Objects contain data (properties) and the code that knows how to manipulate that data (methods).

2. A programming object is a logical block of code and data. You can access the data with the object's properties and manipulate the data with the object's methods. A programming object is often visualized as a real, physical thing, such as a button or a sheet of paper (a form).

3. A method is an externally available procedure that acts on an objects data. "Externally available" means that another procedure outside of the object can execute it. You execute a method by applying it to the object that contains it, as follows:

   ```
   object.method
   ```

4. A property is an object's data value that is available to procedures outside of the object. To read a property's value, place it on the right side of a formula. To change a property's value, place it on the left side of a formula. In both cases, you access the property by applying the property name to the object that contains it, as follows:

   ```
   object.property
   ```

Chapter 3 Answers

1. A collection is a container for all the objects of a specific class. For example, the Workbooks collection contains all the currently open workbooks, and the Worksheets collection contains all the worksheets in an open workbook.

2. You access a collection by using an index number that selects an object according to its position in the collection, or with a string that contains the object's name.

3. You find out how many members are in a collection by applying the Count property to the collection.

4. Select Range objects on the worksheet by using the Range, Cells, or Offset method.

5. If the current active cell is B7 and you want to access cell F12, you could use the following arguments:

   ```
   ActiveCell.Cells(5,6)
   ActiveCell.Offset(4,5)
   ```

Chapter 4 Answers

1. A data type specifies how numbers or other data are stored in memory. It specifies the number of bytes to use, and how to split those bytes so that they can be used with the different parts of a number. A variable type specifies the data type that a variable contains.

2. The Currency data type uses eight bytes of memory.

3. The scope of a variable consists of those procedures and modules where the variable can be accessed.

4. You force yourself to declare all variables in a module by placing Option Explicit at the top of the module.

Chapter 5 Answers

1. An assignment statement causes a value to be stored in a variable's memory location. It assigns a value to a variable.

2. When calculating a formula, Visual Basic first converts all the numbers to the most accurate type in the formula and then carries out the calculation.

3. You must declare an object variable in a declaration statement As Object or As Variant. To assign a value to an object variable, you must use the Set statement.

4. Most operators combine two values in a mathematical operation such as add (+) or multiply (*). The negation operator changes the sign of a value. The concatenation operator combines two strings into one.

5. The precedence of the operators is an ordering that determines which operation occurs first. To change the order of calculation, use parentheses in a formula. Parentheses always override an operator's precedence.

6. To round –3.4 to –3, use the CInt( ) function.

Chapter 6 Answers

1. The smallest usable computer program that you can write in Visual Basic, a procedure is a grouping of one or more Visual Basic statements to accomplish a particular task. A complete application may consist of one or many procedures, depending on the application's complexity.

2. The three types of procedures described in this chapter are general procedures, command procedures, and event procedures. General procedures

Appendix A ◆ Answers to the Review Questions

perform tasks but do not normally modify the cells on a worksheet. A command procedure also performs tasks, but its goal is to modify a worksheet. Recordings of worksheet actions are command procedures. Event procedures are general procedures that are executed when some event occurs, such as the pressing of a button.

3. The Sub statement must come at the beginning of a procedure and the End Sub statement must come at the end.

4. The Macro Recorder creates command procedures.

5. Calling a procedure is the action of passing control to the procedure so that it can execute. You call a procedure by simply placing its name in another procedure, followed by any arguments it needs.

6. You make variables retain their value from one calling of a procedure to the next by placing the word Static in the procedure header.

7. You hide procedures from other modules by placing the word Private in their procedure header.

8. When you pass an argument by address, you pass to a procedure the address in which a variable is stored in memory so that the procedure can modify the value of the variable.

9. When you pass an argument by value, you pass to a procedure the value of a variable, not the variable itself, so that any changes that the procedure makes to the value are not reflected in the value of the variable.

10. To pass an argument by address, you don't have to do anything special, because this is the default method of passing values. To pass a value by value, place the ByVal keyword before the variable name in the procedure header, or enclose the variable name in parentheses in the calling program.

11. To call a procedure in another workbook, precede the procedure name with the other workbook selected in the Workbooks collection.

Chapter 7 Answers

1. A function can do everything a procedure can do, plus it returns a value in its name. Thus you can use a function in a formula.

2. You set the data type of a function by using an As Type clause on the right side of the function header.

3. Before reaching the end of a function procedure, you must have an assignment statement that assigns a value to the function's name. This is the value that the function returns.

4. To execute a program in the Debug window, switch to the Immediate pane and type

   ```
   Run "programname"
   ```

   where *programname* is the name of the program that you want to run.

5. A function that is to be used on a worksheet must only return a value. It must not manipulate the contents of other worksheet cells.

Chapter 8 Answers

1. What differentiates a simple calculator from a computer is the computer's capability to make decisions and change the thread of calculation based on those decisions.

2. The thread of execution is the list of statements that a program executes in the order that it executes them.

3. A compound statement is two or more basic statements separated by colons on a single line.

4. A binary comparison differentiates between upper- and lowercase letters, but a text comparison does not. The default is binary comparisons.

5. The values of the following comparison operations are indicated to their right:

5 >= 5	True
9 < 7	False
27.8 = 27.85	False
13.5 <> 11.3	True
"X" = "x" (binary comparison)	False
"Y" < "y" (text comparison)	False
";" > "a" (binary comparison)	False
"Pat" <= "Wilbur" (binary comparison)	True

Chapter 9 Answers

1. You test for missing optional arguments in a procedure or function call by using the IsMissing function.

2. You should use in procedures constants like DefaultRate rather than literal values so that what you are doing is more obvious, to make the procedures more readable.

Appendix A ◆ Answers to the Review Questions

3. You can have as many ElseIf clauses as you want in a block If structure.

4. You can have only one Else clause in a block If structure.

Chapter 10 Answers

1. The following is *not* a valid Case statement, because you cannot use the Like operator with Is:

```
Case Is Like "??[aeiou]*"
```

2. Given the following two Case statements, if Value = 13, Block 2 is executed, and if Value = 17, Block 1 is executed:

```
Select Case Value
  Case 11, 14, 15 To 19
    Block 1
  Case 11 To 15, 17
    Block 2
End Select
```

3. Enumerated values are a list of options, with each option having a numeric value. Thus you can easily implement the option by using the value to select a branch in a Select Case statement.

4. The code block following a Case Else statement is executed if none of the other Case statements in a Select Case structure is executed.

5. The Excel constant that gives a #NUM! error with the CVErr() function is xlErrNum.

Chapter 11 Answer

1. Given the choice between an unstructured branch and a structured branch, and the unstructured branch looks like it will be easier to code, you should choose the structured branch, because it is easier to understand and to debug.

Chapter 12 Answers

1. A counted loop is a structure that is repeated a fixed number of times. The For-Next loop is a counted loop.

2. The Exit For statement causes a For-Next loop to terminate immediately.

3. If you omit Step *stepsize*, a step size of 1 is used.

4. Normally you should avoid changing a loop variable within a loop. In fact, there is no situation in which changing a loop variable makes good, logical sense.

   The only situation where you might want to change the value of the loop variable is during an error condition, where you have detected and corrected an error and want to reexecute the last iteration of the loop with the corrected values.

Chapter 13 Answers

1. A logically terminated loop is a loop structure that iterates until some logical condition occurs.

2. The While and Until keywords determine how the condition is examined when deciding to execute the loop. The While keyword causes the loop to execute as long as the condition is True, and Until causes the loop to execute as long as the condition is False.

3. The end of the loop that gets the condition determines whether the loop is always executed at least once (condition at end) or could possibly never be executed (condition at beginning).

Chapter 14 Answers

1. An object type loop is a loop structure that executes once for each object in a collection.

2. When applied to a collection of objects, the loop variable in a For Each loop contains one of the objects during each iteration of the loop.

3. If the For Each loop is applied to a single object, the loop is calculated once.

4. You cannot use a For Each loop to change the value of an array element, because only the value of the array element is in the loop variable, not the array element itself.

Appendix A ◆ Answers to the Review Questions

Chapter 15 Answers

1. If you click OK, the MsgBox() function returns the number 1.

2. To have Yes and No buttons on a MsgBox(), use the constant vbYesNo, which equals 4.

3. You display a number with the MsgBox() function by converting the number to text first, and then using the text in the function.

4. To change the title of a dialog box, change the value of the title argument.

5. A modal dialog box is a dialog box that must be cleared before you can continue with an application.

6. The difference between system modal and application modal is that you must clear a system model dialog box before you can do anything, but you have to clear an application modal dialog box only to continue with the application that displayed it.

Chapter 16 Answers

1. You should name the cells on the worksheet and use the names in the Visual Basic procedures instead of using the cell references, so that the procedure still works if you move the cells.

2. The trade-off at runtime between internal data storage in an array and external storage in a disk file is that internal storage is faster but limited in size, while disk file storage is slower but nearly unlimited in size.

3. The `Option Base 1` statement, placed at the top of a procedure, causes all arrays declared without an explicit lower bound to have a default lower bound of 1 rather than the default lower bound of 0.

4. A procedure named Auto_Open is run whenever a workbook is opened.

5. To select a button on a worksheet without executing the procedure attached to it, use the selection tool on the Drawing toolbar, or hold down Ctrl when clicking the button.

Chapter 17 Answers

1. In Excel, display the object by applying the Show method to a custom dialog box object. In Project, use the Form statement to display a custom form.

2. Open a new dialog sheet with the Insert Macro Dialog command.

3. The OK and Cancel buttons are on a new blank dialog sheet form.

4. A label displays text on a form that the user cannot edit. An edit box displays text that the user can edit.

5. You use a group box to segregate parts of a form visually, and to define the members of an option button group.

6. Option buttons are for selecting mutually exclusive options, while check boxes are for selecting independent options. The user can select only one option button in a group, but can check any number of check boxes.

7. Unlike spinners, scroll bars have a slider that enables you to move quickly from one end of a range to the other and that indicates where in a range you currently are.

8. A button with the Default property set is the button that the user automatically chooses by pressing Enter. A button with the Cancel property set is chosen automatically when the user presses Esc.

9. The tab order is the order in which objects on a form are selected whenever you press the Tab key. You use the Tab key to move from field to field while entering data on a form.

Chapter 18 Answers

1. The FreeFile function returns the next available file number for use with the Open statement.

2. In a sequential file, data is stored as a series of text characters, starting at the beginning of the file and continuing to the end.

3. The Append qualifier of the *mode* argument of the Open statement causes the file pointer to move to the end of the file so that any new data printed to the file is added to the existing file instead of overwriting it.

4. To open a file so that you can write data to it, use the Open statement with the For Output or For Append qualifiers. To open a file so you can read from it, use the Open statement with the For Input qualifier.

5. You must close a file with the Close statement when you are done using it.

6. The Print statement writes text to a file as you would expect to read it, while Write places quotation marks around text and commas between values to make reading the data back into a program more reliable.

Appendix A ◆ Answers to the Review Questions

7. The difference between Input and Line Input is that Input loads individual variables from the data in a file, but Line Input reads an entire line as a string.

8. Sequential files are read or written as a single stream of characters from the beginning to the end. Random access files are read and written in fixed-length blocks in any order.

Chapter 19 Answers

1. You open a random access file by using the Open statement with the For Random clause.

2. The Len = specifier specifies the length of a record in bytes when opening a random access file.

3. You read and write random access files with the Get and Put statements.

4. If you read a record from a random access file, you don't have to store it back in the same place.

5. A record variable is a data structure for storing data in a random access file record. The structure contains in a single file record all the individual values that you want to store, not just one value.

6. An indexed record is a method of storing data in a random access file. For this method, the storage location on disk is unimportant, because the ordering of the records in the file is controlled by an array of index values that then point to the individual records.

Chapter 20 Answers

1. You add a new worksheet to the active workbook by applying the Add method to the Worksheets collection.

2. To rename a worksheet, change the Name property of the worksheet object.

3. To open an existing worksheet when you know its name, apply the Open method to the Worksheets collection.

4. To open an existing worksheet when the user knows its name, display the GetOpenFilename dialog box or Excel's Open dialog box so that the user can select and open the file.

5. If the active range object points to cell K13, the `Cells(5,7)` method points to Q17.

Chapter 21 Answers

1. A syntax error is an error in the typing of a command, or in the type of variable applied in an assignment statement. It is usually caused by misspelling a keyword, by misplacing required punctuation, or by using a variable of the incorrect type in a formula or function call. Most syntax errors occur as soon as you finish typing a statement. Others occur when your procedure is compiled the first time that you run it after a change.

2. Runtime errors are all those errors that you cannot find by inspecting the syntax of a single statement. They are caused by the actual values contained in variables being of the wrong type or range for a function, such as taking the square root of minus one, and by problems with file names, paths, and disk drives. Runtime errors also occur in block structures that are incorrectly implemented, such as a For-Next loop that lacks the Next statement or a block If structure that lacks the End If statement. Runtime errors occur while your program is running.

3. A logical error occurs when your program is doing what you told it to do, but not what you wanted it to do. Logical errors can occur anytime in a running program. They do not normally result in your program crashing and an error message being displayed; your program simply does not do what you expect it to do.

4. Debugging is the art of finding and fixing errors or bugs in a computer program.

5. The Procedure box displays the name of the current procedure. If you click it, it lists all the currently active procedures.

6. When you select an instant watch variable, its current value is displayed in a dialog box. You must close the dialog box before you can continue with anything else. A watch variable is displayed in the Watch pane of the Debug window and continuously displays its current value while a program runs. A watch variable can also be an expression that is evaluated at each step in a program, and which stops that program if some logical condition occurs.

Chapter 22 Answers

1. Break mode is where a program stops because it encountered an error or a Stop statement, or because the user pressed Ctrl-Break. A program in break mode is simply paused, with all variables retaining their values at the point that the program entered break mode.

Appendix A ◆ Answers to the Review Questions

2. A breakpoint is a mark placed on a statement in a program. During execution, the program goes into break mode when it encounters the mark.

3. A watch expression displays the value of an expression or variable in the Watch pane of the Debug window. A watch point is a logical expression or value that causes a program to go into break mode if the logical expression becomes True or the value changes.

4. The Stop statement causes a program to go into break mode when it is executed.

5. You can make change for a dollar in 40 different ways.

6. You remove a breakpoint by selecting the marked statement and choosing the **R**un Toggle **B**reakpoint command. To remove all breakpoints, choose the **R**un **C**lear All Breakpoints command.

7. Both the Step Into and Step Over commands execute a single statement and return to break mode. The Step Into command follows the thread of execution from procedure to procedure, while the Step Over command stays in a single procedure, executing a procedure call as a single statement instead of following the thread into the called procedure.

Chapter 23 Answers

1. You enable an error trap in a procedure by placing an On Error GoTo statement in the procedure.

2. The three parts of an error handler are the header, the handler body, and a footer to return to the operating code. The header consists of a label at the beginning of the handler for the On Error statement to point to. The body contains the code that actually handles the error, and the footer contains the Resume statement that returns to the existing program.

3. The Err function returns the error number of the last error and the Error() function returns a text description of each error number.

4. You place an Exit Sub or Exit Function statement between the normal procedure and the error handler to ensure that the code in the error handler is not accidentally executed by a normally executing program.

5. To pass an error back to the system so that the system can handle it, use its error number as the argument of the Error( ) statement. Note that the Error( ) statement is different than the Error( ) function.

6. The three things that turn off an error trap are an `On Error Goto 0` statement, encountering an error, and reaching the end of a procedure.

7. You disable user interrupts with Ctrl-Break by setting the EnableCancelKey property of the Application object to the xlDisabled constant.

Chapter 24 Answers

1. The three objects that make up a menu are the menu bar, the menu, and the menu item.

2. No, you cannot attach a procedure to a menu, only to a menu item.

3. A shortcut menu is a menu that drops down when you click the right mouse button on an object.

4. To activate the Button Editor, follow these steps:

   a. First make sure that the button you want to edit is on a toolbar and is visible onscreen.

   b. Choose the **V**iew **T**oolbars **C**ustomize command to display the Customize dialog box.

   c. While displaying onscreen both the Customize dialog box and the toolbar that contains the button that you want to edit, click that button using the right mouse button. The Buttons shortcut menu is then displayed.

   d. Select the Edit Button Image command from the shortcut menu and the Button Editor dialog box appears.

   e. Use the drawing tool to edit the image on the button. Click the color first, then in the button image click the area that you want to change to the selected color.

   f. After you finish converting the image, choose OK. The new button image replaces your old one on the toolbar.

Appendix A ◆ Answers to the Review Questions

5. To create a custom menu bar, first apply the Add property to the MenuBars collection followed by a name to create the menu bar, as follows:

```
MenuBars.Add Name:="MyBar2"
```

Next add captions to the menu bar by applying the Add method to the Menus collection:

```
MenuBars("MyBar2").Menus.Add Caption:="&Commands"
```

Finally, use the Activate method to display the new menu bar:

```
Application.MenuBars("MyBar2").Activate
```

Chapter 25 Answers

1. A custom object resides in a module.

2. The Property Let procedure creates a function that changes the value of a custom object's property.

3. The Property Get procedure creates a function that returns the value of a custom object's property.

4. The Property Set procedure is similar to the Property Let procedure, but is used when the property is an object rather than a numeric value of a string.

5. To return an object reference to an outside procedure, use a Property Get procedure with the procedure type set to Object or Variant. Be sure to use the Set statement to assign the returned object to an Object or Variant type variable.

6. To create a method for a custom object, simply create a Public Sub procedure with the method's name in the custom object's module.

Chapter 26 Answers

1. DDE is a link between two applications that passes data between them. OLE is a link that passes objects between two applications.

2. A DDE link can pass data only between two applications. When used with Visual Basic for Applications, a DDE link can pass only text and numbers. Other applications can pass more complex objects, such as pictures.

3. An OLE link passes objects between two applications, so to edit a linked object, you use the linked objects methods and properties.

4. You use the DDEPoke statement to send data through a DDE channel to the server, or a DDERequest statement to get the server to send data back to you.

5. To send commands through a DDE channel, use the DDEExecute statement.

6. You don't send commands through an OLE channel to a linked application. Instead, you use the linked application's methods directly.

7. In Word 6.0, you must use CreateObject or GetObject to create an OLE object that refers to a document, because Word 6.0 is not fully object-oriented.

8. When you paste a worksheet table into a Word document, you are pasting the text of the table. If you edit the table, you can change only the text. If you embed a worksheet table into a Word document, you are inserting a Range object that contains the table. If you edit the table, Excel opens to handle the editing, including the recalculation of the cells and the formatting of the results.

APPENDIX B

Table of ANSI Codes

The following table lists the ANSI character codes used to store characters in memory and in files. The ANSI (American National Standards Institute) code table is a super set of the ASCII (American Standard Codes for Information Interchange) codes, which cover the first 128 codes. The ASCII codes were originally developed for teletype communications. The first 32 codes are the control characters, although only four of them are used in Windows applications. The codes from 32 through 127 are the normal typewriter characters, and codes 128 through 255 are the extended characters. Note that the extended codes used in MS-DOS applications differ from those shown here for Windows applications, which use the ANSI standard.

Character	*Hex Code*	*ANSI Code*
Backspace	&H08	8
Tab	&H09	9
Line feed	&H0A	10
Carriage return	&H0D	13
Space	&H20	32
!	&H21	33
"	&H22	34

Appendix B ◆ Table of ANSI Codes

Character	Hex Code	ANSI Code
#	&H23	35
$	&H24	36
%	&H25	37
&	&H26	38
'	&H27	39
(	&H28	40
)	&H29	41
*	&H2A	42
+	&H2B	43
,	&H2C	44
-	&H2D	45
.	&H2E	46
/	&H2F	47
0	&H30	48
1	&H31	49
2	&H32	50
3	&H33	51
4	&H34	52
5	&H35	53
6	&H36	54
7	&H37	55
8	&H38	56
9	&H39	57
:	&H3A	58
;	&H3B	59
<	&H3C	60
=	&H3D	61
>	&H3E	62
?	&H3F	63
@	&H40	64
A	&H41	65
B	&H42	66
C	&H43	67
D	&H44	68
E	&H45	69
F	&H46	70
G	&H47	71
H	&H48	72
I	&H49	73
J	&H4A	74

Character	Hex Code	ANSI Code
K	&H4B	75
L	&H4C	76
M	&H4D	77
N	&H4E	78
O	&H4F	79
P	&H50	80
Q	&H51	81
R	&H52	82
S	&H53	83
T	&H54	84
U	&H55	85
V	&H56	86
W	&H57	87
X	&H58	88
Y	&H59	89
Z	&H5A	90
[	&H5B	91
\	&H5C	92
]	&H5D	93
^	&H5E	94
_	&H5F	95
`	&H60	96
a	&H61	97
b	&H62	98
c	&H63	99
d	&H64	100
e	&H65	101
f	&H66	102
g	&H67	103
h	&H68	104
i	&H69	105
j	&H6A	106
k	&H6B	107
l	&H6C	108
m	&H6D	109
n	&H6E	110
o	&H6F	111
p	&H70	112
q	&H71	113
r	&H72	114

Appendix B ◆ Table of ANSI Codes

Character	Hex Code	ANSI cCode
s	&H73	115
t	&H74	116
u	&H75	117
v	&H76	118
w	&H77	119
x	&H78	120
y	&H79	121
z	&H7A	122
{	&H7B	123
|	&H7C	124
}	&H7D	125
~	&H7E	126
	&H7F	127
Ç	&H80	128
ü	&H81	129
	&H82	130
'	&H83	131
ƒ	&H83	131
„	&H84	132
…	&H85	133
†	&H86	134
‡	&H87	135
ˆ	&H88	136
‰	&H89	137
Š	&H8A	138
‹	&H8B	139
Œ	&H8C	140
ì	&H8D	141
Ä	&H8E	142
Å	&H8F	143
É	&H90	144
'	&H91	145
'	&H92	146
"	&H93	147
"	&H94	148
°	&H95	149
–	&H96	150
—	&H97	151
~	&H98	152
™	&H99	153
š	&H9A	154

Visual Basic for Applications By EXAMPLE

Character	Hex Code	ANSI Code
>	&H9B	155
œ	&H9C	156
¥	&H9D	157
P	&H9E	158
	&H9F	159
Space	&HA0	160
¡	&HA1	161
¢	&HA2	162
£	&HA3	163
⊗	&HA4	164
¥	&HA5	165
¦	&HA6	166
§	&HA7	167
¨	&HA8	168
©	&HA9	169
ª	&HAA	170
«	&HAB	171
¬	&HAC	172
-	&HAD	173
®	&HAE	174
¯	&HAF	175
°	&HB0	176
±	&HB1	177
²	&HB2	178
³	&HB3	179
´	&HB4	180
µ	&HB5	181
¶	&HB6	182
•	&HB7	183
¸	&HB8	184
¹	&HB9	185
º	&HBA	186
»	&HBB	187
¼	&HBC	188
½	&HBD	189
¾	&HBE	190
¿	&HBF	191
À	&HC0	192

Appendix B ◆ Table of ANSI Codes

Character	Hex Code	ANSI Code
Á	&HC1	193
Â	&HC2	194
Ã	&HC3	195
Ä	&HC4	196
Å	&HC5	197
Æ	&HC6	198
Ç	&HC7	199
È	&HC8	200
É	&HC9	201
Ê	&HCA	202
Ë	&HCB	203
Ì	&HCC	204
Í	&HCD	205
Î	&HCE	206
Ï	&HCF	207
Ð	&HD0	208
Ñ	&HD1	209
Ò	&HD2	210
Ó	&HD3	211
Ô	&HD4	212
Õ	&HD5	213
Ö	&HD6	214
×	&HD7	215
Ø	&HD8	216
Ù	&HD9	217
Ú	&HDA	218
Û	&HDB	219
Ü	&HDC	220
Ý	&HDD	221
Þ	&HDE	222
ß	&HDF	223
à	&HE0	224
á	&HE1	225
â	&HE2	226
ã	&HE3	227
ä	&HE4	228
å	&HE5	229
æ	&HE6	230

Character	Hex Code	ANSI Code
ç	&HE7	231
è	&HE8	232
é	&HE9	233
ê	&HEA	234
ë	&HEB	235
ì	&HEC	236
í	&HED	237
î	&HEE	238
ï	&HEF	239
ð	&HF0	240
ñ	&HF1	241
ò	&HF2	242
ó	&HF3	243
ô	&HF4	244
õ	&HF5	245
ö	&HF6	246
÷	&HF7	247
ø	&HF8	248
ù	&HF9	249
ú	&HFA	250
û	&HFB	251
ü	&HFC	252
ý	&HFD	253
þ	&HFE	254
ÿ	&HFF	255

APPENDIX C

Visual Basic Error Codes

The Macro Error dialog box displays the Visual Basic error codes and error messages whenever a program encounters an error and does not have an error handler enabled (see Chapter 23, "Using Error Trapping To Handle Unforeseen Events"). The Err function returns the error code for the last error that a program encounters. The Error( ) function returns the error message for any error code used as an argument, except for codes 1000 through 1006, which do not return error messages in this version of Visual Basic.

Error Code	Error Message and Cause
3	Return without GoSub
	A procedure is attempting to use a Return statement to return from a subroutine without using a Gosub statement to branch to a subroutine.
5	Invalid procedure call
	This error usually occurs when an invalid number is using an argument to a numerical function or an invalid option with a procedure.
6	Overflow
	During a calculation, a number stored in memory became larger than the largest number possible in the data type being calculated.

Appendix C ◆ Visual Basic Error Codes

Error Code	Error Message and Cause
7	`Out of memory`
	Your program needs more memory but none is available. Try reducing the amount of memory used by releasing variables (especially arrays and strings) that are no longer in use.
9	`Subscript out of range`
	You used an index to select an array element that is either larger or smaller than the element numbers that you defined when declaring the array.
10	`Duplicate definition`
	You are declaring a variable that you declared previously in the same procedure. You can use the ReDim statement to redeclare an array variable.
11	`Division by zero`
	A division operation has a zero in the denominator, which is an undefined operation.
12	`Precision lost converting Variant`
	A number stored in a Variant variable was converted to a numeric type that has precision insufficient to display the number correctly.
13	`Type mismatch`
	You tried to store a value in a variable of the wrong type. You can convert most numbers, so this error usually results from trying to store a number in a string variable, a string in a numeric variable, anything other than an object in an object variable, or an object in anything other than an object variable. Variant type variables can store anything. This error also occurs if you call a function using the wrong type of value for an argument.
14	`Out of string space`
	A string could not be allocated because it is too long, or because your program is out of memory. To make memory available, try releasing some existing variables that you no longer need.

Error Code	Error Message and Cause
16	String expression too complex
	Strings returned by functions and those explicitly typed into a string formula are stored as temporary strings. If there are too many of them, this error can result. Try storing the strings in variables and use the variables in the formula.
17	Can't perform requested operation
	This error usually occurs in Break mode when you try to make a change that makes the current state of your program invalid. To make the change, end the program, make the change, and then rerun the program.
18	User interrupt occurred
	The user pressed Ctrl-Break. Use this error to trap user interrupts.
20	Resume without error
	A Resume statement has been encountered but an error has not been trapped. The error is usually caused by the execution point getting into an error handler by mistake.
28	Out of stack space
	Stack space stores the return addresses and local variables for procedure calls. Declare variables at the module level and reduce the nesting of called procedures.
35	Sub or Function not defined
	You called a procedure that is undefined. This error is usually caused by misspelling a variable name or using parentheses incorrectly.
47	Too many DLL application clients
	Too many applications are trying to use the same DLL.
48	Error in loading DLL
	A DLL could not be loaded, probably because you declared it incorrectly or used the wrong file name.

Appendix C ◆ Visual Basic Error Codes

Error Code	Error Message and Cause
49	Bad DLL calling convention
	A DLL is complaining about the arguments that you sent to it. Check whether you correctly stated the procedure's declaration and whether you sent it the correct type values.
51	Internal error
	Something didn't work when attempting to access a file. Try to access the file again.
52	Bad file name or number
	You used an invalid file name, or a file number that was not declared in an Open statement. Check the number and type of characters in the requested file name.
53	File not found
	The file requested in an Open, Kill, or Name statement does not exist. The statement probably has a misspelled file name or specifies the wrong directory.
54	Bad file mode
	You tried to print to a file opened for input or to print from a file opened for output, or you used Get and Put with a sequential file.
55	File already open
	You tried to access a file that is already open. This error can also occur if you restart a crashed program that did not close all its files. To close all open files, type **Close** in the Immediate pane of the Debug window.
57	Device I/O error
	A device is signaling a problem. Try the action again. It could be a hardware problem.
58	File already exists
	You tried to create a new file, but a file with the same name already exists.

Error Code	Error Message and Cause
59	Bad record length
	A record variable that you are using with a random access file is longer than the record length that you specified in the Open statement. You didn't allow for the two-byte specifiers used in all variants and variable-length strings.
61	Disk full
	The disk to which you are trying to write is full. Try a different disk, or remove some information from the disk.
62	Input past end of file
	You tried to read beyond the last record in a file. If you don't know how many records are in a file, use the EOF( ) function to test for the end of the file before attempting to read a record.
63	Bad record number
	You used a record number that is less than zero.
67	Too many files
	You have too many files open at one time, or the disk catalog is full for the root directory of a disk. Close some files, add more file buffers in the CONFIG.SYS file, or try a different directory.
68	Device unavailable
	A requested disk drive or other device is unavailable. This error usually occurs because the media has been removed from a removable media drive.
70	Permission denied
	You tried to write to a write-protected file.
71	Disk not ready
	No disk is in the drive, or the disk drive door is open.
74	Can't rename with different drive
	You tried to rename a file with a different drive letter in the new file name. To move a file to a different drive, copy it instead.

Appendix C ◆ Visual Basic Error Codes

Error Code	Error Message and Cause
75	`Path/File access error`
	The file path or file name is incorrect. Check your spelling.
76	`Path not found`
	A requested path does not exist. Check your spelling.
91	`Object variable not Set`
	You tried to use an object variable that you have not yet defined.
92	`For loop not initialized`
	You have jumped into the middle of a For-Next loop and encountered a Next statement without the initial For statement.
93	`Invalid pattern string`
	You have used a pattern string with the Like statement, which is invalid. Check your spelling.
94	`Invalid use of Null`
	You tried to store the value of a variable or formula that has the value Null. You probably used an uninitialized Variant variable.
323	`Can't load module; invalid format`
	You didn't store a requested Visual Basic module as text. Some versions of Visual Basic store modules in binary format. Resave the module in text format and try again.
423	`Property or method not found`
	An object does not have the requested property or method. Check your spelling or use the Object Browser to see whether the property or method exists.
424	`Object required`
	You have used a number or string, but an object is required.
430	`Class doesn't support OLE Automation`
	You have attached to another application that has class variables but does not support OLE Automation. Check the other application's documentation.

Error Code	Error Message and Cause
438	Object doesn't support this property or method
	An object does not have the requested property or method. Check your spelling, or use the Object Browser to check for allowed methods and properties.
440	OLE Automation error
	An OLE Automation command did not work, and the program that you are attempting to control returned this error code. Many causes are possible. Switch to the other program and see whether it also is displaying an error message.
445	Object doesn't support this action
	An object does not have the requested property or method. Check your spelling, or use the Object Browser to check for allowed methods and properties.
446	Object doesn't support named arguments
	The object does not support named arguments, so you must use positional arguments when calling it.
447	Object doesn't support current locale setting
	The language setting for the object differs from the one that you are using. Check the object's documentation to see whether another version of the object has the correct language setting.
448	Named argument not found
	You used a named argument that does not exist for this object. Check your spelling to ensure that you are using the right library, because objects in different libraries often have the same name.
449	Argument not optional
	You omitted an argument that must be specified.
450	Wrong number of arguments
	You used too many or too few arguments.

Appendix C ◆ Visual Basic Error Codes

Error Code	Error Message and Cause
451	Object not a collection
	You tried to select an element of a collection, and the object that you are attempting to access is not a collection of objects. This error probably is due to a spelling error, because the name of an object and its collection often differs by a single letter, as in, for example, the Sheet object and the Sheets collection.
452	Invalid ordinal
	To select a procedure from a DLL, you tried to use an index number that does not refer to any procedure in the library. Check your number or call the procedure by name.
453	Function not defined in specified DLL
	You referred to a function in a DLL library that does not exist in the library. Check the spelling of the function's name and of the library's name.
454	Code resource not found
	In a Macintosh program, you specified a code resource that the program did not find. Check your spelling.
455	Code resource lock error
	In a Macintosh program, you tried to lock a code resource that cannot be locked. Check your spelling and documentation.
1000	*Classname* does not have *propertyname* property
	An object does not have the requested property. Check your spelling, or use the Object Browser to check for allowed methods and properties.
1001	*Classname* does not have *methodname* method
	An object does not have the requested method. Check your spelling, or use the Object Browser to check for allowed methods and properties.
1002	Missing required argument *argumentname*
	A required argument named *argumentname* is missing.

Error Code	Error Message and Cause
1003	`Invalid number of arguments`
	You called a procedure with the wrong number of arguments.
1004	`Methodname method of classname class failed`
	A method failed, usually because you selected a nonexistent element of a collection and then tried to apply a method to the element, or because the object does not contain data.
1005	`Unable to set the propertyname property of the classname class`
	An attempt to set a property value failed, usually because you selected a nonexistent element of a collection and then tried to set the element's properties, or because an object does not contain data.
1006	`Unable to get the propertyname property of the classname class`
	An attempt to get a property value failed, usually because you selected a nonexistent element of a collection and then tried to get the element's properties, or because an object does not contain data.

GLOSSARY

Glossary

Absolute reference. A reference to a specific worksheet cell that does not change when the formula that contains it is copied. See also *relative reference*.

Active call chain. The list of all an application's procedures that have not completed executing and are waiting for a called subprocedure to return, including the procedure that was active when a program was stopped. The list is called a call chain because one procedure calls the next, which calls the next, and so forth, forming a chain that extends from the first procedure executed to the current procedure.

Active object. The topmost sheet for workbooks and worksheets, the active cell for Range objects, or the selected object for graphic objects.

Assignment statement. A statement that has a variable on the left and an equals sign and a formula on the right. The result of the formula is assigned or stored in the variable.

Biased integer. An integer that can have a positive or negative value.

Bit. The smallest memory element in a computer. It can contain the values 0 or 1.

Block of code. See *code block*.

Boolean. A data type for storing the logical values True or False.

Bug. A programming error that causes your programs to crash or work improperly.

Byte. Eight bits of memory. Most memory transfers are handled in even numbers of bytes.

Call chain. See *active call chain*.

Glossary

Calling a procedure. Executing a procedure by placing its name in another.

CD-ROM memory. Like disk memory, CD-ROM memory stores data and programs while they are not being used. CD-ROM memory cannot be rewritten because an optical process permanently stores the data on it.

Central processing unit (CPU). The integrated circuit chip that performs the control functions and most of the arithmetic calculations in a computer. For the current generation of MS-DOS machines, the CPU is an 80486 processor.

Code block. A contiguous group of statements designed to be executed together as a block.

Collection. A container for all the objects of a specific class.

Command procedure. A procedure that makes changes to another application's documents, expanding the capabilities of those applications.

Construct. A fragment of code constructed from two or more basic language elements that performs a specific function. That function is usually larger than a basic language element but is smaller than a procedure.

Control structure. Any structure that changes the thread of execution, including If statements, structured branches, and repeating structures.

Counted loop. A loop that repeats a single block of code a specified number of times.

CPU. See *central processing unit*.

Currency. A data type that stores currency values, such as dollars and cents.

Data structure. A structure in memory that combines one or more data types into one structure that can be accessed as a single entity.

Data type. A specification as to how a data element is stored in your computer's memory. Data types specify the memory structures for variable types.

Debugging. The art of finding and removing errors, or *bugs*, from a program.

Default button. The button that is chosen automatically when the user presses Enter while its dialog box is displayed.

Design time. The time during which you type your code into the computer and draw your forms. Design time covers everything up to the point that you run your programs.

Discrete mathematics. A mathematical system in which numbers have a fixed number of digits. Computers use discrete mathematics because the number of digits is limited by the hardware.

Disk memory. The memory in which programs and data are stored when they are not being used. Disk memory is like a tape recorder, which can record and rerecord programs and data. Disk memory does not go away when the power goes off.

DLL. See *Dynamic Link Library*.

Double. A data type that stores double-precision floating point numbers.

Dynamic array. An array that you declare at design time but for which you do not allocate memory until runtime. The needs of your program determine the length of a dynamic array.

Dynamic Link Library (DLL). A special kind of library that is linked to an executing program at runtime rather than when the program is compiled.

Edit bar. The horizontal bar that is displayed along the top of a worksheet. When you select a cell, the edit bar displays the contents of the cell and enables you to edit them.

Edit handles. The small, black squares that appear around an object when you select it. To change the shape of the object, you drag the edit handles.

Enumerated values. A list of options in which each option is given an integer value to identify it.

Error handler. A code block in a procedure that is called when a runtime error occurs. It must be enabled with the On Error Goto statement.

Error trap. A trap that captures runtime errors and processes them with an error handler other than Visual Basic's error handler, which crashes a program. To set an error trap, you use the On Error Goto statement.

Event procedure. A procedure that is tied to a specific event, and is executed when the event occurs.

Exponent. A number that indicates where the decimal point is in a floating point number.

"Feature." A polite term for logical errors or omissions in commercial software.

File numbers. Small integer numbers that are associated with a file when it is opened, and are used by the reading and writing commands to specify which file to read or write.

Form. A Visual Basic window. A form is the background for all documents and dialog boxes.

Function. A type of procedure that returns a value in its name.

Glue function. A function procedure that rearranges or modifies the arguments of a function to make it easier to use.

Glossary

Hexadecimal. The base 16 numbering system.

Indexed record. A method of indirectly referencing numbered records using an array of indexes. A record is accessed by accessing the index, which supplies a reference number for a record. The index array enables you to sort the records without having to move the actual records. Only the elements of the index array are actually sorted. Indexed records are often used to reference the records of random access files.

Inheritance. A larger object's assumption of the properties and methods of the smaller objects of which it consists.

Instant watch variable. A variable whose current value is temporarily displayed in a dialog box as a result of the use of the Tools Instant Watch command.

Integer. A data type that stores only whole numbers, and no fractions.

List. A series of items, or descriptions of items.

Literal value. The actual value (number or string) that you type directly into a program. For example, in the formula x = 3, the 3 is a literal value because it is the actual number that you want to assign to x, and not some variable or constant that contains the number.

Logical error. An error in the logic of your program rather than in the syntax of the code itself. When your program has a logical error, it runs but gives the wrong results.

Logically terminated loop. A repeating structure that terminates when a logical condition is met.

Long. A data type that stores double-precision integers.

Mantissa. The numeric part of a floating point number.

Memory. See *random access memory*, *read-only memory*, *disk memory*, and *CD-ROM memory*.

Methods. The tasks that an object knows how to perform on itself.

Modal dialog box. A dialog box that you must clear before you can continue the application.

Modularized code. Code that has been organized into blocks, with each block having a well-specified task to perform, and known inputs and outputs.

Name box. A box on the left end of the edit bar. The name box contains the name of the currently selected object. To change the name of the selected object, you type the new name and press Enter.

Native machine code. Code that is executed directly by the central processing unit (CPU).

Null. The value that indicates that a variable holds no valid value.

Numeric overflow. An error condition in which a formula produces a value that is larger than the largest value allowed for a particular type of variable.

Numeric underflow. An error condition in which a numeric value is inserted into a variable and the value is smaller than the smallest value that the variable's type can represent. This condition does not usually result in an error, because 0 is used to replace the small value, but it can result in invalid data if the small value is important.

Object. A programming abstraction for a structure that contains data and the code that knows how to manipulate it. Objects are often visualized as the physical objects that they mimic, such as a button.

Object Linking and Embedding (OLE). A data communication methodology in which programming objects are passed between applications.

Object-oriented programming (OOP). A programming methodology in which data and the code that knows how to manipulate that data are combined into a structure called an *object*.

Octal. The base 8 numbering system.

ODBC. See *open database connectivity*.

OLE. See *Object Linking and Embedding*.

OOP. See *object-oriented programming*.

Open database connectivity (ODBC). A capability for Excel to access the data files of other, external database applications.

P-code. An intermediate code produced by some compilers. Compilers produce either native machine code or an intermediate p-code. Native machine code can be directly executed by the computer's central processing unit (CPU), but p-code requires an interpreter. An interpreter reads a p-code command and then executes the equivalent machine code commands. P-code makes transporting an application much simpler, because to handle the new processor's commands you need to rewrite only the p-code interpreter.

Path. The list of directory names, separated with backslashes, that specifies the location of a file. A path may include the disk letter on the left and the file name on the right.

Plain procedure. A standard Visual Basic procedure that does not make changes directly in an outside application. Also simply referred to as a *procedure*.

Procedure. The smallest usable computer program that you can write in Visual Basic.

Glossary

Programmer. The person who creates a program, as differentiated from the user, who uses it. The user and the programmer can be the same person.

Project. All the modules in a workbook, plus any workbooks that you attach to that workbook with the Tools References command.

Property. The data contained within a code object. Properties can be the data that the object manipulates or the data that controls how an object looks or behaves.

RAM. See *random access memory*.

Random access memory (RAM). The electronic memory in a computer where programs and data are stored while they are being executed. The contents of RAM go away when your system's power is turned off.

Range object. Any cell or rectangular group of cells on a worksheet.

Read-only memory (ROM). The permanent electronic memory in your computer where the startup code is stored. You cannot change your ROM, and it does not go away when your system's power is turned off.

Record variable. A data structure for storing several different variables in a random access file record.

Relative reference. A reference to a worksheet cell that is relative to the cell that contains the reference. The value of the reference changes when the formula that contains it is copied to a different cell.

Repeating structure. One of several loop structures that execute a block of code more than one time. Counted loops and logically terminated loops are examples of repeating structures.

ROM. See *read-only memory*.

Runtime. The time during which your programs are running.

Runtime error. An error that occurs in a running application when some value is used incorrectly, a block structure is incorrect, or a device indicates a problem. Examples include having a zero in the denominator of a fraction, executing an End If statement without first executing an If statement, or trying to open a file that does not exist.

Scope of a variable. The list of procedures in which a variable is available.

Simple integer. An integer that can have only positive values.

Single. A data type that stores floating point numbers.

SQL. See *Structured Query Language*.

Statement. A single line of code, or a built-in procedure.

Static array. A fixed-length array that you declare and allocate at design time. After design time, you cannot change the length of the array.

Strictly typed language. A language in which you must declare every variable using it.

String. A series of ASCII characters treated as a single unit. When not stored in a variable, a string must be enclosed in double quotation marks. *String* is also a data type that stores strings.

Structured branch. One of several structures that allow one or more different blocks of code to be selected for execution depending on a logical condition. Block If and Select Case structures are structured branches.

Structured Query Language (SQL). The industry standard language for writing queries in database programs.

Substring. A piece of a *string*.

Syntax error. An error that occurs when you mistype a statement, omit a required argument, or use an argument of the incorrect type.

Task List. The list of all running Windows applications. You access the Task List with the Control box on the upper-left corner of a window.

Thread of execution. The sequence of steps that a program executes as it goes from start to finish. The thread is not fixed, and may change from run to run of a program depending on the outcome of control structures in a code.

Truth table. A table that shows the logical output of a logical function for all possible inputs.

Unstructured branch. A structure that can branch to anywhere in a procedure. The GoTo statement creates an unstructured branch. Avoid unstructured branches whenever possible.

User. The person who uses a program, as differentiated from the programmer, who created it. The user and the programmer can be the same person.

Variable. A named storage location in a computer's memory.

Variable type. A specification of the kind of data that a variable can store. The standard variable types are Integer, Long, Single, Double, Currency, Boolean, String, and Variant.

Variant. A special data type that can store any type of value.

Watch variable. A variable whose current value is displayed in the Watch pane of the Debug window.

Index

Symbols

! (exclamation point) in variable
   names, 63
(pound sign)
   Format( ) statements, 255
   variable names, 63
   wild card, 132
$ (dollar sign) in variable names, 63
% (percent sign)
   modifier code, 398
   variable names, 63
& (ampersand)
   concatenation operator, 74
   menu items, 387
   variable names, 63
( ) (parentheses) in arguments, 102
' (single quotation mark) in comments, 72
* (asterisk)
   multiplication operator, 74
   string comparisons, 132
+ (plus sign)
   addition operator, 74
   formulas, 80
   modifier code, 398

, (comma) in Format( ) statements,
   255
- (minus sign)
   formulas, 80
   negation operator, 74
   subtraction operator, 74
. (period) in Format( ) statements,
   255
... (ellipsis) in commands, 385
/ (slash) division operator, 74
; (semicolon) in Print statements,
   254
< (less than) logical operator, 131
<= (less than or equal to) logical
   operator, 131
<> (not equal to) logical operator,
   131
= (equal sign)
   assignment statements, 71
   constructs, 33
   logical operator, 131
   object variables, 73
> (greater than) logical operator,
   131

Index

>= (greater than or equal to) logical operator, 131
? (question mark)
    Immediate pane, 333
    wild card, 132
[ ] (brackets)
    module names, 96
    string comparison, 132
\ (backslash) integer division operator, 74
^ (caret)
    exponentiation operator, 74
    modifier code, 398
_ (underscore)
    macro names, 12
    variable names, 63
{ } (braces)
    arrays, 117
    modifier codes, 398
~ (tilde) modifier code, 398
0 (zero) in Format( ) statements, 255

A

Abs function, 78
absolute references, 11, 485
accessing
    collection members, 40
    structure elements, 68
    worksheets functions, 114
Activate method, 47
active call chain, 335, 485
active objects, 47, 485
ActiveCell property, 47
ActiveWorkbook property, 47
Add method
    collections, 42-43
    menu bars, 395-396
    menu items, 393-395
    menus, 395
    opening worksheets, 307-309
    toolbars, 406-408

Add Watch command (Tools menu), 346
Add-Ins command (Tools menu), 323
addition operator (+), 74
American National Standards Institute code, see ANSI
American Standard Code for Information Interchange, see ASCII
amortization tables, 13-14
ampersand (&)
    concatenation operator, 74
    menu items, 387
    variable names, 63
And operator, 135
ANSI (American National Standards Institute) code, 62, 467-473
    logical operators, 132
Any data type, 123
AppActivate statement, 434, 444
Append mode (sequential files), 253
application dialog boxes, 206-207
Argument not optional error message, 481
arguments
    Cells method, 45-46
    comma-delimited lists, 99
    count, 233
    error messages, 481
    formulas, 101-103
    index, 233
    multiple arguments, 104-105
    named lists, 100
    optional arguments, 103-104
Array data type, 61-62
arrays
    declaring, 66
    dynamic arrays, 175, 487
    error handlers, 363
    For Each loops, 188-189
    indexes, 283-284, 488

passing, 103, 116-121
static arrays, 491
Subscript out of range error
  message, 476
Asc function, 82
ASCII (American Standard Code for
  Information Interchange)
  ANSI (American National
    Standards Institute) code, 467
  strings, 491
Assign Macro command (Tools
  menu), 12
Assign Macro dialog box, 27, 218
assigning values (object variables),
  73
assignment statements, 71-72, 485
asterisk (*)
  multiplication operator, 74
  string comparisons, 132
Atn function, 78
Attach Toolbars command (Tools
  menu), 405
attaching
  buttons to toolbars, 402-403
  procedures to custom dialog
    boxes, 236
  workbooks, 96-97
Auditing toolbar, 401

B

backslash (\) integer division
  operator, 74
Bad DLL call convention error
  message, 478
Bad file mode error message, 478
Bad file name or number error
  message, 478
Bad record length error message,
  479
Bad record number error message,
  479
Beep statement, 348-349
biased integers, 61

binary mode (sequential files), 253
Binary mode files, 281
binary operators, 74-77
bits, 485
block-level errors, 330
Bookmark command (Edit menu),
  435
Boolean data type, 60-61, 485
Boolean operators, 135-136
BorderAround method, 54
braces ({ })
  arrays, 117
  modifier codes, 398
bracket ([ ])
  module names, 96
  string comparison, 132
break mode, 339-342
  breakpoints, 342-343
  Can't perform requested
    operation error message, 477
  running programs, 344-345
  Stop statement, 342
  watchpoints, 345-347
bugs, *see* debugging
built-in data types, 60-63
  Array, 62
  Boolean, 61
  Currency, 61, 486
  Date, 62
  Double, 61, 487
  Integer, 61, 488
  Long, 61, 488
  Object, 62
  Single, 61
  String, 62
  Variant, 62-63, 491
button codes (dialog boxes), 197
Button Image Editor, 404
button object, 228-229
buttons
  adding to worksheets, 218-222
  attaching
    procedures, 27-28, 219
    toolbars, 402-403

Index

creating, 404
dialog boxes, 197-199
sizing, 220
Visual Basic code, 406-408
bytes, 485

C

calculated branches, 162
calculations
   assignment statements, 71-72
   conversion functions, 88-89
calling
   dialog boxes, 206-207
   functions, 111-112
   procedures, 95-98, 486
      modules, 96
         private procedures, 97-98
      workbooks, 96-97
Calls dialog box, 336
Cancel property (buttons), 228
Can't load module; invalid format error message, 480
Can't perform requested operation error message, 477
Can't rename with different drive error message, 479
Caption property, 396
caret (^)
   exponentiation operator, 74
   modifier code, 398
Case Else clause, 154-157
CBool function, 88
CCur function, 88
CD-ROM memory, 486
CDate function, 88
CDbl function, 88
cells
   absolute references, 485
   formatting, 13, 51-54
   Range objects, 43-47
      Cells method, 45-46
      Offset method, 46-47
      Range method, 43-44

   references, 43-44
   relative references, 490
   selecting, 309
Cells command (Format menu), 13-14, 210
Cells method
   Range objects, 45-46
   selecting cells, 309
Central Processing Unit (CPU), 486
Chart menu bar, 384
Chart toolbar, 401
check box object, 231
Checked properties, 396
Chr function, 82
CInt function, 88
Class doesn't support OLE Automation error message, 480
classes, 35
Classname does not have methodname method error message, 482
Classname does not have propertyname property error message, 482
Clear All Breakpoints command (Run menu), 342
clearing forms, 301
CLng function, 88
Close command (File menu), 42
Close method (collections), 42
Close statement, 253, 281
closing
   DDE communication channels, 435
   dialog boxes, 236
   random access files, 281
   sequential files, 253
code blocks, 139-144, 486
   Case Else clause, 154-157
   Else statements, 146-149
   ElseIf statements, 144-146
   executing multiple blocks, 144-146
   Select Case statement, 151-154

Code resource lock error error message, 482
Code resource not found error message, 482
codes
   ANSI (American National Standards Institute), 467-473
   constructs, 486
   modularized code, 488
   native machine code, 488
   p-code, 489
collections, 39-43, 486
   accessing members, 40
   adding members, 42
   Count property, 41
   deleting members, 42-43
   For Each statement, 40
   menu bars, 393
   Object not a collection error message, 482
   object type loops, 185
      For Each, 186-189
combination list-edit object, 234
comma (,) in Format( ) statements, 255
command procedures, 94-95, 486
commands
   ... (ellipsis), 385
   Data menu, 322
   Edit menu
      Bookmark, 435
      Fill Down, 24
      Sheet, 412
   File menu
      Close, 42
      New, 12
      Open, 42, 206
      Save As, 206
   Format menu
      Cells, 13-14, 210
      Object, 229, 238
      Placement, 238
      Sheet, 210, 237

   Help menu, 35
   Insert menu
      Macro, 41, 226, 237
      Names, 210
   Run menu
      Clear All Breakpoints, 342
      Continue, 340, 344
      Start, 83, 343
      Step Into, 344
      Step Over, 344
      Toggle Breakpoint, 342
   Tools menu
      Add Watch, 346
      Add-Ins, 323
      Assign Macro, 12
      Attach Toolbars, 405
      Customize, 226, 236
      Instant Watch, 333-335, 488
      Macro, 12, 174, 335
      Menu Editor, 386
      Options, 14, 64, 222
      Protection, 222
      Record Macro, 11-12, 37
      References, 96, 323, 440
      Run Dialog, 236
   View menu
      Debug Window, 75, 331
      Object Browser, 36
      Toolbars, 27, 219, 402
   Window menu, 12
comments, 22, 72-73
comparing
   objects, 134
   strings, 132-133
compound statements, 130
conditions (loops), 181-182
constants
   built-in constants, 68
   defining, 67
constructs, 33, 486
containers, 32
Content properties, 50
Contents command (Help menu), 35

Index

Continue command (Run menu), 340, 344
control structures, 486
conversion functions, 88-89
converting data types, 88-89
Copy method, 54
Cos function, 78
count argument, 233
Count property, 173
   collections, 41
counted loops, 171, 486
   For-Next, 171-172
   loop counter, 172-177
CPU (Central Processing Unit), 486
Create command (Names submenu), 210
CreateObject( ) function, 442-443
CSng function, 88
CStr function, 88
Currency data type, 60-61, 486
custom data types, 68-69
Customize command
   Toolbars submenu, 404
   Tools menu, 226, 236
Customize dialog box, 28
customizing
   methods, 416
   objects, 411-412, 416-428
   properties, 412-416
   Shortcut menus, 399-400
   toolbars, 402-403
Cut method, 54
CVar function, 88
CVErr function, 88, 360
CVError( ) function, 155

D

data channels, 432
data forms
   creating, 210-211
   initialization procedures, 216
   storing data, 212-215

Data menu commands, 322
data structures, 486
   passing, 103
data types, 59-60, 486
   Boolean, 485
   built-in data types, 60-63
      Array, 62
      Boolean, 61
      Currency, 61, 486
      Date, 62
      Double, 61, 487
      Integer, 61, 488
      Long, 61, 488
      Object, 62
      Single, 61
      String, 62
      Variant, 62-63, 491
   converting, 88-89
   custom data types, 68-69
   functions, 110-111
   long, 488
   single, 490
databases
   error handlers, 363-378
   Microsoft Query, 325
   ODBC (Open Database Connectivity), 323-325, 489
   saving
      external databases, 322-325
      random access files, 284-303
   searching, 246-247
   size, 284
   SQL (Structured Query Language), 323-325, 491
   storing on worksheets, 310-322
Date data type, 60-62
Date function, 86
date functions, 86-88
DateSerial function, 86
DateValue function, 86
Day function, 86

DDE (Dynamic Data Exchange), 431-433
　closing channels, 435
　data channels, 432
　opening channels, 434-435
　requesting data, 435-437
　sending commands, 439
　sending data, 437-438
　Windows, 434
DDEExecute function, 439
DDEIntiate function, 434
DDEPoke function, 437
DDERequest function, 435
DDETerminate statement, 435
Debug window, 331-332
Debug Window command (View menu), 75, 331
Debug.Print statement, 347-348
debugging, 330-332, 485-486
　active call chain, 335
　break mode, 339-340
　Calls dialog box, 336
　Debug.Print statement, 347-348
　editing variables, 332-333
　error codes, 475-483
　error traps, 351-355, 487
　　databases, 363-378
　　delaying processing, 362
　　error handlers, 352, 355-359, 487
　　error trap enablers, 352-353
　　error values, 360-361
　　OLE (Object Linking and Embedding), 446
　　unknown errors, 359
　　user interrupts, 361-362
　　user-defined errors, 359-361
　　variables, 360
　Instant Watch command, 333-335
　logical errors, 331, 488
　runtime errors, 331, 490
　syntax errors, 330

decision making, 129-130
　If statement, 130-131
　logical values, 131-134
declaration statements, 94
declaring
　arrays, 66
　variables, 63-65, 247
　　Dim statement, 64
　　Duplicate definition error message, 476
　　global variables, 65
　　object variables, 73
　　Option Explicit statement, 64
　　procedure headers, 98-99
　　Public statement, 65
　　record variables, 281-282
　　Variant data type, 63
default codes (dialog boxes), 198
Default property (buttons), 228
Define command (Names submenu), 210
defining
　constants, 67
　input ranges, 209-218
delaying error processing, 362
Delete method (collections), 42-43
deleting menu bars
　Menu Editor, 391-392
　Visual Basic code, 396
Device I/O error error message, 478
Device unavailable error message, 479
dialog boxes
　Add Watch, 346
　application dialog boxes, 206-207
　Assign Macro, 27, 218
　attaching procedures, 236
　button object, 228-229
　buttons, 197-199
　calling, 206-207
　Calls, 336

Index

check box object, 231
combination drop-down edit object, 235
combination list-edit object, 234
creating, 196-197, 237
custom dialog boxes, displaying, 236
Customize, 28, 402
default buttons, 198, 486
dialog sheets, 225-227
displaying custom dialog boxes, 236
drop-down object, 234
edit box object, 231
GetOpenFilename, 205-206
GetSaveAsFilename, 205-206
group box object, 231
InputBox( ) function, 201-205
Instant Watch, 334
label object, 229-230
list box object, 232-234
Macro Error, 331, 340, 475-483
modal dialog boxes, 488
MsgBox( ) function, 195-201
Open, 308
option button object, 231-232
Record New Macro, 12
References, 96
Save As, 308
scroll bar object, 235
scroll bars, 244-246
spinner objects, 235
titles, 200-201
Dialog command (Macro submenu), 226, 237
Dim statement, 64, 73
directories, 489
discrete mathematics, 486
Disk full error message, 479
disk memory, 487
Disk not ready error message, 479
Dismiss property (buttons), 228
Division by zero error message, 476
division operator (/), 74
DLL (Dynamic Link Library), 487
  Bad DLL calling convention error message, 478
  functions, 122-123
  Too many DLL application clients error message, 477
Do-Loop loops, 180-183, 204, 275
dollar sign ($) in variable names, 63
Double data type, 60-61, 487
Drawing toolbar, 218, 401
  attaching procedures, 29
drop-down object, 234
Duplicate definition error message, 476
dynamic arrays, 175, 487
Dynamic Data Exchange, *see* DDE
Dynamic Link Library, *see* DLL

E

edit box object, 231, 235
edit handles, 487
Edit menu commands
  Bookmark, 435
  Fill Down, 24
  Sheet, 412
editing
  procedures, 18-26
  variables (debugging), 332-333
ellipsis (...) in commands, 385
Else clauses, 146-149
ElseIf clauses, 144-146
embedding objects, 443-446
Enabled property, 396
End statements, 26
End Sub statement, 94
End Type statement, 68
enumerated values, 152
EOF( ) function, 181, 273, 479

equal sign (=)
   assignment statements, 71
   constructs, 33
   logical operator, 131
   object variables, 73
Eqv operator, 135
error codes, 475-483
Error in loading DLL error message, 477
Error statement, 359
error traps, 351
error values, 155, 360-361
Error( ) function, 156, 355, 475
errors, 141
   numeric overflow, 489
   numeric underflow, 489
   syntax errors, 491
event loops, 180
event procedures, 95, 487
exclamation point (!) in variable names, 63
Excel
   constants, 68
   Macro Recorder, 10-18
      attaching procedures to objects, 27-29
      command procedures, 94-95
      comments, 72
      creating worksheets, 12-18
      editing procedures, 18-26
      formatting cells, 51-54
      references, 11
      running procedures, 18, 22
      start up, 11
   Visual Basic for Applications, 9-10
executing
   methods, 54
   procedures, 95-98
Exit Do statement, 181
Exit For statement, 172
Exit Sub statement, 358

Exp function, 78
exponentiation operator (^), 74
external databases, 322-325

F

File already exists error message, 478
File already open error message, 303, 478
File menu commands
   Close, 42
   New, 12
   Open, 42, 206
   Save As, 206
File not found error message, 478
file numbers, 252
files
   Binary mode files, 281
   error messages, 478
   file numbers, 487
   filters, 206
   random access files, 251-252
      closing, 281
      declaring record variables, 281-282
      indexes, 283-284
      opening, 280-281
      record variables, 490
      retrieving data, 282
      saving databases, 284-303
      storing data, 282
   sequential files, 251-252
      closing, 253
      file numbers, 252
      inputting from files, 258-262
      opening, 252-253
      printing, 254-256
      saving databases, 262-276
      writing to, 257-258
Fill Down command (Edit menu), 24

Index

filters, 206
Fix function, 78
floating-point numbers, 79
For Each loops, 186-189
For Each statement, 40
For loop not initialized error
 message, 480
For-Next loop, 46, 171-172
Form command (Data menu), 322
Format function, 82
Format menu commands
 Cells, 13-14, 210
 Object, 229, 238
 Placement, 238
 Sheet, 210, 237
Format( ) function, 141, 255
formatting cells, 13, 51-54
Formatting properties, 51-54
Formatting toolbar, 401
forms, 487
Forms command (Customize
 submenu), 226, 236
Forms toolbar, 226-227, 401
Formula property, 50
formulas, 80-81
 arguments, 101-103
 conversion functions, 88-89
FreeFile function, 253
Function not defined in specified
 DLL error message, 482
Full Screen toolbar, 401
functions, 109-110, 487
 calling, 111-112
 constructs, 486
 conversion functions, 88-89
 CreateObject( ), 442-443
 creating, 110-112
 CVErr( ), 360
 CVError( ), 155
 data type, 110-111
 date functions, 86-88
 DDEExecute, 439

DDEIntiate, 434
DDEPoke, 437
DDERequest, 435
DLL (Dyanmic Link Library),
 122-123
EOF( ), 181, 273, 479
Error( ), 156, 355, 475
Format( ), 141, 255
FreeFile, 253
GetCurrentTime( ), 123
GetObject( ), 442-443
GetOpenFilename( ), 253
GetSaveAsFilename( ), 271
GetSaveFilename( ), 274
glue functions, 487
InputBox( ), 201-205
InStr( ), 248
IsArray( ), 134
IsDate( ), 134
IsEmpty( ), 134
IsError( ), 134, 156, 361
IsMissing( ), 134
IsNull( ), 134
IsNumeric( ), 134
IsObject( ), 134
LBound( ), 182
Len( ), 282
Log( ), 114
logical tests, 134
mathematical functions, 78-81
MessageBeep( ), 123
MsgBox( ), 175, 195-201
 creating dialog boxes, 196-199
 returning values, 199-200
 titles, 200-201
ODBC (Open Database
 Connectivity), 324
passing arrays, 116-121
Pmt( ), 113
Str( ), 77, 197
string functions, 82-85

time functions, 86-88
TypeName( ), 119
UBound( ), 104
worksheets, 112-116
zLog( ), 114

G-H

Get statement, 282, 293
GetCurrentTime( ) function, 123
GetObject( ) function, 442-443
GetOpenFilename dialog box, 205-206
GetOpenFilename( ) function, 253
GetSaveAsFilename dialog box, 205-206
GetSaveAsFilename( ) function, 271
GetSaveFilename( ) function, 274
global variables, 65
glue functions, 487
GoSub statement, 162
GoTo statement, 161, 491
graphics, 29
greater than (>) logical operator, 131
greater than or equal to (>=) logical operator, 131
group box object, 231

headers (error handlers), 355
Help menu commands, 35
Help property (buttons), 228
Help window, 35
Hex function, 82
Hour function, 86
hyphen (-) in menu items, 394

I-J

icon codes (dialog boxes), 198
If statement, 130-131
Immediate pane (Debug window), 76
Imp operator, 135

indentation in procedures, 105
index argument, 233
indexes, 488
    random access files, 283-284
    Subscript out of range error message, 476
Info menu bar, 384
inheritance, 34-35
inheriting properties, 488
Input mode (sequential files), 253
Input past end of file error message, 479
input ranges, 209-218
Input statement, 258
InputBox( ) function, 201-205
inputting from files, 258-262
Insert menu commands
    Macro, 41, 226, 237
    Names, 210
Instant Watch command (Tools menu), 333-335, 488
instant watch variables, 488
Instr function, 82
InStr( ) function, 248
Int function, 78
Integer data type, 60-61, 488
integer division operator (\), 74
integers
    accessing collection members, 40
    Cells method (Range objects), 45-46
interapplication communication, 431-432
    DDE (Dynamic Data Exchange), 431-439
        closing channels, 435
        data channels, 432
        opening channels, 434-435
        requesting data, 435-437
        sending commands, 439
        sending data, 437-438
        Windows, 434

Index

OLE (Object Linking and Embedding), 431, 440-446, 489
    Class doesn't support OLE Automation error, 480
    creating objects, 442-443
    embedding objects, 443-446
    OLE Automation, 440-442
    trapping errors, 446
    sending keystrokes, 446-448
Internal error error message, 478
Invalid number of arguments error message, 483
Invalid ordinal error message, 482
Invalid pattern string error message, 480
Invalid procedure call error message, 475
Invalid use of Null error message, 480
Is logical operator, 131, 134
IsArray( ) function, 134
IsDate( ) function, 134
IsEmpty( ) function, 134
IsError( ) function, 134, 156, 361
IsMissing( ) function, 134
IsNull( ) function, 134
IsNumeric( ) function, 134
IsObject( ) function, 134

K-L

keywords
    ParamArray, 104
    Private, 97
    Set, 73
    Until, 181
    While, 181

label object, 229-230
LBound( ) function, 182
LCase function, 82
Left function, 82
Left property, 408
Len function, 82, 282
less than (<) logical operator, 131
less than or equal to (<=) logical operator, 131
Like logical operator, 131
Like statement, 480
Line Input statement, 259
LineStyle property, 54
list box object, 232-234
List( ) property, 232
literal values, 488
locating objects
    Help window, 35
    Object Browser, 36-37
locking worksheets, 222
Log function, 78, 114
logical branches, 162
logical errors, 331, 487-488
logical expressions, 135-136
logical tests, 134
logical values, 131-134
logically terminated loops, 179-180, 488
    Do-Loop, 180-183
    event loops, 180
    While-Wend, 183-184
Long data type, 60-61, 488
loop counter, 172-177
loops, 46
LSet function, 82
LTrim function, 82

M

Macro command
    Insert menu, 41, 226, 237
    Tools menu, 12, 174, 335
Macro Error dialog box, 331, 340, 475-483
Macro Recorder, 10-18
    attaching procedures
        buttons, 27-28
        graphics, 29
        menus, 28
    command procedures, 94-95
    comments, 72
    creating worksheets, 12-18

editing procedures, 18-26
formatting cells, 51-54
objects, 37
references, 11
running procedures, 18, 22
start up, 11
Mark Position for Recording command (Record Macro submenu), 11, 37
mathematical functions, 78-81
mathematical operators, 74-77
    precedence, 74-75
    testing, 75-77
members (collections), 42-43
memory
    bits, 485
    bytes, 485
    CD-ROM, 486
    disk memory, 487
    Out of memory error message, 476
    RAM (random access memory), 490
    ROM (read-only memory), 490
    variables, 63-65
menu bars, 383-386
    ... (ellipsis) in commands, 385
    adding menu items
        Menu Editor, 387-389
        Visual Basic code, 393-395
    adding menus
        Menu Editor, 389-390
        Visual Basic code, 395
    attaching procedures, 28
    collections, 393
    creating
        Menu Editor, 386-392
        Visual Basic code, 393-396
    deleting
        Menu Editor, 391-392
        Visual Basic code, 396
    displaying, 391
    Menu Editor, 386

    menu properties, 396
    selecting menus, 385
    shortcut keys, 397-399
    Shortcut menus, 399-400
Menu Editor command (Tools menu), 386
MessageBeep( ) function, 123
Methodname method of classname class failed error message, 483
methods, 23, 33-34, 488
    accessing, 34
    BorderAround, 54
    Copy, 54
    custom methods, 416
    Cut, 54
    executing, 54
    Paste, 54
    PrintOut, 54
Microsoft Query, 325
Microsoft toolbar, 401
Mid function, 82
minus sign (-)
    formulas, 80
    negation operator, 74
    subtraction operator, 74
Minute function, 86
Missing required argument argumentname error message, 482
Mod (modulus) operator, 74
modal dialog boxes, 488
modifier codes, 398
modularized code, 488
Module command (Macro submenu), 41
modules, 32
    calling procedures, 96
Month function, 86
MsgBox( ) function, 175, 195-201
    creating dialog boxes, 196-199
    returning values, 199-200
    titles, 200-201
multiplication operator (*), 74

Index

N

name box, 488
Named argument not found error message, 481
Names command (Insert menu), 210
naming variables, 63
native machine code, 488
negation operator (-), 74
New command (File menu), 12
No Documents menu bar, 384
not equal to (<>) logical operator, 131
Not operator, 135
Now function, 86
numeric overflow error, 489
numeric underflow errors, 489
numerical error handlers, 357-358

O

Object Browser, 36-37
   displaying constants, 68
   error values, 156
   OLE (Object Linking and Embedding), 441
Object Browser command (View menu), 36
Object command (Format menu), 229, 238
Object data type, 60-62
Object doesn't support current locale setting error message, 481
Object doesn't support named arguments error message, 481
Object doesn't support this action error message, 481
Object doesn't support this property or method error message, 481
Object Linking and Embedding, see OLE
Object not a collection error message, 482
Object required error message, 480
object type loops, 185-189
Object variable not Set error message, 480
object variables, 73
object-oriented programming, see OOP
objects, 23, 489
   active objects, 47, 485
   classes, 35
   collections, 39-43, 486
      accessing members, 40
      adding members, 42
      Count property, 41
      deleting members, 42-43
      For Each statement, 40
      menu bars, 393
   comparing, 134
   constructs, 33
   custom methods, 416
   custom objects, 411-412, 416-428
   dialog boxes
      attaching to worksheets, 248
      button object, 228-229
      check box object, 231
      combination drop-down edit object, 235
      combination list-edit object, 234
      drop-down object, 234
      edit box object, 231
      group box object, 231
      label object, 229-230
      list box object, 232-234
      naming, 229
      option button object, 231-232
      scroll bar object, 235

spinner object, 235
edit handles, 487
error messages, 480
inheritance, 34-35
locating
   Help window, 35
   Object Browser, 36-37
Macro Recorder, 37
methods, 23, 33-34, 488
   accessing, 34
   BorderAround, 54
   executing, 54
object type loops, 185-189
OLE (Object Linking and Embedding), 489
   creating objects, 442-443
   embedding objects, 443-446
   opening, 442-443
OOP (object-oriented programming), 489
passing objects, 415-416
passing data, 414-415
properties, 23, 33-34, 490
   accessing, 34
   ActiveCell, 47
   ActiveWorkbook, 47
   Formatting properties, 51-54
   Formula, 50
   LineStyle, 54
   Selection, 48
   Value, 50
Range objects, 43-47, 490
   Cells method, 45-46
   methods, 54
   Offset method, 46-47
   selecting cells, 309
statements, 49
visible data, 33
Oct function, 82
ODBC (Open Database Connectivity), 323-325, 489
Offset method, 46-47

OLE (Object Linking and Embedding), 431, 440-446, 489
   Class doesn't support OLE Automation error message, 480
   creating objects, 442-443
   embedding objects, 443-446
   OLE 2.0, 10
   OLE Automation, 440-442
   trapping errors, 446
On Error Goto statement, 487
On Error statement, 353
OnAction property, 236
OnKey method, 397-401
online help, 35
OnSheet Deactivate property, 95
OOP (object-oriented programming), 31-33, 489
Open command (File menu), 42, 206
Open Database Connectivity (ODBC), 323-325
Open dialog box, 308
Open statement, 252, 280
opening
   DDE communication channels, 434-435
   dialog sheets, 225-227
   files, 487
   objects (OLE), 442-443
   random access files, 280-281
   sequential files, 252-253
   worksheets, 307-309
operators
   logical expressions, 135-136
   logical operators, 131-134
   mathematical operators
      precedence, 74-75
      testing, 75-77
option button object, 231-232
Option Explicit statement, 64, 77, 140
optional arguments, 103-104

Index

Options command (Tools menu), 14, 64, 222
Or operator, 135
Out of memory error message, 476
Out of stack space error message, 477
Out of string space error message, 476
Overflow error message, 475

P

p-code, 330, 489
ParamArray keyword, 104
parentheses in arguments, 102
passing
  arrays, 116-121
  objects, 415-416
  variables
    address, 100
    value, 100-103
Paste method, 54
Path not found error message, 480
Path/File access error error message, 480
paths, 489
percent (%)
  modifier code, 398
  variable names, 63
period (.) in Format( ) statements, 255
Permission denied error message, 479
Placement command (Format menu), 238
plain procedures, 489
plus sign (+)
  addition operator, 74
  formulas, 80
  modifier code, 398
Pmt( ) function, 113

pound sign (#)
  Format( ) statements, 255
  variable names, 63
  wild card, 132
precedence of operators, 74-75
Precision lost converting Variant error message, 476
Print statement, 254
printing sequential files, 254-256
PrintOut method, 54
Private keyword, 97
private procedures, 97-98
Private statement, 412, 427
procedures, 93-94
  active call chains, 485
  attaching to
    buttons, 27-28, 219
    custom dialog boxes, 236
    graphics, 29
    menus, 28
  break mode, 339-342
    break points, 342-343
    running programs, 344-345
    Stop statement, 342
    watchpoints, 345-347
  calling, 95-98, 486
    modules, 96
    private procedures, 97-98
    workbooks, 96-97
  command procedures, 94-95, 486
  comments, 22
  declaring variables, 98-99
  design time, 486
  DLL (Dynamic Link Library), 487
  error messages, 141
  event procedures, 95, 487
  functions, 109-110
    calling, 111-112
    creating, 110-112
    data type, 110-111
    DLL (Dynamic Link Library), 122-123

glue functions, 115
passing arrays, 116-121
worksheets, 112-116
indentation, 105
multiple arguments, 104-105
optional arguments, 103-104
plain procedures, 489
procedure headers, 100-101
Property Get, 414-415
Property Let, 412-413
Property procedures, 412-416
Property Set, 415-416
running, 141
variables
comma-delimited lists, 99
named lists, 100
passing by address, 100
passing by value, 100-103
Static statement, 105
programming modules, 32
projects, 490
properties, 23, 33-34, 490
accessing, 34
Active, 47
Caption, 396
Checked, 396
Content, 50
Count, 173
custom properties, 412-416
Enabled, 396
Formatting properties, 51-54
inheriting, 34-35, 488
Left, 408
LineStyle, 54
List( ), 232
menus, 396
OnAction, 236
OnSheetDeactivate, 95
Selection, 48
setting values, 412-413
Top, 408
Property Get procedure, 414-415

Property Let procedure, 412-413
Property or method not found error message, 480
Property Set procedure, 415-416
Protect Sheet command (Protection submenu), 222
Protection command (Tools menu), 222
Put statement, 282, 295

Q-R

Query and Pivot toolbar, 401
question mark (?)
Immediate pane, 333
wild card, 132
RAM (random access memory), 490
random access files, 251-252
closing, 281
declaring record variables, 281-282
indexes, 283-284
opening, 280-281
record variables, 490
retrieving data, 282
saving databases, 284-303
storing data, 282
random access memory (RAM), 490
Randomize function, 78
Range method, 43-44
Range objects, 43-47
Cells method, 45-46
methods, 54
Offset method, 46-47
Range method, 43-44
selecting cells, 309
range objects, 490
read-only memory (ROM), 490
Record At Mark command (Record Macro submenu), 11, 37

Index

Record Macro command (Tools menu), 11-12, 37
Record New Macro command (Record Macro submenu), 11-12
Record New Macro dialog box, 12
record variables, 490
recording procedures, 10-18
   attaching procedures to objects, 27-29
   creating worksheets, 12-18
   editing procedures, 18-26
   references, 11
   running procedures, 18, 22
   start up, 11
records, 488
redimensioning arrays, 175
references (Excel), 11
References command (Tools menu), 96, 323, 440
relative cell references, 490
relative references, 11
Rename command (Sheet submenu), 210, 237, 412
repeating structures, 490
Resume statement, 358, 477
Resume without error error message, 477
retrieving data (random access files), 282
Return without GoSub error message, 475
Right function, 82
Rnd function, 78
ROM (read-only memory), 490
RSet function, 82
RTrim function, 82
Run Dialog command (Tools menu), 236
Run menu commands
   Clear All Breakpoints, 342
   Continue, 340, 344
   Start, 83, 343
   Step Into, 344
   Step Over, 344
   Toggle Breakpoint, 342
running procedures, 141
   Macro Recorder, 18, 22
runtime, 490
runtime errors, 331, 490

S

Save As command (File menu), 206
Save As dialog box, 308
saving
   databases
      external databases, 322-325
      random access files, 284-303
      sequential files, 262-276
   workbooks, 308
scope, 64-65
scope (variables), 490
screen components, 487-488
scroll bar object, 235
scroll bars, 244-246
searching databases, 246-247
Second function, 86
Select Case statement, 151-154
Select method, 47
selecting cells, 309
Selection property, 48
semicolon (;) in Print statements, 254
SendKeys statement, 446-448
sequential files, 251-252
   closing, 253
   file numbers, 252
   inputting from files, 258-262
   opening, 252-253
   printing, 254-256
   saving databases, 262-276
   writing to, 257-258
servers
   requesting data, 435-437
   sending commands, 439
   sending data, 437-438
Set keyword, 73

setting property values, 412-413
Sgn function, 78
Sheet command
   Edit menu, 412
   Format menu, 210, 237
Shell statement, 434, 447
Short Chart menu bar, 385
Short Worksheets menu bar, 384
shortcut keys, 397-399
Shortcut menus, 399-400
Shortuct Menus menu bars, 384
Show method, 236
simple integers, 61
Sin function, 78
Single data type, 60-61, 490
single quotation mark (') in comments, 72
sizing buttons, 220
slash (/) division operator, 74
Sort command (Data menu), 322
Space function, 82
spaghetti code, 166
spinner objects, 235
SQL (Structured Query Language), 323-325, 491
Sqr function, 78
Standard toolbar, 401
Start command (Run menu), 83, 343
starting Macro Recorder, 11
statements, 175, 490
   AppActivate, 434, 444
   assignment statements, 71-72, 485
   Beep, 348-349
   Close, 253, 281
   code blocks, 139-144, 486
      Case Else clause, 154-157
      Else statements, 146-149
      ElseIf statements, 144-146
      executing multiple blocks, 144-146
      Select Case statement, 151-154

comments, 72-73
compound statements, 130
counted loops, 171, 486
   For-Next, 171-172
   loop counter, 172-177
DDETerminate, 435
Debug.Print, 347-348
declaration statements, 94
Dim, 64, 73
Do-Loop, 204, 275
Else clauses, 146-149
ElseIf clauses, 144-146
End, 26
End Sub, 94
End Type, 68
Error, 359
Exit Do, 181
Exit For, 172
Exit Sub, 358
For Each, 40, 186-189
For-Next loops, 480
Get, 282, 293
GoSub, 162
GoTo, 161, 491
If, 130-131
Input, 258
Like, 480
Line Input, 259
logically terminated loops, 179-180, 488
   Do-Loop, 180-183
   event loops, 180
   While-Wend, 183-184
object type loops, 185-189
On Error, 353
On Error Goto, 487
Open, 252, 280
Option Explicit, 64, 77, 140
Print, 254
Private, 412, 427
Public, 65
Put, 282, 295
ReDim, 175

Index

repeating structures, 490
Resume, 358, 477
SendKeys, 446-448
Shell, 434, 447
Static, 105
Stop, 83, 342
structured branches, 491
Type, 68, 281-282
unstructured branching,
  161-166, 491
    calculated branches, 162
    logical branches, 162
    spaghetti code, 166
With, 26, 49
Write, 257
static arrays, 491
Static statement, 105
Step Into command (Run menu),
  344
Step Over command (Run menu),
  344
Stop Recording toolbar, 401
Stop statement, 83, 342
storing data
  data forms, 212-215
  random access files, 282
Str function, 77, 82, 197
StrComp function, 82
strictly typed languages, 491
string concatenation operator (&),
  74
String data type, 60-62
String expression too complex error
  message, 477
String function, 82-85
strings, 491
  comparing, 132-133
  substrings, 491
structured branches, 491
Structured Query Language (SQL),
  323-325

structures, 68
Sub or Function not defined error
  message, 477
Subscript out of range error
  message, 476
substrings, 491
subtraction operator (-), 74
syntax errors, 330, 491

T

Tan function, 78
Task List, 491
testing mathematical operators,
  75-77
thread of execution, 491
  control structures, 486
  decision making, 129-130
    If statement, 130
    logical values, 131-134
  spaghetti code, 166
tilde (~) modifier code, 398
Time function, 86
time functions, 86-88
Timer function, 86
TimeSerial function, 86
TimeValue function, 86
TipWizard toolbar, 401
titles (dialog boxes), 200-201
Toggle Breakpoint command (Run
  menu), 342
Too many DLL application clients
  error message, 477
Too many files error message, 479
toolbars, 401-402
  adding buttons, 402-403
  attaching procedures, 28
  attaching to workbooks, 405
  Button Image Editor, 404
  customizing, 403
  Drawing, 29, 218
  Forms, 226-227
  Visual Basic code, 406-408

Toolbars command (View menu), 27, 219, 402
Tools menu commands
  Add Watch, 346
  Add-Ins, 323
  Assign Macro, 12
  Attach Toolbars, 405
  Customize, 226, 236
  Instant Watch, 333-335, 488
  Macro, 12, 174, 335
  Menu Editor, 386
  Options, 14, 64, 222
  Protection, 222
  Record Macro, 11-12, 37
  Reference, 323
  References, 96, 440
  Run Dialog, 236
Top property, 408
trapping errors, 352-355, 487
  delaying processing, 362
  error codes, 475-483
  error handlers, 352, 355-359, 487
    array dimensions, 363
    databases, 363-378
    user interrupts, 361-362
  error trap enablers, 352-353
  error values, 360-361
  OLE (Object Linking and Embedding), 446
  unknown errors, 359
  user-defined errors, 359-361
  variables, 360-361
Trim function, 82
truth tables, 135, 491
Type mismatch error message, 476
Type statement, 68, 281-282
TypeName( ) function, 119

U

UBound( ) function, 104
UCase function, 82
Unable to get the propertyname property of the classname class error message, 483

Unable to set the propertyname property of the classname class error message, 483
underscore (_)
  macro names, 12
  variable names, 63
Unhide command (Window menu), 12
unstructured branching, 161-166, 491
  calculated branches, 162
  logical branches, 162
  spaghetti code, 166
Until keyword, 181
Use Absolute References command (Record Macro submenu), 11
Use Relative References command (Record Macro submenu), 11
User interrupt occurred error message, 477
user interrupts, 361-362
user-defined errors, 359-361
user-defined types, 282

V

Val function, 82
#VALUE! error value, 155
Value property, 50
variables, 63, 491
  arrays, 66
  comma-delimited lists, 99
  debugging, 332-335
  declaring, 63-65, 247
    Dim statement, 64
    Duplicate definition error message, 476
    global variables, 65
    Option Explicit statement, 64
    procedure headers, 98-99
    Variant data type, 63
  instant watch variables, 488

Index

loop counter, 172-177
named lists
naming, 63
null, 489
object variables, 480
   assigning values, 73
   declaring, 73
   passing
      address, 100
      value, 100-103
   record variables, 490
   scope, 64-65, 490
   Static statement, 105
   strictly typed languages, 491
   strings, 491
   trapping errors, 360
   user-defined errors, 361
   watch variables, 491
Variant data type, 61-63, 491
View menu commands
   Debug Window, 75, 331
   Object Browser, 36
   Toolbars, 27, 219, 402
visible data, 33
Visual Basic for Applications, 9-10
Visual Basic Module menu bar, 384
Visual Basic toolbar, 401

W

wait mode, *see* break mode
watch variables, 491
watchpoints, 345-347
Weekday function, 86
While keyword, 181
While-Wend loops, 183-184
wild cards, 132
Window menu commands, 12
Windows
   DDE (Dynamic Data Exchange), 434
   Task List, 491
   Windows Software Development Kit (SDK), 122

windows
   Debug, 75, 331-332
   forms, 487
With statement, 26, 49
workbooks
   attaching toolbars, 405
   calling procedures, 96-98
   command procedures, 94-95
   projects, 490
   saving, 308
WorkGroup toolbar, 401
worksheets
   active objects, 485
   adding buttons, 218-222
   attaching procedures to buttons, 27-28
   cells
      absolute references, 485
      formatting, 13, 51-54
      Range objects, 43-47
      relative references, 490
   collections, 39
   data forms
      creating, 210-211
      initialization procedures, 216
      storing data, 212-215
   dialog boxes
      attaching objects, 248
      attaching procedures, 236
      button object, 228-229
      check box object, 231
      combination drop-down edit object, 235
      combination list-edit object, 234
      dialog sheets, 225-227
      drop-down object, 234
      edit box object, 231
      group box object, 231
      label object, 229-230
      list box object, 232-234
      option button object, 231-232

        scroll bar object, 235
        spinner objects, 235
    edit bar, 487
    executing methods, 54
    functions, 112-116
        glue functions, 115
        passing arrays, 116-121
    graphics, 29
    input ranges, 209-218
    locking, 222
    Macro Recorder, 12-18
    menu bars, 384
    menus, 28
    objects, 47
    opening, 307-309
    storing databases, 310-322
    writing data, 309
Write statement, 257
writing
    data to worksheets, 309
    sequential files, 257-258
Wrong number of arguments error
        message, 481

X–Y–Z

XL4 Chart menu bar, 385
XL4 Worksheet menu bar, 385
XOr operator, 135

Year function, 86

zero (0) in Format( ) statements, 255
zLog( ) function, 114

GO AHEAD. PLUG YOURSELF INTO
PRENTICE HALL COMPUTER PUBLISHING.
Introducing the PHCP Forum on CompuServe®

Yes, it's true. Now, you can have CompuServe access to the same professional, friendly folks who have made computers easier for years. On the PHCP Forum, you'll find additional information on the topics covered by every PHCP imprint—including Que, Sams Publishing, New Riders Publishing, Alpha Books, Brady Books, Hayden Books, and Adobe Press. In addition, you'll be able to receive technical support and disk updates for the software produced by Que Software and Paramount Interactive, a division of the Paramount Technology Group. It's a great way to supplement the best information in the business.

WHAT CAN YOU DO ON THE PHCP FORUM?

Play an important role in the publishing process—and make our books better while you make your work easier:

- Leave messages and ask questions about PHCP books and software—you're guaranteed a response within 24 hours
- Download helpful tips and software to help you get the most out of your computer
- Contact authors of your favorite PHCP books through electronic mail
- Present your own book ideas
- Keep up to date on all the latest books available from each of PHCP's exciting imprints

JOIN NOW AND GET A FREE COMPUSERVE STARTER KIT!

To receive your free CompuServe Introductory Membership, call toll-free, **1-800-848-8199** and ask for representative **#597**. The Starter Kit Includes:

- Personal ID number and password
- $15 credit on the system
- Subscription to CompuServe Magazine

HERE'S HOW TO PLUG INTO PHCP:

Once on the CompuServe System, type any of these phrases to access the PHCP Forum:

GO PHCP   **GO BRADY**
GO QUEBOOKS   **GO HAYDEN**
GO SAMS   **GO QUESOFT**
GO NEWRIDERS   **GO PARAMOUNTINTER**
GO ALPHA

Once you're on the CompuServe Information Service, be sure to take advantage of all of CompuServe's resources. CompuServe is home to more than 1,700 products and services—plus it has over 1.5 million members worldwide. You'll find valuable online reference materials, travel and investor services, electronic mail, weather updates, leisure-time games and hassle-free shopping (no jam-packed parking lots or crowded stores).

Seek out the hundreds of other forums that populate CompuServe. Covering diverse topics such as pet care, rock music, cooking, and political issues, you're sure to find others with the sames concerns as you—and expand your knowledge at the same time.

Learn programming
By Example with Que!

C By Example
Jack Purdum

This is the best way to learn C outside the classroom! Short chapters help beginners learn the language one small step at a time.

Version 1.0

$24.95 USA
0-88022-813-X, 650 pp., 7^3/$_8$ 9^1/$_8$

More *By Example* Books from Que

Access Programming By Example
Version 1.1 for Windows
$27.95 USA
1-56529-305-3, 1,024 pp., 7^3/$_8$ x 9^1/$_8$

C++ By Example
Beginner/Intermediate Level
$24.95 USA
1-56529-038-0, 500 pp., 7^3/$_8$ x 9^1/$_8$

Paradox for Windows Programming By Example
Version 1.0 for Windows
$27.95 USA
1-56529-083-6, 500 pp., 7^3/$_8$ x 9^1/$_8$

Turbo C++ By Example
Version 3
$21.95 USA
0-88022-812-1, 650 pp., 7^3/$_8$ x 9^1/$_8$

Visual Basic 2 for Windows By Example, 2nd Edition
Version 2 for Windows
$24.95 USA
1-56529-167-0, 875 pp., 7^3/$_8$ x 9^1/$_8$

QBasic By Example
Version 1.0
$21.95 USA
0-88022-811-3, 650 pp., 7^3/$_8$ x 9^1/$_8$

Turbo Pascal By Example
Version 6
$21.95 USA
0-88022-908-X, 650 pp., 7^3/$_8$ x 9^1/$_8$

que

**To Order, Call: (800) 428-5331
OR (317) 581-3500**

Complete Computer Coverage

Que's 1994 Computer Hardware Buyer's Guide

Que Development Group

This absolute must-have guide packed with comparisons, recommendations, and tips for asking all the right questions familiarizes the reader with terms they will need to know. This book offers a complete analysis of both hardware and software products, and it's loaded with charts and tables of product comparisons.

IBM-compatibles, Apple, & Macintosh

$16.95 USA

1-56529-281-2, 480 pp., 8 x 10

Que's Computer User's Dictionary, 4th Edition

Bryan Pfaffenberger

This compact, practical reference contains hundreds of definitions, explanations, examples, and illustrations on topics from programming to desktop publishing. You can master the "language" of computers and learn how to make your personal computer more efficient and more powerful. Filled with tips and cautions, *Que's Computer User's Dictionary* is the perfect resource for anyone who uses a computer.

IBM, Macintosh, Apple, & Programming

$12.95 USA

1-56529-604-4, 650 pp., 4¾ x 8

que

To Order, Call: (800) 428-5331

Enhance Your Personal Computer System with Hardware and Networking Titles from Que!

Upgrading and Repairing PCs, 3rd Edition

Scott Mueller

This book is the ultimate resource for personal computer upgrade, maintenance, and troubleshooting information! It provides solutions to common PC problems and purchasing decisions and includes a glossary of terms, ASCII code charts, and expert recommendations.

IBM PCs and Compatibles

$34.95 USA
1-56529-467-X, 1,312 pp.

Introduction to Personal Computers, 4th Edition

White & Schafer

IBM, Macintosh, & Apple
$19.95 USA
1-56529-275-8, 512 pp.

Introduction to PC Communications

Phil Becker

IBM PCs
$24.95 USA
0-88022-747-8, 500 pp.

The CD-ROM Book

Sloman & Bosak

IBM, Macintosh, & Apple
$34.95 USA
1-56529-292-8, 480 pp.

Que's 1994 Computer Hardware Buyer's Guide

Bud Smith

IBM-compatibles, Macintosh, & Apple
$16.95 USA
1-56529-281-2, 480 pp.

Que's Speed Up Your Computer Book

David Reed

DOS 5
$29.95 USA
0-88022-761-3, 350 pp.

Using Novell NetWare 4, Special Edition

Que Development Group

Through Version 4
$35.00 USA
1-56529-069-0, 1,100 pp.

---

que

To Order, Call: (800) 428-5331
OR (317) 581-3500

Only Que gives you the most comprehensive programming guides!

DOS Programmer's Reference, 3rd Edition
Through DOS 5.0
$29.95 USA
0-88022-790-7, 1,000 pp., $7^3/_8$ x $9^1/_8$

Borland C++ 3.1 Programmer's Reference 2nd Edition
Latest Versions of Borland C++ and Turbo C++
$29.95 USA
1-56529-082-8, 900 pp., $7^3/_8$ x $9^1/_8$

FoxPro 2.5 Programmer's Reference
Version 2.5
$35.00 USA
1-56529-210-3, 1,258 pp., $7^3/_8$ x $9^1/_8$

Paradox 4 Developer's Guide
Latest Version
$44.95 USA
0-88022-705-2, 800 pp., $7^3/_8$ x $9^1/_8$

Using Visual Basic 3
Version 3
$34.95 USA
0-88022-763-x, 650 pp., $7^3/_8$ x $9^1/_8$

que To Order, Call: (800) 428-5331 OR (317) 581-3500

Que Has WordPerfect 6 Books for All Types of Users!

All Skill Levels

Using WordPerfect Version 6 for DOS, Special Edition
1-56529-077-1
$29.95 USA

Beginners in a Hurry

WordPerfect 6 QuickStart
1-56529-085-2
$21.95 USA

All Skill Levels

WordPerfect 6 Quick Reference
1-56529-084-4
$9.95 USA

Frustrated Beginners

I Hate WordPerfect But This Book Makes it Easy
1-56529-212-X
$16.95 USA

Absolute Beginners

Easy WordPerfect for Version 6
1-56529-311-8
$16.95 USA

All Skill Levels

Oops! WordPerfect What To Do When Things Go Wrong
1-56529-196-4
$16.95 USA

All Skill Levels

Killer WordPerfect 6 Utilities
1-56529-362-2
$39.95 USA

Intermediate-Advanced

Upgrading to WordPerfect 6
1-56529-296-0
$14.95 USA

Motivated Learners

WordPerfect 6 SureSteps
1-56529-242-1
$24.95 USA

For more information or to place an order, call: 1-800-428-5331

Excel—Only from the Experts at Que

Using Excel Version 5 for Windows, Special Edition

Ron Person

Version 5 for Windows

$29.95 USA

1-56529-459-9, 1,120 pp.

Easy Excel

Trudi Reisner

Version 5

$19.95 USA

1-56529-540-4, 256 pp.

I Hate Excel, 2nd Edition

Trudi Reisner

Version 5 for Windows

$16.95 USA

1-56529-532-3, 352 pp.

More on Excel from Que

Excel 5 for Windows QuickStart

Sharel McVey & Cathy Kenney

Version 5 for Windows

$21.95 USA

1-56529-531-5, 608 pp.

Excel 5 for Windows Quick Reference

Chris Van Buren & Shelley O'Hara

Version 5 for Windows

$9.95 USA

1-56529-458-0, 160 pp.

Killer Excel Utilities

Ralph Soucie

Version 5 for Windows

$39.95 USA

1-56529-325-8, 1,000 pp.

Oops! Excel

Michael Miller

Version 4.0 for Windows

$16.95 USA

1-56529-241-3, 300 pp.

To Order, Call: (800) 428-5331 OR (317) 581-3500

A Powerful Dose of DOS for the Everyday User!

Using WordPerfect Version 6 for DOS, Special Edition
Que Development Group

The complete tutorial and reference guide...ideal for users of all skill levels!

Version 6.0
$29.95 USA
1-56529-077-1, 1,200 pp., 7 3/8 X 9 1/8

Easy WordPerfect for Version 6
Shelley O'Hara

The revolutionary, 4-color introduction to the latest version of WordPerfect!

Version 6.0
$16.95 USA
1-56529-311-8, 256 pp., 8 X 10

Using 1-2-3, Release 3.4
Que Development Group

This comprehensive tutorial/reference covers all readers need to know to use 1-2-3!

Release 3.4
$29.95 USA
1-56529-004-6, 1,100 pp., 7 3/8 X 9 1/8

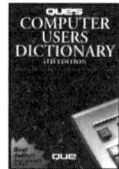

Que's Computer User's Dictionary, 4th Edition
Bryan Pfaffenberger

Completely revised and updated, with more terms than ever before!

All Computer Users
$12.95 USA
1-56529-604-4, 650 pp., 4 3/4 X 8

Quick & Dirty Harvard Graphics Presentations
Bob Benedict

A complete recipe book for a dazzling array of Harvard Graphics charts...plus advice on presentation!

Version 3
$24.95 USA
1-56529-089-5, 320 pp., 8 X 10

Upgrading & Repairing PCs, 2nd Edition
Scott Mueller, et al.

0-88022-856-3, 1,000 pp., 7 3/8 X 9 1/8
$34.95 USA

IBM PCs-Compatibles

Using 1-2-3, Release 2.4, Special Edition
Que Development Group

0-88022-988-8, 1,000 pp., 7 3/8 X 9 1/8
$29.95 USA

Release 2.4

Using Novell NetWare 3
Bill Lawrence

0-88022-756-7, 700 pp., 7 3/8 X 9 1/8
$29.95 USA

Through Version 3.11

Using Paradox 4, Special Edition
Walter R. Bruce, III & Matthew Harris

0-88022-822-9, 900 pp., 7 3/8 X 9 1/8
$29.95 USA

Version 4

Using dBASE IV 2.0, Special Edition
Steve Davis

1-56529-153-0, 1,100 pp., 7 3/8 X 9 1/8
$29.95 USA

Version 2.0

Using Quicken 6
Linda Flanders

1-56529-071-2, 750 pp., 7 3/8 X 9 1/8
$22.95 USA

Version 6

For more information or to place an order, call: **1-800-428-5331**